S0-APN-144

.S33

2015

JUDICIAL REVIEW OF NATIONAL SECURITY

Disclaimer

The views expressed in this work do not represent the views of the
United Nations or any of its bodies.

Judicial Review of National Security

David Scharia

OXFORD
UNIVERSITY PRESS

OXFORD
UNIVERSITY PRESS

Oxford University Press is a department of the University of Oxford. It furthers the University's objective of excellence in research, scholarship, and education by publishing worldwide.

Oxford   New York

Auckland   Cape Town   Dar es Salaam   Hong Kong   Karachi   Kuala Lumpur   Madrid
Melbourne   Mexico City   Nairobi   New Delhi   Shanghai   Taipei   Toronto

With offices in

Argentina   Austria   Brazil   Chile   Czech Republic   France   Greece   Guatemala   Hungary
Italy   Japan   Poland   Portugal   Singapore   South Korea   Switzerland   Thailand
Turkey   Ukraine   Vietnam

Oxford is a registered trademark of Oxford University Press in the UK and certain other countries.

Published in the United States of America by
Oxford University Press
198 Madison Avenue, New York, NY 10016

© Oxford University Press 2015

All rights reserved. No part of this publication may be reproduced, stored in a retrieval system, or transmitted, in any form or by any means, without the prior permission in writing of Oxford University Press, or as expressly permitted by law, by license, or under terms agreed with the appropriate reproduction rights organization. Inquiries concerning reproduction outside the scope of the above should be sent to the Rights Department, Oxford University Press, at the address above.

You must not circulate this work in any other form
and you must impose this same condition on any acquirer.

Library of Congress Cataloging-in-Publication Data

Scharia, David, author.
  Judicial review of national security / David Scharia.
    pages cm. — (Terrorism and global justice series)
  Includes bibliographical references and index.
  ISBN 978-0-19-939336-7 ((hardback) : alk. paper)
1. National security—Law and legislation. 2. Judicial review. 3. Political questions and judicial power.
4. Terrorism—Prevention—Law and legislation. I. Title.
  K3278.S33 2014
  343'.01—dc23
                                                                        2014002193

9 8 7 6 5 4 3 2 1

Printed in the United States of America on acid-free paper

Note to Readers

This publication is designed to provide accurate and authoritative information in regard to the subject matter covered. It is based upon sources believed to be accurate and reliable and is intended to be current as of the time it was written. It is sold with the understanding that the publisher is not engaged in rendering legal, accounting, or other professional services. If legal advice or other expert assistance is required, the services of a competent professional person should be sought. Also, to confirm that the information has not been affected or changed by recent developments, traditional legal research techniques should be used, including checking primary sources where appropriate.

(Based on the Declaration of Principles jointly adopted by a Committee of the American Bar Association and a Committee of Publishers and Associations.)

> **You may order this or any other Oxford University Press publication
> by visiting the Oxford University Press website at www.oup.com**

To Ima who instilled in me the love of learning

21171168aK

Inter arma silent leges—In time of war, the law falls silent

CICERO

"I find the approach when the canons fire, the muses fall silent or, in Cicero's terms, 'In time of war, the law falls silent,' unacceptable. These maxims reflect neither that which is desirable nor that which is prevalent. Particularly when the canons are firing, we need the muses. Particularly in time of war, we require the law."

AHARON BARAK, *President of the Supreme Court of Israel*

"When the trumpets of war blast, the rule of law shall make its voice heard, but we will acknowledge in truth: In those same places, its sound is like the sound of the piccolo, clear and pure but engulfed by the tumult."

JUSTICE MISHAEL CHESHIN, *Supreme Court*

"While we would not want to subscribe to the full sweep of the Latin maxim, inter arma silent leges—in time of war the law is silent—perhaps we can accept the proposition that though the laws are not silent in wartime, they speak with a muted voice."

JUSTICE WILLIAM REHNQUIST, *US Supreme Court*

Contents

Acknowledgments

THIS BOOK COULD not have been completed without the help of so many people. Former president of the Israeli Supreme Court, Justice Dorit Beinish, Judge Nava Ben-Or, Judge Yigal Mersel, Judge Ido Droian, and my former colleagues at the Attorney General's Office in Israel provided me with so much help when presenting cases before the Supreme Court of Israel and later when I decided to engage in this research. Professor Gadi Barzilai of Washington University and Justice Daphne Barak-Erez are the ones who enabled me to transform my chaotic thoughts into an organized and disciplined academic research project.

I would also like to thank the School of Law at Columbia University and in particular [former] Dean David Schizer and Professor Matt Waxmann, and Dean Vera Jelinek and Professor Mark Geleotti from the Center for Global Affairs at NYU for giving me the time, space, support, and warmth of these superb ivory towers in the heart of the city of New York. New York served as a source of inspiration for me when writing this book. Very few cities in the world have suffered more from terrorism than New York. Yet, this city has shown that the best response to terrorism is to stay as we are—committed with the same passion to our values, our freedoms, and our way of life.

I would also like to thank Zachary Goldman and David Unger for the valuable comments they provided me. Kevin Panderkast and Blake Ratcliff at Oxford University Press and Dr. Eve Epstein, Shachar Bar-On, and Ronen Bergman who provided me with much assisatance during the lengthy process of turning this project into a book.

My father Ben-Zion, a brand plunked from the big fire that destroyed Europe Jewry, is the one person I owe most. He dreamt about Zion. He lived in Israel and loved his country. He taught me every day and every night that nothing is more important than education. He encouraged me to write despite all my many other commitments. I miss him every single day and so much more so when I am writing these final notes of this book. My mother is made of the same materials. She taught me how to admire good literature and good scholarship—from early childhood to adulthood. This book is for you Ima—for being with us despite all you have gone through and for all that you gave up for bringing us up.

Last, I would like to thank wholeheartedly my beloved family—my wife, Miri, and my children Amnon, Arielle, and Abigail. Thank you for giving me the will and inspiration to complete this project, and apologies because the time it took me to do so was your time not mine. I owe you this time, and this is one big debt I will never be able to pay back.

One final and personal note. This is book is about court cases but behind each of the cases dealt with in this book there are individuals and very often these individuals are innocent victims of violence. As this book is being sent to print another cycle of violence has erupted between Israel and Hamas. I can not conclude these introductory words without hoping that someday both Israelis and Palestinians will live in peace in this ancient land. Both people suffered from violence. Both people deserve peace. More than anything, both people are entitled to live in a just society respectful of rule of law and human rights and free of war, fear, violence and hatred.

Introduction

IN THE LAST two decades and particularly since 9-11, countries around the world introduced numerous counterterrorism measures and national security programs, and went on military campaigns in order to protect themselves from terrorist attacks. These measures, programs, and campaigns have been the subject of much academic and public debate. Programs and policies such as those dealing with military operations, surveillance, investigation methods, and targeted killings to name a few, have been the subject of academic debate and even much controversy. Yet, very few of these measures have been the subject of judicial review. Several reasons limit the effective review of these measures. The first is that courts tend to defer to the Executive in national security matters, in particular, in regards to military issues. Courts are also reluctant to intervene in times of real or perceived national crisis. When they eventually provide review, courts do so very often many years after the events occurred.

There are other good reasons for this behavior of the courts. Courts need time to learn and assess the impact of policies before they decide. They are better structured to deal with issues ex post facto and much less capable of dealing with issues in real time. Judicial review takes a while. Urgency and the changing dynamic in battlefield or during national security crisis practically prevent courts from exercising the full extent of judicial review powers. Judges also do not always feel they have enough understanding of national security matters. They need very often to understand the threats to our national security before they can decide that a certain measure is unlawful or unconstitutional. Protecting national security is long perceived and constitutionally guaranteed to be the ultimate responsibility of the Executive. Reviewing decisions of the Executive during national crisis runs the risk of putting the nation at greater risk due to a mistaken decision.

Although the reasons for these constraints on the provision of judicial view are clear, the outcome has enormous effect on human rights and on our national security. National security policies impinge on the rights, liberties, and in many cases the lives of thousands and thousands of people. Justified as it may be, deference to the Executive carries a huge price on the protection of human rights and respect for rule of law. Whether we like it or not, it does make a huge difference if the court decides a certain policy to be unlawful or unconstitutional a week or five years after it is applied.

Justice delayed cannot erase the physical and mental scars of those who were subject to violent investigations. It cannot bring back to life those who have lost theirs because of unlawful policies. It cannot repair the damage to the credibility and trust in our values. Justice delayed and too often deferred is also a risky national security strategy. It is therefore in our own national security interest that policies that infringe on our most fundamental values will not serve as recruiting ammunition by our enemies. The sooner courts could make this point the better our national security interests are protected.

It is because of these moral, legal, and strategic reasons that it is important to see how courts could provide a more timely and effective review of national security policies. It is because of these reasons that we need to at least try and create a judicial space in which courts could play a more active and dynamic role in the legal and constitutional deliberation of national security policies. It is not just on the investigative media or government leaks that we should count to disclose controversial programs. It first and foremost should be the role of our courts to review them and to declare that they comply or not with our constitutions, with international law, and with our fundamental values.

Could courts really develop tools that will allow them to provide such review? Although the challenges in providing such review are enormous, the experience of other countries shows it is possible. Learning from this experience could help us look for better solutions or at least to better assess our own.

The Israeli Supreme Court provides an excellent case study in this respect. Its activist approach is known to many. The Court[1] developed jurisprudence on many of the most complex national security policies and measures. It has decided on the use of physical measures in counterterrorism investigations, on the status of "unlawful combatants,"

---

[1] This book deals mainly with the Supreme Court of Israel although it does refer often to other courts including in particular the US Supreme Court. Therefore references to "the Supreme Court" or the Court depend on the immediate context of the passage and, in the absence of such context, refer to the Israeli Supreme Court. When the Israeli Supreme Court discusses constitutional or administrative issues it is referred to as "The Supreme Court, sitting as High Court of Justice" or as it more commonly known in Israel "High Court of Justice." References to the "High Court of Justice" in this book refer to the Supreme Court of Israel as well.

on the legality of targeted killings, and on many more such policies. It provided judicial review for almost every national security policy even if it involved the intelligence, the military, or even special operations units. It has done so when the operations were conducted inside or outside Israel, and it has done so both in times of peace and in times of war.

In order to stand to the challenge the Israeli court developed unconventional judicial review tools and practices. This book will tell the story of how the Israeli Supreme court developed tools that allows it to review the legality of military actions while the forces are still fighting, hostages are still being taken, and bodies are still in the streets. Its aim is to show that it is possible, that courts could play a much more dominant role in reviewing our national security policies, and that they could do so in real time.

This book does not aim to say that everything the Israeli court decided upon is legally right. In fact, this book does not even look into this question. The purpose of this book is to divert the discussion from the solutions the Court has developed and whether the Court's judgment stands in scrutiny or matches the reader interpretation of international law to the question of how courts could play a more dominant role in reviewing national security in real time.

In a nutshell, this book shows that the most important tool that allowed the Israeli Supreme Court to provide judicial review on all national security matters and to do so in real time is intensive real time inter-branch dialogue with the Executive, the Attorney General, the intelligence community, and the military. This book tells the story of this dialogue. Parts of it reached the headlines of world news; parts of it will remain confidential for many years. The important aspect is that through this dialogue the Court was able to provide meaningful even though not always conventional review to the most difficult dilemmas human rights law and international humanitarian law have us face in the twenty-first century.

I hope that after reading this book you will come to the conclusion that judicial review in real time or in close proximity to the adoption of a certain national security policy is feasible and that deference to the Executive in national security matters is not a must. Whether a more rigorous and dynamic Court matches the constitutional system of your country is a different question, which I cannot answer. I will not suggest that this model could be copy-pasted to any other system. In fact, I would caution against it. The differences between legal systems are far too big for such a simplistic approach. However, the fact that one Supreme Court was able to provide meaningful judicial review of national security policies in real time requires some further thinking and perhaps a reconsideration of the conventional wisdom regarding the limits of judicial review of national security.

My hope is that this book will trigger such debate. It is a crucial one. National security policies have a fundamental impact on our lives, our values, and our commitment to human rights and rule of law in times of terror. They are likely to continue doing so in the next century. If we could offer our courts tools to become more dominant in reviewing them, we should not wave off the opportunity to at least consider it. This is the aim of this book.

The book contains 17 chapters. The first chapter is an introduction to the concept of advisory dialogue and provides some historical and legal background on Israel and the Israeli legal system. Chapters 2 to 12 detail the Israeli experience in advisory dialogue. Chapters 2 to 4 focus on the dialogue that occurs while the petition is heard before the Supreme Court. They illustrate how intensive is this dialogue, which begins the moment a petition is served, at times within hours from submission. They show how quick reaction, even in a non-binding manner, allows the Court to intervene in national security policies and in humanitarian situations that stem from military campaigns, very often when the soldiers are still fighting on the battlefield. Chapters 5 to 12 focus on the dialogue the Court developed through its judgments. Chapters 5 and 6 focus on two different methods to convey messages—recommendations and Signaling. Chapters 7 and 8 are dedicated to the tactics the Court developed to convey messages aimed at influencing the application of its judgment. Subsequently, Chapters 9 to 12 discuss the Court's dialogue through the lens of its engagement with different actors—the Attorney General's Office, the military, nongovernmental organizations (NGOs), victims of terrorism, and bereaved families of soldiers.

Chapters 13 to 17 are the analytical chapters of this book. Chapters 13 and 14 analyze how advisory dialogue affects the Court and how the Court uses advisory dialogue to be able to effectively review national security. Chapters 15 to 17 focus on institutional and normative discussion. Chapter 15 and 16 provide, accordingly, arguments in favor and against the use of advisory dialogue in national security matters. Chapter 17 concludes this book with some broader lessons that the Israeli case could teach us on how to apply judicial review in real time and how other systems considering such use in order to better protect human rights in national security matters could make the most appropriate use of such form of judicial review.

1

Decisions Made in Real Time

ON THE NIGHT of May 21, 1994, *Sayeret Matkal*, a top-secret elite commando unit of the Israel Defense Forces, abducted Mustafa Dirani from his home in southern Lebanon. Between the years 1986 and 1994, an additional 21 Lebanese citizens were abducted, like Dirani, by *Sayeret Matkal* and other select commando units. The aim of these abductions was to bring about the release of Ron Arad, an Israeli air force navigator, whose plane was shot down over Lebanon. All of these abductees were held in Israel in administrative detention. They petitioned the Supreme Court with the claim that their detention was unlawful as the sole grounds for their kidnapping and arrest were their status as potential "bargaining chips" toward the possible release of the Israeli navigator.

In a dramatic decision handed down on April 12, 2000, the court ruled that their detention was unlawful and ordered their release.[1] Immediately following the judgment, upon the recommendation of the Ministry of Justice, the Knesset began the process of enacting a law with regard to the imprisonment of unlawful combatants, which concluded with the passing of this law in 2002. A few days later and just several days prior to the release of the Lebanese prisoners, the mother of Ron Arad petitioned the Supreme Court[2] in a final attempt to prevent the Lebanese prisoners' release. The Supreme Court held an urgent hearing on the issue and delayed their release until it gave its decision. On April 19, 2000, the Supreme Court ordered that the petition be dismissed. Incidental to the dismissal of the petition, Justice Barak noted in his decision that he did not view the legislative proceedings, which the Knesset had set in motion following the judgment, as "circumventing" the Supreme Court decision. Two years later, the Knesset passed the

---

[1] Crim FH, 7048/97, Anonymous v. Minister of Defense, PD 54(1) (2000) 721.
[2] HCJ 2967/00, Arad v. the Israel Knesset, PD 54 (2) 188 (2000).

Unlawful Combatants Act which authorized under strict conditions the detention of "Unlawful Combatants". Six years later and eight years after the release of the Lebanese, in a hearing of a petition submitted against the law being constitutional, the Supreme Court ruled that the law does not contradict Israel's Basic Law: Human Dignity and Liberty and there are no constitutional grounds to invalidate it.

For decades, the Israel Security Agency (known also as the Shin Bet) interrogated suspects of terror offenses by using physical force. The Shin Bet did so in accordance with internal directives that permitted investigators to use physical measures such as "violent shaking" and the "*shabah*" position (holding and tying the interrogee in painful positions) in cases where the suspect was considered a "ticking bomb" and in order to save human lives. In a historical decision handed down in 1999, the Supreme Court prohibited[3] the use of physical force by the Shin Bet and determined that in no instance does the government have lawful authority to use physical force vis-à-vis persons being interrogated. At the margins of the decision, the Supreme Court wrote that "*the Attorney General can direct itself with regard to the circumstances under which investigators*"[4] who used physical force in an isolated instance out of a sense of "necessity" will not be indicted. The Court also referred to the possibility that the Knesset will enact a law that will permit the use of physical force in "ticking bomb" cases but wrote that such a law—if legislated—must meet the test of constitutionality.

About a month after publication of the decision, Elyakim Rubinstein, the Attorney General, published a directive in which he specified the situations in which a Shin Bet investigator who uses physical force will not stand trial.[5] Based on this directive and notwithstanding the Court's landmark decision, violent means of interrogation were used (even though in much fewer numbers) against several suspects identified by the Shin Bet as "a ticking bomb." Nonetheless, despite a great deal of pressure to the contrary, the Knesset did not enact a law that permits the use of physical force in Shin Bet interrogations.

On March 29, 2002, the Israeli government decided to implement "Operation Defensive Shield" against terrorist infrastructures in the Occupied Territories.[6] During this action,

---

[3] HCJ 5100/94, The Pubic Committee against Torture in Israel v. the Government of Israel, PD 53 (4) 817, 845 (1999).

[4] *Id.* at 845 (emphasis added).

[5] Elyakim Rubinstein, *Security and Law: Trends*, 44 HAPRAKLIT 409 (2000). Since the HCJ decision, these measures have been applied in dozens of cases. According to a report of B'Tselem, from 2001 to 2010, not one investigator was tried in a criminal hearing with respect to the use of violence in an interrogation. *See* B'TSELEM, THE ABSOLUTE PROHIBITION OF TORTURE AND ABUSE OF PALESTINIAN PRISONERS BY THE SECURITY FORCES OF ISRAEL (2007). *See also* on the same subject HCJ 1265/11, The Public Committee against Torture in Israel v. the State Attorney General.

[6] The term *Occupied Territories* or *Occupied Palestenian Territories* (OT or OPT respectively) refers to the territories Israel occupied in the West Bank and Gaza since the Six Day War in 1967. As Kretzmer notes on numerous occasions, the Supreme Court ruled that the law governing these territories is the law of belligerent occupation. In a recent decision (HCJ 1661/05, Gaza Beach Regional Council et al. v. Knesset of

Israel Defense Forces (IDF) entered Bethlehem. Two hundred Palestinians then proceeded to break into the Church of the Nativity and took up positions in the Church's basilica. In response, the Israeli security forces surrounded the area. Negotiations began to be conducted between the Palestinians inside the church and the surrounding Israelis, in order to reach an agreed-on resolution of the incident. While the negotiations were being conducted, a petition was submitted to the Supreme Court contending that the siege in the church was contrary to international law, and that the condition of those found within the church required the Court's internvention. The petitioners demanded that the Court order the security forces to supply food, water, medicines, and other necessities to the clergymen inside the church. They also requested that permission be granted to remove two bodies found within the area. The Court rejected the petition, determining that it was not justiciable. The Court clarified that its decision that the issue is not justiciable was made solely after it was clarified for the Court that water and food had been supplied to the Church. Accompanying the rejection, the Court added the following comment: "We would like to note that if negotiations are not successfully concluded, the Respondents *should definitely consider* finding a suitable solution to the matter of removing the bodies from the area forthwith, independent of any other arrangement."[7] Two days later, even though the crisis had not been resolved, the army permitted the bodies to be removed from the church's domain.[8]

Nidal Abu Saadeh, a member of Hamas, allegedly conducted, while in prison, a violent "interrogation" of another detainee whom he suspected of cooperating with the prison authorities, and thereby caused that detainee's death. In the hearing on appeal, it turned out that the prosecution at the time of the District Court hearing had screened intelligence according to which the main prosecution witness contended that he did not see who committed the murder. This piece of intelligence that could have been of assistance in Abu Saadeh's defense was not disclosed to the defense due to a certificate of privilege on behalf of national security issued by the Minister of Defense. With the State's agreement, Abu Saadeh was acquitted for this reason. Nonetheless, the Court did not stop at the decision to acquit and wrote a detailed decision relating to the State's conduct in the earlier stages of the proceeding, in which the Court severely censured the State for failing to provide such information. *"The explanation given by the prosecution for the misleading presentation also indicates a failure in understanding the role of an attorney.... This failure of the system of review of classified information is grave and raises serious concern.* [emphasis added]"[9]

Israel et al., 59(2) PD, p. 481, 2005, p. 514), the Court stated that the framework of belligerent occupation has always been accepted by the Court and by all governments that have held office in Israel since 1967. *See* David Kretzmer, *The Law of Belligerent Occupation in the Supreme Court of Israel*, 94 INT'L REV. RED CROSS 207, 210 (Spring 2012).

[7] HCJ 3436/02, Custodia Internationale di Terra Santa v. the Government of the State of Israel, PD 56 (3) 22, 24–25 (2002) (emphasis added).

[8] *See* Felix Frisch & Ali Vaked, *Two Bodies Have Been Removed from the Church of the Nativity*, YNET (Apr. 25, 2002), *available at* http://www.ynet.co.il/articles/0,7340,L-1854331,00.html.

[9] Criminal Appeal 4765/98, Abu Saadeh v. the State of Israel, PD 53 (1) 832 (1999) at 841.

It is important to understand that in this case the Court was not at all required to add the statements of censure. In most cases in which the State agrees to acquit an accused, the Court is satisfied with a particularly brief decision, in which it puts into writing the fact of the State's agreement and gives it the validity of a judgment. Ostensibly, the Court could have been satisfied in this case too with a brief decision that expresses the State's agreement to the acquittal and thereby ends the embarrassing matter. Instead, the Court opted to add voluntarily words of severe censure with regard to all those involved in the review procedure of filtering the classified investigative material. It is difficult to assume that the Court's objective in so doing was other than to direct the future conduct of the prosecutors handling the use of intelligence in criminal proceedings.

Indeed, the prosecution clearly understood the message that was conveyed in this judgment. Following the *Abu Saadeh* judgment, the entire subject of handling classified material by the prosecution was revised. Directives from the State prosecution office pertaining to classified information were updated as well as directives from the Department of Investigations of the Israel Police. Procedures for handling such material were changed, and all internal review processes were made stricter to preclude any such recurrence. The "trauma" that the *Abu Saadeh* judgment caused the prosecution dramatically affected the prosecution's conduct and supervision of the manner in which the Shin Bet collects probative intelligence.

ADJUDICATION AND NATIONAL SECURITY

The main theme of this book is the extent courts could conduct judicial review of national security, very often in real time, in times of crises or national emergency.

Many studies in Israel and throughout the world have analyzed the conduct of the courts at times when they are asked to decide issues of national security. Most studies have concluded that, in this field, the courts make certain to apply maximum self-restraint[10] and attempt to avoid decisions on issues pertaining to the tension ensuing from maintaining a balance among protecting national security, fundamental democratic values, and human rights.[11] Studies have pointed out that in times of crisis judges

---

[10]   *See* Oren Gross, *Chaos and Rules: Should Responses to Violent Crises Always Be Constitutional?*, 112 YALE L.J. 1011 (2003). Gross writes: "Experience shows that when grave national crises are upon us, democratic nations tend to race to the bottom as far as the protection of human rights and civil liberties, indeed of basic and fundamental legal principles is concerned" (at 1019). For a comprehensive review of the studies in this field, *see* Lee Epstein, Daniel E. Ho, Gary King & Jeffrey A. Segal, *The Supreme Court during Crisis: How War Affects Only Non-war Cases*, 80 N.Y.U. L. REV. 1 (2005). *See also* DAVID KRETZMER, THE OCCUPATION OF JUSTICE: THE SUPREME COURT OF ISRAEL AND THE OCCUPIED TERRITORIES (2002), on page 119 and the references in the footnotes there.

[11]   *See in particular* Epstein et al., *supra* note 10, at 71.

apply self-restraint even when they are deciding issues that are not directly related to the emergency situation itself.[12]

The main explanations proposed in the literature to understand this behavior is that in this area, as in other areas that are deeply disputed in society,[13] courts are concerned with the damage to their status due to the considerable possibility of counter legislation.[14] Here, the Executive also benefits from a high degree of autonomy, often guaranteed in the constitution, and the question of justiciability arises in full force. Restraint is also affected by the fact that the public generally does not support liberal adjudication by the Supreme Court on these matters in such times.[15] A very relevant aspect of the reasons for self-restraint is the inability of courts to obtain in real time a full picture of the facts and to evaluate its significance in order to make a rational decision in real time. Another explanation focuses on judges who, in a manner that does not differ from the rest of the population, "convene under the flag"[16] in crises and personally identify with the measures taken by the State in its struggle.[17]

A significant part of this study is devoted, naturally, to the effect of the fight against terrorism, as a particular issue of national security, on the behavior of the Supreme Court. In this regard, the fight against terrorism, specifically since the 1990s, presents a particularly difficult challenge to courts. The impact of terrorism on the State and the civilian population, the serious damage to person and property and impairment of the quality of life, necessarily influence the Court's concept of its function, power, and constraints. As in instances of war, incidental to the discussion of issues related to terror, particularly difficult dilemmas reach the Supreme Court related to the need to balance the protection of life and the protection of basic human rights. Many countries that have fought terror have done so by infringing human rights and using measures that courts in democratic countries would find it difficult to sanction formally. What

---

[12] *See id.* Mark Tushnet is mentioned in this article as the person who named this effect "the elephant in the room phenomenon." As he maintains, judges cannot disregard a state of war just as it is completely impossible to disregard the presence of an elephant in the room. *See also* Mark Tushnet, *Defending Korematsu?: Reflections on Civil Liberties in Wartime*, 2003 WIS. L. REV. 273, 283. *See also* Owen Fiss, *The War against Terrorism and the Rule of Law*, 26 O.J.L.S. 235 (2006).

[13] In relating to the Court's behavior in other areas of case law, *see* STUART A. SCHEINGOLD, THE POLITICS OF STREET CRIME: CRIMINAL PROCESS AND CULTURAL OBSESSION (1991). According to Scheingold, "Judges and prosecutors thus preserve a significant measure of autonomy for dealing with the overwhelming majority of their cases by giving up much of their autonomy in those prosecutions that were inescapably politicized because of the notoriety of the participants or of the circumstances" (at 123).

[14] GAD BARZILAI, DEMOCRACY IN WARS—DISPUTE AND CONSENSUS IN ISRAEL (1992).

[15] GAD BARZILAI, EFRAIM YAAR-YUCHTMAN & ZEEV SEGAL, THE SUPREME COURT IN THE EYE OF ISRAELI SOCIETY 89–94 (1994).

[16] *See* JACK GOLDSMITH, POWER AND CONSTRAINT 65 (2013).

[17] *See* Tushnet, *supra* note 12. Justice Haim Cohen, a legendary Israeli Supreme Court Justice and human rights advocate, said that in times of war "the best of judges bow their heads in view of the sanctity of security and even the daring among them are precluded by the collective anxiety whether it is justified or imagined." NAOMI LEVITZKI, THE SUPREMES: WITHIN THE SUPREME COURT 136 (2006).

distinguishes this area of case law as a distinct national security law doctrine is first that this field has not been fully developed in international law. The laws of war were developed to determine rules of warfare. In interpreting and adjusting them to the counter-terrorism context, the courts are compelled in many cases to be trailblazers. Moreover, the field of terrorism is unique in that it combines routine with urgent situations. This aspect makes it difficult for courts to design doctrines that contain this tension or that are flexible enough to distinguish their application in states of emergency and in states of calm.

With regard to the US Supreme Court, Issacharoff and Pildes[18] and, following them, Epstein and others[19] have demonstrated how the discussion of case law that deals with national security, including those judgments given pertaining to the United States' current war against terrorism following the attacks on 9-11, is directed to the question of whether authority was exercised in accordance with the law and the constitution, rather than the question of actual damage to the citizen, and to maintaining the proper balance between this and the requirements of fighting. Douglas Kmiec[20] noted that the US Supreme Court distinguishes with regard to questions of national security between situations of "cold" war and situations of "hot" war. With regard to the former, the Court manages to review, even if to a limited degree, the conduct of the Executive and to make certain that the country operates according to law. On the other hand, during times of "hot" war, that is, situations in which the Court is required to make judgments during a time of actual fighting, it does not manage to oversee the Executive by way of its judgments. In many instances, the Court waives this capacity and, in other instances, the judgments given grant the Executive the freedom to conduct the fighting without any real constraint on the part of the Court.

JUDICIAL DIALOGUE UNDER FIRE

Several studies have pointed out the various practices developed by courts to address the tensions caused by national security issues. Neal Katyal viewed these difficulties, which characterize the issue of national security and additional problematic areas,

---

[18] Samuel Issacharoff & Richard H. Pildes, *Between Civil Libertarianism and Executive Unilateralism: An Institutional Process Approach to Rights during Wartime*, 5 THEORETICAL INQUIRIES L. 1 (2004). According to these authors, "Historically a significant constitutional tradition of judicial scrutiny in the United States during times of war does exist. But this scrutiny does not take the form of courts making first-order substantive judgments about the content of liberty or other claimed constitutional rights. Nor does it take the form of judicial assessment of how significant or credible the national security claims of the Executive branch might be. Instead, judicial oversight has been focused on preserving the institutional structures and processes through which decision-making on these issues take place" (at 1).

[19] *See* Epstein et al., *supra* note 10.

[20] *See* Douglas W. Kmiec, *The Supreme Court in Times of Hot and Cold War: Learning from the Sounds of Silence for a War on Terrorism*, 28 J. SUP. CT. HIST. 270 (2003).

as a basis for justifying the use of advice-giving by the Court.[21] Katyal writes the following:

> it [Advice-giving, D.S] is therefore particularly helpful in cases that are barred (formally or informally) from binding judicial decision by dint of the political question of doctrine, ripeness, mootness, military deference, and so on. In step one, the Courts make clear that their role is circumscribed by limits on judicial power but that other branches will need to scrutinize the issue because there is a gap between what is unconstitutional and what the Courts may hold unconstitutional. This gap is widest in cases that deal with military affairs or political questions, but it exists in narrower form in many cases because courts do not review legislation for unconstitutionality in a pure sense; they review it to determine whether it is proper for them to declare it unconstitutional. In step two, the Courts give advice to the relevant political actor about the constitutional difficulties engendered by the case and may suggest possible courses of action."[22]

The principal argument of this book, based on the Israeli experience, is that the courts can better deal such jurisprudence by adding to their set of judicial review tools: advisory dialogue. Judicial review through the use of dialogue is likely to provide more than a partial answer to the constitutional, institutional, political, and practical constraints that adjudicating national security matters in particular in real time or in times of national crisis impose on the courts.

The four examples that were presented at the outset of this chapter are ones of attempts to overcome these difficulties. I refer to them as *advisory messages*. The messages that the Supreme Court transmitted in these four cases are part of the judgment but are not part of the ratio decidendi, the binding part of the judgment. These messages offer guidance to the legislature, to the military, or to the Attorney General on how to act or recommend to them how to utilize their authority, and, like binding judgments, seek to affect the conduct of other government agencies. Unlike the binding part of a judgment, through advisory messages, the Court attempts to affect policies by way of guidance, direction, consultation, or authorization, without being obligated to act in accordance with the contents of such messages.

A major part of this book will be devoted to presenting the use made by the Supreme Court of Israel of these types of comments. While examining Supreme Court decisions on national security since the time of the murder of former prime minister Yitzhak Rabin until the present, I will demonstrate that the Supreme Court, particularly in situations where it is required to give its judgments urgently or in relation to states of

---

[21] *See* Neal Katyal, *Judges as Advicegivers*, 50 STAN. L. REV. 1709 (1998).
[22] *Id.* at 1717.

war, often replaces binding decisions with dialogue with other branches. I refer to this as *advisory dialogue*, contending that it serves the Supreme Court to direct, advise, or guide the conduct of actors in other branches. Unlike the theoretical model proposed by Katyal the messages issued by the Israeli Court are not addressed solely to the legislature. They could address anyone from the legislature, the Prime Minister, the Attorney General, the Shin Bet, and even the military. They are also not limited to constitutional advices: their content is varied and much broader.

Indeed advisory messages will be found generally in the obiter dicta of a judgment. However, it is appropriate to underscore at this point that the division between a binding message, the ratio decidendi,[23] and an advisory message, obiter dictum, misses the point of this book. What characterizes obiter dicta as such is that it constitutes a part of a judgment that did not serve the Court for its decision of the issue brought before it.[24] Indicating obiter dicta is a legal interpretive conclusion that is intended to be separate from questions of dialogue or strategy. However, the basic assumption here is that the courts are sophisticated players who use a variety of tactics as part of their strategy to strengthen their influence on other government agencies, including dialogical techniques. As Neal Katyal, in his article on "Judges as Advicegivers," underscores: "Because the Court has put litigants on notice that its dicta are not binding, dicta allow the Justices to mediate the tension between wanting to provide guidance and fearing that such guidance will be misunderstood to be the last word on a matter."[25] The practice Katyal recommends the US Supreme Court to consider is applied broadly and intensively in practice and for decades by the Israeli Supreme Court. Notwithstanding the major differences between the legal systems, the experience and lessons learned from this experience could serve as a basis for discussion over the use of advice-giving in the United States as well as in other countries.

DIALOGUE AND JUDICIAL REVIEW

The concept underlying this study is that in inter-branch dialogue courts use a variety of means beyond final judgments to convey messages to the other branches. They use verbal expressions by judges in the courtroom during a hearing of an action,[26] academic articles

---

[23] For a definition of this term, *see* "Ratio Decidendi," *West's Encyclopedia of American Law* (Jeffrey Lehman & Shirelle Phelps eds., 2d ed. Thompson Gale, 2005; eNotes.com 2006, Aug. 5, 2007, *available at* http://law.enotes.com/west-law-encyclopedia/ratio-decidendi).

[24] *See* http://www.thefreedictionary.com/Obiter+dicta. The *American Heritage Dictionary of the English Language* defines *obiter dicta* as "an opinion voiced by a judge on a point of law not directly bearing on the case in question and therefore not binding."

[25] *See* Katyal, *supra* note 21, at 1801.

[26] *See on this matter*, Yoav Dotan, *Do the Haves Still Come Out Ahead? Resource Inequalities in Ideological Courts: The Case of the Israeli High Court of Justice*, 33 L. & Soc. Rev. 1059 (1999). *See also* Yoav Dotan, *Judicial Rhetoric, Government Lawyers and Human Rights: The Case of the Israeli High Court of Justice during the Intifada*, 33 L. & Soc. Rev. 319 (1999).

written by judges pertaining to the relevant issues,[27] and dialogue with members of the Executive and legislative authorities while sitting on joint committees discussing a variety of reforms. Studies have demonstrated that judges also transmit nonverbal messages expressing perhaps even subconsciously their views on the case before them.[28] Dialogue that occurs by way of advisory messages is one of many forms in which a court could transmit messages to other branches and even to the public.

As we shall see in due course, the Israeli Supreme Court's use of advisory messages is a central feature of its judgments with regard to national security. The intensive use of advisory messages leads to the conclusion that in order to understand the full significance of the Israeli Supreme Court judgments with regard to national security, the advisory messages that the Court conveys must be identified and their significance understood. Reading these decisions without consideration of the advisory message can lead to only partial understanding and, at times, even misunderstanding of the Court's approach to the issue under discussion.

Often such messages can be found only by deep scrutiny of the judgments, by familiarity with the Court's manner of work, and by reading between the lines of its ruling. Therefore, I will focus the discussion particularly on these aspects of a judgment, the sections of a judgment that are less apparent in a quick reading and that are certainly not accessible to a reader who is not familiar with the Court's practice, not to mention readers who are not Hebrew speakers. I will demonstrate how these serve the Court as a convenient platform to convey advisory messages to other branches. What I seek to accomplish in this book is to show how the courts can better contend with the pressures and particular facets of judicial review in times of emergency, through advisory dialogue.

However, before getting into the cases themselves, two more introductions are needed. The first is a historical one that will give the reader some background on the environment in which the Israeli Supreme Court operated. The second is a legal one that will give the reader a better acquaintance with the Court's methods of work.

A SHORT HISTORICAL AND LEGAL BACKGROUND—ISRAEL 1995–2012

I intend to focus in this book on analyzing several national security cases, which the Supreme Court in Israel has discussed from the time of the murder of former prime minister Yitzhak Rabin in 1995 until Operation Pillar of Defense in 2012. The appreciation of this practice goes of course beyond this limited period.

The second half of the 1990s was selected as a point of departure, as the events that occurred then comprise a turning point with regard to everything pertaining to the struggle against terrorism in Israel and around the world. Although the following is not

---

27 *See, e.g.,* Dorit Beinisch, *The Rule of Law during a Period of Fighting,* MISHPAT V'TZAVA 17, 19 (2004).

28 *See* Martin S. Remland, *The Importance of Nonverbal Communication in the Courtroom,* 2 N.J.J. COMMC'N 124 (1994).

a historical overview of this period it provides some important background on the main developments that occurred and were in the background of many of the decisions the Israeli Superme Court and the Israeli society faced.

Following the rise of Yitzhak Rabin to power in 1992, Israel entered into the Oslo Accords with the Palestinians. The Oslo Accords were hotly opposed in Israeli society. In 1994, Baruch Goldstein, a physician living in the settlement of Kiryat Arba, entered the Cave of Machpela, where according to both Jewish and Muslim traditions Abraham is buried, and murdered 29 Moslems praying there and wounded an additional 125 people in a terrorist act known as the Cave of Machpela Massacre. The murders, deemed the worst incident in the history of Jewish terrorism in Israel, shocked both Israeli and Palestinian society. In their wake, the government of Israel designated the Kach movement and the Kahane Lives movement as terrorist organizations.

Another important development occurred earlier in 1992. On December 17, 1992, following the murder of police officer Nissim Toledano, Israel deported 415 Hamas activists to Lebanon. Toledano was kidnapped and murdered in the city of Lod. Immediately after finding his body, Israel arrested 1,200 Hamas and Islamic Jihad activists in an extensive operation. In a very controversial ruling, the Supreme Court decided to leave in place the government decision to deport the 415 Hamas activists to Lebanon. This disputed decision, which will be discussed in further detail, signaled a turning point in relations between the Supreme Court and the security authorities.

In the legal sphere, the 1990s signaled a transformation in the Supreme Court's attitude toward the Knesset. In 1992, two Basic Laws that deal with human rights were enacted in Israel, Basic Law: Human Dignity and Liberty, and Basic Law: Freedom of Occupation. Justice Aharon Barak, while serving as a Supreme Court Justice and later as President of the Court, related to these laws as having a higher normative status in his fundamental judgment, *United Bank Mizrahi v. Migdal Kfar Shitufi*,[29] given two months after he was appointed President of the Court. This decision is Israel's *Marbury v. Madison*.[30] In its decision, the Court ruled that it had the authority to declare a law that contradicts these Basic Laws invalid. The Supreme Court's decision aroused serious opposition to the Court's activity but it also enabled the Court to make sophisticated and strategic use of advisory dialogue and signaling of its intention to invalidate an existing law or a law being legislated without actually invalidating it. During this period, the Supreme Court acted while under serious attack by nationalistic and religious circles, who opposed its fundamental judgments in these areas and, in several instances, the value system that these judgments represented.

The murder of Prime Minister Yitzhak Rabin on November 4, 1995, changed the face of Israeli society and its acknowledgment of the dangers of terrorism and incitement to terrorism that confronted it. In this period, Israel also began to contend with the phenomenon of suicide bombers. In 1994 alone, 38 people were killed in suicide bombings.

---

[29] Civil Appeal 6821/93, United Bank Mizrahi v. Migdal Kfar Shitufi, PD 49(4) 221.
[30] Marbury v. Madison, 5 U.S. 137 (1803).

The mid-1990s is also replete with developments in the international arena. The terrorist attack of the US embassies in Kenya and Tanzania, the attack on the *USS Cole* destroyer, the 9-11 attack and, as a consequence, the United States' war against terrorism led to a sea change in relation to the threat of global terror and the appropriate legal reaction to it. Following the 9-11 attack, the world was exposed to a further series of global terrorist attacks from Bali and Madrid to Istanbul and Beslan. As a result, an extensive legal response was formulated in the international arena. A series of resolutions of the UN Security Council and the conclusion of international and regional conventions against terrorism led to a deep shift in the perception that "your terrorist is my patriot." During those same years, the International Criminal Court (ICC) was set up, demonstrating a broad approach to universal jurisdiction in international law. As a result, countries endorsed the importance of accurately adhering to the rules of warfare and humanitarian law with regard to everything related to the fight against terrorism. These changes also sharpened the tension between the new global reality and the laws of warfare formulated to arrange battles between States. Even if it is too soon to conclude that the legal doctrine known as "Law and Terror" has sufficiently matured, there is no doubt that any historical analysis will record these years as the period in which this doctrine was formulated and consolidated.

All these events and legal developments have been part of what the Israeli Supreme Court had to contend with. Its decisions reflected these tensions, incorporated these developments, and even led to new and innovative approaches to international law. These were all done under the constant pressure of numerous terrorist attacks and the reaction to them of the Knesset, the government, and the Israeli public. The attached timetable provides information on major national security events during these years

TIMETABLE OF MAJOR NATIONAL SECURITY EVENTS, ISRAEL 1993–2013

Deportation of 415 Hamas members to Lebanon	December 17, 1992	In December 1992, Israel deported to South Lebanon 415 Palestinian residents of the Occupied Territories, some for one year and others for two years. The decision to deport was reached after several Israel security force personnel were killed by Palestinians.
Oslo Accords	OSLO I–1993 Oslo II–1995	The Oslo Accords are a set of agreements between the government of Israel and the Palestine Liberation Organization (PLO). They marked the start of the Oslo process, a peace process that aimed to conclude a peace-treaty based on the UN Security Council Resolutions 242 and 338, and fulfill the "right of the Palestinian people to self-determination." The Oslo process started after secret negotiations in Oslo resulted in the recognition by the PLO of the State of Israel and the recognition by Israel of the PLO as the representative of the Palestinian people and as a partner in negotiations.

(*continued*)

The Cave of the Patriarch Massacre	February 25, 1994	The Cave of the Patriarchs massacre was a shooting attack carried out by American-born Israeli Baruch Goldstein, a member of the far-right Israeli Kach movement, who opened fire on unarmed Palestinian Muslims praying inside the Ibrahim Mosque (or Mosque of Abraham) at the Cave of the Patriarchs in Hebron, West Bank. The attack left 29 male worshippers dead and 125 wounded.
Assassination of Prime Minister Rabin	November 4, 1995	Prime Minister Rabin is assassinated by a Jewish extremist while attending a demonstration in support of the Oslo Accords
Second Intifada	Sept. 2000–Feb. 2005	
The Passover massacre in Netania	March 27, 2002	The Passover massacre was a suicide bombing carried out by Hamas at the Park Hotel in Netanya, Israel, on March 27, 2002, during a Passover seder. Thirty civilians were killed in the attack and 140 were injured. It was the deadliest attack against Israelis during the Second Intifada.
Operation Defensive Shield	March 29, 2002–May 2002	Operation "Defensive Shield" was a large-scale military operation conducted by the Israel Defense Forces in 2002 during the course of the Second Intifada. It was the largest military operation in the West Bank since the 1967 Six-Day War. The operation was an attempt by the Israeli army to stop the increasing deaths from terrorist attacks, especially in suicide bombings.
Operation Rainbow	May 12–24, 2004	Operation Rainbow was an invasion and siege of Rafah in southern Gaza. The operation was started after the deaths of five Israeli soldiers in a Palestinian attack, in which an armored vehicle was destroyed. During the incursion, the IDF razed some 300 homes in order to expand the buffer zone along the Gaza–Egypt border. Also a zoo and at least 700 dunams (70 ha) of agricultural land were destroyed.
Sharem el Sheich Summit	February 8, 2005	The Sharm el-Sheikh Summit of 2005 took place on February 8, when four Middle Eastern leaders gathered at Sharm el-Sheikh, a town at the southern tip of the Sinai Peninsula, in order to declare their wish to work toward the end of the four-year Al-Aqsa Intifada.
Israel's unilateral disengagement plan	August 2005–September 12, 2005	Israel's unilateral disengagement plan was a proposal by Israeli prime minister Ariel Sharon, adopted by the government on June 6, 2004, and enacted in August 2005, to resettle all Israelis from the Gaza Strip and from four settlements in the northern West Bank.

(continued)

Those Israeli citizens who refused to accept government compensation packages and voluntarily vacate their homes prior to the August 15, 2005, deadline were evicted by Israeli security forces over a period of several days.

Second Lebanon War	July 12, 2006– August 14, 2006	Following the killing and kidnapping of Israeli soldiers, Israel launches a major 34-day military campaign against Hezbollah. The principal parties were Hezbollah paramilitary forces and the Israeli military. The conflict is believed to have killed at least 1,191–1,300 Lebanese people, and 165 Israelis. It severely damaged Lebanese civil infrastructure and displaced approximately one million Lebanese and 300,000–500,000 Israelis. It ended indecisively with each side claiming a victory over the other.
Operation Cast Lead	December 27, 2008–January 18, 2009	A three-week armed conflict between Israel and Hamas following intensive rocket attacks from Gaza to southern Israel. The conflict resulted in between 1,166 and 1,417 Palestinian and 13 Israeli deaths. According to the Shin Bet, after the conflict, there was a decrease in Palestinian rocket attacks.
The Goldstone Report	September 2009	Following Operation Cast Lead the UN Human Rights Council established a fact-finding mission to investigate violations of international law by Israel and Hamas. The report was highly critical of Israel and accused it of committing war crimes and targeting civilians deliberately. In 2011 in an op-ed, Goldstone retracted his claims that Israel deliberately targeted civilians.
The *Mavi Marmara* incident	31 May 2010	The Gaza flotilla raid was a military operation by Israel against six ships of the "Gaza Freedom Flotilla" on May 31, 2010, in international waters of the Mediterranean Sea. The flotilla, organized by the Free Gaza Movement and the Turkish Foundation for Human Rights and Freedoms and Humanitarian Relief (İHH), was carrying humanitarian aid and construction materials, with the intention of breaking the Israeli-Egyptian blockade of the Gaza Strip. On May 31, 2010, Israeli Shayetet 13 naval commandos boarded the ships from speedboats and helicopters in order to force the ships to the Israeli port of Ashdod for inspection. On the Turkish ship MV *Mavi Marmara*, the Israeli Navy faced resistance from about 40 of the 590 İHH activists. During the struggle, nine activists were killed including eight Turkish nationals and one Turkish American, and many were wounded.

(continued)

Kidnapping and release of Gilad Shalit	June 25, 2006– October 18, 2011	Gilad Shalit served as a soldier of the Israel Defense Forces (IDF) and was abducted inside Israel by Hamas militants in a cross-border raid via underground tunnels near the Israeli border with Gaza on June 25, 2006. The Hamas militants held him for over five years, until his release on October 18, 2011, as part of a prisoner exchange deal.
Operation Pillar of Defence	November 14, 2012	Operation Pillar of Defense was an eight-day Israel Defense Forces (IDF) operation in the Hamas-governed Gaza Strip, officially launched on November 14, 2012, with the killing of Ahmed Jabari, chief of the Gaza military wing of Hamas.
		The operation began in response to Palestinian groups launching over 100 rockets at Israel over a 24-hour period. The stated aims of the military operation were to halt rocket attacks against civilian targets originating from the Gaza Strip and to disrupt the capabilities of militant organizations. The Palestinians blamed the Israeli government for the upsurge in violence, accusing the IDF of attacks on Gazan civilians in the days leading up to the operation, and citing the blockade of the Gaza Strip, and occupation of West Bank, including East Jerusalem, as the reason for the rocket attacks.
		Gaza officials said 133 Palestinians had been killed in the conflict of whom 79 were militants, 53 civilians, and one a policeman, and estimated that 840 Palestinians were wounded. During the operation, Hamas, the al-Qassam Brigades, and the Palestinian Islamic Jihad further intensified their rocket attacks on Israeli cities and towns, in an operation code named Operation Stones of Baked Clay firing over 1,456 rockets into Israel, and an additional 142 that fell inside Gaza itself. Palestinian militant groups used weapons including Iranian-made Fajr-5, Russian-made Grad rockets, Qassams, and mortars. Some of these weapons were fired into the center of Israel including the cities of Tel Aviv and Jerusalem.

Sources: Btzelem, Wikipedia, IDF website*

*Disclaimer: Many of the facts concerning these events are highly contested. The purpose of this timetable is to give the reader general background knowledge on major events affecting the national security of Israel during the researched years. For more information on each of the events, please visit the primary sources as well as other available sources.

THE SUPREME COURT OF ISRAEL AND REVIEW OF MILITARY AND COUNTERTERRORISM ACTIONS

The Supreme Court of Israel is perceived to be a very activist court. As Mersel[31] highlights, it developed a legal doctrine and jurisprudence that allows it to intervene in any national security measures taken by the State including the decisions of commanders in the battlefield. Every person who has a conflict with one of the State's authorities is allowed to bring it before the Supreme Court. If the question has constitutional implications, the Court acts as first and last resort.

The Court may dismiss, in theory, a case due to a lack of standing or based on the political question doctrine. However, the Court rarely does so. In practice, the Court abandoned the demand that petitioners need to demonstrate a personal interest in the case's outcome in order to receive standing. That holds true even with regard to issues relating to counterterrorism, national security, or foreign policy.

The Court also rejected the notion that these measures are non-justiciable. According to the Court's jurisprudence even the decision to go to war is an administrative one that can be adjudicated on the basis of the reasonableness doctrine of administrative law.

The result was that the Court's doors for petitioners and nongovernmental organizations (NGOs) are kept entirely open and they can bring in any case in which they believe the State's national security measures are unlawful or unconstitutional. The only limits on their ability to bring cases to court are those that they wish to put on themselves in picking the right case and the right timing.

The Israeli Supreme Court saw this approach as its contribution to the protection of human rights and rule of law and expressed on several occasions when the State argued that the case is not justiciable that it is fully committed to review every decision of the Executive.

The Court has held strongly to this position both in times of peace and in times of war; in dealing with cases concerning citizens and noncitizens; and in dealing with acts that took place in Israel, the West Bank, or Gaza, or outside Israel.

One of the outcomes of this commitment to an open-door policy was that the Court has found it necessary to provide rulings on all the difficult dilemmas that military actions, national security policies, and counterterrorism measures may raise.

This challenge is further exacerbated as the Court has also been committed to exercising judicial review in real time and as it has dealt with these issues as first instance.

This commitment forced the Court to provide judgments in an urgent manner. That led the Court to develop its accessibility to a point that it is capable of providing

---

[31] Yigal Mersel, *Judicial Review of Counter-terrorism Measures: The Israeli Model for the Role of the Judiciary during the Terror Era*, 38 N.Y.U. J. INT'L L. & POL. 73 (Nov. 2006).

judgments in a very short time and very often while the military or the counterterrorism units are still on the ground waiting to hear whether a specific action is lawful or not.

This commitment to open-door policy, to wide jurisdiction and almost absolute accessibility, did not eliminate the other complexities that providing judgments in times of emergency or on national security matters entail. On the contrary, it made these difficulties even more apparent as the Court at its own will refused to limit the issues and times it is willing to adjudicate.

Very often the Court found itself in a position where it was very difficult if not impossible to provide rulings on these cases. That did not discourage the Court from trying to provide judgments, however. What happened as we will see in this book was that in its search for effective judicial review the Israeli Supreme Court has developed judicial techniques that allow it to provide meaningful review of the State's actions, while refraining from deciding on issues on which it is unable or unwilling to provide judgment. One of the most important strategies the Court developed, in this respect, is the use of non-binding guidance and advisory messages.

DEVELOPING THE DATABASE OF CASES AND IDENTIFYING ADVISORY MESSAGES

In order to locate case law that includes advisory messages, I reviewed thousands of judgments given during the period. The search included all computerized databases, judgments publicized on websites of human rights organizations, and notices to the media that they issued, as well as case law that may be located on the Israeli Supreme Court website. The use of several databases and particularly that of the Israeli Supreme Court, which does not comprise any internal filtering, allowed me to overcome the effect of internal filtering processes by the designers of computerized databases.[32] By the nature of things, judgments whose contents are confidential have not been included in the cases discussed in this book. In order to ensure that essential judgments on the issue have not been omitted, the cases that were located were cross-referenced with cases mentioned in the literature, in news reports from the relevant period, including their computerized archives; in reports of human rights organizations; and in conversations with actors and attorneys active in the field, and with case law that is mentioned in other studies.

Identifying what constitutes national security was not always an easy matter. In most cases, it was clear—issues relating to military campaigns, emergency laws, counterterrorism measures, and alike are very much at the heart of this research. Some others are not.

---

[32] With regard to the legal research methodology, *see in general* Lee Epstein & Gary King, *The Rules of Inference*, 69 U. CHI. L. REV. 1, 106 (2002). For criticism of this approach, *see* Frank Cross, Michael Heise & Gregory S. Sisk, *Exchange: Empirical Research and the Goals of Legal Scholarship: Above the Rules: A Response to Epstein and King*, 69 U. CHI. L. REV. 135 (2002).

One area of particular concern is the issue of settlements considered by the international community[33] as a grave violation of article 49 of the Fourth Geneva Convention. During 1970-1980, the discussion over this issue before the Supreme Court was framed as a national security matter.[34] However, in the early nineties, a shift occurred and the State more or less abandoned this argument by relying on a concept of Ottoman law according to which an unused land reverts back to the Empire. The Court from its side never intervened on this matter, even though no issue is more controversial (and affects human rights and respect for international law) in Israel's policies than the issue of the settlements. It limited its rulings to cases involving the confiscation of private land. When broader issues relating to the settlements came before it, it refused to rule on the settlements' legality, on grounds of lack of standing and on the grounds that the question was non-justiciable. As David Kretzmer notes: "Avoiding ruling on the lawfulness of the settlements has no doubt enabled the Court to avoid a head-on clash with the government and a large segment of public opinion."[35] However, it does remain as an issue that "the Court's refusal to rule on this question has somewhat compromised its position."

Identifying advisory messages requires an in-depth analysis of the legal text. In many instances, the advisory message is eclipsed by the text and cannot be located by searching for keywords. Furthermore, in this process it is impossible to avoid completely personal judgment and subjective interpretations of the judicial text. Accordingly, it is not unlikely that various readers will dispute whether a certain text constitutes an advisory message, and if so what is its content. In order to limit these inherent difficulties, I have expanded the analysis of specific cases that have been located in the study and provided many citations from case law. This extended analysis and abundance of citations is intended to allow the reader to form his or her own impressions, and to evaluate and interpret the text independently.

It will be noted that the aims of the book are not to present quantitative data with regard to the use of advisory messages or to reach quantitative conclusions with regard to the Court's behavior. The aim is to focus on the way the legal text enables and, in practice, serves the Supreme Court to exercise judicial review through advisory messages The discussion in the following chapters will not mention all the instances in which advisory dialogue has been used or provide a representative or random sample of this. As this study is interpretive by its nature, I have opted to present the analysis of several cases that well illustrate the specific tactics the Court has undertaken. Most of the cases analyzed in the study have parallel cases, and several of these have been mentioned in the footnotes. In order to provide a broad and encompassing view, insofar as possible, without being repetitive, the cases selected represent landmark decisions alongside

---

[33] *See* ICJ Legal Consequences of the Construction of a Wall in the Occupied Palestinian Territory, advisory opinion of 9 July 2004.

[34] HJC 610/78, Ayub v. The Minister of Defence, PD 33(2) 113.

[35] Kretzmer, *supra* note 7, at 207.

run-of-the-mill petitions; a variety of justices; different periods; diverse issues; and criminal, administrative, and constitutional cases brought by either repeat petitioners or one-time petitioners.

I will dedicate Chapters 2–12 to demonstrating how the Court implemented its approach in practice. Chapters 13–17 will be dedicated to analyzing the Court's behavior and to assessing its institutional implications and normative merits. However, before entering into a discussion on the Israeli Supreme Court, I will provide an overview of current research in the United States regarding the use of advisory dialogue.

2

Judicial Review in Real Time—Use of Interim Decisions

INTRODUCTION

A court that deems itself obligated to provide judicial review in real time is likely to find it highly advantageous to convey messages at the time of hearing a petition. This enables the court to affect decision-making processes at a time as close as possible to the time these decisions are being made.

The Israeli Supreme Court frequently uses interim decisions to affect policy in decision-making centers in real time even while the petition is still pending. Analysis of Supreme Court decisions instructs that the Court uses several principal tactics to convey messages in interim decisions. In this chapter, I will discuss three elements in Supreme Court decisions that enable the Court to convey messages to parties sometimes already at the time the petition is submitted or on setting the date of the first hearing. Such hearings may be held at times, if the matter justifies this, only one day subsequent to the submission of the petition. These elements are *the timing of the decision, the language of the decision*, and *the procedural platform from which it is conveyed*. Further on, I will discuss the use the Supreme Court makes of *the practice* that developed in hearings before the Court to convey messages to the parties in real time.

TIMING AND ITS EFFECT ON THE MEANING OF THE MESSAGE

For a court committed to judicial review in real time of national security matters, timing is a crucial factor. Legal history in Israel is filled with instances in which the specific *timing* of an interim decision affected the outcome of the proceeding. This is a necessary byproduct of the court's willingness to make decisions that affect the reality being discussed before it. The most famous case pertained to the deportation of Hamas members to Lebanon.[1] On December 16, 1992, following the murder of police officer Nissim Toledano, Israel deported 415 Hamas activists to Lebanon. Toledano was kidnapped and murdered in the city of Lod. Immediately after his body was found, Israel arrested 1,200 Hamas and Islamic Jihad activists in an extensive operation. At the same time, Prime Minister Yitzhak Rabin looked into the possibility of a mass deportation to Lebanon. The Minister of Justice and the Attorney General supported the idea from a legal perspective. However, State Prosecutor Dorit Beinisch vehemently objected and tried to persuade those involved to change their minds because, according to Beinisch, mass deportation was not lawful and would not withstand the test of the High Court of Justice. Her position notwithstanding, on the morning of December 16, the government decided to deport 415 Hamas and Islamic Jihad activists immediately to Lebanon, with no prior notice and while denying their preliminary right to object. A blackout was placed on the decision with the hope that it would be possible to implement it without the matter being brought for a hearing before the High Court of Justice. Nonetheless, rumor of the planned mass deportation spread like wildfire and the Association for Citizens' Rights, a prominent nongovernmental organization (NGO), filed the very same night petitions at the home of Aharon Barak, who served as the justice on duty. Barak issued an interim order that prevented the continuation of the deportation, and the buses, with hundreds of deportees, were stopped at the northern border awaiting the decision of the High Court of Justice.

The hearing on the matter was set for 10 o'clock the next morning, but after the government demanded that the proceedings be expedited, Justice Meir Shamgar, President of the Supreme Court, intervened and, in an exceptional move, set an earlier time of 5 a.m. for the hearing. The panel of judges initially comprised three judges, headed by President Shamgar, and was later expanded to seven judges. Attorney General Yosef Harish was compelled to represent the government as Attorney Dorit Beinisch took the unprecedented position of refusing to defend the State in a proceeding that in her opinion was clearly unlawful. Following a fourteen-hour hearing, during which hundreds of deportees remained on the buses, the panel decided to invalidate the interim injunction and permit the deportation to continue. Later, after the deportees were transferred to Lebanon, a hearing on the petition was held. The deportees were given the opportunity to present their arguments against deportation, but they all decided as one not to exercise this option. The key witness on behalf of the State was the IDF Chief of Staff, Ehud Barak. The hearing prior to adjudication was difficult and almost led to a real split among the Supreme Court justices. Ultimately, a majority appeared in Shamgar's camp, which authorized the deportation and its legality. Aharon Barak, who led the opposing camp,

---

[1] *See* HCJ 5973/92, The Association for Citizens' Rights v. the Minister of Defense, PD 47(1) 267 (1993). With regard to the development of events in the petition, *see* B'Tselem's website, http://www.btselem.org/hebrew/deportation/1992_mass_deportation.asp

wrote the minority decision in which the government's conduct was profoundly criticized. The issue concerned Shamgar, who, due to the gravity of the matter, sought to present a consensus among the justices. Accordingly, Shamgar modified the majority decision and deleted any mention from it that could be construed as if the act of the government was lawful. In return, Barak shelved the minority opinion.[2] There is no doubt that had the decision been made prior to deportation, the results would have been different.

Another example of an incident in which the timing created reality that tailored the decision in the file pertains to a petition that was submitted against the decision of Prime Minister Benjamin Netanyahu to close Orient House on the eve of elections in May 1999. Orient House had for years served as the PLO headquarters in East Jerusalem and a symbol of Palestinian nationalism in the eastern sector of the city. On May 9, 1999, a week before the elections, in what has been described by the media as an attempt to appease right-wing voters, Prime Minister Netanyahu ordered Orient House to be closed. On May 11, 1999, a petition was filed against the decision and, on the same day, Justice Dorner ordered an interim injunction to be granted that prohibited the closing of Orient House.[3] Justice Dorner further ordered that the petition be heard before an ordinary panel of justices on May 30, 1999. Justice Dorner duly believed that the elections did not constitute grounds for setting an early hearing of the petition. The fact that the elections were held on May 17, 1999, led to the complete "neutralizing" of the Prime Minister's course of action. Indeed, the petition was ultimately dismissed after, as a result of Netanyahu's loss of the elections, the State gave notice that it no longer intended to close Orient House.[4]

These two examples illustrate one of the central features of national security adjudication—time is of the essence. Decisions of the Court affect reality on the ground and are being affected by the reality on the ground.

It also shows the level of pressure that such adjudication poses on a court willing to adjudicate in real time. It creates a great deal of pressure on the Court, as demonstrated by the incident of the deportation of Hamas activists. An unrestrained Executive who is concerned about unwanted interference by the Court may decide to tailor reality in a manner that precludes judicial review in real time.

However, deciding in real time also grants the Court opportunities, as demonstrated by the attempt to close Orient House. If not for the elections, the Court would have had to decide the issue, and whatever it decided would have been considered intervention in the elections.

For a court that must decide issues that need immediate attention, timing is of critical significance. It creates limits but also grants opportunities. As we shall see in few a more

---

[2] Naomi Levitzki, The Supremes: Within the Supreme Court 187 (2006)

[3] HCJ 3123/99, Hillman v. the Minister of Internal Security (unpublished, July 7, 1999), decision dated May 11, 1999.

[4] *Id.* in a Decision of June 8, 1999

examples later on, the Supreme Court succeeded in creating opportunities for itself by way of the intelligent use of timing.

USING LANGUAGE TO CONVEY MESSAGES

Another tool the Court uses to convey messages to the other branches in real time is the unique language that serves to convey precisely calibrated messages while a petition is still being heard. The Court carefully chooses the language it employs to accurately express the contents and force of the message it wishes to convey. The language in which the message is formulated or a certain word that is included or is absent from could affect substantially the message.

In fact, as we shall see below, one of the main advantages of advisory dialogue is that it enables the Court, by the sophisticated use of the richness of human language, to choose the precise degree of intensity in which the message will be conveyed. Advisory dialogue, particularly the kind that occurs in real time—as opposed to binding decisions that by nature are binary, post-factum, and absolute—enables the Court to convey its messages with variable degrees of intensity. The Court often uses this capacity to express in quite a precisely calibrated manner the intensity of its preferences on various issues brought before it. This is also true in cases that comprise the briefest decisions consisting of but a line or two.

Case law pertaining to the authority of security forces to prevent a meeting between an attorney and a person suspected of committing terrorist acts for a period of several days can illustrate such sophisticated usage.

Israel's security apparatus is consisted of three major establishments. The military or the Israel Defence Force (IDF); the Shin Bet, which is in charge of internal security, preventing terrorism and counterespionage; and the Mossad, which is in charge of intelligence collection, covert operations, and counterterrorism outside Israel's borders. In the event that an individual is suspected of terrorist involvement, the Shin Bet is authorized to prevent a meeting between the individual and his attorney for several days.[5] The point of this is to enable the Shin Bet to conduct urgent interrogation without any interference where it has information that the detainee possesses information with regard to an imminent terrorist act. Other countries, such as Australia and Canada, have legislated similar laws that allow the taking of preventive administrative measures, whose purpose is to obtain information regarding an expected terrorist act or serious damage to national security. These laws have been the subject of much criticism by Human Rights groups and NGOs.

---

[5] Section 35 of the Rules of Criminal Procedure (Enforcement Powers—Arrests), 5756-1996. It shall be noted that with regard to all that pertains to preventing a meeting of residents of the West Bank and Gaza Strip, the hearing in the Supreme Court occurs as the result of a petition to the High Court of Justice.

The Shin Bet's decision to prevent a meeting with an attorney is subject to judicial review that is immediately referred to the Supreme Court. The appeal is held in the presence of both parties but the Shin Bet has the option of submitting to the Court ex parte privileged material on which the decision to make the arrest is based.

Human rights organizations in Israel routinely tend to submit this kind of appeal even though the absolute majority of these appeals are rejected. It is apt to note that according to law, the Shin Bet is authorized to extend the initial period of preclusion in respect of which the appeal was submitted. Taking into account the urgency and severity of the measures, the Supreme Court is required in these cases to reach its decisions in real time and quite promptly, at times within a day or less. The Court needs to take a decision promptly even though most times there is a high degree of uncertainty regarding the probability of a terrorist act being committed.

A decision taken under circumstances of uncertainty is another inherent element of decision-making in national security matters in real time. The Court generally does not have the time or the tools to clarify the reality of the situation in depth. Yet the Court is required to make a decision often within hours on the question of whether a person's liberty has been significantly infringed with insufficient foundation or whether to allow this person to meet with her lawyer while risking that the information she has will be leaked to her fellow perpetrators or that the Shin Bet will not be able to prevent an act of terrorism. The Court can only estimate whether the suspect has information that can prevent an act of terrorism.

Studying Court decisions on this issue instructs how the Court has developed a language and codes that enable it to mitigate this inherent difficulty.

In practice, most[6] of these petitions are rejected. However, focusing on the bottom line misses the mark of understanding judicial review as applied by the Court. In order to understand the kind of judicial review the Court applies to these decisions, the language the Court uses must be analyzed too.

In many cases, the Court decision in these appeals is formulated with a text that is known in the Israeli professional jargon as "the 'we are satisfied' rule." The "we are satisfied" rule is comprised of a brief and succinct judgment in which the Court determines with no reasons given that "we are satisfied that there is no need for our intervention in the injunction and the privileged material on which it is based may not be exposed. The petition is rejected."[7]

Dan Yakir, General Counsel of the Association for Human Rights, has spoken out in the past regarding his frustration with these "we are satisfied" rulings. He writes that in the basements of the Supreme Court "thousands of judgments lie around…that were swallowed up by a kind of black hole and still await in-depth study. Thousands of failures

---

[6] Shiri Krebs, *National Security, Secret Evidence and Preventive Detentions: The Israeli Supreme Court as a Case Study, in* SECRECY, NATIONAL SECURITY AND THE VINDICATION OF CONSTITUTIONAL LAW (David Cole, Federico Fabbrini & Arianna Vedaschi eds., 2012).

[7] HCJ 9682/03, Abu Jahal v. the Minister of Defense (unpublished, Oct. 30, 2003).

in files…that did not warrant a response, that did not warrant an in-depth hearing, in which petitions were rejected on the subject of human rights in the West Bank and Gaza Strip, at times in a judgment of one page, at times in a judgment of one paragraph, in which the court states we are satisfied that the action of the government agency is lawful and the petition is rejected."[8]

In a number of cases, the Court adds several words to explain the decision and to justify the course of action that the Shin Bet took. For example, in HCJ *Barkan*,[9] the Court formulated its decision as follows:

> We have been persuaded that preventing a meeting between the Petitioner and an attorney was indeed necessary for considerations related to the good of the investigation and for reasons of maintaining security. *We are satisfied* that the Petitioner was made aware of his rights…*From what we saw and heard, it appears that there is a reasonable possibility for the validity of the current order to be extended and, therefore, it seems to us, as well, that the decision is fully justified.* [emphasis added][10]

In this case, the addition of the decision's concluding words conveys a message to the authorities. The appeal was rejected, as expected. However, the Court was not content with the words *we are satisfied*, and added a section that would be lenient toward the Shin Bet with regard to the uncertainty of whether to request a further extension to preclude the meeting. The decision's text is sufficiently clear and, in such a case, it is reasonable that the Shin Bet will not hesitate to request an extension of the initial period preventing the meeting.

Comparing the text of this decision with the one that was accepted in HCJ *Nassar*[11] for example provides an explanation for the question of why such profuse significance is attributed to the language the Court uses when it rejects a petition. The latter is an example of a different text, where at the same time as rejecting the appeal and using the formula "we are satisfied," the Court added another comment:

> *We are satisfied*…that there are no grounds for intervening in the prevented [meeting], insofar as it expires on September 15, 1998. *Nonetheless, insofar as the time is extended, during which the prohibition to meet applies, the onus imposed on the government authorities shall be intensified to persuade the President or the President on duty of the Military Court that the prohibition to meet must be further extended.* The petition is rejected. [emphasis added][12]

---

[8] Interview with Dan Yakir, HALISHKA, Issue 61 (June 2006).

[9] HCJ 4211/03, Barkan v. the Minister of Defense, Tak-El 2003 (2) 1485 (2003).

[10] *Id.*

[11] HCJ 5548/98, Nassar v. the Minister of Defense (unpublished, Oct. 14, 1998).

[12] *Id.* at 2 (of the judgment).

In this case, the petition was indeed rejected but the petitioner warranted "ammunition," which could be useful to him if the Shin Bet requested to extend the prevention of a meeting beyond the several days that the law authorizes. The line the Court added to the routine phrase "we are satisfied" is a partial victory in view of the possibility that the Shin Bet will grasp the advisory message in the Court's decision and will refrain from requesting a further extension. Of course, the Shin Bet is not obligated to grasp the message; the attorneys representing it are intended to assist the Shin Bet with the effective reception of the message.

The Court developed this practice in a sophisticated manner. It uses precisely calibrated messages and codes recognized almost solely by the players appearing before it to influence the question of whether the preventive step that the Shin Bet has taken is to be extended beyond the initial period under its authority until the detainee arrives for judicial review. Thus, for example, in HCJ *Al-Din*[13] the Court rejected the appeal to prevent a meeting, while it added an incidental comment to the routine phrase "we are satisfied" as follows:

> *We are satisfied* that the orders that have been granted by the Respondent to prevent the meeting of the petitioners in the petitions being heard…have been duly issued…*We have noted the declaration of the attorney for the Respondent that the Respondent is aware of the need to enable meetings between the detainees and their attorneys at the earliest possible time. Every effort shall be made to ensure that the orders will be granted for the minimal periods required.* [emphasis added][14]

This text is much more pointed than the text the Court used in HCJ *Nassar*, even though from a formal legal aspect the petitions in both cases were rejected. In this manner, the Court conveys the message that it expects that the meeting between the suspect and his attorney will take place as soon as possible.

Comparing the two texts allows us to see how the Court makes sophisticated and elegant use of language in order to convey messages and suggestions to the Shin Bet in real time, while it precisely calibrates the intensity of the message that it wishes to convey.

The examples brought above clarify why examining judicial work in the field of national security solely in accordance with the results of a proceeding (whether a petition is rejected or accepted) misses the mark of the effect of a principal judicial practice. Comments such as these serve the Court in making it clear to the government what are the possible implications of adopting an approach different from the one to which the Court alludes or advises. The effect of this comment is measured, inter alia, by the question of whether the Shin Bet indeed will refrain from again requesting the prevention of a meeting between a suspect and his attorney.

---

[13] HCJ 2103/96, Al-Din v. The Security Service, Tak-El 96(1) 9 (1996), section 1(c) of the judgment.
[14] *Id.*

Most notably, this practice illustrates a potential model of meaningful yet less traditional model of judicial review in real time. Israel is not the only country that has legislated laws to allow the taking of immediate administrative steps to prevent terrorist attacks or a serious attack on national security. Courts throughout the world are required to decide these questions in real time and to consider the strength of the intelligence material brought to their attention, and estimate the degree of risk to which the State is exposed, if the court orders revocation of the preventive measure. Such decisions put judges in a very difficult situation. They need to protect fundamental rights while almost being practically unable to assess the risk of a terrorist attack hitting a major city due to their reluctance to provide security services with what they want. The Israeli Supreme Court's use of advisory dialogue illustrates how the Court copes with the difficulty ensuing from intervening in real time in conditions of such great uncertainty. The Court rarely intervenes in Shin Bet decisions in such time but conveys a message to the Shin Bet with regard to its position on the issue. This message then affects the future conduct of the decision-maker.

THE PROCEDURAL PLATFORM AND ITS EFFECT ON THE SIGNIFICANCE OF THE MESSAGE

Another tool at the Court's disposal is the use of interim decisions. In the Israeli case, several types of interim decisions are available to the Court to hold a dialogue with the other branches and convey advisory messages to them. In this part, I will focus on *decisions with regard to interim orders*—particularly decisions on the basis of orders nisi. As we will see the Court uses every possible tool to convey carefully calibrated messages to the other branches. Obviously, interim decisions handed down during the hearing are a very useful tool to convey such messages.

Order Nisi

An order nisi is a signal built into legal procedure. According to procedure customary in the Supreme Court of Israel, in any event in which the Court chooses to grant an order absolute, this must be preceded by granting an order nisi, and the State must be allowed to prepare by way of bringing affidavits on its behalf.[15] In most cases in which a decision was rendered against the State, prior to giving the judgment an order nisi was granted that acts as a sort of messenger that heralds the possible coming of an order absolute. This was the case, for example, in the petition pertaining to the legality of the route of the separation fence that was set up to prevent suicide bombers from entering Israeli territory. During the hearing and before deciding that the chosen route is not legal, the Court gave

---

[15] *See* Rules of Procedure in the High Court of Justice 5744-1984.

an order nisi that signaled to the State that the Court is not satisfied with this policy.[16] The Court acted in the same manner in the petition concerning the legality of orders for mass detentions, which the army issued during the fighting in "Operation Defensive Shield."[17] The Court acted similarly at the time the famous petition was brought before it in the matter of Shin Bet interrogation methods,[18] as well as in the petition regarding government authority to hold Lebanese prisoners as bargaining chips.[19]

The contents of the message conveyed by means of the order is generally that the Court sees a difficulty in the State's position as brought before the Court in its preliminary response to the petition. The Supreme Court, which is unable to decide which files it will hear and which it will not hear, uses an order nisi as a signal similar to the signal that the US Supreme Court transmits when it decides to hear a petition. The main difference is that in the Israeli case, such orders could be given within hours or days from the events that led to the petition, thereby affecting the situation on the ground in real time.

This legal state of affairs leads to the fact that for the State, the stage of granting an order is a turning point. If up to this point, the State could adhere to a certain position even when it was not completely persuaded of its lawfulness, from this point onward it must examine its position and adapt it to the questions and difficulties that the Court indicated as the result of the State's written response and the oral hearing.

An obvious case illustrating the use the Court makes of an order nisi for conveying a signal to the parties with regard to its position on an issue was the hearing of a petition that was lodged on the matter of screening the film *Jenin Jenin*.[20] The controversial film deals with fighting in a refugee camp in Jenin and contends that a massacre was perpetrated in the camp by Israel Defense Forces (IDF) soldiers. The film's director, Muhammad Bakri, submitted the film to the Film Review Council to obtain authorization to screen the film commercially in movie theaters in Israel. The Film Review Council decided by an 8 to 3 majority vote to prohibit its screening in Israeli movie theaters. The Council sent notice of the decision to Muhammad Bakri and in it explained the grounds for its decision with the following arguments:

1. The film portrays a distorted view of events under the guise of documentary verity that is likely to deceive the public.
2. The film is a propaganda film that presents one-sidedly the position of the party with which the State of Israel finds itself at war and at the time while this war is still going on and it is inappropriate for the Council to lend a hand and authorize its screening.

---

[16] HCJ 2056/04, Beit Sourik Village Council v. the Government of Israel, PD 58(5) 807 (Mar. 31, 2004).

[17] HCJ 3239/02, Marab v. Commander of IDF Forces in the West Bank, PD 57 (2) 349 (Dec. 15, 2002).

[18] HCJ *On Torture*, sections 6–7 of the judgment.

[19] HCJ 794/98, Obayed v. the Minister of Defense, PD 55 (5) 769 (2001), para. 1 of the judgment.

[20] HCJ 316/03, Bakri v. Film Review Council, PD 58 (1) 249 (2003).

3. The film severely harms public sensibilities. The public is likely to think mistakenly that IDF soldiers systematically and intentionally perform war crimes, absolutely contrary to the truth and the factual findings of investigations carried out by the IDF and by international entities.

4. The presentation of the events borders on incitement and delegitimizes the very existence of the State of Israel.

5. The fundamental principles and nature of a democracy that does not wish to commit suicide require, according to the Council, that it refrain from giving authorization and approval to screening the aforesaid film.

Bakri petitioned the Council's decision to the Supreme Court with the contention that the Film Review Council's decision infringes on freedom of expression and creativity, and deviates from the Council's authority as the Council may not mix in political considerations in its decisions or disqualify films that it believes to be untruthful. On filing the petition, Justice Dorner gave an order nisi the same day the petition was filed. This decision, handed down during a period of intense fighting, without obtaining the government's position, while the Court was yet dealing with dozens of petitions that concerned the actual conducting of the fighting, was a dramatic signal that the Court viewed a genuine difficulty in the government's position.

The Court anticipated that the government would grasp the message and refrain from bringing the matter for judicial decision. Had the government acted accordingly, the film would have been released for public viewing within a matter of days.

Instead, the government, which had understood the message, undertook a countermeasure. It did not respond to the message that the Court conveyed to it but, instead, when the time came for the hearing, in view of the direction of the winds blowing in the courtroom, it requested that the panel be expanded, hoping thereby perhaps to gain time and also additional judges who would support its contentions. Its request was rejected.[21] Ultimately, the petition was accepted and the Court ordered the film to be released for screening.

This case illustrates how the Court could utilize judicial review in the area of national security without waiting for the conclusion of the hearing on a petition—which, at times, can extend for many months. The Israeli Supreme Court does so by transmitting messages and signals. These, if accepted, could lead promptly to a change in policy that the government undertakes and to a faster upholding of human rights, if the government is prepared to grasp such messages and act according to that which is expected of it. Indeed, in this case, the government did grasp the message but opted for its own reasons to fight for its position. However, the tool that was available to the Court exists and, in many cases, as we will see further on, in reality led to a situation that made the hearing

---

21 *Id.*, decision of May 5, 2003.

of the entire petition redundant and to the cessation of controversial policy within a matter of days.

Interim Order

Another interim decision the Court uses judiciously to transmit messages in real time is the interim order. Understanding the Court's patterns of use of interim orders as a means to convey advisory messages requires more complex observation that deviates from the simple question whether to grant an order as the petitioners have requested. In many cases, the order reflects a customary practice of the Court and no more. In making its decision the Court is persuaded by considerations such as the possibility that refraining from granting an order will cause the petitioners a great deal of damage, the possibility that granting the order will endanger human life—and all this before the Court has determined whether the means the government uses is improper. Landmark judgments against the government such as HCJ *On Torture* or Criminal Further Hearing *Bargaining Chips* were taken without interim orders preceding such decisions and, at times, even after the Court was requested to grant an interim order and explicitly refused prior to deciding the petition.

As a rule, the Supreme Court of Israel has a clear and consistent policy on which cases it will or will not grant an interim order. According to such case law,[22] the decision on the matter of interim orders is based on considerations that involve the petition's chances to succeed and the balance of convenience of the parties. For example, in petitions that concerned house demolitions or expelling a person from the West Bank, an interim order was granted as a matter of course even though in fact most of the petitions ultimately were rejected. The granting of an interim order in these kinds of petitions must be construed as the wish of the Court to hold a hearing on the question of a house demolition after the military authorities have already destroyed the house or not to hold a hearing on a petition against an expulsion after the person has been expelled from the territories and thereby to turn the question that pertains to the legality of the conduct of public authorities into a theoretical one.

CASE STUDIES

Use of Violence in Shin Bet Interrogations

While bearing in mind this caveat, analyzing the use of interim orders by the Court can illustrate the sophisticated use the Court makes of decisions in order to transmit messages to the other branches in real time. The most striking example is that regarding

---

[22] *See, e.g.,* HCJ 1715/97, Israel Investments Administrators Office v. the Minister of Finance, PD 51 (4) 367 (1998) and HCJ 6336/04, Mussa v. the Prime Minister, Tak-El 2004 (4) 2737 (2004).

the use of violence against suspected terrorists. For years, petitions were filed with the Supreme Court pertaining to the use of violence against interrogatees. The Court tended to refrain from granting interim orders in these petitions. The rationale provided for this approach was that an interim order that prohibits the use of violence in a "ticking bomb" situation could lead to irreversible damage to many, if the suspect indeed conceals information pertaining to an imminent act of terrorism. The Human Rights NGO, B'Tselem, at the time indicated[23] that the Court's avoidance of granting interim orders that prohibit the use of violence against an interrogate, even though the justices at the Court knew what is happening in the interrogation room, enabled the Shin Bet to use the auspices of the Supreme Court to employ violence against many interrogatees.

When the hearing of the petition in substance was held, several days later, the government would wash its hands clean and declare that no violent measures would be used in the suspect's investigation, that therefore there is no further reason to conduct the proceeding, and that the government requests that the petition be stricken. The Court for many years agreed to such requests as a routine matter and thereby was not required to consider the legality of the use of violence.

A decision that was taken in HCJ *Halef*,[24] close to the Court's precedent-setting judgment on *the Torture* issue instructs how the Court signals by way of an interim order with regard to altering this policy. The decision in *Halef* did not merit a great deal of public attention. This case, which also focused on the use of violence in Shin Bet interrogations, was discussed on the eve of the dramatic decision in the HCJ *On Torture*. Ostensibly, the petition was intended to pass through the ordinary channels through which such petitions are heard, that is, without an interim order being granted and with the Court being satisfied with the government's declaration during the hearing itself that violent measures are no longer being used in the suspect's investigation. From here, the petition was to have moved on to the track of being dismissed. Nonetheless, in this petition the Court veered from this practice. In order to clarify the change that the interim order signaled, we must view the schedule according to which the petition was heard. The petition was filed on May 12, 1999, four months prior to the handing down of the decision in the HCJ *On Torture* and at a time when, behind the scenes, the general picture apparently had already been formed to the effect that the Court intended to move heaven and earth to prohibit the use of violence against interrogatees. The day after the petition was filed, on May 13, 1999, against the dissenting opinion of Justice Terkel, the Court granted an interim order as follows:

> On the matter of the possible use of physical force on the Petitioner, we have decided by a majority vote, against the dissenting opinion of Justice Terkel, to grant an

---

[23] B'Tselem, Legitimizing Torture: HCJ Decision on the Bilbisi, Hamdan and Mubarak Affair; Sources and Comments—Special Report (1997).

[24] HCJ 3195/99, Halef v. Shin Bet (unpublished, May 9, 2000).

order nisi against the Respondent…We have decided by a majority vote—against the dissenting opinion of Justice Terkel—to grant the interim order that prohibits the use of physical force against the Petitioner.[25]

This decision, in a departure from the Court's practice up to that time, signaled a change in the spirit of the Court. The decision also illustrates how in many cases it is not the formal order that creates the signaling but rather specifically the departure from customary practice that was formulated on the same issue—that is what creates the signaling. In this case, the differences of opinion on the panel only intensified the power of the message that the Court conveyed.

The Court sends such signals even when it comes to issues dealing with the battlefield and even at times the battle is still going on. To illustrate this point I will present two cases. One is related to Operation Rainbow. The second one relates to the army's use of neighbors to help it in the capture of terrorism suspects ("Neighbor procedure").

Operation Rainbow

On May 12, 2004, five IDF fighters were killed when the armored personnel carrier (APC) in which they were traveling was hit by antitank fire and exploded due to the large amount of explosive materials in it. The next day, another two fighters were killed in Rafiah close to the corridor, while assisting in a search for body parts of the soldiers of the APC. On May 14, 2004, the IDF commenced intensified fighting in the area of Rafiah, which included the destruction of many houses in the area, known also as the Philadelphi Corridor, in a campaign that was called Operation Rainbow. On the same day, a petition was filed against the army's military actions. The central contention was that the IDF was causing intensive destruction of houses as a punitive measure and campaign of revenge for the killing of its soldiers, completely contrary to the provisions of the Geneva Conventions, which prohibit punitive measures of this kind. The petition was submitted at 9 p.m. Friday evening while the battle was on and most Israelis were having their traditional Sabbath dinner. As there was no justice available in the Court, the petitioners submitted the petition to Justice Mazza at home. At 11:00 p.m., the Attorney General's Office provided his response to the petition. After reading the petition and the response at around 11:30 p.m. Friday night, Justice Mazza ordered the following:

> Following scrutiny of the Petition and the Response, I hereby order that the Petition be set for a hearing before a panel on May 16, 2004, at 1 p.m.….I hereby decide to grant a restrained interim order that shall remain in effect until another decision is taken. The order prohibits the Respondent from the advance planned

---

[25] *Id.*, decision of May 13, 1999, at 1.

demolition of any of the Petitioners' homes … The decision is given *in my home, on the Sabbath eve of May 14, 2004, at 11:30 p.m.* [emphasis added][26]

This decision was taken on Sabbath eve close to midnight, relating directly to war situations and ordering the armed forces, while the public is outraged at the death of seven soldiers, to refrain from demolishing houses during a military campaign. It was given at a time when the fighting forces were yet in the heat of battle.[27] The courageous decision of Justice Mazza demonstrates the difficult conditions under which the Israeli Supreme Court operates and its commitment to judicial review in real time, even if this means ordering the IDF to take or refrain from taking certain actions while still fighting on the front.

Substantively, the decision, even if interim, demonstrates how much the Court was concerned from the reports human rights organizations provided to the justice in the petition regarding the level of destruction in Rafah. The intensity of the message that Justice Mazza transmitted to the IDF may be learned not just from the order itself but also from several more subtle elements in the decision. First, the Court set a date for an urgent hearing of the petition immediately on Sunday after the end of the Sabbath. Second, the timing of the interim order was sigificant—the order was granted at a late hour in the judge's home. Third, the message included the granting of an interim order that restricted the actions of the IDF while the fighting on the front was still going on, in a departure from the Court's declared position that generally it will not intervene in the course of fighting at the time that it occurs, while the combatants are still in the field. The Court repeated and underscored this policy in another judgment given precisely at that time.[28] Fifth, this order was granted notwithstanding the government's contention

---

[26] HCJ 4573/04, Albasyouni v. the Commander of the IDF Forces, Tak-El 2004 (2) 1288 (2004), decision of May 14, 2004.

[27] *See also* HCJ 4969/04, Adallah v. GOC (General Officer Commanding) Southern Command in the IDF, Tak-El 2004 (3) 1786 (2004) (decision of July 22, 2004). The Court related in its decision to the progression of the hearing of the petition: "Yesterday, toward 10 p.m., the chief secretary of the court transmitted to me, to my home, 'an urgent petition on behalf of the Respondent to revoke an interim order.' The petition describes the fighting activities occurring these days in the area of the Philadelphi Corridor—*inter alia*, to locate tunnels that have been excavated for smuggling arms—and it goes on to determine that 'in the course of the operational activities, buildings in the area will be damaged.' The Respondent further contends that contrary to what was argued by the Petitioners in their Petition, IDF forces are unable to locate the homes of the Petitioners 'from among the thousands of homes in the area of Rafiah and its refugee camp.' As this is the case, the Respondent goes on to contend that the Petitioners' Petition must be viewed as a general petition for granting 'a comprehensive order' and, as such, it is not to be granted." The decision concludes with the words "Given this day, 4 Av 5764 (July 22, 2004) at 12:25 a.m."

[28] In HCJ 4969/04, Adallah v. GOC (General Officer Commanding) Southern Command in the IDF, Tak-El 2004 (3) 1786 (2004), the President underscored in his judgment that "the humanitarian issues have been arranged without endangering the lives of soldiers or the activities of the hostilities." *See also on this subject* HCJ 4764/04, Physicians for Human Rights v. Commander of IDF Forces in Gaza, Tak-El 2004 (2) 2183, 2186 (2004) [hereinafter "the *Rafiah* case"]. *See also* HCJ 3114/02, Barakeh v. Minister of Defense, PD 56 (3) 11, 15–16 (2002), in which President Barak notes: "This court certainly will not take any position

that this decision causes difficulties for the IDF forces fighting in the field. Altogether, it signaled that the Court was very concerned from a humanitarian aspect with the manner in which the fighting is being conducted by the IDF and wished, first of all, to convey a strong message to the IDF, by suspending it till Sunday.

Other judgments granted in petitions that were submitted on the subject of Operation Rainbow reinforced this feeling from different directions. For example, on April 18, 2004, Justice Mazza heard another petition that also concerned the question of house demolitions at the time of fighting in Rafiah. On rejecting the petition, Justice Mazza conveyed an additional message pertaining to the Court's dissatisfaction with the manner in which the fighting was being conducted:

Since the beginning of the fighting last week, thirty to forty buildings have been damaged and from the Sabbath eve to date, three abandoned buildings were damaged. *These numbers taken from the petitioners' data, which appear small, provide cold comfort.* However, we would like to assume that the Respondents are aware of the gravity of the responsibility imposed on them and are making every effort to minimize, insofar as possible, the degree of damage to the broad civilian population and the degree of its suffering. [emphasis added][29]

Several weeks later, a judgment was made in a third petition that dealt with the warfare in Rafiah. In this judgment, the Court reviewed the entirety of the army's conducting of the Operation and sharply expressed its views pertaining to the way the army conducted the campaign:

Lessons must be learned from the incident…We must avoid this. This matter must be planned ahead. A clear procedure must be instituted with regard to the different phases that must be undertaken on this matter…It must be assumed that the lessons will be learned, and if it is necessary to amend the orders given to the army, this shall be carried out. [emphasis added][30]

Thus, by way of several interim orders that were strictly formulated and several incidental remarks (obiter dicta) in the judgment on the *Rafiah* case, the Court conveyed a strong message that it was not satisfied with the manner in which the IDF's fighting in Rafiah was being conducted and the extent of the house demolitions taking place.

---

with regard to the manner of conducting the fighting. As long as soldiers' lives are at risk, the decisions will be made by the commanders."

29 HCJ 4694/04, Abu Attrah v. the Commander of the IDF Forces in the Gaza Strip, Tak-El 2004 (2) 1645 (2004).

30 The *Rafiah* case, *supra* note 28, para. 27 of the judgment.

It is important to note that the Court's firm statements in the judgment on the *Rafiah* case with regard to the army's duty to prepare—prior to setting out on an operation—for the difficult humanitarian situation anticipated to be imposed on the local population in Rafiah, were made in the absence of any oral hearing. The focus of the hearing was the legality of house demolitions during the military campaign. The Court conveyed its broader messages without requesting the government to relate in its reply to these questions. The Court entered into the issue of the duty to prepare for the potential suffering of civilian population before going to a military campaign, as a voluntary initiative that was undertaken in a clear departure from accepted practice, in which a verbal hearing is held prior to the Court making a decision on any matter. The message that was understood by the Attorney General's Office as the result of this decision was that this was "a burning issue" for the Court. Attorneys involved in this case stated that the Court felt bound to convey the message and "that it did not feel it could wait even one day with conveying it."[31]

Thus, by way of a series of interim decisions taken on the matter of the fighting in Rafiah, the Court transmitted messages in real time to the IDF, comprising a call for change in its attitude to the humanitarian aspects of warfare and reminding it of its duty to fulfill humanitarian law. The signaling of the Court's dissatisfaction with how the fighting was given in a courageous interim injunction, handed down less than three hours after the petition was submitted, while the fighting was still going on, on Sabbath eve, May 14, 2004, at 11:30 p.m. in the home of Justice Mazza.

The use of Human shields – "Neighbor Procedure"

A further example of the Court's use of interim orders as a signal may be taken from the petition in HCJ *Neighbor Procedure*, which could be referred to as the *Human Shields* case.[32] In May 2002, the Adallah organization, an NGO, lodged a petition that concerned the IDF's use of Palestinian citizens as "human shields" when coming to capture terrorists who ensconce themselves in people's homes. The petitioners contended that the soldiers forced citizens who live near the target to knock on the door of the house and ask the suspects to come out, which is contrary to the Geneva Conventions and places the citizens at great risk. Two days after the petition was lodged, the government informed the Court that "the IDF decided to issue immediately an unequivocal command to forces in the field stating that it is absolutely prohibited for all forces in the field to use civilians, wherever they may be, as a 'live shield' against shooting or terrorist

---

[31]   This was told to the author in a conversation with an attorney who had been involved in the petition of July 20, 2005.

[32]   HCJ 3799/02, Adallah v. GOC (General Officer Commanding) Central Command, PD 60 (3) 67 (2005) [hereinafter "The Neighbor Procedure Petition"].

attacks on the part of the Palestinians."[33] Nonetheless, the government contended that requesting Palestinians to order other Palestinians to leave their homes does not constitute using them as human shields.

On August 14, 2002, while the petition was still pending, Nadal Abu Muhsan, an 18-year-old Palestinian, was killed while participating in "the Neighbor Procedure." As the result of this incident, seven human rights organizations again petitioned the High Court of Justice demanding that an interim order be granted that absolutely prohibits use of this practice. At the beginning of the hearing, Justice Strasburg-Cohen turned to the State representative at the hearing and requested that he explain to the Court exactly how the order would be carried out in the field as "there are many details in it that fall between what is permitted and what is prohibited."[34] The justice also wanted to know how fine distinctions such as this are applied in a complex body such as the IDF.[35] The State replied that the procedure is vital and does not place the Palestinian in actual danger as a military force is backing him up throughout the entire action, and this is always performed with the Palestinian's agreement. The Court was not persuaded by the government's contentions and issued a comprehensive interim order.[36] The order prevented the IDF from using Palestinian civilians for these purposes. This order, also granted at the peak of the fighting during 2002, was again a signal that this petition was heading in a different direction—its timing, as in the case of Rafiah, while the forces were still fighting in the field and actively using this tactic only augmented the message's force.

In January 2003, the State submitted its reply to the petition and presented a softened version of the procedure, which sought to incorporate the Court's reservations. This version, known as "the early warning procedure," introduced several innovations. According to the proposed procedure, the IDF would be permitted to be aided by a Palestinian civilian solely if the Palestinian sent to inspect the house is a family member who lives there and agrees to cooperate. Similarly, he is not to be equipped with any military signs (such as a helmet or bulletproof vest) and it is prohibited from endangering his life.

At this point, the court was faced with two possibilities: one, to go along with the State's proposal and conduct the petition hearing aiming to adopt or modify the softened version of the Neighbor Procedure; two, to conduct the petition hearing aiming to invalidate the entire procedure.

The analysis of the interim decision by the Court again signaled the direction in which the Court opted to go:

In view of the submission of the version of the procedures, formulated by the Respondents, both parties shall complete their pleadings, *inter alia*, by clarifying the

---

[33] *Id. See* the government's response to the petition for an interim order of May 7, 2002.

[34] The Neighbor Procedure Petition, *supra* note 32, decision of May 22, 2005.

[35] *Id.*

[36] *Id.*, decision of Aug. 18, 2002.

situation in international law with regard to the distinction between the use of persons as "human shields" or "hostages" and being aided by them, as contended by the Respondents and as expressed in the procedures they have designed. Furthermore, the parties shall relate to the meaning given to these two concepts in international law. The parties shall relate as well to the question of the legitimacy of the distinction between the use of persons as "living shields" or "hostages" and the manner of activity described in the procedures as permissible.[37]

Later in the hearing, the Court conveyed another signal. While the petition was still pending, Justice Strasburg-Cohen, who headed the panel, retired. However, instead of appointing another justice from the panel to head it, the file was transferred for handling to "the senior panel," the significance of which we will discuss in the next chapter. As the file was transferred to "the senior panel," a hearing was held on September 5, 2004, before President Barak, and he opened the hearing by saying the following:

The Geneva Convention prohibits involving local residents in the actions of a conquering army. Therefore, it is prohibited to implicate any local individual against his will. The case before us indeed involves a willing resident, but my concern is that out of 100 instances of "willing participants," 99 will be instances in which the individual acted unwillingly. It is quite difficult to confirm willingness. The concern is that at night, when a military unit arrives, no neighbor will refuse because he is afraid. The very presence of a military unit at night is threatening. It is rare that consent will be given willingly. I am convinced that your objective is to protect the residents. This is undisputed. However, I am concerned that the military will encounter difficulties. No one will admit to this practice. Therefore, perhaps it is preferable to say, "Distance yourself from the local resident. Don't involve him and don't recruit him, in view of the concern for the security of the person who assents. You do not know how the village will relate to him the next day. He will be deemed a collaborator." These are the difficulties I have with this practice.[38]

There can be nothing clearer than these statements, which were accompanied by a written decision. Studying the decision reveals a different issue that disturbed the Court. In retrospect, it became apparent that this concern significantly affected the justices' decision:

We defer the continued hearing of the petition. The objective of the deferral is to allow the Respondents to present to the court within 90 days a report on their

---

[37] *Id.*, decision of Jan. 1, 2003.

[38] *See* Tal Rosner, *Barak Fears That the IDF Will Encounter Difficulties in the Use of Civilians*, Ynet (Sept. 5, 2004), *available at* http://test.ynet.co.il/articles/0,7340,L-2973057,00.html.

handling of cases that were mentioned in the Petitioners' documents with regard to dealing with the contentions of breaching the practice of early warning.[39]

By way of this interim decision, the Court conveyed a further message. The Court was concerned not just with the question of whether the Neighbor Procedure conflicts with a prohibition in international law on the use of human shields. It was also concerned with the manner in which the current practice is implemented, in view of its depiction during the hearing[40] that commanders do not take care to implement the softened version of this practice. This concern, expressed by Justice Strasburg-Cohen in the courtroom, was reinforced by granting the interim order and later was again expressed by transferring the file to the senior panel of justices, which sought to learn if it is possible to oversee implementation of the practice. Finally, when the Court understood that it was not possible to implement the practice, neither in its original form nor its softened form, it accepted the petition and invalidated the practice. Justice Barak presented this consideration when he stated in the judgment that one of the reasons for invalidating the practices is that "the procedures come too close to the core of the normative prohibition, being found in the unsuitable gray area."[41] Justice Beinisch also clarified this as she explained her legal conclusion is based on the fact that "the risk of slipping toward the prohibited practice with an absolute prohibition is part and parcel of the means that the practice permits,"[42] while Justice Cheshin, who agreed with the judgment, added his own emphasis to the matter:

> However clear and clean the written rule may be, we must not forget that it is carried out, *de facto*, in the field, outside, under pressure, in tense circumstances, in conditions of mortal danger—to residents and soldiers. With any slight deviation from the directive, misunderstanding, or incorrect reading of the conditions in the field, we have strayed off the proper road onto the forbidden shoulders—we have slid from the permitted over to the forbidden. The temptation is great, and the justification will be easily found. Indeed, as the intensity of the danger rises, so rises the intensity of the temptation—in field conditions—to deviate from the procedure.[43]

This case illustrates how advisory messages affect immediately the way the military conducts its operations even before the case is heard. The Court identifies the problem and right away sends a signal that leads the military to change standard operating

---

[39] The Neighbor Procedure Petition, *supra* note 32, decision of Sept. 5,2004, at 2.

[40] *See also* B'Tselem, *Human Shield—The Use of Palestinian Civilians Contrary to an HCJ Order* (Nov. 2002); Human Rights Watch, *In a Dark Hour—The Use of Civilians during IDF Arrest Operations* (Apr. 2002).

[41] The Neighbor Procedure Petition, *supra* note 32, para. 25 of the judgment of then President Barak.

[42] *Id.*, para. 6 of the judgment of then Justice Beinisch.

[43] *Id.*, para. 7 of the judgment of Justice Cheshin.

procedures. This case shows also how in cases in which the Court must decide issues that are related to the manner of fighting in real time, it uses all means of conveying messages that are available to it. The Court does so while the armed forces are fighting on the front to clarify to the military that its manner of conducting warfare disturbs the Court. Ultimately, as the Court remained dissatisfied, it turned the interim order into an order absolute and accepted the petition.

The other unique aspect of judicial review of military actions was exemplified by Justice Barak and Justice Beinisch. These justices clarified in their judgments that what affected them was the fact that even if policy only touches on a prohibition of the Geneva Convention, it must be invalidated, as in the reality of fighting, it is impossible to apply such distinctions. The Court's judgment illustrates how a court committed to reviewing military actions views its role as not only having to decide the lawfulness or constitutionality of steps the military takes. The Court views its role as having to ensure that future conduct of the military will comply with international law. Thus, it orders the invalidation of orders of the military command that border on unlawfulness, if it sees that, in fact, it will not be possible to ensure that soldiers on the front will be able to carry out such orders in this manner.

The justices clarify for the military that it must create procedures to ensure that there will be no loopholes, which cause activity in the field to slide toward illegality. The justices implied two message here: first, they clarify that the Court has been persuaded in its decision to invalidate the procedure by the fact that it was proved at the hearing of the petition that the Neighbor Procedure, in the format proposed by the military, will not be applied by soldiers in the field. Second, it conveys a broader message to the military that, in the future too, if the military does not make certain to maintain the boundaries between the permissible and the forbidden and the strict application of the policy, whose legitimacy it wishes the Court to determine, the Court is likely to invalidate the policy, as it comprises the risk of sliding toward the forbidden practice. As in the *Rafiah* case, the Court used all means of conveying messages available to it rather than waiting for its final judgment to do that. Ultimately, as the Court remained unsatisfied with the issue, the Court changed the interim order to an order absolute and accepted the petition.

3

Supreme Court Practice and Dialogue

THE SIGNIFICANCE OF the language, the timing, and the Court's practice is crucial to an understanding of the ways the Israeli Supreme Court interacts with the other branches. In this chapter, we will present several additional ways in which the Court uses elements in its control to convey messages in real time.

THE PANEL

The Israeli Supreme Court generally sits as panels of three justices. Panels usually are chosen randomly. However, the Court uses three *deliberate* judicial practices pertaining to the panel of judges. Using these practices constitutes a signal to the parties. This refers to the Court's use of three judicial configurations—"a president's panel," "an expanded panel," and "a senior panel." We will first define the terms:

President's Panel—a panel headed by the President of the Court
Expanded Panel—a panel that includes more than three judges
Senior Panel—a panel on which the three most senior justices of the Court sit, including the President and Vice-President of the Court, according to current practice

The decision to hold a hearing with one of these panels is often made according to an explicit decision by the President when a petition is set for a hearing and, when necessary, it states the names of the justices who will sit on the panel. From cases examined, it appears that the President frequently intervenes in selecting a panel through one of the three practices we have indicated. The Court's use of this practice is not concealed from anyone. Use of one of these three formations signals to the parties—already at the time of filing the petition and, in many cases, while the fighting still continues—that the Court wishes to handle this file in a different manner altogether. This message is particularly important in those cases in which the decision to transfer the file to one of these three formations is made ostensibly as if the file is not intended to arouse any difficulty and particularly if the issue has already been decided in the past.

For example, the Court appointed a senior panel to hear the case in HCJ *Targeted Killings*, which we will discuss more extensively further on, even though a short time earlier a judgment had been given with an ordinary panel of the Court that rejected a similar petition. This signaled to the parties that the Court did not intend to continue in the previous judgment's direction.

The panel's configuration is likely to have a considerable effect on the judicial outcome. An analysis of Supreme Court judgments in the field of national security reveals that an absolute majority of judgments during the years 1996–2004—in which landmark decisions were given against the State—was preceded by selection of one of these panels. Appendix A includes most of the landmark decisions made against the State in this field during these years and indicates the panel of judges who gave the decision.

It appears from the table that a decision by the President that a file will be heard by one of the special panels increases substantially the likelihood that ultimately a decision in principle will be made against the State. A special panel makes it easier for the Court to make unpopular decisions and to cope better with the decision's implications in its relations with other branches. Accordingly, the Court's decision to move or not to move a certain petition to a special panel can serve to convey an immediate signal as soon as the petition is received that the Court sees the issue being brought before it as a matter in principle that requires a fundamental decision.

INVITATION TO NEGOTIATE

Another means the Court uses to convey messages to branches of government is "an invitation to negotiate." The Court often conveys comments to the State during the course of a hearing and by way of verbal comments it makes during a hearing urges the State to reach a settlement. In this way, the Court is able to further the rights of petitioners[1] within a relatively short time. These messages deserve special attention.

Petitions on national security matters are generally heard within several days of the date the petition is filed. This enables the Court to bring about a quick settlement that will have an immediate effect on the actual situation on the fighting front. Moreover, the field of national security at times grants the Court a unique framework for dialogue. Several procedures used in many countries pertaining to hearing issues related to national security and particularly administrative proceedings such as immigration,

---

[1] *See* Dotan, *"Do the 'Haves' Still Come Out Ahead?: Resource Inequalities in Ideological Courts: The Case of the Israeli High Court of Justice*, 33 L. & SOC. REV. 1059 (1999).

and designations of terrorist organizations or other administrative measures, include the possibility of holding a privileged hearing ex parte. In such cases, the State presents the Court with the intelligence material on which its response to the petition relies. Generally, only representatives of the Attorney General's Office and the security forces are present in such ex parte hearing. In the Israeli context, in the privileged part of the hearing, judges feel freer to pressure the State to compromise as their comments are stated confidentially to the representatives of the Attorney General's Office and the specific body (intelligence or military) against which the petition is filed.

There are dozens of examples of cases in which the Court uses this channel of communication as a means to further compromise, and the Court has successfully advanced many subjects in this manner. For example, the Court pressed the State to agree to a compromise pertaining to confiscating land for military purposes[2] and visits to mourning families of victims killed in the occupied territories, notwithstanding the closure of the Gaza Strip.[3] The Court acted similarly in HCJ 3109/96,[4] which discussed military checkpoints set up in the West Bank and Gaza Strip.[5] The same was true in HCJ 677/95,[6] which addressed confiscating land by the military for security reasons, in which the Court asked the parties, several times, to reach a settlement and, indeed, such a settlement was promptly attained and notice of it was delivered to the Court within a matter of days.

Another instance in which the Court was successful in promoting negotiations was HCJ 5311/02, which discussed the conditions of detention of security detainees who were arrested in the course of Operation Defensive Shield and the possibility of their receiving family visits. When the petition was filed, in lieu of the ordinary decision in which the State is requested to reply to the petition within a certain period, the Court ordered as follows:

> The Respondent is requested to inform the Court within 21 days of this day if the subject of the petition can be arranged *without the need for a judicial ruling.* [emphasis added][7]

This message was understood well by the State, which agreed to the petitioners' position completely and informed the Court that it would act shortly to complete the construction works and other technical and administrative arrangements that would enable visits by relatives of those detainees.[8]

---

[2] HCJ 5251/02, Arjoub v. IDF Military Commander in Judea and Samaria (unpublished, July 10, 2002).

[3] HCJ 1097/03, Alajouri v. IDF Military Commander in the Gaza Strip (unpublished, Jan. 31, 2003).

[4] HCJ 3109/96, Abu Jabar v. the State of Israel (unpublished, July 7, 2002).

[5] *Id.*, decision of May 19, 1997.

[6] HCJ 677/95, Alzeer v. the Minister of Defense (unpublished, July 10, 1997).

[7] HCJ 5311/02, Abu Hit v. the Commander of the Ketziot Prison Facility, Tak-El 2002(3) 1391 (2002), decision of June 20, 2002.

[8] *Id.*, para. 2.

The Israeli Supreme Court is quite proactive in the dialogue that it conducts during a hearing, which often takes place while the fighting on the front is still going on. Even a serious security situation does not prevent the Court from advising the parties of what, in its opinion, is suitable to be the nature of a settlement and to pressure the parties to accept it. For example, in HCJ 6631/01,[9] which concerned visits of attorneys to security prisoners at the peak of the al-Aqsa Intifada, the Court ordered the State, in an interim decision, to formulate procedures that would allow attorney visits to Israeli and Palestinian prisoners and detainees and even indicated the general direction with regard to the proper contents of the rules. This clear recommendation naturally increases the pressure on the parties because, if the matter fails to end in a settlement, the question also arises as to who cooperated with the Court and who did not. Indeed, in a hearing that was held later on, the State presented the rules it formulated and subsequently the petition was rejected.[10]

Case Study: The Gaza Flotila Raid

A recommendation to compromise could serve well the interests of both the State and the Court. A case that could illustrate this effectiveness is the highly contentious aftermath following the Gaza Flotilla Raid and the appointment of the Turkel Commission to investigate it. The *Gaza Flotilla Raid* was a military operation by Israel against six ships of the "Gaza Freedom Flotilla" on May 31, 2010, in the international waters of the Mediterranean Sea. The flotilla, organized by the Free Gaza Movement and the Turkish Foundation for Human Rights and Freedoms and Humanitarian Relief (İHH), was carrying humanitarian aid and construction materials, with the intention of breaking the Israeli-Egyptian blockade of the Gaza Strip. On May 31, 2010, Israeli naval commandos boarded the ships from speedboats and helicopters in order to force the ships to the Israeli port of Ashdod for inspection. During the struggle, nine activists were killed including eight Turkish nationals and one Turkish American, and many were wounded. The raid drew widespread condemnation internationally including by the United Nations Security Council[11] and resulted in a deterioration of Israel-Turkey relations.

The *Turkel Commission* (officially *The Public Commission to Examine the Maritime Incident of 31 May 2010*) was an inquiry set up by the Israeli government to investigate the Gaza Flotilla Raid, and the blockade of Gaza. One of the questions regarding the rules governing its setup was whether it would be allowed to summon soldiers. In its terms of reference, the government prohibited it from summoning soldiers, commanders, or any members of the Security Forces (Shin Bet and Mossad). Gush Shalom, a human rights nongovernmental organization (NGO), submitted a petition to the High Court

---

[9] HCJ 6631/01, Kuzmar v. the Prison Service, Tal-El 2002(1) 480 (2002).

[10] *Id.*

[11] *See* UN Security Council presidential statement of 31 May 2010 (S/PRST/2010/9). *Also available at* http://www.un.org/News/Press/docs/2010/sc9940.doc.htm.

of Justice against this decision. At the hearing the Court made it clear to the government that without authorizing the summoning of soldiers the Commission would be unable to check the facts surrounding the incident. It proposed to both sides a "compromise": if the Turkel Commission decides to summon military people and the government refuses, the Court will decide the matter, thus making it clear that in such case, the Court will compel the officers to testify.[12] Following this "compromise" the Commission started its work and summoned the Prime Minister, the Minister of Defence, the head of the Mossad, the head of the Shin Bet, and the IDF Chief of Staff. The question whether testimonies of other security or military officials should be brought before the Commission was never raised again before the Supreme Court.

Using this technique of encouraging the State to compromise allowed the Court to increase the credibility of the Commission, and hold soldiers and commanders more accountable to it—all without needing to confront the Prime Minister at the time of a major national crisis.

LEAVING PETITIONS PENDING FOR THE PURPOSE OF OVERSEEING THEIR APPLICATION

In certain cases, the Court's pressure is particularly intensive and includes not only a recommendation to compromise and a comment on the contents of the compromise but also repetition of the recommendation, subsequent to the State's failure to reach an agreement, as advised by the Court. One example is HCJ *Yassin*, which concerned a petition submitted by a lecturer at the American University in Jenin stating that the military did not allow her to work due to a concern that she was involved in terrorist activity. The Court advised the State to compromise.[13] In a later hearing, when it became clear that the Court's recommendation had not produced results, the Court gave an even more concrete and focused decision, which specified the nature of the arrangement that the Court wished the State to reach:

> We have proposed that the Respondents examine a practical way that will allow the Petitioner to fulfill her position at the American University in Jenin, during the course of the current academic year, without acknowledging her right to family unification in the area and without recognizing her right to continue to remain in Israel or in the area after the date of August 31, 2004. *At the request of the*

---

[12] *See* 4641/10 Uri Avneri v. the Prime Miniser of Israel (decision of 12 July, 2010, unpublished). *See also* Press Release by the petitioners, "The IDF Is Not a State within the State"—Another Gush Court Victory, *available at* http://zope.gush-shalom.org/home/en/events/1279061538/.

[13] HCJ 6598/03, Yassin v. the Commander of IDF Forces in Judea and Samaria (unpublished, Apr. 11, 2005), decision of Aug. 10, 2003.

Respondents' attorney and with the agreement of the attorney for the Petitioner, the Respondents are given a stay to consider our proposal. [emphasis added][14]

Clearly, the repeated proposal leaves the State with almost no option. Indeed, following this decision, an agreement along the lines of the proposed arrangement was reached, and, subsequently, the petition was struck.

There are occasions in which the State does not yield to pressure, yet the Court continues to pressure the parties. This was the case, for example, in HCJ 1745/02, which concerned the effect of the separation barrier in the Jerusalem area on the quality of life of residents of Kfar Ekev. The hearings on this petition extended over more than three years, during which the Court continuously pressured the parties to reach a settlement. Even as the parties arrived at an outline of a solution in principle, the Court left the petition pending until it was explained that the settlement agreed on by the parties had already been applied in the field. In one of the interim decisions, the Court called the petition "a rolling petition."[15]

The term *rolling petition* is a unique one. It is doubtful that it is possible to describe anything similar in other legal systems. It accurately explains the pattern of the Court's activity as it exercises judicial review in real time: pressure on the parties to negotiate, intensive intervention in the nature of the agreement, and follow-up of pressure until the Court sees the result it intended be implemented on the ground. The Court sees no difficulty in an intervention that systematically leads the State to achieve the Court's desired results.

The Court's conduct illustrates how dialogue serves the Court for an additional purpose apart from actually reaching a settlement. The Court's conduct is intended in many cases to ensure that the Court's decision is applied. The Court views its role as making sure that State systems designated to protect national security will respect the rule of law, and it does not limit itself to a retrospective examination of the lawfulness of the State's policies. The Court uses dialogue in hearing a petition for an unconventional purpose: overseeing application of the decision. A certain petition may be left pending even though the parties already know the legal resolution, in order for the Court to oversee the implementation of the resolution, and only when its implementation is complete does the Court formally reject the petition.[16]

---

[14] *Id.*, decision of Sept. 7, 2003.

[15] *Id.*, decision of Apr. 14, 2005.

[16] In her book, Naomi Levitzki describes how Justice Beinisch used this practice to cause the State to agree to rectify safety hazards in educational institutions for Beduins in the Negev: "We all understood that until we can see matters for ourselves and check to see that all deficiencies indeed have been rectified, these children will not attend school. This is not a small thing and it is not a waste of time for me to preside over such a file." In an aside, Levitzki writes that Justice Beinisch confided about the considerable difficulty she has as a judge "who has no possibility of following up on the complete and proper execution of judgments that she writes and she regrets this." NAOMI LEVITZKI, THE SUPREMES: WITHIN THE SUPREME COURT 87 (2006).

The Court acted along these lines when petitions were brought before it regarding the behavior of detention authorities toward security detainees in prison facilities. In many cases, there is a wave of mass detentions when the military undertakes a major campaign. In one of the petitions filed against this practice, the Court wrote the following:

> The Reply submitted by the state is a long and detailed Reply...Under these circumstances, it seems to us that it would not be proper that we be required to hear the petition in substance. Since inspection committees have been set up, it would be well for us to await their recommendations *and we shall examine the manner of application of those same recommendations in practice.* [emphasis added][17]

The words that have been emphasized in this decision, "we shall examine the manner of application of those same recommendations in practice," express the Court's willingness to leave petitions pending, even though from a legal aspect their issues have been addressed. The Court is thereby able to follow up through dialogue with government authorities subsequent to the application of its recommendations to ensure that the petitioners' rights will be respected. By employing this technique, the Court uses legal procedures to expand the boundaries of its influence beyond the decision of a legal dispute and to put itself in charge of that decision's application. The Court thereby manages, at times, to bring about the prompt execution of a judgment and halt detrimental policy, all within a relatively brief time. This method of leaving petitions "rolling" serves as a significant tool for the Court, which is determined to have an impact on actual situations in real time or as close as possible to real time.

WRITTEN COMMENTS AND VERBAL COMMENTS

An additional point worth mentioning in this context is that there is a certain dialectic between the message that the Court conveys in its formal decisions and the comments that are voiced verbally during a hearing. On the one hand, in an oral hearing judges feel more comfortable making their remarks, while when matters are presented in writing, judges are careful not to be perceived as having already made a decision on the petition. On the other hand, a signal in a written message is generally more powerful and cannot be ignored by the parties.

A case that illustrates this dialectic is HCJ 3417/03.[18] In this High Court of Justice case, the widow of a Hamas activist, who was involved in three of the most violent terrorist attacks that Israel had known during these years, filed a petition requesting that

---

[17] HCJ 3985/03, Bedui v. the Commander of the IDF Forces in Judea and Samaria Tak-El 2003(2) 3649, 3650, decision of July 14, 2003.

[18] HCJ 3417/03, Elan v. the IDF Commander on the West Bank (unpublished, Feb. 24, 2005).

her husband's body be returned to her so that it could be brought for burial on the West Bank. The State contended that returning bodies is a matter for negotiation between the government and the Palestinian Authority when the battles end. The Court unequivocally clarified in an oral hearing[19] that the State's position is unacceptable and that it expects the State to present a different position. This was so even though legally it is difficult to say that the State's position was erroneous. However, on the conclusion of the hearing, when the decision concluding matters was dictated, the Court ordered the following in writing:

> In light of the exchange, *we have requested that the Respondent reconsider its position*. Notice shall be delivered to us within 30 days. According to the contents thereof, we shall decide on the manner of the continued handling of the petition. [emphasis added][20]

This decision refines the message that had been conveyed verbally, which had been more direct. However, notwithstanding the refined text, the parties understood the decision[21] as a clear instruction to the Attorney General to re-examine his position on the file. Indeed, as a result of this decision, a discussion was held by the Attorney General, at the end of which the government gave notice that it would retreat from its former position and it agreed that the petition be accepted.

POINTING OUT A PROBLEM

Another technique the Court uses in dialogue in a petition is to give an interim decision in which it suggests to the State that there is an actual difficulty with its position, without necessarily indicating a suitable plan for settlement. There are numerous examples of how this type of message is conveyed. One example is the decision in a hearing that was held in HCJ *Natasha*.[22] This case concerned the petitioners' request that the period of maximum detention permitted for security detainees in the West Bank should be curtailed. At the end of the petition's initial hearing, the Court ordered as follows:

> We grant the Respondents' request to defer the continued hearing of this petition. The purpose of the deferral is to enable *a reevaluation* of this policy…– within a

---

[19] Based on a conversation that took place on February 16, 2005, during the period of the hearing of the petition with an attorney who was present at the hearing and well versed in the petition's details.

[20] HCJ 3417/03, Alan v. the Commander of IDF Forces on the West Bank (unpublished, Feb. 24, 2005), decision of July 12, 2004.

[21] *Supra* note 18

[22] HCJ 2307/00, Natasha v. the Commander of IDF Forces on the West Bank, Tak-El 2002(1) 979.

period of four months—supplementary notice shall be delivered to us. According to the contents thereof, we shall decide on the manner of the continued handling of the petition. [emphasis added][23]

The Court's use of the word *reevaluation* signaled that the State's position did not satisfy the Court and therefore the justices required a "reevaluation," which ultimately led to a change in the State's position.

INTERIM DECISIONS AS SIGNALS: CASE STUDIES

The Case of the Use of Violence in Shin Bet Interrogations

An instructive example of conveying an advisory message in this manner may be found in a decision given in HCJ 5304/97[24] that concerned the contention by a Shin Bet interrogatee that violence was used against him during an interrogation. The petition was submitted on September 14, 1997, at the time when the hearings in the HCJ *On Torture* were at an advanced stage. The next day, September 15, 1997, the Court gave the following interim decision:

The case being heard in this petition is *complex*. We commenced a hearing yesterday and we heard from the Respondents, with the agreement of the attorney for the Petitioner, privileged information *Ex Parte. We were not satisfied* and, in a decision given yesterday, we advised that we would like to continue to clarify the matter. To this end, we set an additional hearing for today, for this afternoon, and we requested that prior to the hearing we receive *the position of the Attorney General*. We received written notice today on behalf of the Attorney General and we heard again, this time too with the agreement of the attorney for the Petitioner, privileged information with regard to the suspicions concerning the Petitioner and the development of the investigation that is being conducted at present and will continue in future. We cannot deny the basis on which the investigation is founded. Nonetheless, based on the material that has been presented to us, we see no reason to decide the Petitioner's petition either way. Accordingly, we decide the following:

1. The hearing of the petition will continue in the presence of the parties on September 18, 1997, at 6 p.m.
2. The Attorney General is requested *personally* to follow-up on the course of the investigation of the Petitioner to ensure that no unlawful means are used in the investigation.

---

[23] *Id.*, decision of Dec. 6, 2000.
[24] HCJ 5304/97, Saba v. General Security Service, Tak-El 2000(2) 1869 (2000).

3. The Attorney General is requested to submit to the Court, ahead of the hearing on September 18, 1997, *personal notice that is signed by him*, which responds to the particulars of the Petition and indicates his substantive position with regard to the Petition. [emphasis added][25]

It should be noted that violent measures had been taken against the petitioner during the investigation, and he was defined by the Shin Bet as "a ticking bomb." The advisory message in this interim decision was clear. The Court saw considerable difficulty in the fact that violence had been used vis-à-vis the petitioner. Nonetheless, it refrained from giving an interim order to cease the use of such means. Instead, the Court preferred to advance the subject by way of dialogue with the government's Attorney General. Both the language and contents of the decision indicate the high degree of finesse that the Court uses in the dialogue. Every word in this brief decision has been precisely formulated. At the outset, the Court defines the case as "complex" even though, as we have pointed out, dozens of similar petitions were brought before the Court during that same period, in which the Court refrained from intervening. Second, the Court indicates that "it is not satisfied" with the State's reply. Third, the Court holds two hearings on the same day—one in the morning and one in the afternoon. Fourth, the Court instructs the Attorney General personally to follow up on the course of the petitioner's investigation and submit notice to the Court that the Attorney General has personally signed—a most unusual demand. Those who are attentive might be able to see in decisions of this kind and in others like it[26] that were given during the same period the initial signs of a perceptual change that was developing in the Supreme Court pertaining to the use of violence in Shin Bet interrogations. It should be noted that later, as the result of the acceptance of the HCJ *On Torture*, the Court ordered the State to pay compensation to this interrogatee.[27]

MINORITY OPINION AS A SIGNAL

The Case of House Demolitions

A dialogue of considerable significance also took place during petitions pertaining to house demolitions. In order to understand the significance of the dialogue, it is worth briefly mentioning the development of case law with regard to house demolitions and

---

[25] *Id.*

[26] Another case that also comprised signaling of the Court's various moods was HCJ 6296/98, Hasib v. General Security Services, Tak-El 98(3) 1480 (1998). This case also pertained to violence used against a GSS interrogatee but here the Court indeed refrained from giving an interim order, against the minority opinion of Justice Dorner, who believed that an interim order should be given that would prohibit the State from using violence against an interrogatee.

[27] HCJ 5304/97, Saba v. General Security Services, Tak-El 2000(2) 1869 (2000).

the dialogue between the Court and governmantal authorities on the matter during the years in which Israel maintained this policy.

The use of house demolitions is one of the most controversial administrative measures that Israel wields in its fight against terror. According to most experts everywhere, this measure contradicts the Geneva Conventions because the principal persons who are punished are the terrorist's family members, not the terrorist himself. Therefore, the ethics of taking such measures is also dubious. Additionally, it is highly doubtful whether such measures indeed achieve the objective of deterrence, which is the reason such measures are undertaken.[28] Despite this situation Israeli law is quite clear. Regulation 119 of the Defense (Emergency) Regulations that originated in the days of the British Mandate over Palestine authorizes the military commander to demolish the homes of terrorists and does not limit his authority in any manner whatsoever.

This situation brought the Supreme Court face to face with a dilemma that was far from simple. As this regulation preceded the legislation of the Basic Laws that grant authority to invalidate a law, the Israeli Supreme Court has no authority to determine that this regulation is not constitutional. The question is whether the policy should be declared unlawful even though the language of the law is very clear and broad. The Court's approach to the issue of house demolitions illustrates well how dialogue serves the Court in dealing with this tension. Essentially, the Court attempts to influence, even if not always successfully, the policy of house demolitions without determining that this policy is unlawful, and therefore entering into a head-on confrontation with the other branches of government and risking the Court's credibility due to what could easily be seen as an artificial interpretation.

For years, the Court tended to refrain from intervening in the policy of house demolitions. Normally, the Court would hold a hearing that focused on pressuring the State to restrict the demolition decision to the part of the property that belongs to the terrorist whose house has been slated for demolition. At the same time, the Court for years tended to convey messages on this issue particularly by means of incidental remarks pertaining to the Court's dissatisfaction with this policy and its incompatibility with international law, and with regard to the degree of its effectiveness in the fight against terrorism.[29]

---

[28] *See* Yaniv Ofek, Deterrence in Attrition: The Palestinian Public's Support of Terrorism and Violence (2007) (Master's thesis, Tel Aviv University). In an interview that appeared on the *Ynet* website, someone described as "an entity in the security system" contended with regard to house demolitions, "On the large majority, certainly on the residents in the refugee camps, our measures have no effect. In terms of suicide bombers, supply exceeds demand." Felix Frisch, "The Statements with regard to the War on Suicide Bombers—Are Banal," YNET, Aug. 14, 2003, http://www.ynet.co.il/articles/0,7430,L-2725796,00.html. Amos Harel and Avi Issacharoff related in their book that an internal IDF report stated: "There is no proof of the deterrent effect of house demolitions." The report also indicates, "The number of terrorist attacks [. . .] rose several months after this policy began to be implemented." AMOS HAREL & AVI ISSACHAROFF, THE SEVENTH WAR—HOW WE WON AND WHY WE LOST THE WAR WITH THE PALESTINIANS 163 (2005).

[29] *See, e.g.*, HCJ 8084/02, Abassi v. OC Homefront Command, PD 57(2) 55, 59–60 (2003).

These messages never crossed the line of non-binding remarks. The Court never gave a binding decision to the effect that the State must refrain from house demolitions.

The year 1991 marked a certain turning point regarding this position. Justice Cheshin wrote minority opinions in several judgments,[30] in which he determined that house demolitions are contrary to the reasonable interpretation of Regulation 119 of the Defense (Emergency) Regulations. This minority opinion contradicted consistent case law of the Court and won a certain amount of support only from Justice Dorner.[31] When a wave of suicide-bomb terrorist attacks inundated the country starting in 1994, Justice Cheshin retreated from this position as well. Justice Cheshin explained that he did not change his basic position that house demolitions of suicide bombers constitute collective punishment. However, he concluded that intervention in government policy on the subject has the Court reaching the limits of its capacity for judicial review:

> In war as in war: What business is it of the Court to tell a military commander what he should do and should not do? We will not falter in our efforts for the rule of law. We have sworn by our oath to dispense justice, to be the servant of the law, and we will remain faithful to our oath and to ourselves. *Even when the trumpets of war sound, the rule of law will make its voice heard, but we must admit truthfully: In those same areas, its sound will be as the piccolo, pure and refined, but swallowed up by the tumult.* [emphasis added][32]

Violent reality and the limits of judicial review led the justice to deviate from his original position—not any change in his moral stance with regard to this question. Nonetheless, the impression and intensity of Justice Cheshin's minority opinion served the Court for years. The subtle power of a morally grounded minority opinion served the Court as a signal, prepared the ground, and created legitimacy for it to be overturned so as to become a majority opinion someday.[33]

At the end of 2004, with the cessation of the al-Aqsa Intifada, the petition of Mahmud Ali Nasr, the father of Fuaz Ali Nasr, was heard in the Supreme Court. Fuaz Ali Nasr recruited a suicide bomber who exploded the device in Jerusalem's Café Hillel in a terrorist attack in which seven people were killed. At the opening of the hearing, President Barak turned to the attorney representing the State and asked him if he was "aware of the mood of the

---

[30] HCJ 4772/91, Khizran v. IDF Commander of Judea and Samaria District, PD 46(2) 150 (1992); HCJ 5673/91, Kadr v. Commander of IDF Forces, Tak-El 92(2) 433 (1992); HCJ 2722/92, Elamrin v. Commander of IDF Forces in the Gaza Strip, PD 46(3) 693 (1992); HCJ 6026/94, Nazal v. IDF Commander of Judea and Samaria District, PD 48(5) 338 (1994); HCJ 2006/97, Abu Fara v. OC Central Command, PD 51(2) 651, 654–55 (1997).

[31] HCJ 1730/96, Sabiah v. IDF Commander in Judea and Samaria District, PD 50(1) 353, judgment of Justice Dorner.

[32] *Id.* at 368.

[33] *See with regard to this:* Tracey E. George & Michael E. Solimine, *Supreme Court Monitoring of Courts of Appeals En Banc,* 9 Sup. Ct. Econ. Rev. 171, 199 (2001).

court."[34] When the attorney replied that he was, President Barak told him that it was requested that "he enter into the court's atmosphere,"[35] and for the avoidance of doubt, the President added verbally that unlike in the past, he currently "sees good reason in the minority opinion of Justice Cheshin on the house demolition issue."[36] At the conclusion of a relatively brief hearing, the President, in a concise decision, ordered the hearing to be deferred to another date, without having the verbal statements written down.[37] A similar dynamic was described by persons who were present at a petition heard at the same time[38] that was submitted by the Adallah organization and concerned military authority to demolish houses during fighting. It should be noted that according to B'Tselem, during the years 2001–2004, three thousand homes in the Occupied Territories were demolished for this reason.[39]

It should also be noted that at the time the hearing was held a committee, set up by the military, had already been launched to examine the policy of house demolitions. Committee representatives attended the hearing and heard the President's remarks even though these remarks were omitted in the written decision.[40] Justice Barak was aware of the committee, and it is reasonable to assume that he was also aware that he could not influence the committee by relating to the effectiveness of house demolitions. However, he could influence the committee's conclusions by means of clear statements pertaining to the legality of the demolitions. In this manner, the committee would be compelled to cope with the fact that it was conducting its discussions under the influence of a clear signal vis-à-vis the demolitions' legality. The possibility now existed that the Court would annul this policy, because, ostensibly, a majority had been formed in the Court to overturn the ruling pertaining to the legality of house demolitions. The President's message indeed was grasped by the attorney handling the case and conveyed to the Department of International Law in the Judge Advocate General's Office, and from there to the committee. In February 2005, the committee decided to recommend to the military that it cease house demolitions.[41] Then IDF Chief of Staff Moshe Yaalon and then Minister of Defense Shaul Mofaz accepted the committee's recommendations. Immediately thereafter, the State declared to the Court that it had decided that it would no longer exercise the power prescribed in Regulation 119.[42]

---

34 *Supra* note 18.

35 *Id.*

36 *Id.*

37 HCJ 7733/04, Nasr v. IDF Commander of the West Bank, Tak-El 2005(2) 3855 (2005).

38 HCJ 4969/04, Adallah v. OC Southern Command, Tak-El 2004(3) 1786 (2004).

39 *See on this matter*: B'Tselem, *Demolition Policy: House Demolitions and Damage to Agricultural Areas in the Gaza Strip—Information Sheet* (2002); B'Tselem, *Innocent of Any Crime: Punitive House Demolitions during the Al-Aksa Intifada—Information Sheet* (2004).

40 *Supra* note 18.

41 The committee, appointed by the Commander in Chief of the IDF, decided in February 2005 that the deterrence created by the demolition of homes of terrorists' families is "insignificant" and it is not equivalent to the extent of hatred and loathing that this difficult measure arouses among Palestinians.

42 HCJ 7733/04, Nasr v. IDF Commander of the West Bank, Tak-El 2005(2) 3855 (2005).

At this stage, the petition was rejected. A similar response was delivered in a petition pertaining to house demolitions due to military necessity, and this petition too was rejected.[43] Several months after the petition was rejected, on December 4, 2005, following a terrorist attack on a mall in Netanya in which five people were killed, the Minister of Defense approached the Attorney General to reexamine the policy of house demolitions.[44] Yet, this request notwithstanding, the policy was not amended until 2009.

This case illustrates the extent of the Court's strategic use of dialogue in issues related to national security and human rights. First, the Court clarifies to the players appearing before the Court its position on the legality of the State's chosen course of action without setting this view in stone. Conveyance of this message requires the attorney to return to the political echelon and to propose a new line of action derived from the messages the Court has conveyed. The Court uses all means available at the time of hearing a petition to influence the policy. It even uses a minority opinion given in the past by one of the Supreme Court justices for signaling, and does this with critical timing, precisely at the stage at which a military committee is discussing house demolitions—the very same issue under discussion in the petition.

At this point, we can see how timing affects the Court's messages. Statements by Justice Barak in a hearing pertaining to house demolitions were made at the end of the al-Aqsa Intifada. During the course of the al-Aqsa Intifada, the military demolished hundreds of houses, and the Court did not deviate from its consistent policy that house demolitions were not unlawful. Only after the fighting ended was the Court prepared to intensify the power of its advisory messages and to state matters more clearly on this issue, but again without giving an operative order against the State and risking its credibility as an objective interpreter of law.

To complete the picture and to demonstrate the limits of dialogue that is not binding, it is worth noting in this context that, in 2009 and as a result of the lack of an absolute order on the issue, the State decided to renew its policy of house demolitions. It ordered the demolition of the home of a suicide bomber who had infiltrated a yeshiva in Jerusalem and murdered eight yeshiva students. In a High Court of Justice hearing, the State's position was presented, as it had developed as the result of the hearing in Court and in the committee in 2005. According to the new policy, the military would use this policy solely "in extreme cases."[45] The Court adopted the State's position and permitted the demolition. Another petition submitted against a decision to demolish the house of

---

[43] In a response on behalf of the State of March 20, 2005, the State declared that according to the Prime Minister's notice delivered at the Sharm el-Sheikh Talks, to the effect that "Israel would cease its military activities against Palestinians everywhere" (notice of Feb. 8, 2005), and in view of the current period of calm, the State will refrain from house demolitions in general.

[44] Yehonatan Lis & Amos Harel, *Mofaz Seeks to Renew Demolitions of Terrorists' Homes*, HAARETZ, Dec. 5, 2005.

[45] HCJ 9353/08, Abu Dahim v. OC Home Front Command.

a terrorist, who had driven a tractor into a group of people and caused the deaths of three people, was rejected by the Supreme Court.[46]

USING PER CURIAM DECISIONS AS A SIGNAL

The Case of the Citizenship Law

A final, yet striking, example for conveying an advisory message by way of an interim decision pertains to the amendment of the Citizenship Law that was enacted during the al-Aqsa Intifada and for security reasons prohibited family reunification of Israelis and Palestinians.[47] From the beginning this law was perceived as highly controversial. It prescribed that family reunification would not be allowed for Israelis with Palestinian spouses, unless the age of a male Palestinian spouse was 36 or more or the age of a female Palestinian spouse was 26 or more. The declared aim of this law was security related. It was intended to prevent the danger that had occurred in the past, when a person from the Occupied Territories who was given the option to reside in Israel with his Israeli spouse assisted someone who was involved in hostile terrorist activities. Nevertheless, many believe that the law's true aim was "demographic," and concerned limiting the growth of the Arab population in Israel and maintaining a Jewish majority.

The petition submitted against the law's legitimacy was heard by a highly exceptional panel of 13 justices, during the course of the al-Aqsa Intifada. Following the hearing of the parties' contentions, an interim decision was given per curiam by all 13 justices, the fifth paragraph of which is highly relevant to our matter:

> The petitions before us have introduced constitutional difficulties.... Since we have decided not to rule on these petitions at this time, we will not discuss the particulars of these difficulties in this decision. *What is common to all of us is the acknowledgment that ... the reexamination of this law that the Government decided to undertake, must look most thoroughly at the difficulties that the law arouses, which have found expression in the petitions before us. We all agree that the law before us is not an "ordinary" law. It justifies special attention.* [emphasis added][48]

In this paragraph, the Court conveyed to the government that it views a real difficulty with its position. It warrants attention that in this case, too, the Court ostensibly used neutral language in its written decision, as it did not state directly that the law is likely to be construed as unconstitutional. As we shall see further below, the Court meticulously chooses the language by means of which a signal is conveyed. The power of the message

---

[46] *See* HCJ 124/09, Duwaith v. Minister of Defense, Dinim Elyon 2009 (30) 778.

[47] The Citizenship Law and Entry into Israel (Provisional Order) 5763-2003.

[48] HCJ 7052/03, Adallah v. the Minister of the Interior, Tak-El 2006(2) 1754, a decision of Dec. 14, 2004.

comes from the fact that all thirteen justices signed this interim decision forcing the government to take their view into consideration when reexamining this law.

This interim decision illustrates a particular type of advisory message that may be called "a constitutional signal." This type of signaling will be discussed extensively in Chapter 6. In this case, the signal is directed to both the Government and the Knesset, and the Court clarifies in it that a certain law is likely to be grasped by the Court as being unconstitutional. Subsequent to retirement, Justice Mazza stated the following with regard to signals that ensue from interim decisions on the matter of the Citizenship Law:

> Our hope, as judges, is that the state has understood and shall take action. *When the Supreme Court gives the state leeway*, it is not because the Court believes that the state is acting as required. Rather, it is more correct that the state itself shall rectify the wrong [emphasis added].[49]

These statements illustrate again that Supreme Court justices view interim decisions as a strategic platform for advancing the dialogue between themselves and the State and as a means to influence national security policy within a relatively short time. The Court expects the State to cooperate in this dialogue, to grasp the message included in the decision, and to act according to its contents. In addition, this practice illustrates the Court's use of language to convey precisely calibrated messages to the other branches. The message is carefully formulated so there is not one word in it that attests that the Court believes the law is unconstitutional or that the fate of this petition has been sealed. The strategy that guides the Court is that if the message is understood by the Government and the Knesset, the matter is likely to lead to the immediate cessation of the damaging policy, and no less to preclude potential conflict between the Court and the legislative authority. The platform on which signaling is conveyed and the panel that gives the decision have granted the signaling dramatic impact. The Court and its 13 justices, all lined up as one behind the President, thereby relayed a message of unity and moral cohesion to the Knesset.

---

[49] LEVITZKI, *supra* note 16, at 131.

4

Deviating from the Rules of the Game

STUDIES HAVE DEMONSTRATED that one of the most important ways to convey a message in a dialogue between people is to deviate from the rules of customary communication among the speakers.[1] The surprise effect from this type of deviation causes the recipient of the message to try to understand what caused the shift in the rules of communication that prevailed up to this point and what it might mean. For example, someone who waits for his friend to drop by his office every day and wish him good morning will try to understand why on one particular morning his friend passed by his office without saying anything. A person who anticipates receiving a certain message at a face-to-face meeting will be surprised and will try to discover why this message arrived by mail or e-mail and vice versa.

The rules of communication customary in Court serve as a platform for transmitting messages between the parties and the Court in a formal and predictable fashion. The parties can anticipate the order of the speakers at the hearing, how much time, more or less, will be allotted to hearing arguments, and what the structure of the decision at the end of the hearing will be, more or less. They learn these rules of the game and expect the Court to act accordingly, whether or not these rules appear in the relevant procedural law.

This expectation enables the Court to transmit messages by means of deviating from the rules of the game. The surprise effect that this creates for the parties who appear at the hearing leads them to try to understand what caused the Court to deviate from

---

[1] *See* Paul H. Grice, *Presupposition and Conversational Implicature, in* RADICAL PRAGMATICS 183 (Peter Cole ed., 1981); *see also* Thomas Holtgraves, *Comprehending Indirect Replies: When and How Are Their Conveyed Meanings Activated?*, 41 J. MEMORY & LANGUAGE 519 (1999).

the customary rules of communication and what this departure might mean. Thus, the Court can convey to the parties messages about its frame of mind without necessarily taking a solid position with regard to the questions in dispute or without making binding decisions ahead of time. The parties, who are quite interested in learning the Court's mood, study and consider the deviation, evaluate the motive, and make decisions based on their assessment.

In this chapter, I will present several ways in which the Israeli Supreme Court departs from the rules of the game in order to convey messages to the parties with regard to its frame of mind without having necessarily to decide the issue.

HOLDING A HEARING ON A THEORETICAL PETITION

One of the causes of action that serves the Court to strike out a petition *in limine* as a routine matter is that the hearing of the petition has become theoretical. The Court ruled in this manner in judgments that dealt with the policy of house demolitions.[2] The same was true even when a petition in principle was submitted[3] with regard to the legality of the Incarceration of Unlawful Combatants Law[4] and the State's authority to hold such captives without undertaking criminal proceedings against them or giving them the status of prisoners of war. This petition also raised difficult questions in the areas of criminal law and international law, but it did not compel the Court to deviate from this policy. The Court rejected the petition after Mustafa Dirani and Sheikh Abd al-Karim Obayed, responsible on behalf of Hizballah for the entire region of southern Lebanon, and two central bargaining cards in Israel's hands, were released to Lebanon in a deal. Upon the conclusion of the deal, Elhanan Tenenbaum, an Israeli citizen and reserve officer in the artillery corps with the rank of colonel, who had been abducted by Hizballah, was also released.

Because the Court was so adamant in its unwillingness to hold hearings on theoretical petitions, when the Court deviated from this basic rule, as it did for example in the HCJ *On Torture* case, the deviation is interpreted as a significant signal to the parties that the Court believes that the State's position is not persuasive. Furthermore, it signals that the Court believes that the subject that has been raised in the petition has broad and principled implications regarding which the Court would like to state its position. Usually, the signal implies that the petition "raises a significant constitutional issue."[5]

---

[2] *See* the State's reply of March 20, 2005, in HCJ 4969/04 Adallah v. OC Southern Command, Tak-El 2004(3) 186 (2004).

[3] Criminal Appeal 3660/03, Abayed v. the State of Israel (unpublished, Sept. 8, 2005). Later, the Court was compelled to re-examine this question in a hearing of another petition that was submitted against the legality of this law. *See* Criminal Appeal 6659/06, Anonymous v. the State of Israel, Tak-El 2008(2) 3270.

[4] The Incarceration of Unlawful Combatants Law 5762-2002.

[5] HCJ 2320/98, Mahmud v. IDF Commander, PD 52(3) 346 (1998).

HOLDING A HEARING NOTWITHSTANDING RES JUDICATA

Another rule the Court uses to transmit a message to the parties pertains to upholding res judicata. This rule states that once a decision has been given in a petition on a certain issue, the Court will not agree to discuss it again. One case that illustrates how the Court transmits signals by way of a departure from customary practice with regard to rejecting petitions due to res judicata is the petitions that were submitted to the High Court of Justice against mass arrest orders. These were issued during the course of Operation Defensive Shield, resulting in the arrest of thousands of residents of the Occupied Territories suspected of being involved in carrying out terrorist attacks. The order was issued on April 5, 2002. On the very day it was issued a petition already had been submitted to the High Court of Justice[6] contending that the order was not proportional and was contrary to international law. On April 7, 2002, the Court held a hearing on the petition, and on the same day, the Court dismissed it.[7]

A week later, another petition was submitted against the same order—HCJ *Marav*.[8] The hearing of the petition was held on April 18, 2002, before a President's Panel and, instead of dismissing the petition on the grounds that the issue had already been decided several days earlier, the Court ordered as follows:

> Prior to deciding on the petition (including the preliminary arguments), we request to receive the Respondents' Reply within 15 days of this day, with regard to what is the legal framework within which the military commander acts and what are the criteria that have been determined according to this framework.[9]

In this instance, deviation from the rules of the game comprised a triple message. First, the Court opted not to accept the State's preliminary arguments, the subject of which had already been decided several days earlier. Second, the Court underscored in the interim decision the questions that the order raises for the Court, notwithstanding that the Court had already decided the issue several days earlier. Third, the Court appointed a President's Panel to hear the petition. This decision was a signal that the Court was considering declaring significant parts of the same order as unlawful, as it indeed ultimately did.[10]

---

[6] HCJ 2901/02, Center for Defense of the Individual v. IDF Commander, PD 56(3) 19 (2002).

[7] *Id.* at 20.

[8] HCJ 3239/02, Marav v. The IDF Commander, PD 57(2) (2002) 349.

[9] *Id.*, decision of Apr. 18, 2002.

[10] *Id.*, decision of Dec. 15, 2002.

HOLDING A HEARING NOTWITHSTANDING RES JUDICATA: THE TARGETED KILLING CASE

In a hearing held in Court on the question of the legality of targeted killings, a process occurred that illustrates particularly well the significance of the rule with respect to res judicata and, specifically, the deviation from it.

Since its establishment, Israel has undertaken a policy of targeted killings. During the al-Aqsa Intifada, Israel began applying an official policy for targeted killings. Under this policy, Israel killed hundreds of terrorist activists. Officially, the policy aims to prevent terrorist attacks but it also serves as deterrence, helping promote the disintegration of the leadership of terrorist organizations and damaging their operational activities. The first time that the Court discussed the issue of targeted killings was in a petition submitted by Dr. Siham Thabet, widow of the PLO secretary in Tul Karm, Thabet Thabet, who was killed 10 days earlier by Israel. In the petition, the widow contended that Israel's policy of targeted killings contradicts international law.[11] The petition that was lodged at the peak of the period of terrorist attacks was struck out *in limine* by the Court on the day it was heard, in a brief and particularly resolute decision. The judgment in HCJ 5872/01[12] determined the following:

> We have read and heard extensively the contentions of the Petitioner's attorney. It seems to us that in a notice on behalf of the Respondents an exhaustive reply was given to the contentions of the Petitioners. The choice of weapons used by the government to thwart murderous terror attacks is not a matter in which this Court sees reason to intervene, especially in a petition lacking any concrete factual foundation that seeks a sweeping remedy. The petition is rejected.[13]

The terse and decisive text of the judgment and the immediacy with which the decision was given constitute in and of themselves a message with regard to the degree of the Court's willingness to decide the questions that it raises.

The judgment was given on January 29, 2002. On January 24, 2002, an additional petition was lodged that raised exactly the same question but in a broader format. A major difference between this petition and the previous one was that the petition was

---

[11] The question of the effectiveness of targeted killings in terms of its influence on the support of the Palestinian people was examined recently in an empirical study. The study found that at times of fighting, targeted killings do not affect the support of the Palestinian population on the continuation of military actions, in general, or the continuation of carrying out suicide bomb attacks, in particular. The study surveyed the years 1993–2005. *See* Yaniv Ofek, Deterrence in Attrition: The Palestinian Public's Support of Terrorism and Violence (2007) (Master's thesis, Tel Aviv University).

[12] HCJ 5872/01, Barakeh v. the Prime Minister, PD 56(3) 1 (2002).

[13] *Id.* at 1 of the judgment.

lodged by a human rights organization that came out in principle against the policy. In the first hearing held on the additional petition, only three months after the judgment in the first petition, President Barak entered the courtroom, and following a brief technical discussion, he read out word for word the following decision:

1. Prior to deciding on how to continue handling this petition (including preliminary arguments), we request to receive within forty days the position of the Respondents on the following questions:

   (a) According to the legal classification, to which they agree, what is the system of laws that apply to the issue before us (the laws of war, the laws of armed conflict short of war or another classification). See for example Zengel "Assassination and the Law of Armed Conflict," 134 Military L. Rev. 123 (1991); Beres, "The Permissibility of State-Sponsored Assassination During Peace and War," 5 Temple Int'l and comparative J. 23 (1991); Schmitt, "State-Sponsored Assassination in International and Domestic Law," 17 Yale J. Int'l Law 609 (1992); Jackson, "the Legality of Assassination of Independent Terrorist Leaders: An Examination of National and International Implications," 24 N.C.J. Int'l and Commercial Rev. 669 (1998); Wingfield, "Taking Aim At Regime Elites: Assassination, Tyrannicide, and the Clancy Doctrine," 22 Maryland J. Int'l Law and Trade, 287 (1998); Turner, "Legal Responses to International Terrorism: Constitutional Constraints on Presidential Power," 22 Houston J. Int'l Law 77 (1999).

   (b) What are the "internal" rules of Israeli law that apply to our matter (if there are such rules)? What are the rules of international law that apply in Israel and pertain to our matter? What are the contents of these rules with regard to the matter subject of the petition? What is the criterion that distinguishes between permitted and prohibited acts?

   (c) What is the relation between "internal" Israeli law and international law that applies in our case? Are these two systems of law compatible?[14]

This interim decision is an excellent example of the Court's ability to "break" the rules of the game in order to convey advisory messages to other branches of government. First, this decision comes in spite of the fact that the Supreme Court has already stated its view ostensibly on the issue. The State's representative at the hearing indeed insisted on this when he contended, "that there is already a *res judicata*. This court has already ruled two months ago that choosing means of warfare is not the type of matter in which this court

---

14 HCJ 769/02, The Public Committee against Torture in Israel, Tak-El 2006(4) 3958 (2006), decision of Apr. 18, 2002 [hereinafter HCJ–Targeted Killings].

will intervene."[15] Yet notwithstanding its objections, the Court deviated in this instance from customary practice. Generally, when a petition is rejected with regard to a certain issue, similar petitions that raise the same question may not be submitted. Second, in this decision the Court clarified that it also does not intend to follow the plan outlined in the previous judgment with regard to justiciability. In other words, the Court will not agree to accept the State's contention with regard to the nonjusticiability of targeted killings, a subject that lay at the heart of the decision on the initial petition.[16] Third, the text of the decision, which includes a list of authors in the field to which the parties wish to relate, indicates that the Court has already examined the issue in terms of the law and in principle prior to giving this interim decision. And, this decision was not given inadvertently but rather with the clear intention to decide the matter. Fourth, this text indicates that the Court intends to become considerably involved in the matter at issue, and it completely contradicts the degree of resolve that the Court demonstrated in its initial decision on the subject. Contrary to the punctuation of the initial decision, the message included in this decision principally comprised question marks. Fifth, the conduct of the Court demonstrates that the decision was formulated precisely, word for word, by the panel, before the hearing began, and was not conceived as a result of the hearing. Sixth, it was timed less than three months following the granting of the judgment on the parallel petition and with conscious and demonstrated disregard of the judgment given by another judicial panel of the Court.

Shai Nitzan, the very experienced attorney who represented the State, immediately grasped this deviation from the customary rules of the game and concluded at once that a change in the Court's mood had occurred. He described his feelings at this hearing, stating, "I was slightly embarrassed because I couldn't reply properly on the spot. Accordingly, we asked for an extension to prepare the replies. In view of our request, President Barak gave us a written decision of the three justices that had already been prepared (!), a decision they had written prior to entering the courtroom."[17]

A further development in the file illustrates in another manner the significance of the message transmitted by this departure from the rules of the game. After several hearings had been held and the parties' arguments, including an expert opinion, had been submitted in writing, the State announced, following an agreement that had been made at Taba between Israel and the Palestinian Authority, that the policy of targeted killings would be halted. Several days later, and as the result of the same accord, the State announced that the policy of house demolitions would also be halted.[18] However, following these

---

[15] *See* Shai Nitzan, *The Fight against Terrorism as Warfare—Legal Aspects, in* THE BATTLE OF THE 21ST CENTURY: DEMOCRACY FIGHTS TERRORISM (THE ISRAEL DEMOCRACY INSTITUTE) 130 (Haim Pass ed., 2007).

[16] *See* ISRAEL DEMOCRACY INSTITUTE, IS EVERYTHING KOSHER WHEN COPING WITH TERRORISM: ON ISRAEL'S POLICY OF PREVENTIVE KILLING (TARGETED KILLING) IN JUDEA AND SAMARIA AND IN THE GAZA STRIP 75 (2006).

[17] Nitzan, *supra* note 15, at 131.

[18] *See* the State's Reply of March 20, 2005 in HCJ 4969/04, ***Adallah v. OC Southern Command.***

announcements in the petitions concerning house demolitions, the Court ordered their dismissal after these had become moot,[19] whereas with regard to the petition on targeted killings, the Court refrained from doing so. Instead, and notwithstanding the State's position that the matter had become moot, the Court opted to leave the petition pending.

Ultimately, on the last day that Justice Barak presided in Court prior to his leaving his judicial position, the Court handed down the judgment on targeted killings. In an innovative and groundbreaking judgment, the State's contention that a new status under international law of "unlawful combatants" should be added, was denied. Yet, it was determined that a civilian who is a member of a terrorist organization may not benefit from the immunity from military attack to which civilians are entitled. The Court determined that a terrorist, even though considered civilian under international humanitarian law, could fall into the category of civilian who takes a direct part in hostilities as long as he fights within the framework of an organization and has not left the organization. As such, he may not benefit from the protections granted to civilians under international humanitarian law. Under these circumstances, it is possible to consider carrying out targeted killings. The Court ordered that it is impossible to carry out a targeted killing in cases where it is possible to arrest the "combatant." Similarly, the Court adjudicated that following the execution of a targeted killing, a thorough investigation must be performed (retroactively) with regard to the precise identification of the injured party and the circumstances under which he was injured. This investigation must be independent. In certain cases, it may be possible to consider paying compensation in respect of harm caused to an innocent civilian. In conclusion, the Court determined that each targeted killing must be examined according to the circumstances of the merits of each case, as "it cannot be determined in advance that every targeted killing is prohibited according to customary international law, just as it cannot be determined in advance that every targeted killing is permissible according to customary international law."[20] Nonetheless, the rules create a framework that limits and minimizes the use of this means, leaving it to be applied only in cases in which there is no other option—this too being subject to the conducting of an independent investigation after the fact with regard to the circumstances and merits of the case. The outcomes of the investigation will be subject to the judicial review.[21, 22]

---

[19] *Id.* and HCJ 7733/04, Nasr v. IDF Commander of the West Bank, Tak-El 2005(2) 3855.

[20] HCJ–Targeted Killings, *supra* note 14.

[21] *Id.* para 59.

[22] For an analysis of the Israeli practice see the very important report of Ben Emerson, the UN Special Rapporteur on the promotion and protection of human rights and fundamental freedoms while countering terrorism. A/68/389 Interim report to the General Assembly on the use of remotely piloted aircraft in counter-terrorism operations.

DEVIATING FROM THE STRUCTURE OF A HEARING IN A PETITION AND THE ANTICIPATED SCHEDULE AS SIGNALING

Two additional subtle features of a dialogue that is conducted between people are the rhythm and structure of the dialogue. Every dialogue, even one that takes place via e-mails, has its own rhythm and structure. People develop expectations in relation to that rhythm and structure and come to conclusions with regard to a deviation from it.

This mechanism is relevant in relation to the dialogue between the Court and the parties who appear before it as well. These players will see a deviation from the rhythm or structure expected as being a signal by the Court and will seek to reach conclusions. At times, these conclusions will be correct, but, at times, they will not be. However, the basic rule according to which a deviation from the rules of the game signals the parties with regard to the expected continuation is true also with regard to the structure of the hearing in a petition and how it is scheduled. Generally, a legal procedure has a fixed structure and rhythm according to the petition's nature and degree of urgency. As long as this structure and rhythm are more or less maintained, it is impossible to say that the Court sought to transmit messages in its decisions with regard to scheduling. A deviation from these, particularly if made in a conscious decision, is likely to be construed as an advisory message.

There are some examples that illustrate this dynamic. For instance, there are cases in which the circumstances make it necessary to set up an urgent hearing, as refraining from doing so will cause irreversible damage or will turn the petition into a theoretical one, which the Court seeks to avoid. In such instances, actually setting an urgent hearing does not signify anything. Obvious examples in this context are petitions for habeas corpus orders in cases of persons who were taken from their homes in the middle of the night by security forces,[23] particularly if carried out by soldiers who were not in uniform. In such instances, the Court holds a hearing promptly due to the basic understanding that it is best to avoid a situation in which people can disappear without the members of their families being aware of this incommunicado detention. Moreover, the Court does not hesitate to attribute to the State's detriment any delay, even if slight, of a notice concerning where the detainee is being held, and even to adjudicate costs against the State for this reason. The Court has insisted on this principle in its decisions on the subject more than once.[24]

Nonetheless, there are cases in which the Court departs from a petition's structure and rhythm. Such an action can certainly signal a message to the parties about the Court's attitude toward the petition. This is particularly true in cases where the Court initiates a decision of its own accord without waiting for the parties' initiative. It is the unexpected

---

[23] *See, e.g.,* HCJ 422/03, Abu Dosh v. IDF Commander of Judea and Samaria (unpublished, Jan. 15, 2003); HCJ 2484/03, Ilariyah v. IDF Commander of the West Bank (unpublished, Mar. 18, 2003).

[24] *See* HCJ 7862/02, Alshaf'i v. IDF Commander of the West Bank, Tak-El 2004(1) 972 (2004).

timing of these *voluntary* decisions that creates their great impact. For example, it is possible to see the power of an interim decision that President Barak gave in the HCJ *Targeted Killings* case, which was prepared prior to the Honorable Court entering the courtroom.

Another example of this kind of departure made to advance messages pertains to a petition that was submitted with regard to the activity of Palestinian journalists who survey the course of hostilities in the Occupied Territories. At the end of 2001, the Government Press Office decided that due to the security situation it would not issue any press cards to Palestinian media personnel. The journalists filed a petition against the decision stating that their activities were harmed as the result of it.[25] When the initial hearing on the petition was held, the Court gave an order nisi.[26] The order was the first indication that the Court believes that the State's reasoned position, as presented at the hearing, was not persuasive. The State understood the message. However, it decided nonetheless to stick to its position in principle. As a result, the hearing on the petition was held in full. Eventually, even though the parties had concluded their contentions, prior to the court giving its judgment, it delivered the following decision:

> The petition hearing has concluded. Nonetheless, prior to deciding it, we have asked the State to submit to us a supplementary notice within 45 days (the days of Court recess shall be counted in here) whether in view of the changes that have recently occurred in the country, would the government's position also be amended with regard to the Petitioners or any one of them.[27]

This decision was issued at the Court's initiative, without any hearing that naturally would have led up to this kind of decision having preceded it. The parties expected that the Court would give its judgment at this point and would not ask the State to re-examine its position. This type of departure from the structure of the dialogue that occurs in a judicial hearing and that was given without any preparatory legal procedure having preceded it requires the parties to see it as a message to them. The State replied in its response that it still vehemently objects to the activities of the Palestinian journalists in Israel. Immediately upon receiving the respondent's position, the Court gave an additional decision as follows:

> Following an exchange *and in accordance with our proposal*, the Respondents will examine the possibility of amendments to the procedure and contents of the work permits for the journalists. [emphasis added][28]

---

[25] HCJ 5627/02, Sayef v. the Government Press Office, PD 55(5) 70 (2003).

[26] *Id.*, decision of Jan. 22, 2003.

[27] *Supra* note 25, decision of June 22, 2003.

[28] *Supra* note 25, decision of Nov. 26, 2003.

This decision included an even clearer signal that the Court was not satisfied with the State's position and sought to grant it leeway to retract it. Despite the messages and signals conveyed by the Court, the State adhered to its position, which ultimately led to a decision in principle being given against the State, one of the only ones of its kind, while the flames still raged. This decision came with severe criticism of the State's position:

> In our case, *the absolute refusal* to grant press cards to Palestinians who are residents of the region—including those who hold entry permits to Israel and to work here—instructs that the work of balancing considerations of expression and information with considerations of security *has not been made at all* and, in any event, the balance that has been made has been made unduly. [emphasis added][29]

In the judgment, the Court called the state's position "arbitrary" and even expressed doubts with regard to the reliability of the grounds citing security that were given for the decision not to grant the Palestinian journalists permits.[30]

This case, as many others, proves to what extent it is important for the actors appearing before the Supreme Court to be attentive to the messages issued by the Court even when these are reflected in a deviation from the anticipated rhythm or structure of the dialogue. In the Israeli court practice, an actor's disregard of advisory messages that are conveyed to her or her unwillingness to cooperate in the dialogue are likely to lead to her being subjected to a decision that is difficult not only in terms of its results but also in terms of its formulation. The Court's great interest in advancing and developing advisory dialogue leads the Court "to encourage" the parties to take part in the dialogue with the Court, and to extract "a price" from the party who does not cooperate with the Court in this dialogue and does not comprehend the advisory messages and act accordingly.

MESSAGES IN INTERIM DECISIONS: CONCLUSION

The Supreme Court of Israel is a master craftsman of dialogue. From the moment that a petition is presented to the Court until the moment that a judgment is given, the Court converses with the parties in a variety of ways and forms. Tools that serve the Court include the dialogue that occurs at the time of an oral hearing and its interim decisions. The Court uses precise language and timing as well as the platform for conveying messages, the structure of a decision, the rhythm of a hearing, and the customary practice to convey messages to the parties pertaining to a petition.

At this stage, advisory dialogue generally serves two complementary functions. One is to encourage the parties to reach a settlement. A settlement allows the Court to have a

---

[29] *Supra* note 25, at 78.
[30] *Supra* note 25, paras. 2 and 3 of the judgment of Justice D. Dorner.

prompt impact on what is taking place in the combat arena. It also enables the Court to avoid conflict with other branches during a state of emergency. A second function is to outline or signal to the parties the direction in which the Court is leaning and what its decision is likely to be. These functions are very often complementary as they both allow the Court to affect policy changes and better protect human rights and the rule of law in real time or in close proximity to the events or adoption of a national security policy that led to its review.

At times, there is a third objective—to oversee the application of a policy that the Court wishes to advance and to reject a petition only after it has been clarified to the Court that the policy indeed is being applied. As we have indicated, in this manner the Israeli Supreme Court expands its judicial review from the legal decision on a dispute to an attempt to oversee how resolution of the dispute is being applied, and to promote the rule of law by ensuring that its decision will be implemented, on the ground, prior to disposing of the file. In other words, judicial intervention is not expressed solely or principally in binding decisions. The Court sees its ability to control the procedure as a means to oversee the actual application of national security policy that it wishes to promote.

The Israeli Supreme Court conducts a dialogue with other branches of government that is dynamic, complex, sophisticated, and refined. The Court expects the parties to understand its messages and to have their conduct and procedures correspond with the contents of the messages conveyed. At times, by way of different signals that are layered one on the other, the Court transmits a message with regard to its expectations and trusts that the State primarily will study these messages and will make arrangements, as requested.

In order to fully comprehend the messages that the Court transmits, the parties must be attentive to any deviation from customary practice and be prepared to interpret each decision according to its context. A message's contextual interpretation requires that the interpreter will examine not only the message's contents but also the following: the background, comparing it with other decisions in similar situations; the platform on which it has been given; the language the court used to convey the messages; the decision's timing; the rhythm of the hearing; and the Court's customary practice for conveying such messages.

Several factors facilitate and encourage the development of such sophisticated dialogue. The first factor is legal procedure, which creates such a rigid and formal structure of dialogue that any departure from it immediately calls for its interpretation as an advisory message and potential signal, at times even without any connection to the question of whether the Court intends this. The second factor is that, at least in the field of national security, dialogue in the Israeli legal system generally occurs in a very intimate manner. The number of players in the system, both on behalf of the State and on behalf of the petitioners, is limited, and dialogue repeatedly recurs on a more regular basis. This factor enables the players participating in the dialogue to identify at once any departure, even the slightest, from the rigid procedural structure or the practice that is familiar to them. This was particularly witnessed in the targeted killings case. The fact that dialogue is conducted for the most part by repeat players (both on the part of the State and on the part of human rights organizations active in this field) increases their motivation to avoid risking obtaining a judgment that contradicts the policy they wish to promote. Therefore, these players, more than others, will make more of an effort to study the Court's frame of mind and to be attentive to any message that the Court seeks to convey in its decisions.[31] The Court utilizes brilliantly this situation to transmit messages to the players all the time.

Interim decisions serve as a convenient platform to convey advisory messages for several additional reasons: First, the hearing in the interim stages of a Court hearing, as distinct from the stages of lodging a petition and the judgment, generally takes place at a relatively low level of exposure, as frequently it is only the parties who participate in the hearing. The media focuses its attention on a hearing during times of drama—when a petition is lodged with the High Court of Justice or when a major provisional order is given, or at the time of a final judgment. An additional factor that makes an interim decision a convenient platform for conveying messages is that in these decisions the Court is not required to provide the complete grounds for its decision or to take a stand with regard to its final position, which would otherwise make it difficult to convey advisory messages. Accordingly, interim decisions allow the Court and the parties to re-examine the extent of their obligation to the message and to adapt the course of their conduct to the contents, without having this obligate them later on in the hearing. Conveying advisory messages in interim decisions enables the Court to indicate a possible direction to which it aspires without fearing that it will be perceived as having decided the fate of the petition or having disclosed its final position precipitately, which at times has not been fully formulated at this point. It also allows the Court to learn how firm is the government's stance on the issue in point. Precise signaling in interim decisions, which is correctly interpreted by the actors appearing before it, enables the Court to avoid having to render a judgment.

Through advisory messages, the Court encourages the parties to take part in a dialogue and signals the parties with regard to directions and positions that it expects them to adopt. The Court expects the parties to study the contents of the messages and participate in a dialogue with the Court. It expects them to react quickly and allow it to reach within a few days a decision that will change the reality on the ground. Players who cooperate with this practice are shown esteem or appreciation that finds expression in the Court's judgments even if their views were rejected by the Court. Players who refuse to take part in the dialogue are likely to find themselves "condemned" by the Court.

---

[31] *See on this matter* Marc Galanter, *Why the "Haves" Come Out Ahead: Speculations on the Limits of Legal Change*, 9 L. & SOC. REV. 95 (1974).

5

Recommendations

In the last three chapters, we have discussed the dialogue that occurs during the course of a petition hearing. However, advisory dialogue does not conclude when the hearings for a case are over. The Israeli Supreme Court uses its judgments to continue developing the dialogue with the players in the field, and through them to transmit advisory messages. The following four chapters will be devoted to an analysis of the dialogue that occurs through Court judgments.

In this chapter, we will focus on the Court's use of one type of message—recommendations. I use the term *recommendation* to refer to proposals in the decision in which the Court calls for a certain policy be arranged by way of primary or secondary legislation, that customary policy be amended, or that a particular course of action be taken with regard to the petitioner's issue. The recommendation is part of the advisory dialogue, as the nature of a recommendation is that it also is not binding and is based on the assumption that the player on the other side understands the implied message and how to act accordingly. Recommendations are a highly significant and extremely valuable tool in dialogue pertaining to issues related to national security, and the Court uses them extensively. The Court as we will see further in this chapter uses recommendations not just to improve policy or law, but to try and solve in real time humanitarian problems that arise from the conduct of hostilities.

RECOMMENDATIONS FOR LEGISLATION

The Court uses dialogue for several types of recommendations. The first type was presented above in previous chapters. The discussion in earlier chapters focused on *the*

Court's recommendations made during the course of a hearing generally by way of verbal comments or brief decisions to conclude the file in a certain manner. Another type of recommendation is the recommendations for legislation that concern the need to amend a certain topic or to arrange it in legislation in a certain manner, distinct from the way in which the subject has been arranged up until then. Such, for example, is the recommendation given at the end of the judgment on the Tibi case.[1] Israeli law prohibits parties who support terrorism from participating in the elections. In the case of Ahmed Tibi, an Arab Israeli member of the Knesset, the Court discussed the question of candidates participating in elections whose party platform is likely to be perceived as supporting terrorism. Justice Barak related to the legislative state that distinguishes between the procedure that applies to disqualifying candidates and that which applies to disqualifying parties, with the following statement:

> *We would like to refer the legislative authority's attention* to the problematic issues in the provisions of law that arrange the subject of preventing the participation of parties and individuals in elections. [emphasis added][2]

The Supreme Court indicated at the end of its decision that "we are aware that the reply to these questions is not simple. It would be advisable for the issue to be reconsidered in light of the experience that has accumulated over the years in Israel and in comparative law."[3]

A recommendation of this kind contains two independent courses of action. The first, and perhaps primary, course that generally characterizes judgments to which a recommendation for legislation is attached is the decision on the question of the legality of the policy regarding which a petition has been submitted or the constitutionality of the law that was brought before the Court. In most cases where a recommendation is given, the Court's decision declares that the policy in dispute is lawful or that the relevant piece of legislation is constitutional. The second course that is likely to be associated with such a decision is a recommendation pertaining to arranging the issue in another manner. For example, in the *Tibi* case, the petitioners initially requested that the Court determine that Section 7A of the Basic Law: The Knesset, which permits disqualifying candidates whose party platform supports terrorism, is unconstitutional. The Court rejected the petition on this question but attached to its decision a recommendation to the Knesset to amend the arrangement of the law or to change it in view of the contentions the petitioners raised against its constitutionality.

Legislative recommendations are not a new practice and are not confined to the Israeli Supreme Court. The Court advises the Knesset how to exercise its sovereign authority

---

[1] E.A. 1120/02, The Central Elections Committee v. MK Ahmed Tibi, PD 57 (4) 1 (2003).

[2] *Id.* at 62.

[3] *Id.* at 63.

on many different subjects, and it does this in a manner similar to that of other courts throughout the world.[4]

RECOMMENDATIONS FOR APPLICATION

Another type of recommendation is *recommendations for application*. When we are referring to recommendations for legislation, the message is intended for the legislature. In contrast, recommendations for application are intended to affect the manner in which legislative policy will be applied by the Executive. The Court seeks to do so not by way of a binding decision but rather through dialogue between the Court and the players in the Executive. A look at Israeli Supreme Court judgments in the field of national security shows that the Court often advises government authorities how to apply policy discussed in the Court's judgment. In many cases, in these recommendations for application, the Court draws the government's attention to a certain difficulty that a policy raises even though it is lawful, and calls for the situation to be rectified. These recommendations are included in the judgment and seek, in fact, to extend the Court's influence on the executive branch. Recommendations for application are also not unique to the Supreme Court in Israel. As we will see in upcoming Chapter 6, US Supreme Court justices also tend to use recommendations that pertain to the application of economic or social policy on many issues.

There are two types of recommendations for application. One type includes *concrete proposals*, whereas the second type includes *policy proposals*. Concrete proposals are used when the Court seeks to advise the State to take a certain line of action on a specific matter of the petition, generally humanitarian issues. Policy proposals, however, are by nature much broader. The Court does not only seek a solution for the petitioner by way of such proposals, but rather seeks to instruct the State how it is to act in similar instances in the future. There are numerous examples of concrete proposals. For example, Civil Appeal *Abu Samra*[5] concerns a claim that was filed by residents of Dir el-Balah against the State with regard to property damage caused by settlers. The Court decided to reject the village residents' claim but recommended at the end of the judgment that the State compensate the residents, *ex gratia*.[6] In Administrative Detention Appeal *Federman*,[7] the Court rejected the petition of Kach movement activist Noam Federman for his release from administrative detention but advised the State to re-examine the conditions of the appellant's detention.[8] By making extensive use of these recommendations, the Court does not view itself as bound by the proceeding's procedural framework. The Court's

---

[4] *See* Neal Katyal, *Judges as Advicegivers*, 50 STAN. L. REV. 1709, 1801 (1998).

[5] Civil Appeal 6970/99, Abu Samra v. the State of Israel, PD 56(6) 185 (2002).

[6] *Id.* at 92.

[7] Administrative Detention Appeal 8788/03, Federman v. the Minister of Security, PD 55(1) 176 (2003).

[8] *Id.* para. 20 of the judgment.

practical approach is that if it is possible to assist in a humanitarian matter immediately and to do so in a manner that is non-binding and does not create precedents—then it is warranted to do so.

Recommendation for Application: The Case of Massive Detentions during Military Campaigns

Policy recommendations, by nature, seek to instruct the State how to apply policy in principle. These are broad, fundamental recommendations pertaining to national security that the government has undertaken, which the Court has not determined to be illegitimate. A prime example of the use of such recommendations that illustrates the extent to which the Court is prepared to intervene in policy pertains to the conditions of detention for detainees. The discussion and examples brought below illustrate the nature of the dialogue that is held via Court judgments. It concerns various questions from the most fundamental issues regarding Israel's struggle to protect its national security while maintaining its moral image—to the most prosaic issues such as the height of dining tables and toilet seats in mass detention facilities in the Occupied Territories.

During the First Intifada, 1986–1990, the military arrested thousands of Palestinians who were placed in large detention facilities that were specially set up for this purpose. In the *Sagadiya* case,[9] the Court discussed detention conditions of detainees in the Ketziyot prison during the First Intifada. In the petition, the petitioners protested the highly crowded conditions, the inability to pray, the brutal attitude toward the detainees, the cruel and humiliating means of punishment, and the conditions of hygiene at the facility, as well as the water shortage, the deficient medical treatment, the denial of many rights (such as changing clothes), and the prevention of family visits. The Court heard the petitioners, and instead of ruling with regard to the legality of the contentions, decided to conduct a visit to the site. After the Supreme Court justices visited the detention facility and the parties' claims were concluded, a judgment was given. The structure of the judgment in this case was particularly unusual—President Shamgar examined the petitioners' claims, related to them in principle, and then, following a ruling as required on the question of their legality under international law, the justice advised the military on how to deal with each contention. I shall cite the main section:

> With regard to religious ritual, that is, in connection with the complaint pertaining to assembling for prayers, *it would be warranted* that prior to each decision, a statement of opinion be requested of the competent Muslim religious authority in Israel to examine the actuality in Israel, to examine the reality of the contentions of the detainees vis-à-vis the solutions proposed by the military authorities...With regard to the distribution of books: *There is room for a great deal of expansion and*

---

[9] HCJ 253/88, Sagadiya v. the Minister of Defense, PD 42(3) 801 (1988).

the initiative for this must be taken by the authorities…We have no basis to doubt the arrangements that concern food and water; nonetheless, constant follow-up and supervision are required on the part of the camp commander for the fulfillment of the arrangements in actual practice to prevent any problems in the distribution of food and the distribution of water…*We assume that our general remarks on the matter of the conditions of service require action and arrangements in accordance with the aforesaid.* [emphasis added][10]

In this manner, the Court examined the conditions of the detainees, one complaint at a time. The Court did not find it sufficient to decide the question of whether the current arrangement complies with the minimum requirements provided by international law for detainees. Instead, the Court conducted an on-site visit and later on acted as if it were an oversight committee rather than a court of law. It opted to recommend guidelines for a resolution for the military authorities that would ensure proper conditions, assuming that its "general remarks" would be implemented.

The *Sagadiya* case therefore created a model for judicial review that encompasses advisory dialogue as its principal expression. The Court hears the claims of the detainees. It is not deterred from visiting the detention facilities, and advises the State how to act with the aim of improving the detainees' conditions. The focus of the judgment is not whether the conditions of detention meet the minimum requirements of international law but whether it is possible to improve conditions in order to make them more humane.

In hearing claims pertaining to the detention conditions of detainees who were apprehended in the wave of mass arrests during Operation Defensive Shield, in 2002, the Court continued in this direction. During Operation Defensive Shield detainees were brought to two detention facilities—the Ofer Detention Facility and the Ketziyot Detention Facility.

In HCJ *Ofer* a principle judgment was given on the issue of conditions of detention in the Ofer Detention Facility.[11] While hearing this petition, the Court again sought to view the conditions up close. However, instead of going to see the detention facility on its own, the Court asked the parties to hold a joint visit. Thereafter, the Court turned its attention to hearing the detainees' claims. In this instance, too, the Court analyzed each claim one by one. It reproached the State for not being properly prepared for the operation and continued with the model of the *Sagadiya* judgment by offering recommendations pertaining to the military forces' future conduct vis-à-vis the detention conditions:

Two issues require improvement. First, the question of arranging tables for meals *must be reconsidered*. The explanation we were given—that the prisoners will dismantle the tables and will use them in a way that impairs security—is not

---

[10] *Id.* at 822.
[11] HCJ 3278/02, Hamoked Lehaganat Haprat v. the IDF Commander, PD 57(1) 385 (2002).

convincing. They do not do so with the sleeping planks, and there is no reason to assume that they will do so with tables for meals. These tables may also be built of concrete that is embedded deep in the ground in such manner that it is not possible to dismantle them. The need for a table for meals for those who are used to having this pertains to respect for human dignity. Detainees are not animals and you cannot compel them to eat on the floor....It is possible, of course, that there is not sufficient room in the tents or nearby to arrange tables and this will require expanding the detention facility. *We have not examined the weight of this consideration and its proper place but we request that the matter be reassessed.* [emphasis added][12]

In the *Ketziyot* affair,[13] in which the Court discussed the detention conditions of detainees who were sent to the Ketziyot Detention Facility, the same facility with regard to which the *Sagadiya* ruling was given, the Court continued with this approach. It reproached the State for not having been properly prepared for the operation[14] and then moved on to examine the various claims made by the detainees, one after the other:

Tents...I find it doubtful if the definition of *Pictet* is accurate. It seems that this changes from place to place and from time to time. It all depends on the quality of the tents, on the one hand, and the conditions of the site, on the other. There is also reason to distinguish between a brief detention and a detention that extends for a matter of months or even years. The test ultimately is the test of reasonableness and of proportionality and *we request that the matter be brought for consideration*...The second issue that requires examination is the height of the beds...It has not been clarified to us if the problem has been resolved thereby. *We request that this matter be reexamined thoroughly.* As long as the detainees sleep in tents, everything must be done to provide them with reasonable conditions of accommodation...*From this state of affairs, the duty to resolve the problem is imposed on the Respondents, who must attend to this...* The third issue is the lack of a toilet bowl in the lavatory... *This too requires reevaluation....* The fourth issue is the absence of tables for meals... *We request that this matter be examined in depth and a reasonable solution is to be found.* [emphasis added][15]

Finally, the Court noted that:

We are convinced that our recommendation will be considered by the Respondents and the necessary steps will be taken to rectify the situation. [emphasis added][16]

---

[12] *Id.* para. 28 of the judgment.
[13] HCJ 5591/02, Yasin v. the Commander of the Ketziyot Detention Facility, PD 57(1) 403 (2002).
[14] *Id.*
[15] *Supra* note 13, at 417.
[16] *Id.*, para. 21 of the judgment.

This case strikingly illustrates the willingness of the Court to sacrifice formality over substance in order to get immediate results that will improve the conditions of the detainees. It also illustrates the extent of the Court's willingness to offer recommendations. The Court looks at fundamental constitutional questions with the same seriousness that it examines the height of the tables in the detention facilities and the presence of toilet bowls, and attempts, to the best of its ability, to ensure that humanitarian conditions will be provided in times of hostilities as well.

This case also illustrates the Court's ability to provide recommendations of varying degrees of power. When the Court reached the conclusion that, as regards the tents issue, the State was fulfilling its duties according to international law, it was satisfied with the words "we request that the matter be brought for consideration." Nonetheless, in other cases where the Court was decidedly dissatisfied with the State's conduct, even though it did not find it in violation of humanitarian law, the Court provided recommendations that were formulated more sharply, such as "we request that this matter be reexamined thoroughly."

Indeed, use of these recommendations seems to appear sufficiently significant and does not raise any difficulty in light of the fact that the recommendations are not binding. However, it should be noted that such recommendations do raise a difficulty in terms of the rules of conduct in a democracy. Recommendations by definition create tension between a binding decision and a recommendation that seeks to have the State act in a manner different to that derived from the bottom line of a judgment. The Court accepts the State's contentions that the detention conditions are not unlawful, but advises the State to take further steps apart from that which it ostensibly has been required to do in accordance with the law. The concrete proposals were generally intended to enable humanitarian solutions in the event that the strict application of humanitarian law does not provide one. Nonetheless, broad policy proposals advise the State to act within a sphere defined by the Court as lawful. It may be argued that by way of these policy proposals, the Court in fact "intrudes" into the domain of the Executive and creates spheres of influence that deviate from its authority. We will discuss this issue separately in the concluding chapters of this text.

HCJ *Gush Shalom v. the Broadcasting Authority*[17] provides another example of applying a recommendation that illustrates the disparity, at times, between a binding decision and an advisory message. This petition was lodged by the "Gush Shalom" movement, a human-rights nongovernmental organization, after the Broadcasting Authority banned two of its broadcasts intended for television. The broadcasts were aimed at Israel Defense Forces (IDF) soldiers serving in the Occupied Territories and cautioned them against performing acts that according to the broadcasts constitute war crimes. The Director General of the Broadcasting Authority banned the broadcasts, based on a statement of

---

[17] HCJ 7144/01, Gush Shalom v. the Broadcasting Authority, PD 56(2) 887 (2002).

opinion from the Broadcasting Authority's legal department. This opinion stated that the format of the broadcasts does not constitute "an advertisement" or "a service message" as this concerns a politically controversial message related to IDF activities in the Occupied Territories, "and perhaps asks soldiers to refuse orders."[18] Although this concerns an issue pertaining to questions of freedom of expression, the Court decided not to intervene in the decision of the Authority's Director General, which it found to be lawful in the circumstances of the matter. At the end of the judgment, the Court added a recommendation to the State regarding the method of applying the judgment.

> In conclusion, I would remark that it would be warranted for the Broadcasting Authority to consider the possibility of providing the petitioners with a platform to voice their opinion within the confines of a suitable program at a suitable time.[19]

In this manner, without intervening in the interpretation of Broadcasting Authority Law's provisions, the Court sought to give suitable expression to the message the Gush Shalom movement wished to transmit—in other words, to apply the judgment in a manner different from the legal conclusion it had reached.

A case that patently illustrates the difference in the way the Court uses the operative part of a judgment and the non-binding advisory section concerns military checkpoints that the IDF set up to separate Jerusalem from the Occupied Territories during the al-Aqsa Intifada. In the *Vangensu* case,[20] the status of residents of East Jerusalem was discussed. East Jerusalem residents, who held Israeli identity cards, were entitled to pass through the military checkpoint placed near their place of residence although the checkpoint's position adversely affected the quality of their lives. When the petition was lodged, the Court ordered that it be heard "at the earliest possible time,"[21] and during the hearing the Court maintained the same line as it ordered the State's attorney to inform the Court:

> Within 15 days, what steps the State will take to ensure that the Petitioners will be able to pass through the checkpoint without delays and to enable them passage, subject to a security check as Jerusalem residents, for all intents and purposes.[22]

The State, which understood the implied message, informed the Court: "Following the hearing of this petition, steps have been taken to facilitate matters for the petitioners."[23] It continued, "Soldiers positioned at the checkpoint have received instructions, which

---

[18] *Id.* at 890.
[19] *Supra* note 17, para. 11 of the judgment.
[20] HCJ 6129/02, Vangensu v. the Minister of Defense, Tak-El 2002(4) 747 (2002).
[21] *Id.*, decision of July 15, 2002.
[22] *Supra* note 20, decision of Oct. 2, 2002.
[23] *Supra* note 21.

have recently been revised, that the checkpoint is to remain open to residents of the Petitioners' neighborhood even when a curfew is imposed for security reasons on the residents of Bethlehem."[24] In the judgment that followed these proceedings, the Court distinguished between the binding part of the judgment and the advisory section as follows:

> *We again determine* that those in charge of passage through the checkpoint must respect the orders according to which, apart from a state of specific alerts when the checkpoint is completely closed, the Petitioners will be permitted to pass through the checkpoint as all other residents of Jerusalem who hold Israeli identity cards. *We also advise* that further efforts be made to find a practical way to facilitate the Petitioners' free passage through the checkpoint. [emphasis added][25]

This case illustrates the manner in which the Court separates consciously within the judgment between the binding–authoritative part of the judgment and the advisory part, which does not require immediate binding enforcement. For the binding part the Court used the term *We determine*. For the non-binding part the Court preferred the term *we advise*.

RECOMMENDATIONS DURING HOSTILITIES

Intensive use of recommendations may be seen in judgments in which the Court is requested to decide issues related to fighting that are heard during the actual time of combat. An example of such recommendations may be taken from two petitions that were heard during Operation Defensive Shield. The Court's use of recommendations in these two cases illustrates the many advantages that recommendations afford the Court, which is required to decide legal questions in real time during a period of fighting, but also the complexity of a practice that ostensibly appears trivial.

HCJ 3114/02[26] concerned the evacuation of bodies from Jenin following the fierce battle in the refugee camp during Operation Defensive Shield. The fighting in Jenin occurred at the peak of the operation and was one of its most difficult battles. It attracted media attention as a result of the extensive destruction, the death of 13 soldiers in one day, and the Palestinians' accusations that a massacre was perpetrated in the camp. During the battle, 23 Israeli soldiers and 52–56 Palestinians were killed. In the course of the fighting, Knesset Member Baracha lodged a petition with the Supreme Court in which he requested that the Court order the military to refrain from burying the bodies

---

[24] *Id.*

[25] *Id.*

[26] HCJ 3114/02, Baraca v. the Minister of Defence, PD 56(1), 11(2002).

and to leave the duty to locate and collect bodies to medical staff and representatives of the Red Cross.[27]

The petition was submitted on April 12, 2002, which was a Friday. It was heard on the following Sunday while the operation was still at its height and bodies remained unburied in the field. The international community was closely following the Palestinian claims that a massacre had been perpetrated in the Jenin refugee camp. A judgment was handed down on the same day. The Court's conclusion was that the legal duty under humanitarian law to bury the bodies applied to the military forces. Yet even though the State agreed to include Red Cross representatives, the Court found great practical significance in including representatives of the Red Crescent to collect the bodies for burial. In this case, too, the Court opted to promote this aim, which it did not find legally binding under international humanitarian law, by way of a recommendation:

> The principal starting point is that in the circumstances of the matter, the responsibility of locating, identifying, evacuating and burying the bodies applies to the Respondents....*We recommend that a representative of the Red Crescent will be included, subject, of course, to considerations of the military commanders.* [emphasis added][28]

Later, the Court added:

> *It would be warranted during the phase of locating the bodies to include representatives of the Red Crescent.* It would also be warranted—and this is acceptable to the Respondents—that during the phase of identification of the bodies local entities will be included. [emphasis added][29]

Another case in which the Court sought to promote policy objectives through the use of recommendations during a state of hostilities by creating disparity between the advisory message and the binding part of the judgment was also given during Operation Defensive Shield. This case pertained to the crisis that developed around the siege of the Church of the Nativity. On April 2, 2002, the IDF invaded Bethlehem. Two hundred Palestinians, including 39 wanted men, fled to the church and took members of the clergy and others found in the church hostage at gunpoint. IDF soldiers surrounded the church and demanded that the wanted men surrender and release the hostages. Journalists and television personnel from all over the world followed the hostage situation in live broadcasts. Several countries and organizations attempted to mediate between Israel and the Palestinians. On April 23, 2002, still at the height of the crisis,

---

[27] *Id.* at 15–16.
[28] *Supra* note 26, at 15.
[29] *Id.*

the owners of the premises submitted a petition known the HCJ *Custodia* petition.[30] They demanded that food, water, medicine, and other vital necessities be supplied to the priests found in the church. They also petitioned to have the premises connected to water and electricity and to have a physician who would examine the hostages being held there, and requested the removal of two corpses found in the church. When the petition was submitted, the Court decided to set it for an urgent hearing. The hearing was held the next day at 11:30 a.m. The parties agreed, under the aegis of the Court, that the attorney for the petitioner would submit to the attorney for the respondent a list of food items required for the priests, and the goods would be brought in by IDF forces to the premises where the priests were being held.

The issue of removing the corpses was to be raised during negotiations to be held between military representatives and representatives of the Palestinian Authority in the early afternoon of the same day. Accordingly, the Court decided to halt the hearing until 4 p.m. At 4 p.m., when the Court received a report from the military commanders in the field that the parties had not reached any agreement on the removal of the bodies, it gave its judgment. The Court determined that the issue that had been brought before the Court is not justiciable and therefore rejected the petition. The Court clarified that its decision that the issue is not justiciable was made solely after it was clarified for the Court that water and food had been supplied to the Church. Incidental to rejecting the petition, the Court added the following: "We find it warranted to remark that if the contacts are not able to be successfully concluded, it would be well for the Respondents to consider positively finding a suitable resolution to the issue of the removal of the bodies from the premises forthwith and independent from any other arrangement."[31] Two days later, even though the crisis had not been concluded, the State permitted the removal of the bodies from the church premises.[32]

On the day that the decision was given in the HCJ *Custodia Case*, another petition was submitted that also pertained to the siege of the church.[33] The petition was submitted by the governor of Bethlehem. In the hearing that was held the day after the judgment in the HCJ *Custodia Case*, the State announced that the matter of the collection and burial of bodies had already been resolved. In other words, the State understood the recommendation conveyed to it in the Court decision in the HCJ *Custodia Case* and immediately took action accordingly, even though the message had been given in the absence of a binding judgment on the matter. In these circumstances, the problem remaining was the question of providing food and water. At the hearing, the State announced that it did not object to the departure of Palestinians from the premises and even undertook that

---

[30] HCJ 3436/02 Custodia Internationale di Terra Santa v. the Government of the State of Israel, PD 56 (3) 22 (2002).

[31] *Id.*

[32] *See* Felix Frisch & Ali Wakd, *Two Bodies Were Removed from the Church of the Nativity*, YNET, Apr. 25, 2002, *available at* http://www.ynet.co.il/articles/0,7340,L-1854331,00.html.

[33] *See* HCJ 3451/02, Almadani v. Minister of Defense, PD 56 (3) 30 (2002), a decision of April 24, 2002.

no harm would come to them. As opposed to this, the petitioners argued that according to information they had, the armed Palestinians on the premises were preventing civilians from leaving the area. Thus, the only way to ensure the provision of food for civilians was to bring food in sufficient quantities to the church premises. Accordingly, the State replied that basic foodstuffs were available within the church premises, and there was no possibility of ensuring that any additional food that would be brought in to the church premises would aid only the civilians there. Four days later, when the Court realized that the crisis had not ended, it ordered a hearing to be held in the presence of the parties. At the hearing, the Court advised the State to allow the civilians to leave the premises, to obtain food and water, and to return to the church premises. The State agreed to this. When the State agreed, the Court then gave its judgment in which it determined that the State had fulfilled its undertakings in accordance with international law.

The cases of the Jenin Battle and of the Church of Nativity illustrate how far and deep the Court is willing to go in order to try to make sure that the military complies with international law. These cases could have easily been declared nonjusticiable, as one of them was indeed declared. Yet, the Court declared them so after it tried to solve the crisis and provide the military with some advice on how to conduct the crises in a way that is in compliance with international law (and perhaps also with common sense). The Court indeed rejected the petitions but it did so after making sure that fundamental humanitarian obligations such as the provision of water and food or the involvement of the Red Cross are indeed respected by the military.

CONCLUSION

Recommendations are not trivial as they may sound in first reading. They enable the Court to expand the limits of judicial review of State national security policy. Through recommendations, the Court attempts to encourage a desired policy. It is the same when the Court attempts to improve conditions of detention for detainees beyond that which international law requires, and it is the same when the Court seeks to advance a resolution during a crisis when the reality of combat does not allow the combatants to reach a resolution. The use of recommendations has allowed the Court to demonstrate its willingness to attempt to affect the legitimate decisions of other authorities by way of non-binding advisory dialogue, and the extent to which the Court is prepared to increase its involvement in their discretion, even if it finds that their discretion is being exercised legitimately. The recommendations, specifically those related to the conduct of hostilities, illustrate to what degree the Court is willing to intensify and expand its review and to sacrifice formality in order to enhance humanitarian solutions and respect for international law.

The use of recommendations that are given during a period of hostilities dramatically highlights to what extent the Israeli Supreme Court is prepared to delve into issues pertaining to the actual conduct of war, in real time. The Church of the Nativity crisis was at its height at that time, and the bodies of those killed in the battle in Jenin lay scattered in the area. The Court, of course, ultimately rejected the petitions. Yet prior to doing so, the Court acted in real time at the height of the crises—via recommendations—to attain an arrangement, whether with regard to the evacuation of bodies in Jenin or to the provision of food and water to the hostages in the Church of the Nativity.

Concrete recommendations, policy recommendations, or recommendations during hostilities allow the Court to affect national security policies in real time and to improve the situation of civilians within a few days, without any need for them to serve a petition and to wait months or years until they see any change in their status.

Recommendations appear to be quite a straightforward practice. The Court rules according to the law and adds, as it pleases, recommendations pertaining to what is right and proper. Certainly, as we saw here and shall discuss later, this practice arouses complex questions with regard to relations between the Court and the military surrounding national security issues and the conduct of war.

6

Signaling in Judgments

RECOMMENDATIONS ARE ONE form of non-binding intervention by the Israeli Supreme Court. The discussion in this chapter will focus on the use the Court makes of another type of advisory message: *signaling*. Signaling is how the Court expresses its position on a question of the constitutionality of a certain law or the legality of certain policy without giving a formal binding decision. Although it is true that signaling can have an immediate effect on national security policy, its major significance lies in its ability to produce a long-term effect. This becomes evident when a change in policy or legislation is examined as well as the Court's hypothetical position on an issue.

Like other messages, signaling is not used exclusively in the spheres of national security or Israel's legal system. Studies in the United States have pointed to the use the US Supreme Court makes of signaling. Empirical studies dating back to the 1950s have demonstrated that dialogue is one of the tools used by the courts to influence the manner of formulating policy and conduct of the legislature, the government, administrative entities, the lower courts, and the public at large.[1] A pioneering empirical study in the field of non-binding dialogue between the US Supreme Court and other bodies was conducted by Joseph Tanenhaus et al.,[2] which produced the theory known as Cue Theory. According to it, the dialogue between the US Supreme Court and the other branches and even with the lower courts is conducted by way of "cues." More specifically,

---

[1] For a comprehensive review of the studies in this field, *see* LAURENCE BAUM, JUDGES AND THEIR AUDIENCES: A PERSPECTIVE ON JUDICIAL BEHAVIOR (2006).

[2] *See* Joseph Tanenhaus, Marvin Schick, Matthew Muraskin & Daniel Rosen, *The Supreme Court's Certiorari Jurisdiction: Cue Theory, in* JUDICIAL DECISION MAKING III (Glendon Schubert ed., 1963).

the authors contend that "the cues" that actors convey to the Supreme Court influence the Court when it comes to decide whether to give an order to hear a case (*Writ of Certiorari*).

Several later studies have developed the "cue theory" further by focusing on the signals the court transmits.[3] Perry[4] made use of Signaling Theory, originally developed by the political scientist, Robert Jervis[5] to describe the ways and avenues by which countries communicate with each other in times of crisis. Perry argued that signaling also occurs in inter-branch dialogue and could illustrate the communications between the US Supreme Court and other branches. Signaling Theory assumes that actors tend to convey messages that can be divided into signals and indices.[6] Signals are purposeful messages transmitted by the Court, and indices are signs existing in the Court's behavior that could be studied by the players in order to assess the Court's position on a specific matter. Interpreting signals and indices can help the parties understand what conduct may be anticipated by the Court and also what may happen if the recipient fails to perceive the message, and act according to that which is expected of it. In reference to the manner of decision-making in a *Writ of Certiorari*, Perry wrote the following:

> The cert petition starts a communications process. It is a process where one party is trying to send information and another is trying to evaluate that information.... The notion is that information is transmitted in basically two forms— indices and signals.[7]

Signaling Theory has assisted other scholars in describing the manner in which the US Supreme Court communicates with other authorities. Charles Cameron, Jeffrey Segal, and Donald Songer[8] explained by way of the theory how the Court decides whether to hear a certain file according to signals and indices. The Court relies on signals and

---

[3] *See* Beth Henschen, *Statutory Interpretations of the Supreme Court: Congressional Response*, 11 AM. POL. 441, 447 (1983) and Richard A. Paschal, *The Continuing Colloquy: Congress and the Finality of the Supreme Court*, 8 J.L. & POL., 143, 150–51 (1991).

[4] *See* H.W. PERRY, DECIDING TO DECIDE: AGENDA SETTING IN THE UNITED STATES SUPREME COURT 116–17 (1991).

[5] *See* ROBERT JERVIS, THE LOGIC OF IMAGES IN INTERNATIONAL RELATIONS (1970). Jervis's Signaling Theory differs from another signaling theory developed by Eric Posner to understand and describe the manner of the Court's activity. Signaling Theory as developed by Eric Posner focuses on the relationships created by individuals in society, and how signals affect the development of social norms. *See* ERIC A. POSNER, LAW AND SOCIAL NORMS (2000) and David H. Moore, *A Signaling Theory of Human Rights Compliance*, 97 N.W. U.L. Rev. 879 (2003).

[6] PERRY, *supra* note 6, at 116–17.

[7] *Id.* at 121

[8] Charles Cameron, Jeffrey Segal & Donald Songer, *Strategic Auditing in a Political Hierarchy*, 94 AM. POL. SCI. REV. 101 (2000).

indices, such as whether "Friend of the Court" (amicus curiae) briefs have been filed or the degree of involvement of the Attorney General in the process. George and Solimine[9] used this theory to illustrate the effect on the US Supreme Court of minority opinions and unanimous decisions in lower courts, whereas LeRoy demonstrated that the signaling model is supported by empirical findings.[10]

Signaling Theory is an excellent means to understand the way in which dialogue, used by actors in a system comprising formality, procedure, and hierarchies, structures the framework of communication.

As we will see later in this chapter, what is unique to national security signaling made in real time is the need of the Court to develop a very pragmatic approach to issues of constitutionality. Doing so leaves the State with options to choose from and developing techniques that will not leave the State in the midst of a crisis without the means to handle it.

SIGNALING: THE CASE OF USE OF VIOLENCE IN SHIN BET INTERROGATIONS

The Supreme Court of Israel makes extensive and highly sophisticated use of signaling in its case law with regard to national security. An important precedent was HCJ *On Torture* in which the Court chose a particularly sophisticated way to signal the Knesset. In the background of the decision of HCJ *On Torture* prohibiting the use of violence in investigations of terrorism stood the question of the status of a law that would permit the use of violence vis-à-vis an interrogatee in "a ticking bomb" case. The question remained in the background of the decision as the Court wisely based its decision on the absence of authorization in the existing law to use violence, not on the constitutionality of such a provision.[11] The HCJ decision to prohibit the use of violence in Shin Bet investigations rested not incidentally on the absence of authority in law for the use of violence. In this way the Court was able to refrain from deciding two particularly difficult questions. One was whether a law that would permit the use of violence against an interrogatee under circumstances of "a ticking bomb" would be deemed by the Court

---

[9] Tracy E. George & Michael Solimine, *Supreme Court Monitoring of Courts of Appeals En Banc*, 9 Sup. Ct. Econ. Rev. 171 (2001).

[10] *See* Michael H. LeRoy, *Institutional Signals and Implicit Bargains in the ULP Strike Doctrine: Empirical Evidence of Law as Equilibrium*, 51 Hastings L.J. 171 (1999).

[11] For an analysis of the Supreme Court's decision in HCJ *On Torture* based on the theory of dialogue and judicial minimalism, *see* Cass R. Sunstein, *Not Deciding*, New Republic at 41 (Oct. 29, 2001) (reviewing Lisa Koppenberg, Playing It Safe: How the Supreme Court Sidesteps Hard Cases and Stunts the Development of Law). *See also on this subject* David Scharia, *On Torture Chambers and Acoustic Walls*, 10 Politica 61 (2003). *See also* Oren Gross, *Are Torture Warrants Warranted? Pragmatic Absolutism and Official Disobedience*, 88 Minn. L. Rev. 1481 (2004).

as unconstitutional. The second referred to the difficult legal and moral dilemma of whether the use of violence in the event of "a ticking bomb" is defensible under the criminal law doctrine of necessity, and if not whether an investigator who used violence in such circumstances should be prosecuted.

Accordingly, in the judgment the Court refrained from deciding the issue of the constitutionality of such a law, if it were to be legislated, but the question hovered in the background of the discussion of the petition and aroused extensive public debate after the judgment was rendered.[12]

Scrutiny of the judgment and reading between the lines demonstrates that the Court related most judiciously to the question of the constitutionality of a law that would permit investigators to use violence. The Court's signaling on the constitutionality of a future "torture" law was complex and cautious, but restrained the Knesset. On the one hand, the Court related incidentally (in other words, in a non-binding manner) to this issue as it referred to the use of violence vis-à-vis an interogatee as constituting an infringement of his basic rights to an extent that is excessive.[13] On the other hand, when the Court related directly to the question of the constitutionality of such a law, if it were to be legislated, it chose to use ostensibly cautious and neutral language stating that the final decision on such a law is in the hands of the Knesset.[14]

The judgment in the petition HCJ *On Torture* was written with each word in the judgment meticulously chosen by the Court. It should not be assumed that certain matters in the judgment were left to chance. The Court intentionally sought to transmit an ambivalent message with reference to the question of constitutionality. On the one hand, the Court determined that the use of violence infringes a suspect's basic rights.

---

[12] *See on the subject* B'TSELEM, LEGISLATION THAT PERMITS PHYSICAL AND MENTAL FORCE IN GSS INVESTIGATIONS (2000).

[13] "A reasonable interrogation is an interrogation without torture, without a cruel or inhuman approach vis-à-vis the interogatee and without his humiliation… This conclusion complies with international agreement law—to which Israel is a party—which prohibits the use of torture… Such prohibitions are 'absolute.' There are no 'exceptions' and there is no balancing thereof… There is no doubt that shaking is an invalid means of interrogation. It harms the body of the interrogatee. It is disrespectful of him. It is a violent method, which does not constitute part of a lawful interrogation. It exceeds the necessary measures… It has been contended before us that one of the methods used in the interrogation was that in which the interrogatee crouches down on the tips of his toes for five minute intervals at a time. The State did not deny the use of these methods. This is an invalid method of interrogation. It serves no purpose that is inherent to the interrogation of a person. It is humiliating and disrespectful of human dignity…. The same is true of the method of having the interrogatee sit in the '*shabach*' position … *All these methods do not fall within the sphere of a 'fair' interrogation. These are not reasonable methods. They infringe the suspect's human dignity, his bodily integrity and his basic rights in an excessive manner.*" *See* HCJ *On Torture*, HCJ 5100/94 The Pubic Committee against Torture in Israel v. the Government of Israel, PD 53 (4) 817, 838 (1999).

[14] "…there are those who argue that Israel's security problems are too numerous, and require the authorization of physical means. Whether it is appropriate for Israel, in light of its security difficulties, to sanction physical means is an issue that must be decided by the legislative branch, which represents the people. We do not take any stand on this matter at this time." *See id.*, para. 39.

On the other hand, the Court recognized and declared that the moral decision regarding this question lies with the Knesset. The ambivalent signaling, as it were, which the Court transmitted blocked the possibility of legislating a law that permits the use of violence, even though the Court's decision did not determine that the use of violence is immoral or contrary to the Basic Law: Human Dignity and Liberty. Accordingly, those in favor of the legislation could not rely on the HCJ decision as a basis for legislation of a law that would permit the use of violence, despite the fact that the Court's ruling was based on lack of authority in the existing law.

In a lecture delivered by Justice D. Dorner, one of the justices on the panel that handed down the judgment in HCJ *On Torture*, about five years after the judgment was given, she relates to this complicated signaling. Justice Dorner views this as one of the reasons the Knesset refrained from legislating a statute that would permit the use of violence:

> Nevertheless, the Court stated that it abstains from expressing its opinion regarding the question of the constitutionality of a statute explicitly authorizing the Shin Bet to use physical pressure in certain interrogations, mainly those conducted in situations of a "ticking bomb," where by withholding the information he possesses, the terrorist endangers lives in an immediate sense. *The Court did emphasize, however, that such legislation must adhere to the requirements set forth in Basic Law: Human Dignity and Liberty.* When the issue was raised in the Knesset, it rejected the suggestions to enact such a statute. The reason for the rejection, apart from the moral dilemma, was mainly the fear that the statute would not comply with the requirements of the Basic Law or survive the comprehensive review of the High Court of Justice. [emphasis added][15]

This neutral formulation, as it were, that the Court selected was part of the complex message that the Court sought to transmit. The judgment in HCJ *On Torture* included, therefore, sophisticated signaling that comprised two apparently conflicting elements.[16] On the one hand, it included a seemingly neutral statement that the legislative authority is the one that must decide the moral dilemma of the use of violence in the event of "a ticking bomb." On the other hand, constitutional limits were set in the judgment for the scope of action of the Knesset by including signaling to the effect that the use of violence in Shin Bet interrogations is likely to be construed by the Court as conduct contrary to the constitutional rights of the suspect being interrogated.

---

[15] Dalia Dorner, *The Protection of Human Rights in the New Age of Terror*, 11 Hum. Rights Brief (2003). For the full version of the lecture, *see* http://www.wcl.american.edu/hrbrief/11/1dorner.cfm.

[16] *See* Scharia, *supra* note 2, at 72.

"POSITIVE SIGNALING": THE CASE OF DETENTION OF "UNLAWFUL COMBATANTS"

A comparison of the signaling that the Court transmitted in HCJ *On Torture* with the signaling that it transmitted several months later in its judgment in the *Bargaining Chips* affair further supports this conclusion. It is also instructive with regard to the Court's degree of sophistication and precision in formulating the signaling. The issue of the *Bargaining Chips* was reviewed repeatedly by the Court over the years during which Israel held under administrative detention 21 Lebanese citizens for the purpose of their possible exchange for Israeli captives and missing persons in Lebanon. The dilemma in this case was rather novel at the time of the hearing, although today as we know the issue of prolonged detention of individual members of terrorist organizations is something many countries are dealing with in what is often referred to as the detention of "unlawful combatants."

The Court's decision to order that the detention contradicts the Administrative Detentions law was given after it had ratified this practice several years earlier. Nonetheless, as we saw with regard to the torture issue, years before a judgment was given that revokes a national security policy, the Court transmitted signaling that heralded the coming of the change and suggested to the State that it better alter its policy so that a decision in principle would not have to be made against it. Yet in 1996, four years before the Court's fundamental judgment, the Court added the following, at the end of one of the decisions in which it ratified the detention:

> Nonetheless, the question again arises in this appeal: Until when is it possible to hold persons in administrative detention, with regard to whom the public authorities in charge of applying the law have no possibility and no intention of prosecuting them? ... *Indeed the emphasis in decisions of this kind must be placed on utilizing a sense of proportion. Such orders are not to be extended or renewed as a routine matter. On the contrary, these must be reexamined each time, not only in terms of whether the order was justified initially, but whether the continued utilization thereof is really vital to attain the objective of safeguarding the security of the state.* [emphasis added][17]

It is true that in this decision the Court did not relate to the question of whether the detention of Lebanese citizens was legal, yet the decision did express the Court's dissatisfaction with their prolonged detention by suggesting that this policy arouses a difficult question of proportionality.

---

[17] Administrative Detention Appeal 6/96, Anonymous v. the State of Israel, PD 50 (4) 45, 48–49 (1996).

A year later, a fundamental judgment was given in which it was determined that the State has authority under the Administrative Detentions Law to detain the Lebanese citizens as bargaining chips in exchange for the release of the captive navigator Ron Arad.[18] This decision was given against the minority opinion of Justice Dorner, who believed that the State does not have the authority to detain persons and hold them as bargaining chips. The petitioners submitted a petition for a Further Hearing with regard to this decision. A Further Hearing is a rare procedure in which the Court upon its own discretion decides to rehear a case due to the fundamental constitutional question it raises. The Court decided to accept this petition and hear this case before a panel of nine justices.

The hearing took place over a period of three years. In December 1999, five of the detainees were released and, in March 2000, another detainee was released. On April 12, 2000, the final judgment was given, in which the prior decision of the majority opinion was overturned and the minority opinion of Justice Dorner was adopted as a binding ruling. In the Further Hearing, a majority of the justices of the Supreme Court determined that the State has no authority to hold bargaining chips. With great drama, Justice Barak decided as well to retract his position and join the opinion of the justices who believed that the State has no authority to hold "bargaining chips."

During the petition hearing, the question arose, as in the *On Torture* case, of what is the constitutional position of a law that will specifically permit holding "unlawful combatants." An analysis of the opinions of the justices demonstrates that at the same time as the precedent was determined that the existing law[19] does not allow holding bargaining chips, several justices signaled the legislative authority with regard to the question of the constitutionality of a specific law on the subject. Justice Barak, for example, emphasized that he did not base his decision on the determination that there is no authority for such arrests in international law or the Basic Laws of Israel, but solely on the absence of lawful authority for incarceration. These grounds are similar to those on which the decision on the question of torture was based. Certainly, as distinct from the torture issue, Justice Barak signaled what would be his opinion if the Knesset opted to enact a law on the subject:

> In conclusion, *since the Respondent does not contend that there is a lawful way to detain the petitioners in custody except by way of administrative detention according to the Detentions Law* and since we have reached the conclusion that, pursuant to the Detentions Law, there is no authority to incarcerate a person who does not pose a risk to state security, it appears that there is no authority for the Respondent to detain the Petitioners in custody. The result is that we accept the petition, and declare that the Respondent may not hold the Petitioners in custody by virtue of the Detentions Law. *In the absence of other grounds for the arrests,* the Petitioners

---

[18] Administrative Detention Appeal 10/94, Anonymous v. the Minister of Defense, PD 53 (1) 97 (1997).

[19] Emergency Powers Law (Detentions) 5739-1979.

shall be released from custody and arrangements shall be made forthwith for their release from custody and their return to Lebanon. [emphasis added][20]

Justice Shlomo Levine, who agreed with Justice Barak, decided to add several words in a concurring opinion. A concurring opinion offers an excellent platform for signaling. For players in the field, it immediately raises the question of why the justice decided to distance himself from the remaining judges of the majority opinion, even though he agrees with the result that they reached, and what message he seeks to transmit by these means. In his concurring opinion, Justice Levin suggests to the legislative authority in clear language to consider enacting a law that would permit holding bargaining chips in Israel. Citing from his very short opinion:

> The State did not enact suitable legislation and, as aforesaid, did not indicate to us another source that establishes the power to arrest the Appellants. *For this reason alone,* I have agreed to accept the petition. [emphasis added][21]

In this manner, Justice Levine suggested, following on the statements of Justice Barak, that the Knesset's decision to enact a statute that would grant lawful authority to detain the Lebanese detainees would likely be considered as constitutional, in his opinion.

Comparing the version of signaling in the judgment of Further Hearing *Bargaining Chips* with the signaling transmitted in HCJ *On Torture* demonstrates how the Court can influence a plan for potential legislation via signaling. It demonstrates as well the Court's particular use of language to transmit precisely calibrated messages. Indeed, although in both cases, the decision for intervention was based on an absence of authority in existing law, in HCJ *On Torture* the Court extensively discussed the question of the constitutionality of a possible law and incidentally remarked that such a law would constitute an excessive infringement of human rights. It thereby prevented the Knesset from legislating a law that would permit the use of violence. As opposed to this, in the judgment in Further Hearing *Bargaining Chips*, the Court did not make an unequivocal statement with regard to the question of the possible unconstitutionality of future detention by virtue of a specific law. Furthermore, it also went on to suggest that a legitimate course that would grant such authority would not be deemed necessarily as unconstitutional. The Court thereby paved the way for enacting a law for incarceration of unlawful combatants.[22]

The Court's judgment in the *Bargaining Chips* affair illustrates a specific type of signaling, which may be called "positive signaling" or invitations to override a decision, a

---

[20] Further Hearing *Bargaining Chips*, at 745–46.
[21] *Id.* at 755–56.
[22] The Incarceration of Unlawful Combatants Law 5762-2002.

practice also not unique to the Israeli Supreme Court.[23] Lori Hausegger and Lawrence Baum bring, as an example, the judgment of the US Supreme Court in *McCarty v. McCarty* (1981) in which the Court rejected a petition to compensate the ex-wife of a military man. However, along with the rejection, Justice Blackmun added the following comment: "We recognize that the plight of an ex-spouse of a retired service member is often a serious one… Congress may well decide, as it has in the Civil Service and Foreign Service contexts, that more protection should be afforded a former spouse of a retired service member. This decision, however, is for Congress alone."[24]

Baum and Hausegger[25] contended that "invitations to override a decision" enable US Supreme Court justices to convey the fact that they find the conclusion they have reached to be unsatisfactory. These authors also illustrate how such "invitations" can be given at varying levels of intensity, according to the wish of the Court in overriding its decision. Invitations to override enable Supreme Court justices to convey that they have reached a conclusion they find unsatisfactory by way of a message that the legislative authority's overriding of the decision will not be deemed "a radical change."

Development of the discussion in the *Bargaining Chips* affair can illustrate this idea. If the signaling to the Knesset had not been sufficiently clear in the judgment given in the Further Hearing, an additional later decision of Justice Barak clarified to what extent the Court seeks to signal the Knesset positively on the question of the constitutionality of a law that would permit holding "Unlawful Combatants." On April 12, 2000, a Court decision was made in Further Hearing *Bargaining Chips*.[26] On April 18, 2000, a ministerial committee commenced the legislative process. At the same time, on April 19, 2000, the Minister of Defense ordered the release of 13 of the Lebanese citizens being held in custody (except for Mustafa Dirani and Abd al-Karim Obeid). The mother of navigator Ron Arad (who was believed to be held captive by Hizbullah during that time) filed an urgent petition against this decision in a final attempt to halt the release of the Lebanese, which would eliminate any possibility of learning the fate of her son.[27] As expected, in its decision in the Further Hearing, the Court rejected the petition and ordered the prisoners' release. However, Justice Barak added the following comments:

> Accordingly, we have reached the conclusion that the petition must be rejected… With regard to this matter comes the initiative to set in motion a legislative process that would allow the incarceration of "unlawful combatants." *As regards this matter, we would note that we do not view such legislation as*

---

[23] Lori Hausegger & Lawrence Baum, *Inviting Congressional Action: A Study of Supreme Court Motivations in Statutory Interpretation*, 43 AM. J. POL. SCI. 162 (1999).

[24] McCarty v. McCarty, 453 U.S 210 (1981), *cited in* Hauseger & Baum, *supra* note 14, at 1.

[25] *See* Hauseger & Baum, *supra* note 14, at 1. Later, because of this comment, the law was indeed amended accordingly.

[26] Criminal Further Hearing *Bargaining Chips*.

[27] HCJ 2967/00, Arad v. the Israel Knesset, PD 54 (2) 188 (2000).

circumventing our judgment in Criminal Further Hearing 7048/97. The Court has stated its view on the current case. This is its power and this is its mission. The Knesset may alter the current situation. This is its power and its mission. This is the right separation of powers. [emphasis added][28]

The Court clearly spells out that it does not view the proposed statute intended to permit the custody of "unlawful combatants" in certain circumstances as "circumventing" the Court, as opponents of the legislative process contended,[29] but rather precisely the opposite. By means of positive signaling in its decision, the Court "blessed" the future legislative process, invited the Knesset to override the Court's decision, and granted the proposed law constitutional backing. The Court could not have given any clearer signaling.

This case illustrates how signaling and judicial review in general on issues related to national security do not have to be limited to reviewing the legality of current policy or the constitutionality of an existing statute. Through signaling, the Court can outline a path for the legislative authority to cope with the threat with which the law is intended to cope in a constitutional manner. In the *Bargaining Chips* case, signaling was intended to pave the way for the Knesset to enact a specific statute that permits holding "bargaining chips" in certain circumstances, by signaling that the Court would not interpret such a statute as unconstitutional. Indeed, two months later, an "Incarceration of Unlawful Combatants Bill" was brought for a hearing in the Knesset and, a year later, a statute that granted the Chief of Staff the power to order the arrest of "an unlawful combatant" under judicial review was enacted.[30]

The law defined *unlawful combatant* as a person who has participated either directly or indirectly in hostile acts against the State of Israel or is a member of a force perpetrating hostile acts against the State of Israel, and therefore that the conditions in Geneva conventions regarding prisoners of war do not apply to such a person.

The law authorizes the person's incarceration for a first period of up to six months, subject to judicial review. Once every six months from the date of issue of an order the prisoner has to be brought before a judge of the District Court. If the court finds that the person's release will not harm State security or that there are special grounds justifying

---

[28] *Id.* at 191–92.

[29] *See* B'Tselem, *Position Paper on the Proposed Law: "Incarceration of Combatants Not Entitled to Prisoners of War Status"* (2000), *available at* www.btselem.org/Download/2000_Hostages_Law_Position_Paper_Heb.doc.

[30] The bill was brought for a Knesset hearing in June 2000, and the Knesset ratified it on the third reading on March 4, 2002. Section 2 of the Incarceration of Unlawful Combatants Law, 5762-2002 permits, under the conditions determined therein, the incarceration of "an unlawful combatant," who is defined as follows: "A person who took part in hostile acts against the State of Israel, whether directly or indirectly, or belonged to a force carrying out hostile acts against the State of Israel, and the conditions that grant prisoner of war status under international humanitarian law are not fulfilled with respect thereto, as specified in the Third Geneva Convention of August 12, 1949, with regard to the treatment of prisoners of war."

the person's release, it will quash the incarceration order. Any decision by the District Court could be appealed to the Supreme Court.

In 2008, a petition was served challenging the constitutionality of this act. However, as was already planted in the Supreme Court's original decision, the Court determined that the law "fulfills the conditions of the limitation article and there are no constitutional grounds to intervene therein."[31]

CONSTITUTIONAL PRAGMATISM

In analyzing the Israeli Supreme Court adjudication one can see that one of the main features of its national security adjudication is its commitment to try and find practical solutions. When a country is in crisis or under serious threat to its national security, the Court can be satisfied with a determination of the constitutionality of a law, but it can also go further. Via signaling and advisory messages, the Court can propose solutions that may be applied within a relatively short time without its judgment necessarily leading to a security vacuum in the country. In this manner, the Court avoids the concern that its decisions will lead to seriously harming the country's national security. A case that illustrates the constitutional pragmatism of the Court is the HCJ *Marab* case[32]. HCJ *Marab* discussed the question of the legal status of the provisions for arrest determined in Order 1500, which GOC (General Officer Commanding) Central Command issued in Operation Defensive Shield, and the positive signaling conveyed there, which was directed this time at the Executive.[33]

Order 1500 was given while the military was initiating Operation Defensive Shield. The Order amended the powers of arrest that were customary on the eve of the Al-Aqsa Intifada, in view of the waves of mass arrests that followed during the campaign. There were many new provisions in Order 1500 and, without going into detail, we would note that the Order permitted detention for up to 18 days without the need for a remand order of a military judge, judicial review, or a meeting between the detainee and his or her attorney. By virtue of this Order, thousands of Palestinians were held in custody in the course of Operation Defensive Shield. The Court determined in its judgment that the relevant provisions of Section 2 of the Order are void. In other words, a military commander does not have the authority to order remand for such a long period without

---

[31] Criminal Appeal 6659/06, Anonymous v. the State of Israel, Tak-El 2008 (2) 3270, para. 49 of the judgment of Justice Beinisch. *See further on this subject* the judgment of Justice Rubinstein in Criminal Appeal 1226/06, Iyad v. State of Israel (unpublished, Feb. 19, 2006).

[32] HCJ 3239/02 Marab v. Commander of IDF Forces in the West Bank, PD 57 (2) 349 (2002) [hereinafter HCB *Marab*].

[33] It will be noted that according to the law applied in the Territories, the GOC (General Officer Commanding) is sovereign in the field and has primary legislative authority. Accordingly, for the purpose of our discussion, he may be deemed as a kind of legislative authority.

judicial review. The grounds for the Court's decision were that judicial review is part of the process of formulating the legitimacy of an administrative detention order and part of formulating the legality of its extension. As the Order's provisions do not include judicial review, they must be invalidated.

What is interesting to see in this case is that, incidental to invalidation of the Order, the Court paved the way by positive signaling for finding a suitable legislative arrangement, which, if brought before the Court, apparently would be deemed lawful. At the end of its decision, the Court proposed a practical solution to implementing mass detention orders during a period of combat:

> How might it be possible to resolve the difficulty?…As we have seen, everything depends on the variable circumstances, which cannot always be anticipated in advance. *In the same way, due to the special circumstances before us, it would be justified to apply the approach taken by international law, which avoids determining fixed periods, and determines instead the duty to approach a judge forthwith. In any event, this is a matter for the Respondents, not for us.* [emphasis added][34]

In this case, we see how the Court invalidates the provisions of a lawful arrangement but at the same time advises the State how to formulate the order so that it may be construed by the Court as lawful. This type of positive signaling has been referred to in the US literature as *constitutional road maps*[35] or *exemplification*.[36] The Court invalidates the current arrangement, but instead of asking the legislative authority to override its decision, it proposes an alternate resolution of the issue already in its judgment. In certain aspects, this signaling has even more far-reaching consequences than those of Further Hearing *Bargaining Chips*. In the *Bargaining Chips* case, the Court suggested that it would be possible to enact a statute to arrange the subject under discussion, and this would not appear unconstitutional to the Court or as a procedure that circumscribes the High Court of Justice. However, the Court refrained from intervening in the question of what the contents of such a law would be and only placed constitutional limits on its contents. As opposed to this, in HCJ *Marab*, the Court invalidated the existing arrangement, and incidental to this "formulated" an alternative.

It is worth noting in this context how the language the Court uses in the signaling conveyed in HCJ *Marab* demonstrates to what extent the Court views itself as a partner in formulating national security policy, specifically in times of national crisis. The Court could have satisfied itself with invalidating the existing order. However, it was important to it to advise the State how to handle the arrest of thousands of people in a manner that is respectful to the rule of law and international law. Therefore it added language that

---

[34] HCJ *Marab, supra* note 23, at 376.
[35] Eric Luna, *Constitutional Road Maps*, 90 J. Crim. L. & Criminology 1125 (2000).
[36] *See* Neal Katyal, *Judges as Advicegivers*, 50 Stan. L. Rev. 1709, 1718 (1998).

will guide the State on how to redraft this order. The worldview that arises from such signaling, as well as from other instances of signaling, is that the Court does not view its function as being limited to the question of whether the State's national security policy is lawful or unlawful. The Court views itself as having the duty to assist the State in finding lawful solutions to the difficult dilemmas that new national security challenges raise.

CONSTITUTIONAL PRAGMATISM IN REAL TIME: THE CASE OF EMERGENCY REGULATIONS

As we have seen before a minority or dissenting opinion can serve as an excellent platform for conveying advisory messages. Tracey E. George and Michael E. Sulimine demonstrated that the US Supreme Court is more inclined to issue a *Writ of Certiorari* where a dissenting opinion has been given in the lower court. According to these authors, "figures suggest that dissents do serve as a signal to the Supreme Court."[37]

In the Israeli context, the significance of signaling given by way of a minority opinion may be learned particularly in a case where the Court refrained from providing a dissenting opinion. The famous case in this context is the Supreme Court judgment on the issue of the expulsion of 415 Hamas members following the murder of the military reserve soldier Nissim Toledano. On the eve of the judgment, three justices debated the question whether to validate the expulsion. Justice Barak believed that it was important for the Court to demonstrate institutional solidarity in this case, and the other justices agreed with his opinion. Subsequently, Justice Mazza regretted that Justice Barak had succeeded in persuading him. In Justice Mazza's opinion, it was important that particularly in this case a dissenting opinion would be expressed. "Even though he is well aware of the fact that a minority opinion would not alter the result, he knows that it would serve as a significant moral statement."[38]

A dissenting opinion is unique as signaling because, even if it does not bind anyone, it provides a lawful and moral alternative to the consensus established by the Court. It exposes an internal conflict that occurs in the Court. Judges can cite it and rely on it. Players in the field on the defeated side can based on a dissenting opinion endeavor to direct the course of legislation and policy change.[39]

A dissenting opinion bears a clear message—an alternative line of thought is legitimate on the question brought before the Court for a hearing. Accordingly, the defeated party can plan its course of action. The defeated party can choose to move the discussion

---

[37] *See on this matter* Tracey E. George & Michael E. Solimine, *Supreme Court Monitoring of Courts of Appeals En Banc*, 9 SUP. CT. ECON. REV. 171, 199 (2001).

[38] NAOMI LEVITZKI, THE SUPREMES: WITHIN THE SUPREME COURT 126 (2006).

[39] *See, e.g.,* the reliance of the B'Tselem organization on the minority position of Justice Cheshin on the matter of house demolitions. B'TSELEM, THROUGH NO FAULT OF THEIR OWN—PUNITIVE HOUSE DEMOLITIONS DURING THE AL-AQSA INTIFADA 39–40 (Nov. 2004).

to the public arena by relying on the dissenting opinion. It can attempt to present the question again in a different petition that will reach the Court at a more convenient time, from the Court's point of view, or perhaps justify a Further Hearing. Players on the winning side of the petition are also aware that a victory that is based on a disagreement among the justices of the Court is not an absolute one, and there is a chance that in time the ruling may be overturned.

A dissenting opinion also affects how a ruling that the majority judges have determined is applied. Players on the winning side, particularly where this concerns the State, are aware that if they pull the rope too hard, the dissenting opinion is ultimately likely to become the majority opinion. There are many examples of minority opinions whose effects over time have trickled onto center stage. The use Justice Barak made of the dissenting opinion of Justice Cheshin regarding the issue of house demolitions, discussed above, illustrates the use of a dissenting opinion to signal the parties.

Another instance of a dissent serving as signaling is the discussion that was held regarding the government's authority to enact emergency regulations to arrange issues that go beyond urgent national security matters.

National security at times requires using methods that are not under the government's authority as a matter of course. It is not always possible to foresee what methods are likely to be required by the State. In order to cope with emergencies, Israel (as well as many other countries) legislated Emergency Regulations Laws or Executive Orders Laws that grant the government or the Executive the authority to enact regulations that are actually primary legislation for handling emergencies. These broad but essential powers naturally generate difficulties in a democratic regime, and courts throughout the world have more than once discussed the proper limits of such authority.

In Israel, this issue is intensified due to the Court's willingness to examine government decisions not only in retrospect but also in real time. The commitment of the Court to being available almost unreservedly leads to a situation in which the Court is required to decide on government powers to enact emergency regulations, at times at the height of a crisis. The Court thereby arrives at a point in which it must decide not only whether the resolution the government has chosen is lawful but also the pragmatic question of whether, within the state of emergency the government has declared, the government may take a certain line of action even before it has practically taken it. Discussion regarding the use of emergency regulations illustrates how the Court uses advisory messages, specifically in minority opinions, to deal with this tension.

The question of the limits of government authority in using emergency regulations arose in the *Paritzky* case, which dealt with a rather civilian matter: elections of local authorities in 1998. That year the elections were set for November 10. Several days prior to the elections a strike broke out at the Ministry of the Interior in which employees of the Ministry refrained from issuing Identity Cards to voters. On November 5, the government resolutely decided to hold the elections on time and to enact emergency regulations that would allow voters to use passports and drivers licenses as identification. The same day MK Paritzky decided to file a petition to the High Court of Justice in which he argued that the government had overstepped its authority in enacting emergency regulations to arrange an issue that is essentially a civil administrative one.

The Court decided to hear the petition immediately, two days before the date set for the elections. At the time of the petition hearing, it was clear that it was impossible for the Knesset to dispose of this issue by means of legislation. The Court was left facing the dilemma of whether to allow such overly extensive use of emergency regulations with all the inherent difficulties or to refrain from intervening and thereby grant the strikers the power to veto the democratic election process.

The Court gave its decision on the same day, immediately after hearing the parties. All of the justices on the panel viewed disposal of this issue by means of emergency regulations as a real difficulty. Nonetheless, Justice Barak and Justice Dorner, of the majority opinion, refrained from invalidating the regulations that had been enacted. As opposed to them, Justice Cheshin, the dissenting opinion, believed that the government had overstepped its authority on this issue and that the regulations should be invalidated. I will not expand on the differences of opinion among the justices or on the grounds that served them in reaching their respective decisions, as this is not the principal point here. What is important for the purpose of our discussion is the technique the Court used to convey its disapproval of the practice without leaving the country in chaos or in the hands of the strikers. In his concluding paragraph Justice Barak wrote the following:

> I have reached the conclusion that the emergency regulations regarding the means of identification have been duly enacted. This was not a simple conclusion...I hope that our judgment herein—*both that of the majority opinion and the dissenting opinion together*—will indicate the many difficulties that mount up before the Government when enacting emergency regulations. *I expect that* the use of emergency regulations will not constitute a first choice of action but rather a last. [emphasis added][40]

The conversational tone of this concluding comment allows us to see, first of all, how the judges directly address the government in their judgment, conduct a dialogue within the judgment, and transmit messages to the government, as if the judgment were correspondence. The Court signals to the government that it is dissatisfied with the use made of the emergency regulations in this case but in order not to leave the state in chaos is willing to refrain from exercising the full power of its review. Moreover, Justice Barak employs the minority opinion of Justice Cheshin in order to convey that there is a dissenting opinion on this matter, which the government should take into consideration.

---

[40] HCJ 6972/98, Paritzky v. Minister of the Interior, PD 53(1) 763, 785–786 (1999).

Including the dissent in the majority opinion judgment allows Justice Barak to signal the government that the minority opinion may become a majority opinion, if the government does not learn to place reasonable limits on enacting emergency regulations. Justice Dorner, who joined Justice Barak, also added a concluding paragraph of her own with a similar message:

> Nonetheless, the Court's refraining from granting a relief in this matter shall not constitute a precedent. *The Government should not rely on the fact* that in future its omission of approaching the Knesset in time with a bill will provide grounds for this court to refrain from granting a relief against emergency regulations that are passed unduly.[41] [emphasis added]

Justice Dorner, even more decisively than Justice Barak, indicated that the government should not view the Court's judgment as a binding ruling. It only meant to prevent chaos and hijacking of the democratic process. In other words, judicial review in real time unlike normal times requires often the Court to offer pragmatic and rule of law based solutions to society. The Court committed to such role can not limit itself to detached, post facto review of questions of legality and constitutionality.

FROM SIGNALING TO RULING: THE RIGHT TO BE WARNED BEFORE INTERROGATION IN COUNTERTERRORISM INVESTIGATIONS

Another example of the sophistication with which the Court uses signaling can be seen in the way the Court can transmit a signal to the legislative authority in a decision in one file and turn the signaling into a binding decision in another file.

One of the difficult dilemmas facing investigators of terrorist acts is the question of whether to warn a suspect of his rights prior to his interrogation. On the one hand, warning a suspect with regard to the significance of his version of the event and, in particular, that it may serve as evidence against him, and informing him of his right to remain silent in the investigation so as not to incriminate himself is one of the fundamental rights of an interogatee, if not his most basic right. On the other hand, where an investigation is intended to prevent a future act of terrorism, if the suspect is warned, and if it is explained to him that he may remain silent during the interrogation, it is possible that he will choose to remain silent, at least until the terrorist act is performed by his partners in crime. Israeli law at that time had not determined this matter decisively. At that time, according to case law,[42] the rule that determines that obtaining a

---

[41] *Id.* at 818–19.
[42] Criminal Appeal 5614/92, State of Israel v. Messika, PD 49(2) 669 (1995).

confession from a suspect without issuing a warning will lead to the inadmissibility of the confession did not apply in Israel.

The dilemma was brought to the Court in the *Smirk* matter.[43] The Court's approach here illustrates a proficient use of dialogue and signaling. Steven Smirk, a German citizen who converted to Islam in 1994, traveled to Lebanon in the service of Hezbollah. In Lebanon, Smirk underwent instruction and training in operating weapons and explosives. Upon concluding his training, he was given a sum of money, a camera, and film. His instructions from his Hezbollah operators were to arrive in Israel as a tourist and collect information with regard to potential sites for carrying out suicide attacks. In November 1997, Smirk arrived in Israel and immediately was arrested by the Shin Bet after receiving a warning by the security services in Germany and Holland.

During his investigation by the Shin Bet, Smirk was not cautioned with regard to his rights. The Shin Bet investigators gave the following reasons for this. As this concerned an investigation to thwart a terrorist attack, an investigation intended to prevent Smirk, and perhaps his operators as well, from executing a terrorist attack in the immediate future, the investigators preferred not to caution him with respect to his rights so as to prevent him from taking refuge in his right to remain silent, prior to terminating the operatives of the countdown to the terrorist attack.

It should be noted that during the hearing in the Supreme Court of the *Smirk* case, a principal deliberation was held in the *Issacharov* matter[44] by an extended panel of nine justices, concerning precisely this fundamental question of the evidentiary standing of a confession obtained without warning the interogatee of his rights. The accused in the Issacharov matter was represented by attorney Avigdor Feldman, a prominent human rights advocate, who, at the same time, served as defense attorney for Smirk. Supreme Court Justice Dorit Beinisch was the justice who led the hearings in these two appeals that were conducted at the same time in the Supreme Court. In the course of the hearing of the *Issacharov* petition, the Court transmitted signaling to the Knesset that it would be better if the Knesset arranged the matter in legislation rather than the Court having to decide the issue.

When the date for the decision in the *Smirk* case arrived, the Court was compelled to give its judgment. The Court devoted key sections of this judgment to a discussion of the question of the evidentiary status of a confession that was obtained without warning the accused of his rights. Ultimately, the Court decided to base its conviction of Smirk on another confession that he made, of which there was no doubt that it was given of his own free will and following warning of his rights. However, Justice Beinisch added the following remark:

> *As for myself, I lean toward the opinion that the trend in interpretation ensuing from the Basic Law requires a renewed examination of the balance between the rights of the*

[43] Criminal Appeal 6613/99, Smirk v. State of Israel, PD 56(3) 529 (2002) [hereinafter the *Smirk* case].

[44] Criminal Appeal 5121/98, Issacharov v. the Chief Military Prosecutor, Tak-El 2006 (2) 1093.

accused and the need to protect the public interest.... The nature of cases, in which a confession will be invalidated due to the absence of a warning [of the rights of the accused], requires a comprehensive discussion best left to the future. [emphasis added][45]

What sets this comment apart is that Justice Beinisch is not satisfied with leaving this difficult issue as requiring further consideration, as the Court tends to do from time to time or as would have been possible considering the ruling that the matter awaits determination by the Knesset and does not require a decision in this file, or because the matter is pending before the Court in a hearing before a different panel. Instead, Justice Beinisch signaled that there is reason to review the principal ruling on this issue. She explained that the Court's position on the question of the admissibility of a confession obtained without a warning of rights had changed and added that she herself leaned toward the opinion that the rule must be changed but preferred to leave this to a suitable case. At the time that the *Smirk* judgment was given (March 4, 2002), the parties' contentions had already been heard in the *Issacharov* case. Furthermore, Justice Beinisch led the hearings in both cases. Accordingly, it is possible to see here signaling indicating the Court's frame of mind on this issue and its signaling to the Knesset that it might wish to take action or that the Court might decide it applying a new balance.

As noted above, this signaling was not made in a vacuum. While hearings were taking place in the Supreme Court on this issue, the Knesset was considering several bills to arrange the issue of admissibility of a confession obtained without warning the accused of his rights. The Supreme Court was aware of the Knesset discussions. This led the Court to wait in the *Issacharov* case no less than four years from the conclusion of hearing the parties' claims, without giving a judgment—all in the hope that the Knesset would be required to decide the principle and state its opinion, subject to the constitutional constraints the Court indicated by the signaling transmitted in the *Smirk* judgment.

Ultimately, the judgment in the *Issacharov* case was given on May 2, 2006, after the appeal on the matter had been pending for almost six years and after the Knesset did not manage to formulate a law on this issue. In this fundamental judgment, also given by Justice Beinisch, the Supreme Court determined as precedent that it has discretion to invalidate the admissibility of evidence in a criminal matter, if the Court learns that the evidence was obtained unduly and that admitting the evidence in court will essentially infringe the right of the accused to a fair hearing. Justice Beinisch relied in her judgment on the normative framework determined in the *Smirk* case, and even referred to statements she made in the same incidental remark, stating that as the Court had signaled the Knesset, but the Knesset had not acknowledged the signal, the inherent counsel was being fulfilled.

---

[45] *Smirk* case, *supra* note 34, para. 8 of the judgment of Justice Beinisch.

JUDICIAL SUNSET: THE CITIZENSHIP LAW

A final type of constitutional signaling to be presented in this chapter is that which Neal Katyal calls *Judicial Sunset*.[46] This is essentially a message from the Court that its decision not to declare a law unconstitutional will be valid only for a certain period or as long as certain conditions are fulfilled.

Judicial Nullification is a possible pragmatic solution for dilemmas ensuing from states of emergency, in which society finds it difficult to formulate norms for the long-term. In national security legislation of many countries throughout the world, expiration procedures are present that enable a country to re-examine from time to time whether the balance reached at a time of emergency still is warranted. Judicial Sunset allows the Court to operate in a similar manner. The Court may give a ruling during a state of emergency but at the same time can transmit a message to other branches that when the battle or state of emergency has ended, the Court will again review its decision on the matter. If the arrangement has not yet been amended, the Court may then reach the conclusion that it is unconstitutional.

A good example of the use of Judicial Nullification is the Court's judgment on the matter of the *Citizenship Law* discussed above.[47] As may be recalled, the Supreme Court justices were split in their opinions between the minority opinion, which believed the law is unconstitutional and the majority opinion, which believed the law is not unconstitutional. Justice Levy, who sided with the majority opinion, decided finally after a great deal of hesitation[48] to reject the petition. However, he added the following remark at the end of his judgment:

> In conclusion, I would propose to my colleagues that subject to the aforesaid, we will reject the petitions with regard to all that pertains to making the order, which orders revocation of the Citizenship Law due to its being unconstitutional, at this time absolute. *Nonetheless, I would underscore that if the Respondents do not manage to fulfill that which they have been requested to do, I doubt that the law will be able to continue to do well with judicial review in future, too.* [emphasis added][49]

---

[46] *See* Neal Katyal, *Changing Laws of War: Do We Need a New Symposium; The Sunsetting Judicial Legal Regime after September 11*, 79 NOTRE DAME L. REV. 1237 (2004). On the same matter, *see also* GUIDO CALABRESI, A COMMON LAW FOR THE AGE OF STATUTES 148–50 (1982). As opposed to this, a disparate method operates in Canada where parliamentary decisions to circumvent judicial decisions by the use of Section 33 of the Charter are valid solely for five years. Subsequently, if Parliament wishes to implement the matter, it must revive the law.

[47] *See* Chapter 3 next to note 46 and beyond.

[48] HCJ 7052/03, Adallah v. the Minister of the Interior, Tak-El 2006(2) 1754, para. 1 of the judgment of Justice Levy.

[49] *Id.*, para. 10 of the judgment of Justice Levy.

Analysis of Justice Levy's judgment leads to the general conclusion that his principled ruling is that the proposed arrangement in the Citizenship Law is unconstitutional. However, his pragmatic constitutionalism leads him to the conclusion that due to the difficult security situation prevailing at the time the judgment was given, he was not prepared to determine that the law must be revoked. Instead, Justice Levy left the law in place for a period of nine months so that the Knesset would be able to establish another more balanced arrangement. He even signaled the Knesset that the failure to accept an "improved" arrangement within a period of nine months was likely to lead the justice to a completely different conclusion, that is, that the law must be revoked.[50] As part of the dialogue, we may understand Justice Levy's judgment as follows: the judge reached the general conclusion that the arrangement was unconstitutional. Nonetheless, "*due to strong security requirements,*" at the time the judgment was handed down, Justice Levy was willing to leave the current arrangement in place. This arrangement would terminate if the Knesset failed to extend it under improved conditions within nine months. In this manner, the justice transmitted a message to the legislatature that it must take steps to arrange the matter or the justice may be likely to join the minority opinion, which believes that the law must be revoked. Underscoring the words *nine months* in the body of the text by Justice Levy himself reinforces the conclusion that the justice sought to signal the legislative authority explicitly and to make certain that it understood this message.

In conclusion, the solutions the Court offered in both the case of the emergency regulations and in the Citizenship Law illustrate some of the unique challenges associated with judicial review in real time and some of the pragmatic constitutional solutions developed by the Court. The Court may decide that a certain policy is unlawful or certain act is unconstitutional yet withhold the practical implications of its decision in order to prevent chaos or leave the State in a vacuum in times of a national security crisis.

Judicial review in real time affects the language, structure, and justification of the judgment. However, the changes are much more dramatic, it brings reality into the courtroom and a court committed to enhancing the rule of law by giving decisions in real time must take into account the effect of its decisions on the national security reality within which it operates. It must take into account that such adjudication affects itself as well.

---

[50] In the judgment on the matter of *United States v. Then*, 56 F.3d 464 (2d Cir. 1995), Justice Calabresi transmitted a similar message. The issue discussed there was discrimination in penalty tables between a person convicted of the possession of cocaine and a person convicted of possession of "crack." Justice Calabresi determined that it was not proved that the differences in penalties result from discrimination. Nonetheless, he determined that the disparity is troubling and that the government must take into account on updating the tables that: "Constitutional arguments that were unavailing in the past may not be foreclosed in the future." On page 467, in the same place, the judge raises this rhetorical question: "Precisely at what point does a court say that what once made sense no longer has any rational basis?"

7

Dialogue on Policy Application—I

INTRODUCTION

In the next two chapters, I will illustrate how the Court communicates with other branches of government to influence how laws are applied. The discussion will center on strategies of influence applied without the Court's intervention in constitutional questions or interpretation of statutes. The intention here is to present messages that the Court transmits regarding its expectation of how the State will apply a certain policy, even if the policy is recognized as lawful and even if the Court does not intend to intervene in how the authorizing law is interpreted.

At the outset of the discussion, it would be well to highlight a significant distinction: the dialogue regarding policy application to be presented in this chapter differs in essence from the Court's ordinary administrative supervision of public bodies. As we shall see further on, by using dialogue with respect to how policy is applied, the Court seeks to influence the conduct of the Executive beyond the formal legal standard of exercising reasonable discretion, in good faith and without extraneous considerations. Several cases to be mentioned later in this chapter will illustrate this distinction.

The discussion of dialogue in these two chapters will include five ways in which the Court influences how policy is applied, which are not based on the recognized grounds of administrative supervision:

1. **Statements advising public agencies**—Dialogue that advises public bodies with regard to the way in which the Court expects they will apply the law or the Court's judgment.

2. **Imposition of conditions on the application of policy**—Conditions that limit in practice the ability of the Executive to apply policy.

3. **Messages that advise how a judgment is to be applied**—Messages pertaining to a judgment, which indicate how the Court expects the Executive to implement the judgment.

4. **Transmission of messages of application by means of an operative order**—Messages that indicate by the structure or text of an operative order how the Court expects the Executive to apply the judgment.

5. **Expression of approval or censure**—Messages with regard to how the Executive applies the law to influence the manner of its application.

This, of course, is not a complete list of ways to transmit messages pertaining to the application of policy, but only primary examples of strategies that have been identified.

STATEMENTS ADVISING THE EXECUTIVE: THE CASE OF INCITEMENT TO VIOLENCE AND TERRORISM

A case that can illustrate the meaning of dialogue with regard to policy application pertains to offenses that impose limits on freedom of expression. This issue can explain how the Court contends with the tension between the desire to maintain a free society and the concern that freedom of speech will be exploited to incite to violence or terrorism.

An analysis of the development of case law regarding incitement to terror, and particularly the question of the relation between terrorism and political violence and freedom of speech during the stormy period following the murder of Prime Minister Yitzhak Rabin, can illustrate how the Court employs advisory statements in this area of case law.

As opposed to the United States, European countries and the State of Israel chose to directly criminalize incitement to terrorism. Incitement to terrorism as a criminal offense differs from most other terror-related offenses in several aspects: First, by its nature it constitutes a restriction of freedom of speech. Accordingly, the Courts must contend with the question of proper enforcement.[1] Second, this offense is a preventive offense. In order to convict a person of incitement to terrorism it is not necessary that a terrorist act indeed must take place. The inciter's statements do not have to cause another person to perform an act of terrorism for it to be possible to convict the inciter of the offense. However, this offense assumes that incitement to terror is likely to cause individuals exposed to such statements to perform acts of terrorism. The question of the degree of probability that links a statement of incitement with the occurrence of a

---

[1] For a more extensive view of this subject and a review of international and comparative law, *see* Daphne Barak-Erez & David Scharia, *Freedom of Speech, Support for Terrorism and the Challenge of Global Constitutional Law*, 2 HARV. NAT'L SEC. J. 1 (2011).

future act of terrorism has occupied many courts all over the world. It is clear that the higher the degree of probability, required in the law, between statements of incitement and the occurrence of an act of terrorism, the more difficult it will be for the prosecution to prove that such link exists. As opposed to this, the more hypothetical and distant the degree of probability needed between the statement and potential act of terrorism, the easier it will be for the prosecution to file indictments. However, this will result in a greater restriction of freedom of speech in society. These features of the offense have occupied the courts in Israel over the last 20 years. In this chapter, I will focus on the ways the Israeli Supreme Court uses to transmit messages to the prosecution regarding the proper enforcement of these offenses. In the next chapter, I will demonstrate how the Court has employed other tactics to mitigate this tension.

The point of departure for this question was the murder of Prime Minister Yitzhak Rabin. Rabin's murder deeply disturbed Israeli society. It unleashed a profound public debate on the liability for the incitement that preceded the murder, the liability of political figures and religious leaders for the murder, and the relation of the law enforcement system, and principally the State Attorney and the courts, to the question of political violence and the limits of freedom of speech. Up until 1995, the policy of the Attorney General Office was almost to refrain absolutely from prosecuting individuals with respect to their statements, even if such statements comprised incitement to violence or terrorism. The policy relied on provisions of law that included a requirement for the Attorney General's authorization prior to filing an indictment and a quite brief period of limitation. This warranted the full support of the Supreme Court.[2] The policy did not change even when the public mood with respect to government actions turned oppositional and hostile. This was the case, for example, in HCJ *Schlanger*,[3] which was lodged against the Attorney General's decision not to open an investigation against former chief Rabbi Goren, who determined that Jewish law requires a soldier to refuse an order from his commander to evacuate a settlement in Judea. The Attorney General provided the following grounds for his decision:

> These times are times of highly significant policy returns; these are times of critical debate among various political movements; times in which momentous decisions are being made that are likely to affect the fate of many people; times in which a deep concern arises about creating a split among different groups in society. In these sensitive times, the Attorney General believes that a policy of "forbearance" is preferred. An indictment is likely to increase the tensions currently prevalent among different sectors and add another point of contention to the many disputes that presently divide the nation. Public interest justifies the decision not to indict

[2] *See* HCJ 292/86, Ha'etzni v. the State of Israel, PD 42(4) 406 (1989).
[3] HCJ 588/94, Schlanger v. the Attorney General, PD 48(3) 40 (1994).

Rabbi Goren, with respect to the need to endeavor to moderate the public mood and preclude its exacerbation.[4]

The grounds for the Attorney General's decision warranted the full support of the Supreme Court.

This policy changed after the murder of Yitzhak Rabin. In the wake of profound criticism by the Israeli public with regard to the handling of incitement offenses by law enforcement agencies, the prosecution began to indict persons who incited to violence before the murder or who expressed support for or glorified the murder. This policy, too, was criticized, as many viewed it as a response that came too late and too slow, and even as vindictive against a wide public in an attempt to silence the criticism.

Several of the justices believed that the method for handling such tension was narrow interpretation that reduces the capacity of law enforcement bodies to utilize the incitement provisions of the Prevention of Terrorism Ordinance and relevant provisions of the Penal Law. As opposed to this, Justice Mazza, in a dissenting opinion, rejected this approach. The statements of Justice Mazza illustrate the use he chooses to make of dialogue regarding the application of policy to oversee the Executive. He writes as follows:

> I do not believe that in the current political and social reality, considering the independence that the prosecuting authorities enjoy and the internal system of balances of the Government of Israel, we need to give much weight to this concern. Submitting an indictment due to an offense of publishing incitement to racism indeed is not a trivial matter and solely in the most particular and appropriate cases should the prosecution submit such an indictment. *Nonetheless, experience teaches that the prosecution has always acted thus in practice in relation to all offenses that express a restriction on freedom of speech. There are strong grounds to assume that particularly ethical considerations and not difficulties of the onus of proof dictate such policy...Indeed, to date the prosecution has refrained, almost absolutely, from submitting indictments in respect of offenses of publishing incitement to racism; it is presumed that the prosecution...[and] as long as circumstances do not require conducting a different prosecutorial policy, should continue to submit such indictments cautiously, with restraint and moderation.* [emphasis added][5]

Justice Mazza's approach advises, therefore, that the best way to balance freedom of speech with preventing incitement to violence and terrorism is not by burdening the prosecution even further by a restrictive interpretation of the Incitement Law. Instead, he prefers to "talk" to the prosecution in his judgment and convey a more moderate

---

[4] *Id.*

[5] The Criminal Appeal, Alba v. the State of Israel, PD 50(5) 221, 264–65 (1996).

message that encourages the prosecution to continue with its policy of caution that has directed it to date, a policy that will in any event lead to a restrictive outcome.

It should be underscored that Justice Mazza does not employ the recognized legal grounds for review, to transmit this message. The assumption that has guided him is that the prosecution in any event will apply its discretion with reasonableness and without bias. In his judgment, Justice Mazza sought to transmit a message to the prosecution that he expects it to use its discretion with "caution, restraint and moderation"—requirements that exceed this.

Accordingly, in keeping with the approach of Justice Mazza, effective dialogue between the Court and law enforcement bodies is the best means to ensure that the policy of enforcing the laws of incitement indeed will be applied "with caution, restraint and moderation."

Another instance that illustrates the range of possibilities that advisory dialogue grants the Court pertains to the disagreement that erupted among Supreme Court justices on the question of whether Knesset Member Azmi Bishara could benefit from substantive immunity against accusations with regard to controversial speeches in which he expressed support for Hezbollah activities. During the course of 2000, Bishara gave a series of controversial speeches. Inter alia, he participated in the Hezbollah Victory Festival that was held in June 2000, following Israel's withdrawal from south Lebanon. At the conference Bishara stated, "Hezbollah has won, and for the first time since 1967 we have tasted victory. Hezbollah has the right to be proud of its achievement and to humiliate Israel…Israel suffered defeat after defeat, and was forced to leave south Lebanon. This is the truth…Lebanon, the weakest of the Arab states, has presented a tiny model, which if we look at in depth, can lead us to draw the necessary conclusions for success and victory."

The hearing regarding the substantive immunity of Knesset members saw unusual development in 2002, when, during the amendment of Section 7A of the Basic Law: The Knesset, discussed above, Section 1A of the Knesset Members (Immunity, Rights and Duties) Law was also amended at the same time. The amended Section 1A stipulates in which cases a Knesset member will not benefit from parliamentary immunity. According to this section:

(1A) *For the avoidance of doubt*, an act including an expression of a Knesset member that is not indiscriminate and comprises one of the following shall not be deemed on the matter of this section as an expression of opinion or an act made in the course of carrying out his duties or for the purpose of carrying out his duties as a member of the Knesset

(1) Commits an act or expresses an opinion rejecting the State of Israel as the state of the Jewish people;

(2) Rejects the democratic nature of the State;

(3) Incites to racism due to color or belonging to a race or to a national-ethnic origin;

(4) Supports the armed struggle of an enemy state or acts of terror against the State of Israel or against Jews or Arabs, due to their being Jews or Arabs, in Israel or outside of Israel. [emphasis added][6]

This amendment provides a rare disclosure of dialogue from the legislature to the Court. Section 1A of the law promotes a possible course of interpretation for the Court in the choice of words of the text and includes words intended to influence such interpretation. Use of the words *for the avoidance of doubt* is more consistent with the text of a contract that anticipates the parties' interpretation of its provisions than with a sovereign act of the legislative authority,[7] even if all that was intended was to clarify the current state of the law.[8] In many senses, the legislative authority's choice of these words illustrates to what extent the approach of dialogue in constitutional law has taken root with the legislative authority as well.

The question of the interpretation of Section 1A stood at the forefront of HCJ *Bishara* as the Court deliberated the immunity of a Member of Knesset. As the result of these and other statements he made, an indictment was submitted against Bishara alleging that he committed the offense of incitement to terrorism. The Supreme Court justices were divided as to whether these statements were made within the confines of his position as a Knesset member, therefore falling within the limits of substantive immunity. This question again touched on the tension between freedom of speech and incitement to terror. Justice Barak believed that the Court had to choose the interpretation that would restrict the ability to intervene in freedom of speech of Knesset members. In his approach, it is specifically the broad language of the provisions of law on the subject of incitement to terror that requires the Court to employ a strategy of interpretation that restricts its ability to apply these provisions.[9] The technique that will bring about such results is secondary in his opinion.

---

[6] Knesset Members (Immunity, Rights and Duties) Law (Amendment No. 29) 5762-2002.

[7] In a Knesset hearing ahead of a second and third reading, considerable parts of the discussion were set aside for the meaning of this term. Even the chairperson of the Knesset Committee expressed doubts about this wording. He explained his hesitation as follows: "The Ministry of Justice and the party presenting the bill wrote here 'for the avoidance of doubt' because the Ministry of Justice says that if the current law does not allow indicting a Knesset member, then how did we indict MK Azmi Bishara? Is he right with regard to his contentions? Therefore, they wrote in the bill 'for the avoidance of doubt.' This is not good legislation. In a contract between attorneys, one writes 'for the avoidance of doubt'; in a statute of the State of Israel, it is proscribed to write 'for the avoidance of doubt.' This is not customary nor appropriate nor advisable. Accordingly, MK Dehamshe and I have submitted reservations and, to a certain extent, we have adopted the idea of the Ministry of Justice to link this with the Basic Law: The Knesset. However, we have deleted the words 'for the avoidance of doubt.'" See Divrei Knesset 16, 3440 (5762). See www.knesset.gov.il/Tql// mark01/h0003293.html#TQL.

[8] *See further on this matter* HCJ 11225/03, Bishara v. the Attorney General, Tak-El 2006 (1) 1398, para. 10 of the judgment of President Barak.

[9] *Id.*, para. 9 of the judgment of President Barak.

As opposed to this, Justice E. Hayuth, in a minority opinion, considered that Bishara was not entitled to benefit from substantive immunity. Justice Hayuth did not disregard the dilemma of freedom of speech but thought, like Justice Mazza that it is possible to transmit messages to law enforcement bodies that will cause them to cautiously enforce these provisions of law without restricting their scope:

> It is important to remember and emphasize that a long way separates the finding that a certain statement does not enjoy the protection of substantive immunity from a criminal conviction for that statement. *This route includes three important stations at which legal and public discretion should be exercised wisely and responsibly in order to determine whether there is a basis for bringing the elected representative to trial for those statements before he is convicted in a criminal trial for them.* The first station is the attorney-general…The second station…is the deliberations of the Knesset Committee…The last station on the route that we have outlined is the criminal trial itself. [emphasis added][10]

From the statements cited above, it appears that both Justice Hayuth and Justice Mazza prefer not to choose an interpretation that would restrict the abilities of law enforcement bodies to apply the law. They choose to leave room for the flexible application of policy by law enforcement agencies while the Court closely monitors how such policy is applied. Justice Mazza prefers to transmit a message by the use of the words *cautiously, with restraint and moderation*, taken from a world of content that does not fall within recognized legal categories. Justice Hayuth assumes that the prosecution will grasp this message and will exercise its discretion accordingly. She is prepared to rely on the message being understood and internalized by law enforcement bodies, and views it as one guarantee out of three that are sufficient to prevent an overly broad application of the law.

Both justices offer a judicial approach with regard to the balance between national security and individual liberties, primarily based on dialogue, whose purpose is directing the future conduct of law enforcement agencies, and judicial oversight of the way in which such policy is applied. The focus on dialogue with the Executive instead of rigid interpretation of the authorizing law allows the Court to apply a flexible review of this delicate balance—a huge benefit in a turmoil society such as Israel.

IMPOSING CONDITIONS ON THE APPLICATION OF POLICY: THE CASE OF
HOUSE DEMOLITIONS

The Court has the ability to influence how policy is applied not only by means of messages to the Executive as to how it would be advisable for it to exercise its discretion.

---

[10] *Id.*, para. 13 of the judgment of Justice Hayuth.

The Court can indirectly make it difficult for public bodies to apply policy by imposing restrictions on this ability.

In the past, the most famous example in this context comes from the implementation of deportation policy. For years, Israel tended to deport suspects of terrorist activity. This policy was carried out, notwithstanding that it was highly doubtful that it complied with international law. The Supreme Court never determined that the deportations were contrary to the Geneva Conventions. Instead, the Court preferred to apply policy aimed at restricting the ability to employ it, by making certain that prior to employing it, several conditions would be fulfilled. Yoav Dotan writes the following about the effect of the threshold conditions the Court dictated with regard to practical application of the deportations policy:

> Enforcing the right to a hearing prior to execution of demolition orders or deportation orders may have various implications: delaying execution of the activity in terms of time and therefore damaging its effectiveness, or neutralizing the ability to carry it out due to the creation of political circumstances (such as world public opinion or U.S. intervention).[11]

The Court's requirement that, prior to executing a deportation order, certain threshold conditions must be met led in practice to restricted application of the policy, whether or not the Court intended this to occur.

The Court acted in a similar manner, as indicated above, with regard to house demolitions. It is also highly doubtful that these comply with international law, and regarding this issue as well, the Supreme Court never ruled that the policy of house demolitions was unlawful. Nonetheless, the Court often expressed its dissatisfaction with this policy. In a lecture that Justice Barak gave at the height of the Al-Aqsa Intifada, he stated the following on this matter:

> House demolitions, for example. We rule according to the law, but I am conscience-stricken every day and every hour of every day. I would be pleased if the Knesset would intervene and state that it is prohibited to demolish houses.[12]

At the same time, over the years, the Court developed constraints that limited application of this policy by subjecting it to a variety of threshold conditions. B'Tselem, a

---

[11] See RUTH GAVISON, MORDECHAI KREMNITZER AND YOAV DOTAN, JUDICIAL ACTIVISM—FOR AND AGAINST: THE ROLE OF THE HIGH COURT OF JUSTICE IN ISRAELI SOCIETY 57([Hebrew] 2000). See also Amnon Strashnov, Justice under Fire—The Legal System during the Intifada 105 (1994) as well as B'Tselem, Deporting Families in the Territories, Israel's Policy and Application (1993), available at www.btselem.org/Hebrew/Family_Separation/Implementation.asp.

[12] Moshe Gorali, Barak: "I am Conscience-Stricken" with Regard to House Demolitions, HAARETZ, June 20, 2003.

leading nongovernmental organization that monitors the human rights situation in the Occupied Territories, indicates that these constraints had a real effect on the policy of house demolitions in the 1990s. B'Tselem noted that studying High Court of Justice case law from the early 1990s demonstrates that the Court indeed limited the discretion of the military commander to a certain extent in order to restrict application of Regulation 119, the regulation that authorizes house demolitions.[13]

The discussion on this issue allows us to see how the Supreme Court justices choose different tactics to arrive at restrictive results. Justice Cheshin, as may be recalled, objected for years to the policy of house demolitions. He proposed attacking the issue via narrow interpretation of Regulation 119(1) even though the language is quite clear and ostensibly determines[14] that a military commander has the authority to confiscate (and in any event to demolish) a house in which it is suspected that damaging activity has taken place. Nevertheless, Justice Cheshin also thought that the authority to apply the regulation must be intentionally restricted by means of strict construction and the Court must determine that the policy may be applied solely in the event that the house is the home of the individual who is guilty of the terrorist act. In other words, Justice Cheshin does not wish to leave discretion with regard to the use of the authority defined in law with the military authorities and the agencies of their supervision, and prefers to direct them by strict construction even if it is not consistent with the plain language of the law.

In 1994, and in view of the dissenting opinion of Justice Cheshin, the Supreme Court held an extended hearing with a panel of five justices on the policy of house demolitions. True to his approach, Justice Cheshin chose a strict construction that limits the application of the section of law. Justice Mazza, who wrote the majority opinion, confronted the approach of Justice Cheshin head-on. Their disagreement to a large degree demonstrates that imposing rules, binding and justifiable in and of themselves, on a restrictive implementation of the house demolitions policy was a strategic move on the part of the Court. Justice Mazza writes:

> Indeed, our case law also imposed many constraints on the conditions under which a military commander may exercise his authority, which the regulation defined in

---

[13] B'Tselem further indicates that as the result of another petition heard in 1992, the authorities limited the use of house demolitions to the home of the nuclear family of the person because of whom the demolition was carried out. *See* B'Tselem's Internet site: www.btselem.org/Hebrew/Punitive_Demolitions/Legal_Basis.asp. *See also* DAVID KRETZMER, THE OCCUPATION OF JUSTICE: THE SUPREME COURT OF ISRAEL AND THE OCCUPIED TERRITORIES 160–61 (2002).

[14] Regulation 119(1) of the Defense (Emergency) Regulations 1945 determines: "A Military Commander may by order direct the forfeiture to the Government of Israel of any house, structure, or land from which he has reason to suspect that any firearm has been illegally discharged, or any bomb, grenade or explosive or incendiary article illegally thrown, or of any house, structure or land situated in any area, town, village, quarter or street the inhabitants or some of the inhabitants of which he is satisfied have committed, or attempted to commit, or abetted the commission of, or been accessories after the fact to the commission of, any offence against these Regulations."

broad sweeping language; … *In practice (in fact and not in theory), the power and authority of the military commanders to act within the confines of the regulation were diminished.* [emphasis added]¹⁵

This citation demonstrates that the judicial policy to impose a variety of constraints on implementation of house demolition policy was influenced by the conscious wish to restrict the State's ability to apply this authority. Justice Cheshin chose to restrict the State's authority by strict construction of the regulation. The majority opinion justices chose the path of "restrictive application"—in other words, strictly ensuring that procedural requirements are fulfilled in full prior to application of the policy, which would lead to the practical outcome of restricting the use of Regulation 119 without intervening in the interpretation of the regulation. Justice Mazza goes on to state:

> We have not hesitated to express our position on any suitable case in the course of the hearing; and more than once our comments have prompted the security agencies to agree (without waiting for a judicial decision) to mitigate the damage to the residences of others found within the area of the structure slated for demolition.¹⁶

Justice Mazza's statements illustrate how the Court used dialogue with the Executive to achieve in practice a strict application of the house demolitions policy. The majority position, as expressed in Justice Mazza's judgment, is that the Court must lead the State by way of dialogue to a restrictive application of the policy without "artificial" interpretation of the provisions of law. More accurately, the Court primarily transmits messages that it insists that all preliminary requisite conditions will be met prior to military authorities making use of such policy. Justice Mazza underscores that the restriction was *not* achieved *in theory, but was achieved in practice.* This, as may be recalled, was the approach of Justice Mazza also with regard to the means of achieving the proper balance on the question of incitement to terrorist activity.

We can learn about the effect of "dialogue regarding the application of policy" that occurs by determining threshold conditions for house demolitions specifically from the period in which the Court did not apply such restrictions. In 2002, at the height of the Al-Aqsa Iintifada, Israel officially decided to renew the house demolitions policy by means of Regulation 119. The decision was made at a State Security Cabinet meeting in July 2002,¹⁷

---

¹⁵ HCJ 6026/94, Naazal v. IDF Military Commander in the Region of Judea and Samaria, PD 48(5) 338, 346 (1994).

¹⁶ *Id.*

¹⁷ According to a report of B'Tselem, the house demolition policy was renewed in practice in October 2001. *See* B'Tselem, Guilty of No Wrongdoing: House Demolitions as Punishment during the Al-Aqsa Intifada 6 (Nov. 2004). Also according to B'Tselem, the first demolition following the actual renewal of the policy was carried out on October 23, 2001, in Qalqiliya. That day IDF Forces demolished the family home of Said Hasan Al-Huteri, who executed the suicide terrorist attack at the Dolphinarium

following a terrorist attack at the Hebrew University of Jerusalem in which five Israeli civilians and four foreign residents were killed.[18] Immediately after the Cabinet decision was made, the Israel Defense Force (IDF) began to carry out the policy of house demolitions and, in most cases, this was done with no advance warning. Four days after the Cabinet decision, dozens of families of suicide bombers lodged a petition on this matter. The petition was directed solely against military policy not to provide advance warning to the petitioners. When the petition was lodged, the Court ordered the State to submit its reply immediately. In its reply, the State contended, "The provision of warning of anticipated operational activity in hostile territory is liable actually to jeopardize the lives of our forces and to thwart the success of the activity, since advance warning would enable the enemy to booby-trap these houses or to lay ambushes for the approaching said forces."[19] It must be noted that this exception was indeed recognized in case law[20] as justification for refraining from giving advance warning. However, the Court made certain that the exception would be applied in a highly restricted manner.[21] The Court determined that if immediate action is necessary, the military must be satisfied with a reversible action, such as evacuation and sealing, and must wait on the demolition until after judicial review of the matter.

In this petition, the question under discussion was how broad the exception to the updated test was to be. In other words, the question was whether the Court would insist on restricted use of this exception and, in any event, continue to make the application of the policy of house demolitions difficult in practice, or whether the Court would expand

---

in Tel Aviv, which killed 18 Israeli civilians, including 12 minors, two foreign residents, one minor, and an IDF soldier. The next day in Tulkarm, the family residence of Raid Al-Karmi, suspected of the murder of two Israeli citizens, was demolished. On that same day, as part of IDF Forces' activity in the village of Beit Rima, three houses were destroyed in which Palestinians, suspected by Israel of involvement in terrorist activity against Israelis, lived.

[18]   *See* section 9 of the State's Reply to HCJ 7473/02, Bahar v. IDF Commander in the West Bank, PD 56 (8) 488 (2002). *See also* Maj.-Gen. Ben, *Actions against the Families of Suicide Bombers Have Been Authorized: Deportation and Forfeiture of Property*, HAARETZ, Aug. 1, 2002, *available at* www.haaretz. co.il/hasite/pages/ShArt.jhtml?itemNo=193192&contrassID=0

[19]   HCJ 6696/02, Amar v. Commander of IDF Forces in the West Bank, PD 56 (8) 110, 113–114 (2002) [hereinafter HCJ *Amar*].

[20]   In HCJ 358/88, The Association for Civil Rights in Israel v. the Central District Commander (Israel), PD 43 (2) 529, 541–42 (1989), it was decided: "Indeed, there are operational military circumstances in which judicial review is not compatible with the conditions of the time and place, or the nature of the circumstances; for example, when a military unit carries out an operational activity in which it has to remove an obstacle or overcome opposition or respond on site to an attack on military forces or civilians that occurs at the same time, or other such circumstances in which the authorized military authority sees an operational need for immediate action. According to the very nature of the matter, in such circumstances, there is no room for delaying military action, the performance of which is necessitated on the spot."

[21]   "My opinion is that ways must be found to have the right to contest to be exercised prior to making a decision…If action is required at once, we may be satisfied with an action that is reversible, such as evacuation and sealing, and delay the matter of demolition until subsequent to judicial review. In other words, I see reason to distinguish between sealing and demolition. The first may be implemented at once if circumstances require this. Prior to taking action of the second type (demolition), time shall be given to evacuate in an objection or petition, as the case may be." *Id.*

the exception and thereby enable the military to apply the policy expansively. The Court determined in its judgment that in cases "where there is a serious concern that granting a right to contest the order may jeopardize the lives of soldiers and thwart the action itself, the right to contest is denied due to the vital needs of combat."[22] In fact, with these words the Court restricted one of the means that in practice allows it to limit the use of the house demolition policy.

The decision was given in August 2002 and, on that day, several dozen residents of the territories, who were concerned that their homes were about to be demolished, lodged another petition.[23] In its ruling, the Court proposed that the residents, who feared that they would not be given a warning of demolition, approach the army and provide it with a diagram of the house so that the army could plan, prior to the operation, which sections to demolish.[24] This process of review that until that time occurred in the Court was transferred, as a result of this decision, to the military authorities. Attorney Shai Nitzan, who represented the State in a major portion of the hearings on the subject, discussed the effect of this message on the application of the policy of house demolitions:

> In the fascinating hearing on the question [whether] it is possible to demolish without a hearing, we explained our position: In a state of war, as distinct from an *intifada*, it is not always possible to grant a right to a hearing. We declared that if there is no concern that the hearing procedure will jeopardize soldiers or thwart the action, we will allow the family a right to a hearing. The Court accepted our position, *and this caused a dramatic change*: Since August 2002 and to date, a right to a hearing has not been granted prior to the demolition of 250 homes. In these cases, the IDF military commanders determined that granting a prior hearing is liable to impede the soldiers and jeopardize the success of the mission… The right to a hearing is a significant right, but it is not central at a time when the laws of war apply. [emphasis added][25]

These Supreme Court decisions from August 2002 included two messages that led to the permissive result. One message was to remove procedural constraints, which had to be fulfilled prior to demolitions, and to extend the possibilities of application of the limited exception. The second message conveyed was to transfer the center of gravity of the hearing taking place prior to demolition from the Court to the military authorities, who were to decide in which cases the right to a hearing would be granted. This transpired

---

[22] HCJ *Amar*, *supra* note 19, at 115.

[23] HCJ 6868/02, Tzalah v. the Commander of IDF Forces, Tak-El 2002 (3), 258 (2002).

[24] *Id.* at 259.

[25] *See* Shai Nitzan, *The Fight aAgainst Terrorism as War—Legal Aspects, in* THE BATTLE OF THE 21ST CENTURY: DEMOCRACY FIGHTS TERRORISM (FORUM IYUN—THE ISRAEL DEMOCRACY INSTITUTE) 138 (Haim Pass ed., 2007).

even though the hearing in Court and the dialogue that took place during its course, as Justice Mazza indicated, "in practice" led to a more limited application of the policy.

The message conveyed to the IDF was not just technical and apparently was not understood by them as such. The result, in practice, of the cessation of this dialogue was the broad application of Regulation 119 during the years 2002 to 2004 and the intensive demolition of houses. In most cases, no sealing or partial demolition was implemented and the families were not given advance warning.[26] According to information from B'Tselem, since the outbreak of the Al-Aqsa Intifada, Israel, by virtue of Regulation 119, demolished 628 houses in which 3,983 people lived. Only in 17 cases (3 percent) did the IDF inform the families of the intent to demolish their home. The de facto cancellation of the dialogue between the Court and the military authorities during the course of the hearing of a petition led to the State's greater ability in practice to demolish houses. It is likely that this practical outcome was what stood behind the change that occurred in the Court's approach in 2004 with regard to house demolitions. As already indicated, in a hearing that took place in 2004, Justice Barak stated that he was considering adopting the minority opinion of Justice Cheshin on this issue.

---

[26] *See* B'Tselem, Through No Fault of Their Own: Punitive House Demolitions during the Al-Aqsa Intifada (Nov. 2004). *See also* Zeev Segal, *Judicial Restraint Encourages Initiating a Path to Bypass the Law*, Haaretz, Aug. 7, 2002.

8

Dialogue on Policy Application—II

MESSAGES THAT ADVISE HOW A JUDGMENT IS TO BE APPLIED: THE CASE
OF THE SEPARATION FENCE

Another tactic developed by the Supreme Court in order to expand its judicial review
of national security issues is to convey messages to the State incidental to the giving of
a judgment that pertain to the manner in which the Court expects the State to apply
its judgment. The most celebrated example of this type of message in the United States
is the judgment in *Brown v. Board of Education*.[1] In this case, the US Supreme Court
ordered the gradual termination of the separation of the races in the US education system, notwithstanding the determination that this separation is unconstitutional. At
the end of the judgment, the Court added the famous words in the operative order: *"all
deliberate speed."*[2] The practical significance of this addition was that the policy of equality in education could be applied with all due speed without the Court having to fix a
date for this. Bradley Canon wrote on this matter as follows:

> *Certainly, for example, the Court was a restrained cheerleader at best in Brown v.
> Board of Education* (347 U.S. 483, 1954) when it put off a final decree for a year and
> then announced an ambiguous policy of "all deliberate speed."[3] [emphasis added]

---

[1] Brown v. Board of Education, 347 U.S. 483 (1954).

[2] These words were written as a proposed compromise. Justice Black believed that the operative order was to
be formulated using the word *immediately. See with regard to this* L. MILLER, THE PETITIONERS: THE
STORY OF THE SUPREME COURT OF THE UNITED STATES AND THE NEGRO 351, 356 (1966). *See also*
Charles L. Black, *The Unfinished Business of the Warren Court*, 46 WASH. L. REV. 3, 22 (1970).

[3] *See* Bradley Canon, *The Supreme Court as a Cheerleader in Politico-Moral Disputes*, 54 J. POL. 637, 642
(1992). For an empirical study on this subject, *see* Jon Gould, *The Precedent That Wasn't: Collegiate Hate
Speech Codes and the Two Faces of Legal Compliance Theory*, 35 L. & SOC. REV. 345 (2001).

Canon, one of the important scholars of judicial influence, proposed a theoretical model that he called "Judicial Cheerleading." According to this model, the US Supreme Court expresses its position regarding highly controversial issues in American society by way of "cheerleading." Cheerleading can take the form of an incidental remark or advisory messages that have no immediate legal consequences. "Cheerleading" may be performed also by signals or recommendations that have no immediate legal consequences. The use of "cheerleading" enables the US Supreme Court to transmit messages to government bodies, including Congress, or the public at large, yet doing so while refraining from rendering decisions on issues that are deeply disputed in society. According to Canon:

> Much judicial cheerleading is deliberate. Deliberate cheers are found in dicta. That portion of an opinion that is not necessary to its rationale. In dicta, the court may suggest action by congress…question the viability of a doctrine or prior holding…or invite further litigation.[4]

Canon's model is significant to our study because it highlights a broader expanse of means for transmitting messages available to the US Supreme Court other than signals or indices. Cheerleading could include: inviting Congress to intervene in policy, summoning petitioners to return with an issue again for a hearing in court, and more. These messages constitute part of the broad repertoire of tactics discussed in this book. Canon guides us through the processes by which the US Supreme Court influences legal and policy matters apart from formal decisions. Incidentally, Canon calls attention to the difficulty of proving the impact of dialogue on the conduct of the Executive or Congress. At times, an act of the Court along one path leads Congress or the Executive to focus efforts in alternative contexts where no opposition is anticipated. In other cases, it is not at all clear that court decisions, even binding ones, indeed affect policy.[5]

The use of cheerleading enables the US Supreme Court to mitigate tensions in highly controversial issues in society. The Court, which understood that by this decision it set itself up for serious confrontation, preferred to convey a softened message regarding the judgment's application without the matter affecting its ruling pertaining to the lawfulness of the policy or the interpretation of the US Constitution. In place of direct confrontation, the Court preferred that the decision be applied gradually, and conveyed messages in this spirit to the Executive.[6]

---

[4] Canon, *supra* note 13, at 641.

[5] GERALD N. ROSENBERG, THE HOLLOW HOPE: CAN COURTS BRING ABOUT SOCIAL CHANGE? (1991).

[6] William N. Eskridge & Philip P. Frickey, *The Supreme Court, 1993 Term Forward: Law as Equilibrium*, 108 HARV. L. REV. 27, 87 (1994).

Use of this practice in national security matters in Israel may be seen in the Israeli Supreme Court decisions concerning the separation fence. The separation fence (or separation wall) is a barrier constructed by Israel in the Occupied Territories in 2002, intended to prevent passage without permission of Palestinian residents to Israeli population centers, with the aim of averting infiltration of Palestinian terrorists, including suicide bombers. The separation fence, which in part included territories taken over to the west (of Jerusalem), is the subject of numerous judgments and even an opinion of the International Court of Justice, which determined that it was illegal due to the fact that parts of it invade the Occupied Territories.

The Israeli Supreme Court did not accept the ruling of the International Court of Justice. However, in two central judgments given on the subject—HCJ *Beit Sourik*[7] and HCJ *Alfei Menashe*,[8] handed down in the height of the intifada—parts of the route of the fence were excluded.[9] However, in neither of the judgments did the Court fix a specific date to change the route of the fence. In HCJ *Beit Sourik*, the Court returned the discussion to the Committee without determining a specific date for the elimination of the route,[10] and in HCJ *Alfei Menashe*, the Court refrained from giving a time-limited order and was satisfied with giving the following decision:

> Accordingly, we make the order *nisi* absolute in the following manner. Respondents 1–4 must reconsider *within a reasonable time* the different alternatives for the route of the separation fence in Alfei Menashe. They must examine secure alternatives, which intrude less on the lives of the local inhabitants. [emphasis added][11]

It seems that the Court formulated these decisions because of its wish that the judgment be applied with care, while preventing infiltration of terrorists during a period that coincided with the height of the suicide bomber attacks. In this regard, it is another illustration of how dialogue regarding the application of a judgment could help the Court decide on national security matters in real time without being worried that it leaves the State without the means to protect itself.

Nonetheless, it is impossible to disregard the result of these advisory messages, which consisted of the quite limited application of the judgments by public bodies, if not more than this as in practice the State was rather slow in planning and erecting the alternative

---

[7] HCJ 2056/04 Beit Sourik Village Council v. the Government of Israel, PD 58(5) 807 (2004) [hereinafter *Beit Sourik*].

[8] HCJ 7957/04, *Maraba v. the Prime Minister of Israel*, Tak-El 2004 (3) 2982 (2004) [hereinafter *Alfei Menashe*].

[9] To get the full picture, see the map of the various routes of the security fence on the website of the Ministry of Defense: http://www.secuityfence.mod.gov.il/Pages/Heb/mivne.htm

[10] *Beit Sourik, supra* note 5, from para. 85 and on of the judgment.

[11] *Alfei Menashe, supra* note 6, para. 116 of the judgment.

route.[12] It should be noted that the Court changed this practice in later judgments dealing with the separation fence and ordered removal of the route within a specific time that was defined for performance of the Court order.[13]

Another tool the Court uses to convey messages pertaining to application of its judgment returns the discussion to HCJ *On Torture.* As is known, the Court determined in this judgment that the Shin Bet has no authority to use violence in its interrogations, and that the defense of "necessity" in the Penal Law cannot serve as a source of authority for this. In its conclusion the Court related to the significance of its decision as follows:

> Just as the existence of the "necessity" defence does not bestow authority, so too the lack of authority does not negate the applicability of the necessity defense or that of other defences from criminal liability. *The Attorney General can instruct himself regarding the circumstances in which investigators shall not stand trial, if they claim to have acted from a feeling of "necessity"*...we declare that the "necessity" defence, found in the Penal Law, cannot serve as a basis of authority for the use of these interrogation practices, or for the existence of directives pertaining to GSS investigators, allowing them to employ interrogation practices of this kind. Our decision does not negate the possibility that the "necessity" defence be available to GSS investigators, be within the discretion of the Attorney General, if he decides to prosecute, or if criminal charges are brought against them, as per the Court's discretion. [emphasis added][14]

Precise reading of the operative order instructs that along with determining that use violence is unlawful and that these acts were committed without authority, the Court transmitted a calibrated advisory message to the Attorney General. The Court stated that the Attorney General is authorized to decide not to indict an investigator who used

---

[12] Following the failure to apply the judgment of the Court in the *Alfei Menashe* case, the Association for Civil Rights in Israel petitioned the High Court of Justice a second time (HCJ 10714/06, *Maraba v. the Government of Israel,* Tak-El 2007 (3) 3434). However, the petition was rejected. *See on this matter* the website of the Association for Civil Rights in Israel: www.acri.org.il/hebew-acri/engine/story.asp?id=1444

[13] *See* HCJ 2732/05, Hassin v. the Government of Israel, Tak-El 2006 (2) 3672 (2006) and HCJ 1748/06, The Mayor of Dahariya v. the IDF Commander in the West Bank, Tak-El 2007(3) 1109 (2007).

[14] HCJ 5100/94, The Pubic Committee against Torture in Israel v. the Government of Israel, PD 53 (4) 817, 846 (1999).

violence vis-à-vis an interogatee if he believes that in the circumstances of the matter the investigator's action is protected by the defense of necessity.

Another judgment that was given subsequent to HCJ *On Torture*, and which merited almost no publicity even though it is closely related to it, illustrates the meaning of the application of this remark. HCJ *Harizat*[15] concerned the question of indicting Shin Bet investigators who were involved in the "shaking" (a violent technique used by the Shin Bet), of Abdul Harizat while under investigation. During the course of the violent interrogation, Harizat lost consciousness and ultimately died of his injuries. One can assume that the death of Harizat and the use of "shaking" in his investigation influenced the Supreme Court justices in their principled decision on the issue of torture. During the fundamental hearing in HCJ *On Torture*, Harizat's brother submitted a petition in which the Court was asked to order the Attorney General to indict the investigators with the charge of causing death after the Attorney General ordered that the file of criminal charges against them be closed.[16] The hearing on this petition extended over no less than seven years, among other reasons because in 1998 the Court ordered that a decision on this petition would be given solely after the fundamental judgment in the *On Torture* case.[17] After the fundamental judgment was given, the Court turned its attention to hear the *Harizat* case and requested that the State submit an updated position. Following this, the actual hearing of the petition was held. Ultimately, the Court decided not to intervene in the position of the Attorney General. The Court referred to HCJ *On Torture* and deemed a marginal remark in the operative order as an instruction to the Court regarding the question of how to review Attorney General's exercise of discretion. Based on the same remark that was added to the end of the operative order and while fully citing it in its judgment, the Court accepted the Attorney General's position not to criminally charge the investigators of *Harizat*.[18]

---

[15] HCJ 2150/96, Harizat v. the Attorney General (unpublished, Feb. 21, 2002) [hereinafter HCJ *Harizat*].

[16] See the State's Reply in *id.*, section 2. The Reply may be viewed at this Internet site: www.hamoked.org. il/items/8051.pdf. Haaretz reported at the time that no one of the investigators of Harizat was criminally charged, but the person in charge of his interrogation, M, was brought in 1996 for a disciplinary hearing after then State Attorney Dorit Beinisch did not find sufficient evidence to indict him criminally for causing death by negligence. The Shin Bet tribunal determined that "the Service failed in the investigation" but determined that M's part in the alleged offense was minimal and decreed a penalty of a warning only. *See* Moshe Reisenfeld, *HCJ: Shin-Beth Investigators Are Not to Be Charged with the Death of an Interogatee Who Was Shaken*, HAARETZ, Mar. 26, 2002.

[17] In a decision of September 10, 1998, in a hearing on HCJ *Harizat*, the Court determined: "It seems to us that the petition must be left pending, while we shall discuss it—if there is still need for this—in light of the judgment to be given in petitions pending with respect to the necessity defense (including HCJ 4054/95 *The Association for Civil Rights in Israel v. the Prime Minister of Israel*, PD 98 (3) 796, HCJ 5100/94 *The Public Committee Against Torture in Israel v. the Government of Israel*, PD 53 (4) 817 and the files that have been joined with these)."

[18] In HCJ *Harizat, supra* note 13, the Court determined that "one of the central pillars on which the decision of the Attorney General is based—which joins the complex of other considerations that led to the formulation of its decision—is the 'necessity' defense, which in the circumstances of the case would have

In actual fact, under cover of this calibrated message, the Attorney General decided not to indict the Shin Bet investigators who used violence in dozens of cases dealt with in the years following the judgment. The Attorney General believed that the investigators were entitled under the circumstances of the matter to benefit from the necessity defense. B'Tselem noted that the numbers of investigations in which violence was used has indeed been reduced dramatically following the judgment. However, despite hundreds of complaints that were submitted in the years following the judgment on the use of violence during investigations, no investigator was criminally charged.[19]

The Court's messages on the torture issue throughout the years illustrate how the dialogue of practicability was not necessarily intended to restrict the application of the provisions of the law, as was done with regard to deportations or house demolitions. The dialogue of practicability may also serve an opposing objective—to extend or broaden the discretion granted to law enforcement authorities by conveying various messages to the prosecution regarding the way it exercises its discretion on a variety of issues.

Ten years after the judgment, in 2011 several human rights organizations submitted a petition to the Supreme Court. They argued that the means for review set up following HCJ *On Torture* that left the Shin Bet involved in the investigations of violence and the lacunae that this judgment left do not comply with the law or with international law, as the detainee's right to a remedy has been violated and as there is a duty to hold an investigation following complaints of torture. The Court examined the petition and, even though it did not find the arrangement authorizing the Attorney General to use his discretion to be unlawful, it encouraged the State to amend the current arrangement and transfer the means of internal review pertaining to complaints of detainees from the Shin Bet to the Ministry of Justice.

---

been available to the investigators, in the opinion of the Court, had they been criminally charged. The petitioners contended that the Attorney General's use of the necessity defense departs from the realm of reasonableness, due to its *ex ante* legal authorization of a criminal act. According to this contention, such *ex ante* legal authorization cannot ensue from a defense for criminal liability. On this matter, the attorney for the petitioners demonstrated a facet that is not in accordance with the law with regard to statements of this court on *the Public Committee* matter. It was stated there, 'The authority to establish directives respecting the use of physical means during the course of a Shin-Beth interrogation cannot be implied from the "necessity defense."' (HCJ 5100/94 The Public Committee Against Torture in Israel v. the Government of Israel, PD 53 (4) 817, paragraph 36 of the judgment). This is not the approach to be applied in an individual case, where, as part of the considerations of the Attorney General pertaining to the question of indictment, he may consider the necessity defense in order to assess the probability whether an accused is likely to be convicted, if charged. This does not involve *ex ante* legal authorization. This concerns a defense *post factum* and it was thus stated there: 'Just as the existence of the "necessity defense" does not bestow authority, the lack of authority does not negate the applicability of the necessity defense or of other defenses from criminal liability. The Attorney-General can establish guidelines regarding circumstances in which investigators shall not stand trial, if they claim to have acted from "necessity."' (HCJ 5100/94 The Public Committee Against Torture in Israel v. the Government of Israel, PD 53 (4) 817, 845)."

19. According to B'Tselem, "From the beginning of 2001 to the end of March 2011, more than seven hundred complaints alleging ISA (Shin-Beth-D.S) abuse of interrogees have been filed with the State Attorney's Office. The State Attorney's Office did not order a criminal investigation into any of the complaints." *See* http://www.btselem.org/torture/impunity.

The Court thereby signals the petitioners and the State that if the mechanism for review is not amended and its independence reinforced, the Court will conclude that the current mechanism for checking complaints is unlawful. The President also suggested: "Along with the aforesaid, I would add that the general contention of the petitioners—which has not been refuted—has not disappeared from my sight. As a rule, the mechanism of preliminary examination by the person in charge of detainees' complaints does not lead in practice to opening a criminal investigation, despite the large number of complaints that have been submitted within the confines thereof. This fact justifies examination of the decision-making process in substance."[20]

The President of the Court, Justice Grunis, also added a strong advisory message in his concurring opinion, stating: "I would underscore that this institutional change is of critical significance from my point of view. Insofar as it becomes clear that the change has not been put into effect, this shall be a reason to renew the hearing."[21]

The judgments on the use of violence following illustrate the extent to which the Court's practicable comments are significant for understanding advisory dialogue and its effects on human rights.[22] In this case, a brief comment at the end of the operative order included a message to the Attorney General that substantively changed the practicable meaning of this judgment, enabling the continuation of the policy, even though in much more limited numbers and even though it is entirely unclear that this was the real intention of the Court when handing down its judgment. About 10 years after the judgment, the Court was required to hear again the issue and conveyed messages pertaining to the extent of the lacunae that it created in the *On Torture* judgment and ordered it to be diminished, signaling that something does not make sense in the way the judgment is applied. The Court expressed a certain doubt regarding the way complaints over the use of violence are handled. The Court signaled that 10 years after the giving of the judgment, not even one case was found that justified opening a criminal investigation, and this informs as to the credibility of the decision-making process itself.

Another instance in which a Supreme Court justice suggested taking a similar tactic is the judgment in HCJ *The Neighbor Procedure*. As may be recalled, in this case Justice Barak and Justice Beinisch prohibited use of the procedure even in its restricted format as the military forces had proposed because in practice it amounts to the use of human shields. Justice Cheshin, who had serious doubts on this question, joined the majority opinion but added the following statements:

If, notwithstanding all these, I said I would join the opinion of the President, I decided so once I considered the text that was adopted in the Public Committee against Torture affair. *The wording of the text uses "in advance" and "in retrospect"*

[20] *Id.*, para. 3.

[21] HCJ 1265/11, The Public Committee Against Torture et al. v. The Attorney General (to be officially published), para. 1 of the judgment of President Gronis.

[22] *See on this issue* David Scharia, *On Torture Chambers and Acoustic Walls*, 10 POLITICA 61 (2003).

and, in our case, also by way of "all the more so." It is possible that life will instruct us otherwise and the wheel will turn back again . . . Routine, by nature, erodes, even with the necessary sensitivity and caution, the performance of the procedure and it is of great concern that that which is unusual and rare will become ordinary and routine, merely a bureaucratic deed. We encountered this same difficulty in the Public Committee against Torture in Israel case and in the "ticking bomb" incident. *It is only that the format of "in advance" and "in retrospect," even though its strength is limited, may be of use to us, even if only of partial use.* [emphasis added][23]

With these words, Justice Cheshin conveyed a message to law enforcement authorities by borrowing the wording that was used in HCJ *On Torture* for HCJ *The Neighbor Procedure*. In other words, just as in HCJ *On Torture* the Court conveyed a message to the Attorney General that the prohibition of using violence in Shin Bet interrogations does not lead immediately to the general conclusion that every investigator who used violence must be criminally charged, in the same way Justice Cheshin conveyed a similar message in *The Neighbor Procedure* case. He explains that according to his approach, the Attorney General may order that a commander who used the Neighbor Procedure not be charged if he believed that under the circumstances of the matter the procedure was undertaken under conditions in which the commander may avail himself of the necessity defense. Much like in the Torture case the Court warns against using its applicability messages as a means to turn the isolated incident into the rule.

EXPRESSING CENSURE OR SUPPORT REGARDING HOW THE EXECUTIVE
APPLIES THE LAW: THE CASE OF FAILURE TO REPORT A PLANNED
TERRORIST ATTACK

As part of the use the Court makes of precisely calibrated messages to other branches, the Court occasionally expresses censure or support regarding how these bodies apply the law in order to influence their future conduct. The important feature with regard to our discussion is that in the cases presented in this section, a change in tone in order to direct the State's conduct occurs without the ruling on the matter necessarily being altered. The binding ruling remains the same, but policy in practice is influenced by the advisory message conveyed by the Court's expression of censure or support regarding the manner of application.

---

[23] HCJ 3799/02, Adallah v. GOC (General Officer Commanding) Central Command PD 60 (3) 67 (2005), para. 7 of the judgment of Justice Cheshin.

An example of this may be found in the Attorney General's policy of indictment. As a rule, the decision to charge suspects of terrorist offenses does not evoke particular dilemmas. The gravity of the acts attributed to the suspect generally does not raise any doubt of whether there is a public interest in charging the suspect. A more difficult quandary arises with regard to preventive offenses, such as material support, recruitment for terrorism, passive assistance, or incitement to terrorism. In the discussion above, we saw that the dilemma related to indicting inciters of terrorism led the Court to make use of advisory dialogue. A similar dilemma arises with regard to the possibility of charging a person who was aware of certain activities of a terrorist organization but refrained from disclosing this to the authorities—in other words, a person who by omission expressed passive support for an act of terrorism.

The dilemma involved in charging a person for knowingly not disclosing a planned terrorist attack[24] arises because in such case a person may be convicted of failing to act. Criminal liability and the accompanying penalty are imposed because the individual did not "inform on" the intentions of others. The Supreme Court related to this offense most ambivalently and used the tone and language of its judgments to convey precisely calibrated messages to the Attorney General about whether it is right to charge a person criminally with respect to this offense. A significant point for our discussion is that in this case the changes in the Court's mindset and its directing the policy of enforcement by way of advisory messages were accomplished without amending the law on this issue or even by way of narrowing or broadening the interpretation of the relevant statutes by the Court. Binding law remains the same but the policy of pressing charges for the offense has been dictated by the advisory message that was conveyed by the Court in the margins of its decisions.

In order to understand the development of dialogue on this issue, we must review the background of judgments from the 1970s. In 1973, a case was brought before the Court in which a member of a terrorist organization approached the accused and sought to recruit him to the organization. However, the accused refused. The State Attorney's Office decided to indict him on a charge of misprision of felony (the failure to report knowledge of a felony), as the accused was aware that the person contacting him was a member of a terrorist organization but refrained from reporting this to the authorities. The majority opinion opted to convict the appellant.

The important point for our interests is specifically the minority opinion of Justice Haim Cohen, who believed that the Court must acquit the accused. Justice Cohen did not conceal his dissatisfaction with the prosecution's decision to charge the accused, and chose two ways to convey this message. On the substantive level, he believed that the offense of the failure to prevent a terrorist act must be given a strict and narrow interpretation "in order not to create the prospect of a duty to inform that is redolent of

---

[24] Section 95 of the Penal Law 5737-1977.

totalitarian oppression."[25] In addition, he severely castigated the State with regard to its decision to press charges:

> Until I can clarify the legal question whether the appellant did indeed commit the offense of which he has been convicted, *I cannot deny my amazement* that the authorities deemed it well, fair and just to charge this appellant criminally. [emphasis added][26]

Six months later in the *Disoki* case,[27] which concerned a similar issue, when it appeared that the State had moderated its approach to the offense, Justice Haim Cohen noted this, as he stated: "To the credit of the Deputy Attorney General it must be said that she did not insist on upholding this conviction."[28]

Justice Haim Cohen's judgments may be understood as framing the use of two methods of directing the Executive's conduct with one purpose—the narrow enforcement of the offense of the failure to prevent an act of terrorism. The first is interpretation, that is, choosing an interpretation that will lead to a narrow outcome even if the language of the law, as the justices of the majority indicated, is ostensibly clear and leads almost necessarily to the outcome of a conviction. The second method Justice Cohen uses is to convey a message "of censure" of the State's decision to press charges against this accused. In this manner, Justice Cohen created a negative incentive to filing indictments on this offense.

Indeed, following this judgment, and although the majority opinion gave validity to the prosecution's policy of pressing charges, the prosecution submitted very few charge sheets in cases of a person who was aware of terrorist activity but failed to report this to the authorities. The famous case in which it was decided to indict a person occurred in 1986. Aharon Gilo, an officer of the Civil Administration in the Ramallah district, was charged with being aware of the intentions of members of the Jewish underground to place explosive charges in the car of the mayor of El Bireh, but failing to report this.

The judgment of Justice Haim Cohen illustrates how the Court's criticism of certain policy can influence the decision of the Attorney General, even when the ruling determined on the subject allows the indictment of suspects who fail to prevent a felony. The effect of a reprimand, understood by the relevant players with regard to their conduct, is at times more effective than the majority opinion, which permitted making extensive use of this offense, principally due to the players' unwillingness to suffer such criticism again. For years, the prosecution's policy was influenced by Justice Cohen's minority

---

[25] Criminal Appeal 496/73, Anonymous v. the State of Israel, PD 28 (1) 714, 719–20 (1974).

[26] *Id.* at 716–18.

[27] Criminal Appeal 307/73, Disoki v. the State of Israel, PD 28 (2) 802 (1974). The judgment in the *Anonymous* case was given on February 27, 1974. The hearing of the *Disoki* matter was held on June 12, 1974, and the judgment given on August 15, 1974.

[28] *Id.* at 804–05.

opinion, which included a reprimand, more than it was affected by the ruling determined in the majority opinion, which legistimized the decision to press charges.

Years later, the Supreme Court was again required to hear this issue in the case of Margalit Har-Shefi. Har-Shefi was accused of being aware of Yigal Amir's intent to assassinate Prime Minister Yitzhak Rabin, but of not contacting the authorities about it. Justice Cheshin and Justice Tirkel disagreed on this matter. Justice Tirkel, following the approach of Justice Haim Cohen, thought that it was fitting that the lawful duty imposed by the provisions of the section of misprision of felony in the Penal Law "*shall be eliminated from our code of law and shall remain solely as a moral duty.*"[29] As opposed to him, Justice Cheshin, who wrote the majority opinion, disagreed with Justice Cohen's narrow interpretation and allocated part of his judgment to the argument that the prosecution should not enforce this offense. The difference between Justice Cheshin's approach and the approach of the justices of the majority opinion in case law of the 1970s is that Justice Cheshin presented a moral position that recognizes the legitimacy of the prosecution's use of this offense in suitable cases. The message that Justice Cheshin conveyed in the judgment was clear—in suitable cases the prosecution may not only make use of this section to indict persons who saw others about to commit acts of terror, but is even obligated to do so. In other words, the advisory message that Justice Cheshin conveyed to the prosecution was that it will not encounter the Court's reprimand, such as Justice Cohen conveyed, if in suitable cases it opts to make use of this section of the Penal Law.

The Court's attitude to the failure to prevent a felony illustrates how the dialogue between the Court and the prosecution authorities frequently takes place by an expression of support for or by censure of the manner in which the provision of a law is applied, and not necessarily by amending the case law in effect. In the past, Justice Haim Cohen's position significantly affected the conduct of the prosecution and, as a result, it was possible to see the restrained enforcement of this offense. This ensued from the moral invalidation that Justice Cohen attached to the offense and his censure when the prosecution made use of it. The judgment of Justice Cheshin expresses a change in approach and grants moral legitimacy to the enforcement of this provision. Thus, by way of dialogue, the Court brought about a more restrained approach during the 1970s and a change in the prosecution's policy with regard to this offense in the 1990s. This dialogue extended over a period of more than two decades, and took place without a change in case law on the issue.

When the al-Aqsa Intifada erupted, the issue of indicting on misprision of felony for failing to prevent a terrorist attack again arose to confront the Court. The prosecution authorities were compelled to contend with relatives and friends of suicide bombers who knew of the bomber's intent but failed to report this to the authorities and failed to

---

[29] Criminal Appeal 3417/99, Har-Shefi v. the State of Israel, PD 55 (2) 735, 813 (2001) (emphasis added).

prevent a terrorist attack. The nature of terrorist attacks in those years changed, and terrorists acting alone or in small cells often carried out such attacks. In many cases, underlying support for terrorism was found in the close circles of these terrorists, who lent their support and assistance to carry out the attack. The need to find new ways to impede the plans of potential suicide bombers, who operated as part of networks of this kind, led law enforcement officials once again to require the use of this offense. Judgments given during these years are characterized mostly by the elimination of any traces of ambivalence in the charge sheets submitted. The message the Court conveyed to the prosecution was one of backing and support of its policy. The Court's tone sharply and clearly condemned the omission of those who were aware of terrorist acts and who did nothing to prevent them, and it adopted a decisive and unequivocal tone vis-à-vis everything that pertains to the use of this offense to deter relatives and friends from covering up, even if passively, for suicide bombers.

For example, in the *Bargouti* case,[30] the Supreme Court decided that a person who refrains from reporting terrorist activity even though he knew of it is dangerous to the extent that this does not allow for his early release from incarceration. The same was true in the case of Tajiri Latifah Saadi.[31] In this case, the appellant knew of a terrorist attack that was about to be carried out and even talked to the terrorist on her way to the scene of the attack. In the terror attack that took place at the Mahane Yehuda market in Jerusalem, six people lost their lives and dozens more were injured. The appellant was convicted of the offense of failure to report a terrorist act. The Court rejected her contention that even if she had contacted security authorities, it was not certain that the terrorist attack would have been averted. In the view of the Court, a reasonable chance that the attack could have been prevented was sufficient to convict her of the offense. In the *Rejabi* case,[32] the Court strongly expressed its revulsion toward a person who knew of his brother's intention to carry out a suicide bombing in Haifa in which 17 people were killed, mostly children. The Court stated the following on this matter, which sealed off any expression of moral ambivalence with regard to the possible use of this offense by the Attorney General:

> The same hatred also led the Appellant not to act in a reasonable manner in order to prevent the terrible terrorist attack, which was ultimately executed, although without his active involvement and which sowed death and bereavement in our streets. The gravity of these acts and omissions of the Appellant and the need to deter persons who reside among us from perpetrating acts that aid the enemy, as well as the need to condemn the silence under cover of which those who plot

30 Leave for HCJ Appeal 1443/04, Bargouti v. the Attorney General (unpublished, Apr. 22, 2004).
31 Criminal Appeal 2131/03, Saadi v. the State of Israel (unpublished, Dec. 23, 2003).
32 Criminal Appeal 1932/04, Rejabi v. the State of Israel, Tak-El 2005 (2)187 (2005).

against us manage to injure the innocent in order to take out their anger—all these justify the penalty that has been imposed on the Appellant in the case herein.[33]

In conclusion, a change in circumstances and changes in the nature of the terror threat caused the Supreme Court to direct and guide the prosecution on the question of how to enforce offenses related to passive assistance for acts of terror. This change occurred principally by means of advisory dialogue, while the law and interpretation of the section have not changed over the years. The law remained as it was, but the manner of applying the law was influenced by the Supreme Court through dialogue with the prosecution that focused on providing censure or expressing moral support for its position. During the 1970s, the Supreme Court's messages centered on expressing revulsion from the very whiff of informing that arose from the offense. As the wave of terror intensified, followed by the murder of Yitzhak Rabin and the entry of suicide bombings into the arena, the understanding took root that in many cases only those found in the close environs of the terrorist could prevent that person from perpetrating the offense. As a result, the Supreme Court altered the nature of its messages, and granted the prosecution moral and lawful legitimization to press charges against those who were aware of an act of terror about to be committed but failed to do anything to prevent it.

This case illustrates how the disparity between endorsing and granting moral validity to policy to censuring is critical to understanding the subtle mechanisms of influence of the Court. Often, it is possible to discover this message just by reading between the lines of a judgment or by comparing the text with the text the Court uses in similar cases. The cases indicated above illustrate how at times the real question is whether the Court disapproves of a policy or approves it and recognizes its necessity in the fight against terrorism. In other words, sometimes, the real message, even if concealed, is to be found in the absence of moral justification for the State's conduct in the judgment of the Court. This absence is highly salient to the players who represented the State and did their best to persuade the Court that the State's position is not only lawful but also justified and ethical.

We will clarify matters. When the Court discusses national security policy, it can determine that the policy that the State applies is not unlawful and, accordingly, the Court will not intervene in it. However, the Court—and in many cases this is expected—can deliberate the necessity of the relevant policy to the State's national security interests. The expectation that the Court will deliberate the necessity of policy is required as often policy is involved in impingement of basic rights. Accordingly, it is reasonable that the Court will also seek to justify policy ethically and not only approve its lawfulness.[34] The Court is also aware of these "rules of the game." In most cases in which the Court determines that a certain policy is lawful, it also affords it moral justification, in one way

---

[33] *Id.*

[34] *See on this* ROBERT PAUL WOLFF, THE RULE OF LAW (1976).

or another. As opposed to this, there are cases in which, as we have seen, the Court is satisfied with a determination that a policy is not unlawful but is unwilling to provide moral justification to it.

The use of advisory messages in the case of failure to report a terrorist attack illustrate nicely the advantage of such messages from the point of view of the flexibility they provide the Court. When the level of terrorist threat it relatively low the Court could send soft messages that will disincentivize the Attorney General from bringing more such cases to courts. When the level of terrorism threat is heightened that Court could provide more legitimacy to the need to bring these cases to justice. The change in both cases occurs without a need to change case law or to provide a too narrow or too broad interpretation to a needed yet controversial offense.

CONCLUSION

In the last two chapters, I have presented several methods of judicial review that the Court developed the influence the application of national security policy, without the Court having to intervene in constitutional questions or even the interpretation of law.

As a strategy, these messages must be examined distinct from the question of whether the Court's ruling is legally accurate. Such tactics allow the Court a way out in cases in which it is unable to rule in the manner in which it would perhaps like to rule, whether because of the emergency state the country is in or because in its opinion the law does not allow the Court to rule in this manner.

Israel's court has developed several strategies for these situations, all of which are based on dialogue with the other branches. By the messages that the Court conveys, it clarifies its expectations with regard to the manner in which lawful policy should be applied. The Court conveys messages that would restrict the application of policy and make its application more difficult. The Court can influence how policy is applied also through messages included in an operative order, whose purpose is to clarify for the Executive what the Court expects of them when applying the Court's judgment. Another tactic used by the Court is to influence application of policy by messages that support the manner in which the Executive applies policy or by messages that censure this.

Messages with regard to a policy's application can lead to a restricted application of a judgment, as we have seen with regard to various issues such as house demolitions or passive support for terrorism, but not necessarily. The messages can also lead to a "broadened" application of policy as may be seen in HCJ *On Torture* or with regard to house demolitions during the al-Aqsa Intifada.

We see how different justices developed different points of view regarding the use of dialogue pertaining to application of policy as a tool to formulate judicial policy. On questions related to freedom of speech, Justice Barak, for example, was not prepared to rely on dialogue regarding the application of policy in order to protect basic liberties. As opposed to this, other justices viewed such dialogue as sufficient guarantee, or at least, one of several guarantees available to the Supreme Court in order to ensure individual liberties.

As regards the dialogue of the application of policy, the Supreme Court combines messages that are not taken necessarily from the world of recognized legal content. The Court introduces into the State's procedure of decision-making in cases of incitement to terrorism a different set of values based on "reason,"[35] "liability,"[36] "restraint,"[37] "moderation,"[38] and "caution."[39] Through such directives regarding application, the Court creates a conscious disparity between the law (*the Law of the Books*) and the manner in which the Court would like the Executive to apply the judgment (*the Law in Action*).[40]

From the Court's perspective, influence by dialogue regarding application gives it two important advantages. First, it prevents a conflict with the other branches in times of national crisis or heightened tension. Second, it allows it to promote a policy that is flexible enough to be adjusted if security situation requires so or if the Executive misuses its discretion.

---

[35] HCJ 11225/03 Bishara v. The Attorney General, Tak-El 2006 (1) 1398, para. 13 of the judgment of Judge Hayuth: "*Legal and public discretion must be exercised reasonably and responsibly, and it must be decided whether there is reason to exploit the law with the public representative*" (emphasis added).

[36] *Id.*

[37] Criminal Appeal Alba v. the State of Israel, PD 50(5) 221 (1996), para. 20 of the opinion of Justice Mazza: "*It is presumed that the prosecution ... will continue with the procedure of filing such indictments, with caution, restraint and moderation*" (emphasis added).

[38] *Id.*

[39] *Id. See also* the HCJ 6698/95, Kadan v. Israel Lands Authority et al., PD 54(1) 258, 285 (2000).

[40] For further discussion of the issue, *see* STEWART MCAULAY, LAWRENCE M. FRIEDMAN & ELIZABETH MERTZ, LAW IN ACTION: A SOCIO-LEGAL READER (2007).

9

Dialogue with Military Authorities

INTRODUCTION

This chapter and the following three differ somewhat from the preceding ones. Although they still deal with messages conveyed in Supreme Court judgments, instead of focusing on the contents of the messages, these chapters will consider the ways the Court communicates with various parties addressed by the Supreme Court messages. We will divide the discussion according to four "addressees." First, we will discuss dialogue that the Court conducts in its judgments with *the military*. As I will demonstrate, such dialogue serves the Court principally to create an additional means of influencing policy in real time that joins the other methods the Court developed by using advisory dialogue, which has been presented above. Subsequently, we will discuss the nature of the Court's dialogue in its judgments with *prosecutors and attorneys who represent the State*. This will be followed by an examination of the dialogue that occurs in judgments and decisions with *petitioners and human rights organizations*, which represent the injured party or the party likely to be injured by actions of the State. Finally, we will discuss the Court's messages to *victims of terrorism, families of combatants, and bereaved families*.

As we will demonstrate below, the Supreme Court of Israel, as distinct from any other Supreme Court in the world, conducts an intensive, direct dialogue with these players. The dialogue commences in the courtroom by way of verbal remarks in the course of a hearing. However, in many cases it continues and occurs within judgments as well. What sets this dialogue apart is the fact that it is not just inter-organizational dialogue. It occurs through the prism of dialogue the Court conducts with living persons to whom the Court was introduced during a hearing. The Court wishes to converse with these persons or to convey a message to them by way of its decisions and judgments. It is so direct that in many ways it is similar in nature to an ordinary conversation among people, and the messages conveyed often originate in worlds of content that look very similar to interpersonal communication.

EDUCATING THE MILITARY TO RESPECT HUMANITARIAN LAW THROUGH JUDGMENTS

The Supreme Court holds intensive dialogue with military authorities. Its principal purpose is to influence the military in another way apart from Court judgments so that it will make certain to respect the rules of international law that apply to the situation under discussion. One of the ways in which this is done is by the use of "educational" messages, intended to influence the conduct of commanders and soldiers.

Educating the Military: The Case of Major General Dan Halutz

Probably the most prominent example pertaining to the Supreme Court's use of its decisions as a tool to promote "educational" messages is the petition that was submitted against the appointment of Major General Dan Halutz to Deputy Chief of Staff.[1] Decisions to appoint officials, in Israel, like in most states, are made by the Executive. However, in a landmark decision in 1993 the Supreme Court decided that it has authority to nullify the appointment of an official by the Executive if the decision is so extremely unreasonable that it could be considered unlawful.[2]

The case leading to this decision was the appointment of Yossi Ginosar, a former Shin Bet Executive to the position of Director General of the Ministry of Housing. Ginosar was a member of an inquiry commission charged with investigating the execution of two Palestinians who were among the kidnappers of a line 300 bus carrying passengers from Tel Aviv to the southern city of Ashkelon, in what later became known as the Line 300 affair. Ginosar was charged with obstruction of justice due to his leaking of information from the meetings of the commission to the Shin Bet. The leakings allowed Shin Bet officials suspected of being involved in the execution to coordinate their testimonies and to accuse, in the murder, Yizchak Mordechay, the commander of the parachute elite unit who conducted the operation for the release of the hijacked passengers. After his indictment, Ginosar, in a very controversial decision, was pardoned by the President of Israel. When Ginosar was appointed to become the Director General of the Ministry of Housing a petition was submitted to the Court, and the outrageous appointment was declared by the Court as so unreasonable that it could be considered illegal. Since then

---

[1] HCJ, *Hess v. Halutz*, PD 59 (6) 97 (2005) [hereinafter HCJ *Halutz*].
[2] HCJ 6163/03 Eizenberg v. The Minister of Housing PD 47(2) 229.

several petitions have come before the Court inviting it to nullify senior appointments of officials involved in criminal activity.

The circumstances for lodging the petition in the case of Halutz was an air force mission of July 22, 2002, in which Salah Shehadeh, a prominent Hamas activist, was targeted in an air attack. The attack was executed by dropping a one-ton bomb that hit his secret hideout. Shehadeh and another Hamas activist who was staying there were killed, along with another 15 Palestinian civilians, most of them children, and more than 150 people were wounded. On August 23, 2003, the *Haaretz* daily newspaper published an interview with Halutz, entitled "We're Fed Up with You, Noble Souls." Major General Halutz repeated statements he had made at a meeting with air force personnel related to the operation against Shehadeh. The petition focused on several statements Halutz made during the same interview. At the beginning of the interview he said, "Sleep well at night. Incidentally, I, too, sleep well at night." At the end of the interview, when he was asked if it is legitimate to ask a pilot, who executed an attack in which children were unintentionally killed, how he feels, Halutz responded, "No. That question is not legitimate and it should not be asked. However, if you nonetheless want to know how I feel when I release a bomb, then I will tell you that I feel a slight bump to the airplane as the result of the bomb's release. A second later, it's gone—and that is all. That is what I feel." The central contention of the petitioners was that the moral failing that adhered to Halutz was so grave that it would be best to refrain from allowing the appointment to stand.

In this case, the petition had already acquired an "educational" nature in its initial stages. At the first hearing that was held on November 18, 2004, Justice Levy, who headed the panel of judges, made the following statement:

> *I have an uneasy feeling, to say the least*, from these statements. It is difficult for me to come to terms with this, particularly since he does not express any misgivings. We would like to have his position in writing. His moral stance is important to us. Because if this is his position—I do not wish to develop.... [emphasis added][3]

The Court did not stop at explanations that the State representative gave orally at the hearing, and ordered the following in an interim decision:

> After we heard the contentions of the litigants, *we deliberated with the attorney for the Respondents* whether it was not warranted, prior to this court deciding how to deal with the petition, to have the response of the Deputy Chief of Staff (Respondent 1) presented to the Court with regard to the statements attributed to

---

[3] The precise quotation is brought as it was reported in the press. *See* Efrat Weiss & Tal Rosner, *HCJ to Maj.-Gen. Halutz: Present Your Moral Position*, YNET, Nov. 18, 2004, *available at* http://www.ynet.co.il/articles/1,7340,L-3006245,00.html..

him in the press and cited herein in the petition. *Adv. Nitzan stated he was willing to consider the matter* and to bring it before the entities pertaining to the matter. Accordingly, our decision on the petitions will be deferred so that a supplementary Reply on behalf of the Respondents may be submitted within 15 days. We expect to read in this same Reply not only a confirmation or denial of the statements attributed to Respondent 1 but also *his moral position* with respect to the statements he is alleged to have made. [emphasis added][4]

Two issues in this decision are notable. First, the dialogue style in which the decision is worded is salient. The decision is not formulated in an imperative manner but in the form of an inclusive dialogue and, ostensibly, the Court and the State together formulate its contents. Second, it is warranted to underscore the educational-operative significance of the decision. Like a chastised schoolboy, Halutz is requested by the Court to explain his moral position concerning the questions on the agenda.

Following the decision, Halutz indeed submitted an affidavit in which he clarified the meaning of the statements he made and expanded on the matter of his moral position with regard to the issues at stake. Furthermore, Halutz apologized for the fact that it appeared from his statements that he seemed not to sympathize with the deaths of innocent civilians. On January 26, 2005, a judgment was given in HCJ *Halutz*, which rejected the petition. The Court extensively analyzed the legal situation pertaining to senior appointments in public service and reached the general conclusion that there is no legal basis to grant the request of the petitioners. After this, the Court added the following statements:

> *We must taper the tenor of the interview and even of part of the statements made therein, which it would have been best had these not been made, and particularly coming from an IDF major general, serving as the commander of the Israel Air Force.* [emphasis added][5]

And, if these statements by Justice Edmund Levy were not sufficient, Justice Naor added her own opinion:

> In any event, even when matters are read in their full context, and while noting the explanations given in the letter of Respondent 1, the little that may be said with regard to his statements in the newspaper article is that these concern expressions that, in part, are unwarranted and are likely to be construed, as the Major General himself indicated, as imperviousness to the results of the bombing.[6]

---

[4] HCJ *Halutz, supra* note 1, decision of Nov. 18, 2004.
[5] *Id.* at 114.
[6] HCJ *Halutz, supra* note 1, at 116.

The judgment in the *Halutz* case illustrates how the Court is willing to undertake the role of educator and to hear petitions even if the results of the hearing are predictable. The fact that from the outset the petition had no significant chance of being accepted was not concealed from anyone. The Court indicated this in its judgment in the *Halutz* case as it related to *"the difficulty in reconciling the relief requested by the petitioners within the confines of this petition with the conclusion they seek to reach from the interview conducted with Maj.-Gen. Halutz."*[7]

When it comes to judgments dealing with the military, the Court assumes that its judgment will be disseminated among soldiers and commanders. Therefore, the Court allocates extensive parts of its judgments in the field of national security and in particular where moral or humanitarian law issues relating to the military are discussed, to explain to military commanders the nature of their conduct, to berate them, or to compliment them. This type of "educational" message is separate from the judgment in the petition and generally is not included in the judgment's operative part. The difference between the messages discussed in this chapter and those with regard to the application of policy that were discussed in Chapters 7 and 8 is that the Court does not seek through these "educational" messages to instruct the State on how to apply certain policy. Instead, the Court again underscores messages whose contents are not in dispute, but it does so in a manner and language whose purpose is "to educate" military authorities as to their conduct. In other words, in this context the Court does not seek *to create* new legal rules. By conveying an educational message, the Court seeks *to instill* proper norms of combat among soldiers and their commanders.

"Educating" the Military: The Case of Checkpoints in the Occupied Territories

The conduct of soldiers at checkpoints that were erected in the Occupied Territories and the numerous complaints of human rights organizations along with the grave reports in the media regarding the tough and humiliating attitude toward Palestinians who are compelled to pass through the checkpoints led the Court in several instances to convey "educational" messages to the military. In HCJ *Alouna*[8] the Israel Defense Forces (IDF) blockaded three villages proximate to the city of Nablus, which prevented the passage of residents of these same villages into the city. The petitioners contended that the blockades are exceedingly burdensome. In substance, the Court accepted the State's contention that "the ring" imposed on the area in which the three villages are located was imposed due to the difficult security situation and to the fact that many suicide missions to Israel originated in Nablus. However, along with rejecting the petition, or more precisely toward the end, the Court ordered the military authorities to explain the

---

[7] *Id.* at 109 (emphasis added).

[8] HCJ 2847/03, Alouna v. Commander of IDF Forces in Judea and Samaria, Tak-El 2003 (2) 3829 (2003).

procedures in order to ensure that soldiers at the checkpoints would behave properly with local residents.

> Attorneys for the Petitioners contended before us that soldiers at the checkpoints do not properly obey the rules that obligate them. However, we are unable to accept such a vague and general contention as this. *All that we can advise the Respondent is solely this—the officers in charge of the checkpoints shall not tire of continuing to instill in the soldiers at the checkpoints that they act with patience and humanely as required, and do not make matters difficult for the village residents beyond that which is necessary. We decide to reject the petition.* [emphasis added][9]

We would note that notwithstanding the use of the term *advise*, this comment does not define for the State how to apply the policy the Court discusses in its judgment. In place of this, the Court addresses the military by way of the remark and requests of its commanders that they "educate" the soldiers to act patiently and humanely while they are on duty at the checkpoints. As already indicated above, patience, moderation, and restraint are not legal norms and, accordingly, they do not have operative legal significance. It is clear that the effectiveness of such messages is dependent on the military's willingness to accept the Court's messages, to disseminate them, and to implement them as an "educational" message among its soldiers and commanders.

JUDICIAL REVIEW "UNDER FIRE"

Judicial Review "Under Fire"—Operation "Defensive Shield"

Intensive use of "educational" messages may be found in judgments given during Operation Defensive Shield. In March 2002, Israel suffered the highest losses of the entire period of the al-Aqsa Intifada. During this time over 120 Israeli soldiers and civilians were killed. The height of the terrorist attacks was the attack on the Park Hotel—a suicide attack perpetrated at the Park Hotel in Netanya on Passover Seder night in which 30 holiday guests were killed. As the result of the drastic increase in suicide attacks, the government decided on a broad and extensive military campaign to be carried out in the West Bank. The campaign began on March 29, 2002, with an incursion of regular forces and reserve troops into the major cities of the West Bank and refugee camps. During the campaign, the IDF destroyed the organizational infrastructure of the Palestinian Authority and laid siege to the Mukata'ah, where Yasser Arafat resided at that time, and destroyed the Hamas infrastructure. The IDF also captured numerous arms and weapons, and arrested thousands of suspects of terrorist activity. The campaign ended on May 10, 2002.

---

[9] *Id.*

During the period of the campaign no fewer than 29 petitions were submitted to the Supreme Court concerning the military's conduct and its ramifications for the civilian population. This figure is particularly striking due to the fact that six years later during Operation Cast Lead, only a very few petitions were lodged pertaining to that campaign. Only two petitions, which were joined, concerned humanitarian aspects of conducting warfare (evacuating the wounded and attacking medical teams).[10]

With regard to all the petitions that were filed during Operation Defensive Shield, except for two,[11] a hearing was held within several days, generally within a day or two, while hostilities were still ongoing. There was constant contact between the military forces operating in the field and the attorneys and military representatives appearing at the hearing. Metaphorically speaking, the work of the Supreme Court during the military campaign may be described as a kind of judicial war room that was set up alongside other war rooms instituted during the campaign.

Notwithstanding the legal, practical, institutional, and political difficulties in contending with such petitions, the Court opted to confront, and perhaps more accurately insisted on confronting, the issues that these petitions sought to raise in "real time."

Analysis of the 29 petitions led to the following findings. In three cases, the petition was struck out *in limine*. In one case,[12] in which the Court was requested to order the military forces to refrain from the use of airplanes or tanks during the fighting in the Jenin refugee camp, the Court accepted the State's position that the petition is not justiciable. However, in almost all the other cases, the Court added advisory messages to its decisions.

Two of the 29 petitions that were submitted were accepted.[13] In these two a judgment was given long after the campaign ended. The significance of this timing will be addressed separately. In all the petitions, except for those that were accepted, the discussion was conducted and the decision given during the period of the military campaign or several days following its conclusion. All petitions decided during the military campaign or proximate to it were rejected.

The conclusion that arises from an analysis of these petitions is that the chief way in which the Court applied judicial review during the campaign was through dialogue.

---

[10] HCJ 209/09 and HCJ 248/09.

[11] HCJ 3460/-2, Dror HaLevy—Chairman of the Separation Movement v. the Prime Minister (unpublished, July 1, 2002) concerned the need to establish a separation barrier due to the terrorist attacks. Perhaps because the government had already discussed the issue, the Court did not deem it necessary to decide the matter urgently and even determined that the petition was premature. In HCJ 3761/02, Hadir v. the IDF Commander in the Gaza Strip (unpublished, May 28, 2002), the government declared at the same time as the petition was submitted that until a decision would be given in the petition, no actions to implement the order for seizing land issued by the commander of the IDF forces would be taken. It is reasonable to assume that this was the reason the Court did not see any urgency in hearing and deciding the petition.

[12] HCJ 3022/02 Canon v. GOC (General Officer Commanding) Central Command PD 56(3) (2002) 9.

[13] HCJ 3799/02 Adallah v. GOC (General Officer Commanding) Central Command PD 60 (3) 67 (2005) and HCJ 3239/02, Marav v. the IDF Commander, PD 57(2) (2002), decision of Dec. 15, 2002.

This feature is extremely dominant with regard to the use of judicial review during Operation Defensive Shield and in other military campaigns that followed,[14] to the point that it may be said that the Supreme Court's chief means of review during times of combat is advisory dialogue. The Court's conduct in practice, even if it is not its declared position, was that during times of combat, the Court, despite its willingness, is unable to intervene effectively in how combat is being conducted, and the absolute majority of petitions submitted in this situation were rejected.[15] However, instead of concluding the hearing with this position and ordering that the petition be rejected, the Court in many cases added messages to the army intended to convey to the commanders the Court's view of how to educate IDF soldiers to conduct themselves properly.

Thus, for example in HCJ 2977/02,[16] two human rights organizations contended that the military was violating court orders as it demolished houses in the Jenin refugee camp without giving preliminary warning and without offering the right to a hearing. The Court rejected the petition and accepted the State's position that this concerns combat actions in which at times damage to residential houses is unavoidable. However, at the end, the Court added the following comment:

> Nonetheless, it is clear that everything must be done—as required according to the conditions of the place and the requirements of the campaign—to minimize possible injury to civilians…The military authorities must fulfill the rules of humanitarian law and refrain from injuring civilians unnecessarily. *It is surely presumed that the Respondent—and it has not been contended before us otherwise—has instructed and will instruct the combatant forces to do all that is necessary to avoid the possibility of unnecessary injury to the innocent.* [emphasis added][17]

In another petition submitted on the same day (HCJ 2936/02[18]), the petitioners contended that IDF forces were shooting at Red Cross and Red Crescent medical personnel who were operating ambulances and in hospitals. The petitioners also contended that the IDF was preventing evacuation of the wounded and sick to hospitals to receive medical care, and the evacuation of the bodies of the dead to hospitals and from there

---

[14] HCJ 4764/04, Physicians for Human Rights v. Commander of IDF Forces in Gaza, Tak-El 2004 (2) 2183, 2186 (2004) [hereinafter the *Rafiah* case].

[15] *See, e.g.*, the *Canon* case, *supra* note 12, at 10–11 as well as HCJ 2977/02, Adalah v. the Commander of IDF Forces in Judea and Samaria, PD 56 (3) 6, 7–8 (2002). "The position of the Respondent is that this concerns effective combat actions in which, at times, damage to residential houses is unavoidable as these houses turn into a kind of bunker that serves as shelter for shooting at IDF forces. Under these circumstances, the power of the Court to intervene in campaign actions by way of judicial review is limited. HCJ 358/88 PD 43 (2) 529. Indeed, this does not concern ordinary static conditions in which it is warranted to give a party early warning prior to damaging its property, when the party seeks to operate against it."

[16] HCJ 2977/02, Adalah v. the Commander of IDF Forces in Judea and Samaria, PD 56 (3) 6 (2002).

[17] *Id.* at 7–8.

[18] HCJ 2936/02, Physicians for Human Rights v. Commander of IDF Forces, PD 56 (3) 3, at 5–6 (2002).

for burial by their families. The petitioners also contended that the IDF was preventing the supply of medical equipment to Christian hospitals. The State replied that in view of the brief time allotted to it, and, in particular, in view of the combat being conducted at the time the petitions were being clarified in the courts, it was not possible to investigate the contentions relating to concrete incidents mentioned by the petitioners. Substantively, the State agreed that the objective situation with regard to all that pertains to caring for the sick, the wounded, and the bodies of those killed is not easy. However, the State claimed that this ensued from the actual combat conditions. In this case, too, the Court rejected the petition in its judgment on the grounds that it is impossible, practically speaking, to relate to the incidents mentioned in the petitions. However, in this judgment as well, the Court added an "educational" message to the military authorities:

> Without relating to the specific incidents mentioned in the petitions, which ostensibly appear to be difficult, *we see fit to underscore that our fighting forces are obligated to fulfill humanitarian rules pertaining to care for the wounded, the sick and the bodies of those killed. . . . This obligation of our forces, as required by law, morality—and according to the state also utilitarian considerations—must again be presented to the fighting forces, down to the rank of the lone soldier in the field, through giving concrete instructions that will prevent, to the extent possible, even in severe situations, incidents that are inconsistent with the rules of humanitarian assistance.* [emphasis added][19]

In fact, a striking feature of these kinds of petitions is that it is clear to the petitioners, the State, and the Court that there is no practicable way that the Court will be able to—or will agree to—influence actions being executed on the battlefield while hostilities are still going on. Nonetheless, human rights organizations in Israel choose to submit these petitions. In HCJ 2936/02 mentioned above, the Court referred openly to this practice:

> *The relief requested in the petitions was to obligate the state to provide an explanation. When the explanation was given, in which it was clarified that IDF soldiers were instructed to act according to humanitarian rules and that they also act so, then the petitions must be rejected.* [emphasis added][20]

Also, in HCJ 2117/02 the Court indicated:

> *The petition before us looks ahead to the future. Accordingly, since this is so, we have not been requested to grant relief that pertains to the specific incidents. These have*

---

[19] *Id.*
[20] *Id.*

been brought to establish the factual infrastructure of the petition. [emphasis added][21]

These two statements illustrate one of the most important aspects of judicial review "under fire," in Israel. They show that one of the practical aims of these petitions is to hone the Court's normative message to the military authorities. The petitioners do not focus their petition on provision of a practical relief, and the Court for its part does not see any difficulty with this. The Court is prepared to cooperate with petitions whose principal purpose is to refine messages to the military and have them understood by the fighting forces, without the petitioners realistically expecting the Court to intervene by providing some type of operative relief. In the choice between nonintervention at all at a time of combat and striking out the petition *in limine,* and cooperating with petitions whose practical purpose is to sharpen educational messages to the military offering a potential operative relief each time, the Court chooses the second option. *These petitions may be understood as petitions in which human rights and humanitarian assistance organizations request that the Court act as mediator in the dialogue occurring between them and the military during times of combat, assuming that the Court is entirely capable, or at least more capable than they are, to convey effective messages to the military.*

As with other bodies, in certain cases the Court is not satisfied with conveying general educational messages such as in the examples brought above, and it employs a strategy of intensifying the tone in this "educational" dialogue. The Court censures the military and compliments it, all the while considering to what extent its conduct measures up to the norms that the Court seeks to target. Thus, in reference to the conditions of incarceration of thousands of Palestinians who were arrested during the initial days of the campaign, the Court wrote the following:

> Nonetheless, in this state of affairs as well, everything must be done to maintain minimum requirements for conditions of incarceration. *This was not done at the time of arrest in the temporary facilities, while the detention order was violated, [as well as] the rules of international law that apply to the region and the fundamental principles of Israeli administrative law. It is sufficient if I mention several grave violations: ... This requirement was known in advance. It was expected. Operation Defensive Shield was planned ahead. It was intended, inter alia, to arrest as large a number as possible of suspects of terrorist activity. The need to maintain minimum standards of detention was therefore a natural result of the campaign objectives. There was no surprise in this area. It was possible to prepare in advance proper spaces for detention under suitable conditions. What was accomplished several days following commencement of the campaign should have been done several days prior to its*

---

[21] *Id.* at 28.

commencement. Indeed, security requirements—which must always be taken into consideration—did not justify the impaired detention conditions that occurred at the time of arrest and interrogation in the temporary facilities.....Several minimal requirements were breached with regard to the detention conditions...All these fell below the minimal standards of detention conditions. There was no justification of security for this. [emphasis added][22]

Statements similar in tone were made in the judgment given in the *Ketziot* case:[23]

The detention conditions that the first detainees encountered—whose affidavits were attached to the petition—fell below the requisite minimum conditions. There was no justification for this. Operation Defensive Shield was planned in advance...It was clear to all—in any event it ought to have been clear to all—that this meant, inter alia, a large number of detainees. Therefore, detention facilities ought to have been prepared in advance, which fulfill the minimum criteria with regard to detention conditions. This was not done. [emphasis added][24]

Judicial Review "Under Fire"—Operation Rainbow

Two years later, the issue of the military preparing for combat campaigns and the humanitarian aspect again reached the Court in a judgment when the military initiated a further campaign in the Gaza Strip.[25] The petition was submitted to the Supreme Court on Thursday (May 20, 2004). It was set for a hearing the next morning (May 21, 2004). Ahead of this hearing, the Court requested and received a written Reply on behalf of the respondent. In an oral hearing, in addition to the parties' representatives, the head of the Coordination and Liaison Administration in the Gaza Strip and the chief military advocate were also present. These officers presented information orally to the Court with regard to the various issues brought before it. When the information was not available to them, they requested a brief delay in order to ascertain what was taking place in the Rafiah sector. They telephoned commanders on the front lines, who provided information with regard to events occurring there, which they then relayed to the Court.

The Court's judgment in this instance is an excellent example of how dialogue was conducted with military authorities while the fighting was ongoing. The dialogue took the form principally of educational messages of a normative nature, compliments and censure, according to the conduct that the Court expected the military to instill in its soldiers and commanders.

---

[22] HCJ 3278/02, Hamoked Lehaganat Haprat v. the IDF Commander, PD 57(1) 385, 399–400 (2002).
[23] HCJ 5591/02 Yasin v. the IDF Commander of Camp Ketziot PD 57(1) 418 (2002).
[24] *Id.* at 415.
[25] The *Rafiah* case, *supra* note 14, at 115.

A large part of the judgment is devoted to expressing dissatisfaction with the manner in which the military prepared for the humanitarian crisis that was anticipated as a result of the fighting in Rafiah. For example, the Court related to the evacuation of the bodies from the combat zone and bringing them for burial as follows:

> The development in the Respondent's position, as would have arisen from the Reply of the Attorney before us, attests to the fact that *the matter apparently was not taken into account in advance and the solutions proposed constituted on the spot improvisation. This is to be avoided. This matter must be planned in advance.* [emphasis added][26]

These cases illustrate how educational dialogue with military soldiers and commanders is colored distinctively by censure, without the Court's intervention ultimately in decisions taken by the military echelon. It appears that without the ability to influence how combat is conducted by means of operative orders, the Court uses other tools that are available to it. The Court conveys "educational" messages, including censure of military commanders, and offers compliments to other commanders in order to affect the manner in which the State combats terrorism.

The Court is aware that it is exercising judicial review at a time when the forces are still fighting in the field. However, according to the Court's way of thinking, as long as judicial review does not jeopardize the fighting forces, nothing will prevent the Court from exercising judicial review. These contentions have been raised with regard to judgments in the course of Operation Defensive Shield and those in relation to Operation Rainbow. In the case of Operation Defensive Shield, the Court related to this contention with the following statements:

> The case before us is special in that judicial examination occurs prior to the conclusion of military operations, while IDF soldiers are still at risk due to the fact that battle is still being waged. On this matter, we must restate and underscore, "It is certain that this court will not take any position with regard to the manner of conducting combat. As long as the lives of soldiers are at risk, the decisions will be made by the commanders. In the case before us, it was not claimed that the arrangement we have reached jeopardizes our soldiers.[27]

And, in the *Rafiah* case, the Court restated its firm position:

> The humanitarian issues have been settled without jeopardizing the lives of the soldiers or military operations. Subject to this constraint, our case is no different

---

[26] *Id.* at 404.
[27] HCJ 3114/02, Baraca v. the Minister of Defence, PD 56(1), 11(2002), at 16.

from other cases in which this court investigates whether military activities are conducted within the framework of the law.[28]

Judicial Review "Under Fire"—Operation Cast Lead

On December 27, 2008, the IDF commenced an extensive military campaign in the Gaza Strip, called Operation Cast Lead, which aimed at damaging Hamas infrastructure and restricting rocket attacks on Israel. During this campaign, the Israeli air force attacked targets that served Hamas authorities in the Gaza Strip. On January 3, 2009, armored personnel, infantry, and the engineering corps of the IDF joined the combat in the Gaza Strip. The campaign included heavy fighting under difficult conditions. In the course of the campaign, several petitions against the military were submitted regarding the conduct of the fighting. Examination of the petitions and the manner in which these were handled by the Court leads to the conclusion that the Court's approach of serving as a bridge between the human rights community and the military in times of combat is the preferred practice of the Court.

In two petitions lodged in the course of the campaign, the petitioners contended that the military does not fulfill its obligations to allow local inhabitants to receive medical treatment, that it injures medical teams contrary to the Geneva Convention, and that it precludes local inhabitants' access to electricity and water. Accordingly, proper operation of hospitals, medical clinics, the water system, and the sewage system is not possible. In order to hold a hearing on the petition, the Court summoned the commander of Military Coordination Administration to Jerusalem, obtained an affidavit from him, and requested his replies to questions that the petition raised. All this took place while fighting on the front was still ongoing.

Ultimately, after examining the petitioners' claims one by one, the Court rejected the petition. An interesting point is the remark the Court added toward the end of the judgment:

> Every now and then, the role of the Court in such cases is *to encourage* and monitor compliance with the provisions of Israeli and international law, *even where it knows and trusts that the authorities are unreservedly committed to the appropriate legal framework*; it does so, however, from the judicial perspective aimed at capturing the comprehensive picture. There is therefore constant need for judicial review. [emphasis added][29]

With these words the Court discloses the guiding principle that directs it when hearing these petitions and how it comprehends the role of judicial review during times of

---

[28] The *Rafiah* case, *supra* note 14, at 115.
[29] HCJ 201/09, Physicians for Human Rights v. the Prime Minister, Tak-El 2009 (1) 565.

intensive hostilities. It appears that the central aim of hearing the petitions is to hold a dialogue with military authorities in which the Court can urge them to abide by the indisputable provisions of humanitarian law. The Court "admits" that it is prepared to hear petitions even though there is no legal dispute with regard to the question being brought before the Court. It also "admits" that it is impossible to provide conventional judicial review in such times. However, the Court views the maintenance of such educational dialogue with military authorities so that they will strictly ensure the fulfillment of the provisions of international law as a central constituent of judicial review, which it utilizes in times of hostilities. This constituent is of such significance to the Court that the Court is willing during a time of hostilities to hear petitions that deal with the conduct of the fighting.

The Court also noted, in some cases dealing with the conduct of combat, that the petitioners do not always realistically expect the Court to intervene by binding judicial decisions. Sometimes, they do not dispute the legal questions the petition raises. What matters to them and to the Court is the ability to influence through the proceedings the behavior of the military and its adherence to humanitarian law.

This is one of the main reasons, as the Court itself "admitted" that the Court converses with soldiers and their commanders all the time—including in time of war. If necessary, the Court also summons for a hearing commanders who arrive from the battlefield to report to the Court on the events taking place and then return to the war zone with the Court's message. The Court does not strike out the petitions *in limine* even though it could do so, but rather makes use of them as an impetus and means to convey educational messages to the IDF and its commanders.

10

Dialogue with the Attorney General's Office

RELYING ON ATTORNEYS TO ASSIST THE COURT IN IMPLEMENTING ITS DECISIONS

A notable phenomenon relating to advisory dialogue is that which takes place between the Israeli Supreme Court and the Attorney General's Office, particularly the use the Court makes of dialogue with attorneys who appear before the Court on the Executive's behalf. The intensive and intimate dialogue that the Supreme Court conducts with these attorneys is quite exceptional. It is doubtful whether any parallel may be found in other legal systems. As we shall demonstrate, this mechanism enables the Court to influence decision-making processes in the Attorney General's Office within a short time, as well as the application of court judgments and policy-making in national security matters, without necessarily adjudicating that the policy is unlawful.

HCJ *Saleh*, which discusses the appropriation of land by the military, provides a good basic example of this practice. The Court rejected the petition after accepting the State's declaration that the petitioner's right to make partial use of the land shall be reserved. The Court then added the following remark:

> *Mr. Helman agrees that if the Petitioner should encounter difficulties on this matter, he will be able to contact Mr. Helman and request his assistance.* The parties further agree that the Petitioner is entitled to payment of compensation due to the appropriation. Subject to the aforesaid, the petition is dismissed. [emphasis added][1]

---

[1] HCJ 5422/01, Salah v. The Commander of IDF Forces in Judea and Samaria (unpublished, Aug. 9, 2001).

The significance of the judgment is that Attorney Helman must ensure that the petitioner will be able to work his land. If the petitioner encounters difficulties, he is to contact Attorney Helman, who will use his influence with military authorities so that the judgment will be implemented. Relying on the attorney is an integral part of the operative decision. The Court requests that he continue to handle the petitioner's affairs, even though the hearing has concluded.

In several cases, the Court goes even further and replaces a binding operative decision with an informal undertaking of the attorney representing the Executive at the hearing to try to arrive at an agreed-upon resolution of the dispute. A distinctive example of this practice may be seen in HCJ 4462/03,[2] which also deals with land appropriation by the military. The Court rejected the petition after receiving the State's declaration that compensation and fees for use will be paid to the landowners, and the barrier planned to be constructed in the area will have openings to allow access to the land in coordination with the owners, so that they will be able to work the land. Then, the Court added the following remark:

> The attorney for the State, Attorney Yuval Roitman, further declared at the hearing before us that the Attorney General Office undertakes to assist with safeguarding the right of the local inhabitants who own land to work their lands undisturbed. Of course, this response does not satisfy the petitioners, who undoubtedly are harmed by appropriation of the land. However, in view of the purpose of the appropriation, which is, as aforesaid, security, we see no possibility of intervening, even though, as aforesaid, measures have been taken to minimize the damage. The petition is rejected, accordingly. [emphasis added][3]

The Court therefore gives a judgment in which one of the operative directives is that the attorney appearing before the Court, whose name is stated in the decision, will continue to assist "with protecting the right of local inhabitants who own land to work their land undisturbed." The attorney himself and the entire Attorney General's Office are understood in this judgment not as representing a party but as representing the long arm of the Court, and one of the Court's objectives is to ensure that military authorities will implement judicial policy as determined in the judgment. The message's effectiveness depends on the ability and willingness of the attorney handling the case to see the point of the message and to take measures so that its contents will be realized.

There are numerous additional examples of the Court's reliance on attorneys who represent the Executive to continue handling different issues that the Court did not complete. What we see from these cases is that the Court includes in its decisions assurances

---

[2] HCJ 4462/03, Fanon v. Commander of IDF Forces, Tak-El 2003(3) 543 (2003).

[3] Id.

and declarations of attorneys to safeguard petitioners' rights—with and without the agreement of the petitioners. In several cases, the matters constitute the completion of the judgment and, in other cases, they serve as a replacement for the ruling in the petition.

These judgments are highly significant in understanding the central place of dialogue to judicial review of national security. The practical significance of these judgments is that dialogue between the parties continues without the normative umbrella of the hearing pending in court. The judgment has been given. However, the dialogue between the players continues as the Court acts as mediator.

Activities that serve the Court in its dialogue with prosecutors can also illustrate this unique manner of advisory dialogue. In operative judgments, there is no room seemingly for "clarifications."[4] Ostensibly there is also no room for "requests," "assistance," or "assurances."[5] The judgment is intended to ensure the finality of the ruling on the question in dispute. Nonetheless, the Israeli Supreme Court conducts an intensive and intimate dialogue with attorneys who appear before it. The Court assigns them tasks to promote the implementation of good policy. Using attorneys from the Attorney General's Office enables the Court to attempt to further objectives even after the hearing of a petition has concluded. These Attorneys act in this context as the long arm of the Court or as its "agent" vis-à-vis other State authorities. The agent brings the Court's words to government bodies and serves as its mouthpiece at internal hearings. The examples we have presented attest to the fact that the Court, which is not secure that its judgment will be applied precisely as written, relies on assurances from State attorneys that a judgment will be implemented as the Court would like it to be. Moreover, it expects the Attorneys to do so even in the absence of a binding formal order.

The Supreme Court's dialogue with attorneys who appear before it influences the manner in which the Court formulates its judicial rulings. The use of advisory dialogue gives the Court the option to reject the petition formally, subject to resolving the issue by way of advisory messages conveyed to the relevant authorities during the hearing of a petition or upon its conclusion. The notion that this is a strategic practice on the part of the Court is supported in statements made by Justice Dorner in a lecture she gave on human rights in the age of terrorism. She stated the following:

> There are also cases where the petition is formally rejected, but *the Court includes in its decision instructions that in practice allow for the complete or at least partial realization of the aspirations of the petitioners.*[6]

---

[4] *Id.*

[5] *Id.* at 386.

[6] *See* Dalia Dorner, *The Protection of Human Rights in the New Age of Terror*, 11 HUM. RIGHTS BRIEF (2003) (emphasis added).

This practice grants the Supreme Court several alternatives for exercising judicial review. One way is to accept the petition and grant it the effect of a binding judgment with regard to the proper policy to be applied in the circumstances proved before the Court. A second alternative that the Court may choose, should it be justified, is to reject the petition without adding any incidental remark that is not lawfully binding. A third option is to reject a petition, but attempt to promote the interest of the petitioners by means of advisory messages to attorneys appearing before the Court that are given in interim decisions during the course of the hearing of a petition and in the judgment as well. There are several cases where use of this practice stands out. The Court has available the legal option of formulating the judgment as accepting the petition. Yet the Court prefers to formulate the bottom line of the judgment as "the petition is rejected" even when in fact the practical significance of its decision is accepting or adopting the petitioners' position on most of the matters that have been presented.

The Court often selects this option, which reduces the intensity of the conflict between it and the Executive while at the same time leading to prompt results in the field. A petition that was heard in 2013 on the use made by the military of white phosphorus in its military activity illustrates this point. The petitioners contended that this material has the potential to injure seriously anyone who is exposed to it and continues to have a damaging effect long after it has been launched. The petitioners further contended that the use of white phosphorus by its nature makes it impossible to distinguish between military and civilian targets. Therefore, even when it is aimed at legitimate targets, it is likely ultimately to injure civilians. The petitioners' principal legal claim was that the use of white phosphorus constitutes a violation of international law because of the inherent disability to use this ammunition in a way that distinguishes between civilians and combatants. As the bottom line, the Court indeed rejected the petition. However, the Court did so only after conducting a dialogue with the attorneys, in which the Court instructed the military to issue new guidelines that will drastically reduce the use of white phosphorus and leave it as an alternative to be used solely in the most extreme cases, which leaves "the most effective and extensive prohibition of use in place, so that it is doubtful whether this issue will arise ever again in practice."[7]

For its part, the Court exploits this motivation and encourages attorneys to cooperate with the Court in this way. The Court could rely on this dialogue, because without a doubt, attorneys in State service are motivated to fulfill these instructions and serve as the long arm of the Court due to their being repeat players whose conduct is dictated according to strict rules of conduct[8] and who know that their relations with the Court are important to their success. An attorney who represents the State put it this way, in a conversation with the author: "We look for these signalings. In their absence,

---

[7] HCJ 4146/11, Hess v. the General Chief of Staff (unpublished, 9 July 2013), para. 5 of the judgment).
[8] Marc Galanter, *Why the "Haves" Come Out Ahead: Speculations on the Limits of Legal Change*, 9 L. & Soc. Rev. 95 (1974).

we become concerned. This is part of the game. We see a decision that is given without signaling as a breach of the rules of the game."[9]

CENSURE AND COMPLIMENTS

One of the principal tactics the Court employs to "encourage" State attorneys to serve as the long arm of the Court is the use of censure and compliments in its judgments. The term *censure and compliments* in this regard focuses on the individual who represented the State and not the policy itself. The Court generally conveys such message at the end of a judgment, when the Court may compliment the attorney or may censure him with regard to his conduct. Through this form of dialogue, the Court "encourages" attorneys to act in a certain way or to refrain from acting in a certain way, not by way of a binding absolute order but rather by creating the motivation to undertake the required action in this spirit.

A judgment that illustrates this practice concerns fighting that occurred around the Karnei Netzarim traffic artery in the Gaza Strip. On May 28, 2002, about three months after Operation Defensive Shield, HCJ *Gussin*[10] was heard, on the decision of the military commander to demolish two buildings from which numerous shooting incidents had taken place aimed at users of the traffic artery. Close to issuing the demolition order, two shooting incidents occurred from the direction of the factory in which four IDF soldiers were wounded. During the hearing, the State continued the line of argument that had been authorized in the judgments given in the course of Operation Defensive Shield and argued that the case is not justiciable.[11]

The Attorney thereby relied on one of the Court's decisions from three months earlier in which the Court was prepared to hear this argument.[12] However, in this instance a surprise awaited the Attorney: the Court refused to accept this threshold argument. Moreover, the Court also censured the attorney who dared to raise it:

The Respondent infringed the right of ownership of the petitioner. He did so by issuing a demolition order. He granted him the right of a hearing. He stayed the execution of the order for fourteen days. *I am astonished, given this backdrop, at what the attorney for the respondent found to claim before us, that the case before us*

---

[9] An interview on July 20, 2005.

[10] HCJ 4219/02, Gussin v. Commander of IDF Forces, PD 56 (4) 608 (2002).

[11] "IDF combat actions that are carried out within the confines of incidents of hostilities that occur in the areas clearly are operational. *The case before us is listed among the same cases that lead judicial review to the outer limits of justiciability. The Court must be doubly cautious in determining the degree of its intervention*" (emphasis added); HCJ 4764/04 Physicians for Human Rights v. Commander of IDF Forces in Gaza, Tak-El 2004 (2) 2183, 2186 (2004) [hereinafter "the *Rafiah* case"].

[12] HCJ 3022/02 Canon v. GOC (General Officer Commanding) Central Command PD 56(3) (2002) 9.

stands at "the outer limits of justiciability"; that it comprises issues that introduce the Court "into the war zone"; and that we are requested in this petition to monitor "combat activities." [emphasis added][13]

In this case, what is important is not only the Court's operative decision not to accept the contention of lack of justiciability but also the tone in which it was given. The Court sought to convey a message pertaining to its ability to oversee the manner in which the State fights, including during a time of hostilities. The Court chooses to do this by way of "censure," which clarifies to the Executive that it must refrain from bringing before the Court the claim that the Court is unable to apply judicial review at a time of hostilities.

The term *censure and compliments* includes a relatively wide range of responses in which the Court gives "a grade" to the State's position. It is clear that a player who merited such a remark on the part of the Supreme Court, which in many cases is publicized and in a few cases even earns media coverage, will be prepared to invest a great deal of energy in ensuring that her moves in the future meet the Court's expectations. This form of dialogue has advantages in that it offers another way in which the Court manages to direct the conduct of the Executive by way of non-binding dialogue, as it disciplines the attorneys appearing before the Court and mobilizes them to assist the Court in promoting good norms of behavior by the military.

The "cost" of this tactic to the Court is quite low. The risk of confrontation is also quite minor. In contrast, the representing attorney whose conduct is driven by considerations of a repeat player is highly motivated to make his conduct correspond to the Court's expectations. It should be noted that a compliment or censure of an attorney handling a case has no connection necessarily with the outcome of the case or with the Court's approach to the issue in dispute. In many cases, the Court distinguishes between the conduct of the attorney who appears in court and her position vis-à-vis the question in dispute. For example, in the *Rafiah* case, the Court clearly distinguished between the conduct of the military and the conduct of the players who represented the military before the Court. The Court seriously censured the military for its lack of preparedness regarding the campaign's humanitarian aspects but at the hearing clearly complimented the players who represented the State on their conduct:

Prior to concluding, we would like to thank the attorney for the petitioners, Adv. Fatma Elajar, who represented the position of the petitioners clearly and responsibly, and the attorneys for the respondent, Adv. Helman and Adv. Roitman, who succinctly provided us with detailed and updated information, insofar as possible. Our thanks also go to Colonel Y. Mordechai, who was so good as to explain to us the data about the

---

location and activities of the respondent and made every effort to translate the humanitarian norms into practical language. [emphasis added][14]

DIALOGUE WITH THE PROSECUTION AND OVERSEEING SHIN BET INVESTIGATIONS

One of the most difficult areas for judicial review is the method of collecting intelligence by the intelligence services. In Israel the law[15] differentiates between wiretaps conducted for the purpose of preventing or investigating conventional crimes and those conducted for security purposes. Whereas the former are subject to prior judicial authorization the latter require only Executive (Prime Minister or Minister of Defence) approval. The law stipulates that except for very specific circumstances, information gathered not in accordance with this law will be inadmissible. When it comes to other covert investigation techniques such as covert searches in premises or in computers, the law governing the collection is the General Security Service Act of 2002, which authorizes the Shin Bet to conduct such search subject to prior approval by the Prime Minister.[16] The Shin Bet does not need to get such prior approval in order to gain access to information collected by telecom providers. In such cases the license itself will clarify what information the service provider needs to retain and the Director of the Shin Bet could order the provider to provide the Shin Bet access to this information. The only meaningful oversight mechanisms that exist are that of the Shin Bet ombudsperson office and a quarterly report by the Shin Bet to the Knesset's Committee on security and foreign relations.

The lack of direct judicial authorization before a wiretap is issued makes the judicial review of national security wiretaps in Israel very limited in scope. A petition seeking information on the number or wiretaps authorized for national security reasons based on the freedom of information act, is pending before the Jerusalem District Court at the time of writing of this book.[17]

A more robust review takes place whenever the wiretaps lead to criminal investigation. In such cases the Supreme Court itself will review the intelligence gathered and will look into the lawfulness of the collection method as well as to the usefulness to the accused of the gathered information. In today's world more and more surveillance programs lead to criminal investigations. Courts throughout the world invest a great deal of effort in monitoring intelligence gathering and ensuring that the material brought to a hearing in a criminal procedure is consistent with the norms that have been formulated with regard to its admissibility. Scrutiny of Supreme Court case law in Israel demonstrates how the

---

[14]   The *Rafiah* case, *supra* note 11, at 408.
[15]   The Wiretaps Act (1979).
[16]   Section 10 of the General Security Service Act [2002].
[17]   Administrative Petition 19501-90-13 (Jerusalem) The Association for Civil Rights in Israel v. the Prime Minister (Pending).

Court has learned to use the practice of compliments and censure to increase oversight of the Shin Bet. One example that illustrates this pertains to the Damien Pakowitz case.[18] Pakowitz was convicted because on September 4, 1997, he placed the head of a pig in a Muslim cemetery. He was interrogated by the Shin Bet, and he contended at his trial that violence had been used against him in his interrogation. It must be noted that during his trial, the interrogator who investigated him admitted that various measures were used such as covering the accused's head with a sack.[19] The date of the hearing in the *Pakowitz* case is of considerable significance as the hearing of the appeal before the Supreme Court occurred immediately following the judgment in the HCJ *On Torture* case. Although in the judgment the Court did not relate to the question of the admissibility of the confession that was obtained by the use of violence, such a determination, even if it was not the binding result of the judgment on the question of violence in practice, was necessary.

The State, which apparently had considered *prior* to the hearing that this possibility might come up, immediately declared at the outset of the hearing that it was not seeking to rely on the confessions of the appellant to the Shin Bet investigators and the police. In its judgment, the Court related to this as it complimented the State representative on his approach:

> (J) *It appears that the prosecutor did well* in that he saved time for the Court by omitting a discussion of the dispute between the parties with regard to the admissibility of the confessions and, principally, by seeking to remove from the basis of the conviction any shred of evidence, the admissibility and credibility whereof is in doubt. [emphasis added][20]

Thus, by means of "a compliment," the Court encourages the prosecution to adopt a policy in the future that the State, at its own initiative, will refrain from bringing confessions of accused for the Court's deliberation, if there is any doubt that these were given freely and willingly, even though the Court did not decide this question substantively.

The gathering of probative intelligence, in preparation for a criminal proceeding is another major challenge and one of the most sensitive issues in a national security case. In accordance with procedure customary in criminal law, the State may refrain from delivering to an accused in a criminal proceeding material that may impair national security. The condition precedent for the failure to transmit such material is that such

---

[18] Criminal Appeal 3338/99, Pakowitz v. the State of Israel, PD 54 (5) 667 (2000).

[19] *See* Criminal File 109/98 (Jerusalem), State of Israel v. Pakowitz, Tak-Mahozi 99 (2) 3415 (1999), session of Apr. 29, 1998, at 26 [citation taken from B'Tselem Position Paper—Legislation Allowing the Use of Physical Force and Mental Coercion in Interrogations by the General Security Service (Jan. 2000), *available at* http://www.btselem.org/Download/200001_Torture_Position_Paper_Heb.doc.]

[20] CA 3338/99 Pakowitz v. the State of Israel PD 54(5) 667 (2000), para. 7 of the judgment of Justice Beinisch.

material cannot assist the accused in his defense.[21] The primary person who is supposed to examine whether the intelligence entities have material that could assist in the defense of the accused is the prosecutor who files the indictment. The Court, much like in Classified Information Procedure Act[22] proceedings in the United States, is intended to oversee the prosecutor's work, if and insofar as the accused submits a petition in which the Court is requested to remove the certificate of privilege. The concern that at any stage of the proceeding investigative material that can lead to the acquittal of an accused may hide or be concealed in the cellars of the Shin Bet requires all supervisory systems to maintain constant vigilance and strict monitoring of their own conduct. The history of intelligence services in the world as well as the enormous quantity of material that is collected, and the sophisticated means of collection available to them, make such monitoring extremely difficult. Both the prosecution and the Court must assume that the Shin Bet's independent supervisory methods will lead to the disclosure of any evidentiary material that it possesses, which could assist the accused.

In one aspect, Israeli law differs from that of most common law countries. According to Israeli law, it is a Supreme Court justice that will decide on the discovery of any such material. Aside from developing a robust procedure to decide on disclosure, Supreme Court case law in this field illustrates how the Court has learned to use tactics of censure and compliments in order to augment oversight of intelligence gathering prior to filing an indictment. An important judgment in which the Court made use of this tactic is the *Abu Saadeh* matter.[23] In this case, the conviction of Nidal Abu Saadeh, a member of Hamas, was discussed. He allegedly conducted a violent "interrogation" of another detainee whom he suspected of cooperating with the prison authorities and thereby caused that detainee's death. In the hearing on appeal, it turned out that the prosecution at the time of the District Court hearing had screened intelligence according to which the main prosecution witness contended that he did not see who committed the murder. This piece of intelligence that could have been of assistance in Abu Saadeh's defense was not disclosed to the defense due to a certificate of privilege on behalf of national security issued by the Minister of Defense. With the State's agreement, Abu Saadeh was acquitted for this reason. Nonetheless, the Court did not stop at the decision to acquit and wrote a detailed decision relating to the State's conduct in the earlier stages of the proceeding, in which the Court severely censured the State for failing to disclose such information.

In its decision, the Court wrote the following:

Acquittal of the appellant does not serve to rectify the grave faults that marred the conviction thereof and the proceedings that preceded it. These faults essentially negated the

---

[21] Section 44 of the Evidence Ordinance [New Version]5731-1971; *see also on this matter* Misc. Civil App. 838/84, Livni v. the State of Israel, PD 38 (3) 729 (1984).

[22] Classified Information Procedures Act (CIPA), 18 U.S.C. app. 3 §§ 1–16 (2006).

[23] Criminal Appeal 4765/98, Abu Saadeh v. the State of Israel, PD 53 (1) 832 (1999). *See also* recent Criminal Appeal 7281/12 Hacohen v. the Minister of Defence (unpublished yet, 4 December 2012).

right of the accused to conduct a defense... In our matter, the said review failed on all three levels thereof... The prosecution objected to the removal of the privilege, which, as aforesaid, was not at all necessary. And more serious, the prosecution even presented at the public hearing before the District Court, in the presence of the appellant and his defense attorney, a misleading representation pertaining to the contents of the classified information.... The explanation given by the prosecution for the misleading presentation also indicates a failure in understanding the role of an attorney.... This failure of the system of review of classified information is grave and raises serious concern. [emphasis added][24]

This case demonstrates how the Court uses severe censure to "encourage" the State through the prosecutors who appear before it to examine every shred of intelligence so as to avoid a situation in which such material, which may be of assistance to an accused, is not disclosed to the defense. It also illustrates the Court's strategic use of advisory dialogue. It is important to understand that in this case the Court was not at all required to add the statements of censure. In most cases in which the State agrees to acquit an accused, the Court is satisfied with a particularly brief decision, in which it puts into writing the fact of the State's agreement and gives it the validity of a judgment. Ostensibly, the Court could have been satisfied in this case too with a brief decision that expresses the State's agreement to the acquittal and thereby end the embarrassing matter. Instead, the Court opted to add voluntarily words of severe censure with regard to all those involved in the review procedure of filtering the classified investigative material. It is difficult to assume that the Court's objective in so doing was other than to direct the future conduct of the prosecutors handling this subject.

Indeed, the prosecution clearly understood the message that was conveyed in this judgment. Following the *Abu Saadeh* judgment, the entire subject of handling classified material by the prosecution was revised. Directives from the State prosecution office pertaining to classified information were updated as well as directives from the Department of Investigations of the Israel Police. Procedures for handling such material were changed, and all internal review processes were made stricter to preclude any such recurrence. The "trauma" that the *Abu Saadeh* judgment caused the prosecution dramatically affected the prosecution's conduct and supervision of the manner in which the Shin Bet collects probative intelligence. Edna Arbel, the State Prosecuting Attorney at that time, expressed this as follows:

Since the judgment in the Nidal Abu Saadeh matter, in which the Court criticized our conduct, we have held many deliberations and countless consultations. Responsibility has been strictly assumed, rules and procedures have been prepared

---

[24] *Id.* at 841.

regarding a matter that obligates all and ensures the maximum means of control. Nonetheless, as aforesaid, many concessions have been made.[25]

There are also examples of dialogue in which the Court compliments the prosecution with respect to the use of classified material. For example, in the matter of Tali Fahima, the Court opted to compliment the prosecution on the manner in which it handled classified information. In 2004, an indictment was filed against Tali Fahima, which attributed to her several security offenses in view of her contacts with activists in a terrorist organization. Fahima was also accused of delivering material about a military campaign to activists in "the al-Aksa Brigades," which is a designated terrorist organization in Israel. A considerable part of the material held by the prosecution was collected from various classified sources. Tali Fahima petitioned the Supreme Court against the decision not to disclose this material to her. The Supreme Court rejected her petition, and in its judgment related to the prosecution's manner of examining the material in her case, complimenting it as it stated:

> *The manner, in which the prosecution handled the selection and classification of the information, and the disclosure of parts of it, was serious, intelligent, and most punctilious. It is evident from the manner of the prosecution's work in this matter that it has considered each document substantively, and generally led to the disclosure of parts of the classified information in places where this was required for the petitioner's defense.*[26]

The Court acted similarly in the case of Raad Salah and the file of the Islamic Resistance Movement who was suspected of funneling money to Hamas charity funds in what has become known as the Holy Land Foundation Case. The judgment in the *Salah* case discussed the question of privilege of the intelligence material amassed by the Shin Bet for the case, in which senior members of the Islamic Resistance Movement were charged with collecting money to finance Hamas charity funds. In this instance, the Court was satisfied with the manner in which the prosecution handled the classified material and indicated this explicitly as it complimented the State. The Court stated the following:

> I was persuaded that, in the case under discussion, the prosecution and members of the Shin Beth made wide-scale efforts in which they punctiliously and pedantically examined every piece of information included in the classified material. *I was also persuaded that the prosecution acted in the said manner sincerely out of the wish*

---

[25] Following the judgment in the Abu Saadeh case, *see* Edna Arbel, *The Prosecution Copes in a Time of Crisis*, 16 MISHPAT VETZAVA 37, 89 (2002).

[26] Misc. Crim. App. 4857/05, Fahima v. the State of Israel, Tak-El 2005 (3) 479 (emphasis added).

to fulfill its duty to disclose to the defense any pertinent information, the disclosure of which does not actually impair state security.[27]

In conclusion, overseeing the collection and potential use of probative intelligence is one of the most difficult tasks that the Court is required to undertake. In order to perform its work faithfully, the Court, and not just the Israeli court, practically depends on the prosecution as it lacks any real capacity to oversee what is taking place in the basements of the intelligence agency or agencies involved in the collection of this intelligence. The Court has no real access to the intelligence databases. The Court also lacks the personnel to examine this type of data as the quantities of material collected in these files frequently are huge. The Court also is not well versed in the methods of collecting intelligence. Nevertheless, the risks are great that an innocent individual will be convicted and that there will be damage to the credibility and legitimacy of the judicial system caused by a failure to locate material that has the potential to acquit, and a failure to disclose such information to the defense.

Accordingly, particularly in this dark and difficult niche, the Court is interested in having reinforcement players overseeing the procedures of intelligence collection. Consequently, particularly in this context, the Court intensively utilizes dialogue as a tactic that is intended to provide an incentive to prosecutors and to discipline them, so that they will monitor the Shin Bet precisely in accordance with the Court's wishes.

This is a unique dialogue. The Court conducts its dialogue with prosecutors representing the State in these cases, in an intimate manner that is unique in comparison to any other judicial system. The Court's approach toward prosecutors is personal, and the contents of this dialogue depart in many instances from the narrow legal domain. The Court converses with these players, clarifies a variety of issues with them, accepts their assistance, berates them, compliments them, requests their assistance in applying its judgments and advises them on the direction of policy. By complimenting prosecutors, the Court encourages them not to bring confessions of subjects of investigation in cases where it is concerned that the confession may have been attained in a way not recognized by the rule of law. The Court severely censures the persecution when its acts do not meet the Court's expectations that it would fulfil its duty to disclose every piece of information that could assist the accused.

The Court's intensive conversation with these players is a clear departure from classic adversarial procedure and, even more so, from any recognized legal formalism. From the Court's point of view, the advantages of this type of practice are clear and justifiable. By disciplining prosecutors, the Court is able to cause prosecutors to perform their duty to screen intelligence gathered by the Shin Bet with fear and trepidation, and to ensure that every shred of evidence that could be of assistance to the defense will be disclosed to it.

---

[27] Misc. Crim. App. 11493/03, Mahajana v. the State of Israel, PD 59(4) 193 (2004) (emphasis added).

11

Dialogue with Petitioners and Human Rights Organizations

UNTIL NOW, THE discussion of advisory dialogue has focused on the relations between the Supreme Court and the legislative authority and executive authority, including players on their behalf. These actors are practiced in understanding the sophisticated and delicate messages the Court conveys to them and are accustomed to transmitting these messages to the decision-making echelons. However, as we shall now demonstrate, the Supreme Court conducts a dialogue via its judgments as well with petitioners and the human rights organizations representing them.

The Supreme Court is aware that the Israeli and international human-rights communities read and examine its judgments, and it sets apart sections of its judgments for this audience. HCJ *On Torture* and the Court's judgment in the *Operation Cast Lead* affair include content primarily intended for this audience.[1] Supreme Court judgments pertaining to national security are translated and disseminated in other languages, and, in cases of landmark judgments, the judgment is very often translated at the time it is handed down in the courtroom. The Supreme Court is aware of this and allocates sections of the judgment for this audience. The hearing of the petition on *the Separation Barrier* is an excellent example. The hearing took place at the time that a hearing on the legality of the barrier was being conducted before the International Court of Justice. The Supreme Court had considerable interest in rendering its judgment prior to the decision from the International Court of Justice.[2] The Supreme Court also related in its judgment to issues and questions that the parties raised in the hearing at The Hague. Israel's unique international situation and the claims that pertain to its commitment to human

---

[1] *See on this subject* David Scharia, *On Torture Chambers and Acoustic Walls*, 10 POLITICA 61 (2003).
[2] NAOMI LEVITZKI, THE SUPREMES: WITHIN THE SUPREME COURT 335 (2006).

rights and humanitarian law influence the contents of Supreme Court judgments and the timing of its decisions.

The Court also utilizes this unique situation to remove objections to its use of judicial review during times of hostilities. In a lecture given by Justice Barak, for example, he made the following statements:

> In view of this, I would like to raise a question for your consideration: What is the proper degree of intervention of the Supreme Court in questions that arise while the state is fighting terrorism? Should we have discussed the question of how to deal with the bodies in Jenin and whether to allow the Red Cross to enter the [refugee] camp (the court discussed this, which led to agreement on this matter)? Should we have adjudicated the matter of the Church of the Nativity premises (this matter was heard and we decided that the state was acting in accordance with international law regarding the blockade of the church it maintained, but that the state must ensure food for unarmed civilians)?...Another petition pending before us concerns conditions of detention. In an additional petition, it was contended that IDF soldiers are shooting at medical teams of Red Cross organizations. The court heard this petition and rejected it. Is the actual hearing of the petition lawful? In another petition, the petitioners—the Physicians for Human Rights Association—complained of shooting by IDF soldiers at Red Crescent ambulances and injuring medical teams riding in the ambulances. The court obtained explanations from the military and rejected the petition. Was there room to obtain explanations?...In the Jenin case, I wrote: "This court shall not take any position with regard to the manner of conducting the fighting." And, in the case of the Church of the Nativity premises, I noted: "This court does not conduct negotiations, and does not attend such. The state's liability for this matter is imposed on the executive authority and those acting on its behalf." However, where should the limit be placed? Is it not good that the State of Israel can quote from the Supreme Court judgment in the Jenin case, in which I wrote: "The petitions contended that a massacre was perpetrated in the Jenin refugee camp...A massacre is one thing. A difficult battle is another. The respondents repeatedly indicate to us that they have nothing to conceal, and they do not seek to conceal anything. The arrangement that we reached is an expression of this position." And, it can cite from the judgment on the Church of the Nativity premises, in which I wrote: "We have examined the parties' contentions with regard to international law. We have been persuaded that with regard to all that pertains to armed Palestinians, there is no violation of these rules."[3]

---

[3] Aharon Barak, Between National Security and Individual Liberty, Address before a conference of the Israel Bar Association in Eilat (May 6, 2002).

With these statements intended for an audience likely to find in its judicial review constraint with regard to the manner of conducting the fighting, the Court clarifies the interest of this audience in conducting judicial review, if and when contentions pertaining to the military committing war crimes are brought before international forums. The Court and the audience are aware of the fact that in such cases the question of complementarity[4] and independent judicial review will be thoroughly examined.

However, the Court's dialogue with petitioners and the human rights community is not summed up by its effect on the text or rhetoric of the Court's decisions or their timing. HCJ *Cn'aan*[5] raises several additional features of the dialogue that the Court conducts with petitioners. This petition discussed the question of land appropriation by the military to arrange an area where merchandise in trucks from Israel and from the Palestinian Authority is transferred. The State's claim was that due to the fighting in the Occupied Territories, finds it difficult to deliver goods to local inhabitants to fulfill the immediate need for vital supplies for Palestinian Authority residents. In order to carry out this requirement, areas of land on which the petition turned were appropriated. The Court accepted the State's position and approved appropriation of the land. Incidental to this, the Court made the following statements:

> The question of compensation did not arise before us. Nonetheless, it seems to us that the landowners are deserving that the authorities shall compensate them for the damage caused to them. At the end of the day, the general public will benefit from the damage, which the petitioners will bear; it would therefore be right that the general public should bear the [cost of the] damages that the landowners will sustain.[6]

Two entities are addressed in this judgment. One is the Executive, which is asked to act *ex gratia* toward the petitioners and compensate them for their losses even though they have not raised this issue in their petition. A second addressee is the petitioners. Court added a text in which it addresses the petitioners, and expresses empathy with regard to the harsh effect the Court's decision has on them. Indeed, empathy and an attempt to relieve the distress of petitioners when their petition is rejected are principal elements in the Court's dialogue with petitioners.

Another case in which the Court acted in a similar manner is HCJ *Bary*.[7] This petition was lodged against the military's decision to order the cutting down of 20 trees located in an olive orchard belonging to the petitioner from which shooting at a military

---

4 According to the Rome Statute the international criminal court will only hear cases the national courts are unable or unwilling to handle. This is known as the principle of complementarity. *See* Rome Statute, Article XX.

5 HCJ 2461/01, Cna'an v. IDF Military Commander in Judea and Samaria, Pador Elyon 01 (6) 424 (2001).

6 *Id.* at 426.

7 HCJ 1321/04, Bari v. Commander of IDF Forces on the West Bank, Tak-El 2004 (1) 2394 (2004).

vehicle had occurred. The trees at this site apparently served as shelter for the perpetrators. In this case, too, the Court rejected the petition in substance. However, the Court added the following remark at the end of the judgment:

> The attorney for the state declared that if a claim for compensation due to the damage is filed, the Attorney General Office will examine it substantively and, it may be assumed, *in a sympathetic spirit*.[8] [emphasis added]

The State did not dispute its actual duty to compensate the owners of the orchard. However, the Court added the words *in a sympathetic spirit* to signal the Executive that it must act generously when the question of compensation was heard.

The Court again acted similarly in HCJ *Al'ouna*, which discussed the question of the legitimacy of checkpoints that were set up around the city of Nablus in view of the large wave of terrorist attacks that originated there. The Court rejected the petition but incidental to the rejection added the following statements:

> *We have heard the contentions of the attorneys of the petitioners. With all the empathy we have vis-à-vis the petitioners—and, all, or at least most, of them have not transgressed—we have not found grounds to inform the respondent that the acts it performed diverge from the realm of reasonableness or proper proportionality.* [emphasis added][9]

Expressing empathy is one of the central messages that the Court conveys to petitioners who appear with claims regarding human rights violations. This stands out in view of the fact that the absolute majority of their petitions are rejected.

INVITATIONS TO OVERRIDE

Another type of message that the Court conveys to petitioners bears more substantive contents. This is when the Court invites petitioners to challenge its decision: "invitations to override" could be transmitted to the Executive or Legislature but they could also be transmitted to petitioners. An "invitation to override" is a message conveyed alongside the Court's decision to reject a certain petition, in which the Court invites the petitioners to challenge its decision. In a discussion in previous chapters, we saw how the Court "invites" the other two branches to alter its decision by way of "positive signaling" pertaining to the possibility of legislating an arrangement that will overturn, in practice, the Court's decision. With respect to petitioners, the occasions on which the Court proposes to petitioners to challenge its decision can be varied and diverse.

---

[8] *Id.* at 2395.
[9] HCJ 2847/03, Al'ouna v. the Commander of IDF Forces in Judea and Samaria, Tak-El 2003 (2) 3829 (2003).

One tactic for an implied invitation is to reject petitions without creating a precedent, by giving a judgment that does not relate to the depth of the legal questions ensuing from the petition. These are judgments consisting of two lines in which the Court rejects petitions at times by the use of the well-known term *we are satisfied*.[10] In this manner, the Court enables the return of the petitioners or of other petitioners to court with the same actual issue. In many cases, the Court gave a judgment that was summed up by the words *we are satisfied* even though the Court held an in-depth discussion of the matter. Rejecting the petition in the absence of an actual judgment precludes the State from relying on it when the subject is raised again for a hearing and from contending res judicata. Such conduct may be construed as a message to petitioners that the Court indeed did not want to decide the matter in their favor at this time. Nonetheless, the Court is not interested in having those petitioning on this issue stay away from court.

In this way, petitioners can bring the matter for a hearing a second time. In the event that the Court feels it cannot accept the petition, whether due to circumstances of security or the state of hostilities, or because the Court is unable to obtain a sufficiently clear, factual picture due to the intense fighting, it could feel open enough to do so if and when the petitioners accept this invitation. Indeed, one of the most important advantages of advisory dialogue is that it allows the Court to time landmark decisions to calmer periods where it could get all the information it needs and minimize opposition to its decision.

The tactic works as follows: On the one hand, the Court signals the parties and, in particular, the petitioner, that it has not yet concluded its say on the matter, and its conclusion may change in the future. On the other hand, this message is conveyed without the Court having to introduce itself at the stage of "the summons" into a conflict with the Executive or legislature. This allows the Court "to intimate" to the petitioners that due to the state of hostilities, the political situation, or the lack of information, the Court is unable to grant their request now. However, perhaps at a future date, the Court may be able to re-examine the matter raised in the petition.

In judgments pertaining to national security given in a time of heightened hostilities, several examples have been found in which the Court not only encourages the petitioners to return the issue for a hearing before the Court or intimates its willingness to re-examine its decision, but also explicitly invites the petitioners to do so. We have seen, for example, how the Court invited the petitioners to bring the issue of the method for oversight of Shin Bet investigations for another hearing, if this method were not removed from the influence of the Shin Bet and transferred to the Ministry of Justice. Another instance in which the Court used this tactic was during Operation Defensive Shield. When the operation began, a petition was lodged against the legitimacy of the order

---

[10] Michael Sfard, a prominent human rights advocate representing many of these nongovernmental organizations, told the author that he calls these decisions "the Satisfaction Rule" (borrowed from the use the Court makes of the term *we are satisfied*).

that directed mass arrests, at the end of which, as may be recalled, the Court revoked principal parts of the order. It is interesting to note that several days earlier, a similar petition was lodged that sought to have the order canceled. The petition was submitted on Friday, April 5, 2002, at the height of the fighting and was heard and already decided on April 7, 2002. In this judgment, the Court rejected the petition. Nonetheless, the Court "invited" the petitioners to raise the subject for a hearing at another time that would be more convenient. I cite the following statements of the Court:

> In our opinion, it is inconceivable that while hostilities are ongoing and proximate thereto, the respondent will allow a meeting with attorneys for persons with respect to whom there is concern that they jeopardize or are likely to jeopardize the security of the area, the security of the IDF forces or the security of the public, as long as conditions are not ripe, which would enable consideration of the individual circumstances of each and every detainee. And, we have found no grounds—within the confines of the general petition that was submitted to us—to give the petitioners an order *nisi*.
>
> *Nonetheless, it is clear that, within a reasonable time, when conditions come about that will allow taking into account the individual circumstances of a detainee, the respondent shall be obliged to consider whether there are grounds to give an order prohibiting a meeting with regard to any particular detainee.* [emphasis added][11]

Indeed, about a week later the human rights organizations lodged an additional petition that generated a similar discussion. It was heard primarily following the conclusion of Operation Defensive Shield, and, as stated above, the Court eventually revoked principal sections of the order.[12]

Another case that illustrates this approach is HCJ *Elrazi*,[13] which concerned the possibility of study abroad for students who are residents of the Occupied Territories, and who may be suspected of terrorist activity. The Court sensed that in view of the difficult security situation at the time of the hearing, it was not possible to accept the petition, but, at the same time, it invited the petitioners to raise the subject again at a later date. Justice Mazza delivered an advisory message at the end of his judgment that the Court's position was likely to change, as he indicated the hope[14] that when circumstances did change, it would be possible to allow the petitioners to depart for their studies.[15]

---

[11] HCJ 2901/02, HaMoked: The Center for the Defense of the Individual et al. v. the Commander of IDF Forces in the West Bank, PD 56 (3) 19, 21–22 (2002).

[12] HCJ 3239/02, Marav v. the IDF Commander, PD 57(2) (2002).

[13] HCJ 7960/04, Elrazi v. the Commander of IDF Forces—Gaza Strip (unpublished, Sept. 29, 2004).

[14] "We must hope that with a change in the times, some of the petitioners, whose sole objective is indeed to study occupational therapy, will be able to renew their applications with regard to the programs of study at Bethlehem University." *Id.*

[15] Naomi Levitzki notes that Justice Mazza later regretted this position. LEVITZKI, *supra* note 2, at 129.

A rare example of the practice of inviting petitioners to return with an issue for a hearing is seen in the case of *Natasha*.[16] This petition concerns the question of the length of detention periods of security prisoners until they are brought before a judge. The petition itself was heard on February 26, 2002. That particular month was one in which terror claimed a high price in terms of the number and intensity of terrorist attacks that Israel suffered during the al-Aqsa Intifada; a total of 31 Israelis were killed. The Court rejected the petition after receiving the affidavit of the head of the Investigations Department of the Shin Bet. According to the affidavit, it was impossible to curtail the period of detention due to the difficult security situation that prevailed in the occupied territories. However, on rejecting the petition, the Court added the following words:

> After studying the contentions of the parties…we have reached the general conclusion that there is no reason *__at this time__* for the intervention of this court in curtailing the period of maximum detention until a detainee in the territories is brought before a military judge.[17] [emphasis in original][18]

It is worth highlighting three points here. First, the emphasis on the words *at this time* and underlining them as well appeared in the original decision—which is unusual and exceptional in the Israeli court practice at that time. This can reveal the Court's frame of mind with regard to the question under discussion, and the Court's wish that the petitioners grasp the message that at a suitable time, it would be well if they would bring the matter again for a hearing before the Court. When a Supreme Court justice emphasizes a certain message in her original decision by stressing the written word and adding underlining to further highlight it, this can only be understood as a wish that the petitioners will read this message and reach the appropriate conclusions. Second, adding the words *at this time* and underscoring them is a clear signal not only to the petitioners but also to the players who represent the Executive that the decision is likely to change in the future. Third, this invitation comprises an indication that the Court is most likely aware of the question of timing and its effect on judicial decision-making, at least within the realm of national security. In this case, the Court "has confessed" that the difficult timing makes intervention unsuitable. However, at another time, which is more convenient, the Court is likely to intervene in the matter.

---

[16] HCJ 2307/00, Natasha v. the Commander of IDF Forces in the West Bank, Tak-El 2002 (1) 979 (2002).

[17] *Id.*

[18] In the Takdin law cache, the words *at this time* appear without emphasis. However, in the original judgment of the Court, as it was publicized on the website of the Supreme Court and as it was distributed to the parties, these words are emphasized by being underlined.

12

Dialogue with Victims of Terrorism, Families of Soldiers, and

Bereaved Families

A DISCUSSION OF Supreme Court dialogue cannot conclude without a look at the dialogue that the Court conducts with victims of terrorism, families of Israel Defense Force (IDF) combatants who were captured, or IDF soldiers who fell in battle.

In Israeli society, the status of terror victims and bereaved families has undergone a major transformation. In the 1950s and 1960s, the bereaved were deemed part of national culture. Wars, such as the Yom Kippur War and the Lebanon war, led to a loss of faith in the government's ability to make decisions with regard to entering into war as well as avoiding it. This, in addition to other changes in Israeli society, led to a view of bereavement that emphasizes the individual, at times as distinct from the State and, at times, even in opposition to the State.[1] Together with the changes that occurred, we can include the willingness of bereaved families to approach the Supreme Court to seek relief there. At times, the victims or their families, groups of victims, or organizations for victims will approach the Court directly. Petitions submitted by bereaved families help the families to insist on their rights, no less than voicing their concerns to the Court and expressing pain and protest. Often the proceeding in the Supreme Court serves as a basis for a discourse of anger and bitterness directed at the government or its representatives. The Court is not only aware of this but frequently accommodates such petitions by conducting a direct dialogue with the families and allowing them to utilize the judicial

---

[1] *See further on this subject* Oz Almog, *Monuments to War Victims in Israel: A Semiological Analysis*, MEGAMOT 34 (2) 179 (1992) as well as Eliezer Witztum & Rut Malkinson, *Bereavement and Memorialization: The Dual Face of the National Myth, in* LOSS AND BEREAVEMENT IN ISRAELI SOCIETY 231(Eliezer Witztum & Rut Malkinson eds., 1993).

proceeding, which receives a great deal of exposure, as a platform for airing their claims, pain, and anger.[2]

Although most of the petitions submitted by bereaved families are rejected in the end, this dialogue nevertheless has an important aspect to it. Terror victims, terror victims' rights organizations that represent them, and families of fallen soldiers have a unique and sacred status in Israeli society. Many in Israel have lost a family member or a friend in a terror attack or war. In addition, they have the ability to affect processes that are conducted outside of the courtroom and the formation of national policy.

The Court conducts an intensive dialogue with terror victims and families of fallen soldiers. As I will demonstrate here, the Court assigns considerable parts of its judgment for this dialogue. Although, the pragmatic aspect does not escape the eyes of the Court, the center of gravity of such dialogue lies in the parts of its judgment dedicated to assuaging the pain of the victims of terror and their families and persuading them of the justice of the decision. These are these sections of the judgment that serve the Court to express empathy and identify with the victims' grief and anguish.

An article published by judge and theoretician Richard Posner[3] suggests distinguishing between two typical writing styles of judges. He calls the first style "pure" and the second style "impure." Posner argues that the pure writing style is characterized by text that is focused on a legal-technical analysis of the issue brought for hearing, and it is intended for cases in which the audience of readers to whom the judge directs the judgment is proficient in law and legal analysis. Posner refers to this audience as *Legal Insiders*.[4] This style is characterized by legal-technical language, numerous reference citations, analysis of the issue, and neutral writing. In contrast, judges tend to formulate judgments with impure wording where the target audience is a broader circle that includes people who do not understand legal nuances. In such cases, the text is characterized by writing whose purpose is to persuade those who are not skilled in the mysteries of the law of the correctness of the legal conclusion. The text lacks references and the Court attempts to address the reader's feelings in order to persuade him or her to take the legal outcome to heart. Posner writes the following:

> "Voice" goes with "ear." We should therefore expect the choice of styles to be influenced by the "implied audience" for a judicial opinion—the audience at which the judge seems particularly to be aiming. For many judges the implied audience consists primarily of the judge or judges of the lower court whose decision is being

---

[2] *See, e.g.*, the words of the Court in HCJ 3900/02, Israel Trauma Center for Victims of Terror and War v. Ariel Sharon (unpublished, May 8, 2002). "We understand the hearts of the petitioners. Their pain is harsh. Their fury is great… The pain and anger of the petitioners in these circumstances may be expressed to political and social entities. As for us—we are unable to redeem them."

[3] *See* Richard A. Posner, *Judicial Opinion Writing: Judges' Writing Styles and Do They Matter?*, 62 U. Chi. L. Rev. 1421 (1995).

[4] *Id.* at 1431.

reviewed and the lawyers for the parties. Anyone else is an (authorized) eaves-dropper. The lawyers and the lower court judge are the most knowledgeable and interested professional consumers of the appellate court's opinion. Consummate insiders, they are adept in reading (including reading between the lines of) a "pure" judicial opinion. The author wants to persuade them that in reaching its result the Court has carefully considered all the points in the case and has not deviated from "the law" in the typical sense in which the lawyers and the lower court judge will have conceived it—has not pulled any rabbits out of hats...At the other extreme of the stylistic spectrum, the primary implied audience of the most boldly impure judicial stylist consists not of legal insiders but of those readers, both lay people and lawyers, who can "see through" the artifice of judicial pretension.[5]

This distinction is particularly appropriate when analyzing judgments of the Israeli Supreme Court that deal with national security, and particularly those in which the victims of terror or families of fallen soldiers are part of the proceeding. These judgments illustrate how the Court at a certain point abandons the "pure" legal writing style and opens up direct discourse with the broad circle of the persons involved in the petition in an attempt to persuade them of the justice of the judicial ruling. The dialogue accurately demonstrates to what extent the Supreme Court's viewpoint is ingrained—that its judgments are part of a discourse whose humaneness, sensitivity, and expression of empathy are clearly evident.

The *Bargaining Chips* case[6] provides a good example of direct dialogue that is focused on expressing empathy. Here, the Court conducted an intensive dialogue in its judgment with families of soldiers being held hostage and families of soldiers missing in action in an attempt to persuade them of the ruling's justice and necessity:

> I am aware of the suffering of families of IDF captives and of those missing in action. Their pain is vast. The passing of the years and the uncertainty wound a person's soul. Even more painful is the situation of a hostage, who is being held clandestinely in hiding, torn away from his home and country. Indeed, this pain, together with the supreme interest of the State of Israel to return its sons to its borders, is not unknown to me.... We bear the human and social tragedy in being held hostage and in being missing in action on our shoulders day in and day out. However, as much as the objective of freeing hostages and those missing in action is important, it is unable—within the framework of the law under discussion in this hearing—to justify any means. It is unfeasible—in the legal situation before us—to rectify a wrong with another wrong. I trust and I am certain that the State

---

[5] *Id.* at 1431.
[6] Crim FH, 7048/97, Anonymous v. Minister of Defense, IsrSC 54(1) 721 (2000)

of Israel will not rest until it finds a way to resolve this painful issue. As a state and as a society, we may take comfort in knowing that the path toward a solution will befit our fundamental values.[7]

This "public speaking" almost sermon-like tone is very typical to judgments dealing with such cases.

The same was true later in this affair with reference to the request of Dirani and Obeid (HCJ *Obeid*)[8] for permission to meet with representatives of the Red Cross. In this case, the families of IDF soldiers who were missing in action or being held hostage expressed outrage at the Court's decision in view of the fact that IDF prisoners held by Hezbollah were not granted this basic right. The legal question up for discussion was whether Section 143 of the Fourth Geneva Convention applies with respect to the protection of civilians during times of war; this section grants a right to prisoners of war to meet with Red Cross representatives. At the beginning of the hearing, the Court was informed that the IDF Chief of Staff believed that petitioners should not be granted meetings with Red Cross personnel. The position of the Attorney General differed, as he maintained that taking into consideration all the circumstances of the matter, the meeting ought to be permitted. The petition was heard in view of these differences of opinion, and the family of the kidnapped navigator Ron Arad requested to join as a respondent to the petition.

While the petition was pending, three IDF soldiers were abducted by Hezbollah. Soon after, Hezbollah also abducted Colonel (Reserve) Elhanan Tenenbaum. Hezbollah refused to transmit to Israel any information with regard to the abductees, including their health and welfare. In addition, Hezbollah refused to allow any Red Cross representatives to visit. Under these circumstances, the Attorney General concluded that it was unreasonable to allow Red Cross representatives to visit the petitioners and retracted his original position. In its judgment, the Court rejected the Attorney General's position and decided to allow the meeting with the Red Cross. The Court determined that the meeting ought to be permitted; however, at the end of the judgment, Justice Barak added the following statements:

> *It was not easy for us to reach our decision.* We are aware of the efforts being made in the matter of Ron Arad and our abducted soldiers and citizens. We are convinced that our judgment herein will not harm these efforts. Being convinced as such allows us, in the comprehensive balance of considerations, to determine that humanitarian considerations shall prevail. [emphasis added][9]

---

[7] *Id.* at 744–45.

[8] HCJ 794/98, Obeid v. Minister of Defence, PD 55(5) 769 (2001).

[9] *Id.* at 773–74.

And, in a personal note to the Arad family, the Court added the following:

> *In reaching this conclusion, we understand the feelings of the Arad family. We listened with emotion to the pleadings of Ron Arad's mother and brothers.* In any dispute with them, their view shall always have the upper hand. However, the State of Israel has no dispute with the Arad family. The State has made every effort in the past and will continue to do so in future to obtain information with regard to our men being held in captivity and our men missing in action. [emphasis added][10]

From the contents of these statements and the language the Court used, it appears that Justice Barak sought to mollify the families of the men being held in captivity, even if minimally, by addressing them directly.

The discussion, as well, of the question of permission to screen the film *Jenin, Jenin* mentioned above was held with the active involvement of families of soldiers who were killed in the battle and their comrades-in-arms. Several of these families and some of the combatants joined the petition as respondents and contended that the film constitutes a blood libel against them. During the hearing, the Court allowed family members and combatants to speak. In the course of the hearing Hagi Tal, brother of Ro'i Tal who was killed in Jenin, made the following statements:

> You are judges but you are also human beings. You should understand what we as bereaved families are experiencing. When my brother was killed, my life stopped and moved onto another track completely, to a path of darkness. I searched for something to hold onto and I am here to protect my brother's legacy, who, at that time, fought to protect me. If he were here today, he would have wanted to say that he has the right to defend his good name. I watched the film. It is entirely a blood libel, maliciously intended to turn the soldiers and my brother into war criminals. My little brother could have been the son of any one of you. He was aware of where he was going and for what values he was fighting. He went, and so did the others, in the knowledge that they are going to give their lives and we are forbidden to forget who sent them. Is this film our certificate of honor for them? I am not standing in a court of law in Belgium. I am standing in a court of law in Jerusalem.[11]

The judgment in the *Jenin, Jenin* case centered for the most part on questions of the limits of protecting freedom of speech. Nonetheless, the Court was not satisfied solely with the binding legal conclusion that the movie should be published, and responded in

---

[10] *Id.*

[11] *See* Efrat Weiss, *The Bereaved Families against "Jenin, Jenin"*, YNET, Mar. 20, 2003, *available at* www.ynet. co.il/1,7340,L-2507177,00.html.

the judgment to arguments of the bereaved families and the families of combatants by using language intended to persuade them of the necessity of the legal conclusion:

> We understand the pain of the bereaved families and the difficult feelings of the combatants. The failure to disqualify the film does not constitute indifference to these sensibilities or any diminishing of the appreciation and esteem for their contribution to the security of the State. The matter also does not signify the provision of any approval for the contents of the film. Only that it is proper that the respondents shall also focus their efforts—as they have indeed done and with a considerable measure of success—on coping with the claimed injury, in the arena of freedom of speech.[12]

The Court converses with families and combatants in the *Jenin* case and explains in non-legal language that the Court is a partner to their pain and that its decision by no means signals approval of the film. The judgment departs to a large degree from that which is customary, as the Court "invites" the families and the combatants to deal with the film in other areas outside of the sphere of influence of the High Court of Justice.

Another subject that has repeatedly arisen before the Court for many years is the release of prisoners in accordance with various political arrangements that the State of Israel has reached with other governments or at times with terrorist organizations. The Supreme Court has never intervened in such decisions, and the judgments it has given over the years do not leave any opportunity for future intervention of any kind. Nonetheless, notwithstanding the foreseeable outcome, there is a fixed ritual in Israel where, together with media reports of impending deals of prisoners' exchange, victims of terror and their families, who fear that the perpetrators of terrorist attacks against them will be released in the impending deal, lodge petitions in the Supreme Court. These petitions generally attract a great deal of public attention. The petitions may be filed only following a government decision to enter into an agreement to release terrorists held prisoner and are heard between the date of the decision and the date of actual release. By the nature of things, from the moment the government has entered into an agreement, it is in its interest to carry out the agreement at the earliest possible time. The only obstacle remaining at this point between the government's decision and the actual prisoner release is the petition that has been submitted to the Court on this matter.

Despite the Court's reluctance to intervene in a government decision on this issue and its clear position that such decisions are for the Executive to make without almost any room for a court intervention, the Court makes certain to summon an urgent hearing; conduct oral briefings where it allows the victims' families to speak, usually before dozens of journalists attending the hearing; and devote several paragraphs in its judgments

---

[12] HCJ 316/03, Bakri v. Film Review Council, PD 58 (1) 249, 270 (2003).

to a dialogue with the bereaved families. In these sections, the Court addresses the families directly and attempts to persuade them of the justice of the Court's decision not to intervene in the government decision to release the prisoners.

Most of these judgments are constructed of a brief presentation of the legal grounds clarifying why there is no cause for the Court's intervention and making the families partner to the difficulty the Court faced in reaching this decision not to cancel the government's decision. The Court acted in this manner with regard to petitions submitted during the release of prisoners pursuant to the Oslo Accords, when it described the argument of the representative of the families as "difficult, extremely difficult—difficult and onerous"[13] and similarly again when prisoners were released following an agreement reached with the Palestinian Authority on achieving a period of calm during the intifada.[14]

One of the most difficult hearings ever to take place in the Supreme Court on this issue occurred on the eve of the release of IDF soldier Gilad Shalit, who was held hostage by Hamas. On October 11, 2011, the government of Israel made the decision to enter into an agreement with Hamas for Shalit's release. Immediately thereafter, representatives of bereaved families lodged a petition with the aim of preventing the agreement, which called for the soldier's release in exchange for the release of 1,027 Hamas activists, most of whom had been convicted of terrorist activities. The details of the prisoners slated for release were published only on October 15, 2011, in the late hours of the evening, and the agreement was to be carried out on October 18, 2011. On October 17, 2011, during the Sukkot holiday, the Court held a hearing on the petition while the eyes of the entire world were waiting for its judgment. The petitioners contended that their rights as terror victims had been violated as the government decided to pardon these convicted terrorists. This schedule, as the Court indicated, obliged the Court to give its judgment "within a matter of several hours,"[15] as the schedule was part of the agreement, and any amendment was likely to thwart implementation of the agreement and might jeopardize the life of Gilad Shalit.

The Court was not deterred by this schedule. The Court opened its judgment with the following words, as it stated that the hearing of this file was "one of the most charged and disturbing hearings that ever came before this court." Thereafter, the Court deliberated with regard to the legal arguments, which the petitioners brought, and rejected each and every one of them. The Court explained that only in the rarest cases would the Court intervene in a government decision to enter into a political agreement, and then went on to explain to the families and to the public why it had no choice but to reject the petition.[16]

---

[13] HCJ 9290/99, M.M.T. Center for Victims of Terrorist Attacks v. the State of Israel, PD 54(1) 8, 17 (1999).

[14] HCJ 1671/05, Almagor—Terror Victims Association v. the Government of Israel, PD 59 (5) 913, 916 (2005).

[15] Para. 2 of the judgment.

[16] HCJ 7523/11, Almagor Terror Victims Association v. the Prime Minister, para. 4 of the judgment.

The fact that the Court's policy of nonintervention in these issues is well established illustrates how its judgments serve as a platform for discourse with bereaved families and an opportunity to express empathy with their pain, each time the government decides to release prisoners from incarceration.

A final example of how far the Court is willing to go in identifying with bereaved families and expressing empathy relates to the terrorist attack that occurred on March 5, 2003, on Sderot Moriah in Haifa. In this incident, Munir Rajabi was indicted for having the knowledge that his brother was planning a suicide attack in Haifa and driving him to his destination, where the suicide bomber finally exploded on a bus and caused the deaths of 17 people—most of whom were children and adolescents on their way home from school. In the hearing in the District Court, the prosecution reached a plea bargain with Munir Rajabi, according to which he admitted the offenses with which he was charged—a confession that led to his conviction and a life sentence.[17] One of the bereaved parents, Benjamin Fierstetter, father of Smadar Fierstetter who was killed in the attack, was furious with the prosecution's decision to reach a plea bargain and submitted on behalf of himself and his family an appeal to the Supreme Court. The father claimed that the State's decision to reach a plea bargain ensued from its wish to shield a complete failure of the Shin Bet, which was aware of the impending terrorist attack but failed to prevent it.

It should be underscored that according to criminal procedure in Israel, family members of terror victims have no formal standing in criminal law except for the rights granted to them according to the Rights of Victims of Crime Law.[18] Therefore, the appeal ostensibly should have been struck out *in limine*. However, the Court (with the government's consent) decided to deliberate the evidence disclosed in the file and examine the classified material gathered by the Shin Bet, all to try to placate even minimally the rage and shock of the bereaved father. The Court even indicated in its judgment expressly that in the hearing of this matter:

> *We have unloaded, as an unusual and exceptional instance due to the circumstances, and in light of the agreement of the respondents, the onus of the rules of procedure,* with the intention of addressing the principal issue and not with legal questions that are important in and of themselves. [emphasis added][19]

The entire aim of the unusual proceedings was to placate the petitioner, even though, unfortunately, and as the Court attested in the judgment, it did not succeed in doing so. At the end of the judgment, the Court related to the proceeding that it heard as follows:

---

[17] *See* Haifa Criminal File (Haifa) 189/03, State of Israel v. Rajabi, Tak-Machozi 2004(1) 873 (2004).

[18] The Rights of Victims of Crime Law, 5761-2001.

[19] Criminal Appeal 2046/04, Fierstetter v. the State of Israel, Tak-El 2005 (1) 3903.

We are unable to offer any relief for the gaping wounds. However, in these circumstances, in order to alleviate even minimally the burden of the grave tragedy that has befallen the families who have lost their loved ones, we have deemed it proper to accede to the appellants request. We shall examine, with the agreement of the State, the material of the investigation, *notwithstanding that the proceeding undertaken by the appellants before us has no anchor in the rules of procedure.* Subsequent to performing this investigation, we shall be able to say to the appellants and by way thereof to the other families as well that the terrorist attack on Bus Line 37 in Haifa was investigated most diligently by the various investigating bodies. [emphasis added][20]

In conclusion, in judgments that concern the loss of relatives and loved ones, the Court often breaks through the customary limits of dialogue or legal practice and directly addresses the petitioners—the victims of terrorism, bereaved families, or soldiers—and converses with them. The judgment serves the Court as a means of dialogue with the families and, by way of the judgment, to convey a sense of empathy, identification, and sharing on the Court's part, even if the message that is conveyed has no operative meaning apart from this. This discourse allows the Court to persuade the bereaved families of the justice of the decision or at least of its being unavoidable. The Court seeks to persuade the families that the Court shares in their pain, and the decision not to grant their petition has been made, nonetheless, out of a sense of a shared common fate and pain. Often, the profound sensitivity that the Court demonstrates in the dialogue it holds with the victims of terrorism leaves one with the sense that in cases where these families are involved, the legal hearing and subsequent judgment are intended primarily as a conversation, as one person to another. In most cases, the Court does not give these bereaved families the relief that they have sought. Nonetheless, focusing on the bottom line overlooks what actually transpired in the proceeding that was held in court. The proceeding demonstrates the Court's commitment to provide relief in real time to the party that requires it. It also illustrates its commitment to hearing the claims of the victims of terrorism and to confirming their feeling that there are justices in Jerusalem who are willing to listen to their pain and sorrow.

---

[20] *Id.* at para. 10 of the judgment; *see also* Criminal Appeal 1932/04, Rajabi v. the State of Israel, Tak-El 2005(2) 187 (2005).

13

Judicial Review through Dialogue in Israel

JUDICIAL REVIEW OF national security issues poses significant challenges for every legal system. It requires adjudication of complex questions under a veil of uncertainty and in the knowledge that, generally, the public, the goverment, and the security forces will not support their position, certainly not when a large terrorist attack has recently occurred or when the country is in a state of emergency. It is even more challenging for a court seeking to make use of judicial review in real time and inclined not to be satisfied with rulings made after the fact that are given years after the relevant events. The Israeli Supreme Court sees itself committed to full judicial review of how the State handles decisions concerning national security, and it hastens to give its decisions at a time as close to the events as possible, with the intention of influencing national security policy and protecting human rights in real time. This is a huge challenge that requires tactics of judicial review that are not exhausted by conventional methods.

Debate over inter-branch dialogue is not unique to Israel. Other countries face similar dilemmas. India and[1] Germany,[2] for example, secured in their constitutions the authority of their Supreme Courts to offer advice and make recommendations on constitutional questions. In England, the Human Rights Act secures a concept of dialogue in relations between the courts and Parliament,[3] whereas Canada secured it in its Charter of Rights and Freedoms. Canada's Charter not only uses language that encourages inter-branch dialogue[4] but also offers means that allow the legislative authority to respond

---

[1] Article 143 of the Constitution of India.
[2] Article 83 of the Constitution of Germany.
[3] Conor A. Gearty, *Reconciling Parliamentary Democracy and Human Rights*, 118 L.Q. REV. 248 (2002).
[4] Articles 1 and 33 of the Canadian Charter.

to court judgments.[5] As a result, extensive literature has developed that discusses the dialogue between the Supreme Court of Canada and the parliament or the Executive.[6]

Certain US states[7] also have a state constitution that allows the courts to provide an advisory opinion, but such opinions are generally not deemed as binding.[8] In contrast, the US federal judicial system assumes that the Supreme Court must refrain from offering advice to other government agencies with regard to how they are to use their powers. As Ronald J. Krotoszynski notes, the prohibition has been in effect in the United States almost as long as the US Constitution. On July 18, 1793, Thomas Jefferson, on behalf of George Washington, wrote to Justice John Jay, Chief Justice of the Supreme Court at that time. Jefferson asked Justice Jay to convene a meeting of the Supreme Court justices so that they could present their positions to him with regard to the effect of the war between Britain and France on the United States. In response, Justice Jay wrote that Washington's request conflicts with Article 2 of the US Constitution, which sets up the Executive authority and defines the separation of powers among it, the legislature, and the judiciary.[9]

More than a hundred years later, in the *Muskrat* case,[10] the Supreme Court gave effect to this position, as it dismissed a claim submitted to it, on the grounds that in the absence of "a real dispute" on the issue that the Supreme Court had been asked to decide,

---

[5] A further means to encourage constitutional dialogue is the determination that the validity of parliamentary decisions, which rescind judicial decisions by making use of Article 33 of the Charter, is limited solely to five years. Thereafter, if parliament so wishes, it must revive the law. *See further* Christine Bateup, *Expanding the Conversation: American and Canadian Experiences of Constitutional Dialogue in Comparative Perspective*, 21 TEMP INT'L & COMP. L.J. 1, 7 (2007).

[6] *See* Tsvi Kahana, *Understanding the Notwithstanding Mechanism*, 52 UNIV. TORONTO L.J. 221 (2002); as well as Robert C. Post & Reva B. Siegel, *Popular Constitutionalism, Departmentalism and Judicial Supremacy*, 92 CAL. L. REV. 1027, 1041 (2004). *See also* KENT ROACH, THE SUPREME COURT ON TRIAL (2001) and Kent Roach, *Constitutional and Common Law Dialogues between the Supreme Court and Canadian Legislatures*, 80 CAN. BAR REV. 481 (2001). For an empirical study examining the dialogue in the Canadian context, *see* Peter W. Hogg & Allison A. Bushell, *The Charter Dialogue between Courts and Legislatures*, 35 OSGOODE HALL L.J. 75 (1997).

[7] States in which this authority is granted are: Colorado, Maine, Florida, Massachusetts, New Hampshire, Rhode Island, South Dakota, Alabama, and Delaware. In North Carolina, the court gives directed opinions without there being explicit authorization for this in the state constitution. *See also* Jonathan D. Persky, *Ghosts That Slay: A Contemporary Look at State Advisory Opinions*, 37 CONN. L. REV. 1155 (2005). *See also* Cynthia R. Farina, *Supreme Judicial Court Advisory Opinions: Two Centuries of Interbranch Dialogue*, in THE HISTORY OF THE LAW IN MASSACHUSETTS: THE SUPREME JUDICIAL COURT 1692–1992, at 353 (Russell K. Osgood ed., 1992).

[8] The customary concept is that on giving such an opinion, the court does not act as a court of law but rather as a legal adviser to the government. *See* Ronald J. Krotoszynski, *Constitutional Flares: On Judges, Legislatures and Dialogue*, 83 MINN. L. REV. 1 (1998). According to him, "In giving such opinions, the Justices do not act as a court, but as the constitutional advisers of the other departments of the government, and it has never been considered essential that the questions proposed should be such as might come before them in their judicial capacity" (at 28).

[9] *Id.* at 16.

[10] Muskrat v. United States, 219 U.S. 346 (1911).

any outcome that the Court would reach would be deemed as advisory and contrary to Article 3 of the US Constitution. Article 3 requires the Supreme Court to decide real disputes.[11] The rationale at the basis of this clear position of the US legal system is that judges are not intended to participate in legislative acts and apply the force of legislation directly or indirectly. Separation of powers according to this decision of the US Supreme Court requires that the three branches (judiciary, legislature, and Executive) must refrain from intervening in each other's powers. Accordingly, the courts too must refrain from giving advice to the Executive or Congress. It should be noted though that despite the decision in the *Muskrat* case, US Supreme Court justices continued to give advice on many different issues.[12]

FEATURES OF INTER-BRANCH DIALOGUE IN NATIONAL SECURITY CASES IN ISRAEL

Although not the only Court relying on dialogue as a tool, the approach adopted by the Israeli one is unique and most likely could not be adopted as-is by any other legal system. It is characterized by intensive use of dialogue alongside of and, at times, as an alternative to conventional judicial review. The centrality of dialogue follows from the various means that serve the Court to transmit messages, the significance of the messages conveyed through dialogue, the multiplicity of players participating in the dialogue, its intensity, and its influence on the manner of the use of judicial review.

In order to meet the challenge of reviewing national security in real time the Court conducts dialogue with any player who can have an impact on Israel's national security policy. This dialogue is not limited to "constitutional" players and does not necessarily include constitutional messages. In many cases, the messages bear policy contents addressed to the bodies intended to apply the judgment. The Court transmits messages repeatedly to the Attorney General, the prosecution, or the military. Often the addressees of the messages are not entities and organizations but rather flesh-and-blood specific players, who appear before the Court. The Court does not hesitate to convey messages directly to the players representing these bodies, who are intended to act so that the specific body pertaining to the matter (Shin Bet, military commanders, etc.) will apply the Court's decisions. The Court also expands the limits of dialogue to include petitioners,

---

[11] Article 3 of the US Constitution prescribes that the Supreme Court has the power to hear "controversies to which the United States shall be a Party." In the *Muskrat* case, the term *controversy* was interpreted so that the power of the court is conditioned on the existence of a real and pending dispute.

[12] *See, e.g.*, Lori Hausegger & Lawrence Baum, Inviting Congressional Action: A Study of Supreme Court Motivations in Statutory Interpretation, 43 Am. J. Political Sci. (1999); Neal Katyal, *Judges as Advicegivers*, 50 Stan. L. Rev. 1709 (1998); Ronald J. Krotoszynski, *Constitutional Flares: On Judges, Legislatures and Dialogue*, 83 Minn. L. Rev. 1 (1998).

human rights organizations representing petitioners, soldiers, military commanders, and members of their families, as well as the families of the victims of terrorism.

In most other countries inter-branch dialogue is viewed as abstract inter-organizational dialogue. According to this view, the Court makes decisions that stimulate response of the Executive or legislature, and these bodies respond by applying the judgment, construing the messages included in a decision or overturning the judgment by way of new legislation. Here, a Supreme Court decision that a certain law is unconstitutional or that a certain policy conflicts with the interpretation of the law is the principal means of expression. This approach to dialogue further assumes that a court decision that invalidates a policy or that determines that a certain law contradicts the constitution is part of the ongoing dialogue that occurs in this manner. First, a law is enacted or a policy is adopted; then, the Court may determine that the law is unconstitutional or that the policy is unlawful; finally, the legislature or the Executive formulates a new law or policy in response to the Supreme Court proceeding, and so on. Each such course of action is part of an ongoing dialogue that takes place among the different branches of government.

However, the discussion in previous chapters demonstrates that the classic theory of dialogue does not aptly describe the Israeli Supreme Court's practical conduct with regard to national security. The discussion above indicates that the Supreme Court, along with classic dialogue, conducts a conscious, concrete, and active "conversation" with other branches. This dialogue occurs during the course of a legal proceeding and upon its conclusion. One such example, out of many, was, as we saw, a dialogue that actually occurred as a conversation in the judgment of Justice Barak in the *Paritzky* case. Here, Justice Barak directly addressed the goverment and stated, "I expect that the use of emergency powers regulations shall not constitute a first option but rather a last choice of action."[13] This approach is not part of a metaphorical dialogue but rather a real dialogue that occurs between players, and the judgment serves as a platform for holding such a conversation. The actual dialogue taken in this case is not so different from a written letter. The reality of the discourse appears as well in judgments in which the Supreme Court directly addresses military commanders in a certain position, soldiers, petitioners, and prosecutors, and even bereaved families, and converses with them.

The dialogue is also real in the sense that it is interactive. The Supreme Court initiates a variety of moves and cooperates with other branches in conducting and developing this discourse. The Court has considerable interest in conducting effective dialogue with the other branches, and it has developed a variety of methods to convey these types of messages. Furthermore, the Court has developed tools "to encourage" players in other branches to cooperate in dialogue with the Court. Players who do so earn compliments or appreciation that is expressed in the judgment. Players who refuse to cooperate in dialogue are likely to find themselves "penalized" by the Court.

---

[13] HCJ 6972/98, Paritzky v. Minister of the Interior, PD 53(1) 763, 785–86 (1999).

MESSAGES CONVEYED BY THE SUPREME COURT ARE NOT LIMITED
TO LEGAL NORMS

A further characteristic of the use of judicial review in Israel in the field of national security pertains to the fact that in many cases the Supreme Court conveys messages to other branches that do not fall into recognized legal categories. Rather, the messages bear ethical, moral, or humanitarian contents. The term *humanitarian* in this context refers to the humanitarian relief that the military is requested to grant, not based on humanitarian law that, of course, constitutes a legal norm.

These messages constitute part of a judgment's normative structure but differ in purpose and in the way in which they seek to influence. The advisory messages used by the Supreme Court seek to instill norms of behavior that depart from application of the rules of law. For example, the Supreme Court's approach to the Attorney General with regard to indicting elected public officials with respect to statements supporting of terrorism which they may have made, in which the Attorney General is asked to exercise his discretion with "caution," "moderation," "restraint," "deliberation," and "responsibility," departs from the legal requirement of applying administrative discretion. The use of non-legal language is particularly salient also in the Court's dialogue with Israel Defense Forces (IDF) soldiers and their military commanders. Instead of legal language, the Court uses "educational" language in its discourse with them. For example, the Court addresses IDF military commanders and requests that they instruct soldiers at checkpoints to conduct themselves "with restraint."[14] The Court behaves similarly toward victims of terrorist attacks, in a dialogue intended to comfort and mollify or to express empathy with their pain.

Furthermore, judgments in which the Supreme Court uses attorneys representing the State illustrate how, in many cases, the Court replaces the imperative text with operative directives that are "soft," discursive—based on a sense of cooperation between the Supreme Court and other branches. Positive judgments are intended, generally speaking, to conclude with clear imperative directives that regulate the relations between the parties. The text of a judgment is intended to create a legal reality—"This policy contradicts international law" or "This law is unconstitutional"; however, the domain of verbs that serves the Supreme Court in dialogue incidental to combat illustrates the manner of integrating additional contents in the case law of the Supreme Court. In judgments, ostensibly there is no room for "clarifications"[15] or

---

[14] HCJ 2847/03, Al'ouna v. the Commander of IDF Forces in the West Bank, Tak-El 2003 (2) 3829(2003).

[15] *See, e.g.,* HCJ 2307/00, Netasha v. the Military Commander of IDF Forces in the West Bank, Tak-El 2002(1) 979 (2002). "We asked the attorney for the Respondents whether the detainee can be apprised of his right to approach a military judge with regard to his detention, and he has told us that he will clarify this with the competent authorities" (emphasis added).

"assurances."[16] The person implementing the decision is not intended to act in "a supportive spirit,"[17] "with caution,"[18] "moderation,"[19] "restraint,"[20] "deliberation,"[21] or "responsibility."[22] He or she must apply the judgment precisely as it is written and no more. Nevertheless, the Supreme Court inserts into its decisions, in many judgments, directives that do not fall into the category of "an imperative." These messages can come, at times, along with an operative order and, in several cases, even as a replacement for it, and provide an in-depth expression of the Supreme Court's view, which looks at a court hearing as discourse.

The approach of the Israeli Court to dialogue is similar to what has been defined in the literature as discursivism. Christopher Peters defines *discursivism* as follows:

> A recent trend in constitutional scholarship that is closely related to minimalism (and may even be a species of it) is what I will call "discursivism." The core idea of discursivism is that the judiciary, and particularly the Supreme Court, should attempt to resolve constitutional issues by engaging in some form of dialogue or give-and-take with the political branches rather than by imposing final and authoritative decisions of those issues.[23]

The principal idea of a discursivist approach is that the Supreme Court must attempt to resolve constitutional crises by means of dialogue with other branches instead of subjecting them to the resolutions that it prefers. The principal argument of writers attributed with this view is that the Supreme Court must acknowledge the limits of its influence and, where it cannot influence policy by conventional means, it must attempt to influence policy by way of dialogue with other branches. Authors who identify with this view consider the Supreme Court to be an equal partner to other branches in formulating social principles and social values.

---

[16] HCJ 5311/02, Abu Hit v. Commander of the Ketziot Detention Facility, PD 02 (2) 385 (2002). And in HCJ 6834/02, Abu Hit v. Commander of the Ketziot Detention Facility, PD 02(2) 385 (2002), "the attorney for the respondent *promised* to look into the possibility that relatives of the detainee petitioners in the aforesaid files, who are citizens or residents of Israel, would be permitted to visit their relatives."

[17] HCJ 1321/04, Bari v. the Commander of IDF Forces in the West Bank, Tak-El 2004 (1) 2394 (2004). "The attorney for the State declared that if a claim for compensation for damages is filed, the claim will be examined in substance and it may be assumed *in a supportive spirit*." [emphasis added]

[18] Criminal Appeal, Alba v. the State of Israel, PD 50(5) 221,264–65 (1996). "It is presumed that the Prosecution…will continue to act when submitting such indictments *with caution, restraint, and moderation*." [emphasis added].

[19] *Id.*

[20] *Id.*

[21] HCJ 11225/03, Bishara v. the Attorney General, Tak-El 2006 (1) 1398HCJ, para. 13 of the judgment of Justice E. Hayut. "Legal and public discretion must be exercised *with deliberation and responsibility* to decide whether there is reason to exhaust the law with the elected public official."

[22] *Id.*

[23] *See* Christopher J. Peters, *Assessing the New Judicial Minimalism*, 100 Colum. L. Rev. 1454, 1471–72 (2000).

Accordingly, it is accurate to call the Supreme Court's approach in this area of case law a discursive or conversational one. The discursive approach to judicial review is expressed in highlighting the significance of dialogue as a way of overseeing other branches, particularly dialogue that occurs without the use of binding messages. "The Supreme Court of Israel views this is an immanent and principal part of judicial review of national security".

MESSAGES ARE CONVEYED BY A VARIETY OF MEANS AND FORMATS

One way to understand how central dialogue is to the Supreme Court of Israel is to look at the variety of means and formats used by the Court to convey messages. Judicial dialogue that the Supreme Court conducts with other branches occurs through messages that are usually conveyed within the framework of a petition. Part of the dialogue is conveyed in official decisions, part in oral remarks. The Court transmits binding messages to other branches (in the ratio decidendi and in operative orders), and it transmits advisory or non-binding messages to them. Figure 13.1 below schematically presents the principal methods that serve the Supreme Court in transmitting messages to other branches.

We can see that at one end of the scale the Court engages with other branches by patently informal means. Justices may convey these messages in lectures they give, in academic articles on relevant issues, in direct dialogue they conduct with players in the Executive and legislative authorities, in correspondence with Members of Knesset or

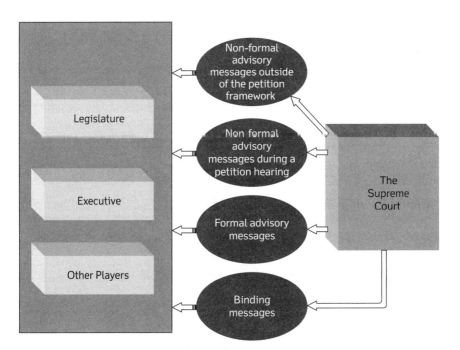

FIGURE 13.1 The Means by Which the Supreme Court Communicates with Other Branches

others, in joint committee meetings with players of other public authorities, and in other informal frameworks that allow them to convey messages outside of the formal seat of justice. The Supreme Court uses all these methods to transmit advisory messages.

At the other end of the scale, we can see how the Supreme Court engages with other branches by means of its binding decisions. Messages that are included in the operative order or in the *ratio* of a judgment also constitute a form of dialogue that the Supreme Court conducts with other branches. This is the classic form of the dialogue.

Between these two extremes, intermediate types of dialogue occur. One format occurs by way of messages that are conveyed verbally during a hearing; another format of dialogue occurs in formal interim decisions.

The discussion in previous chapters demonstrates that messages transmitted by the Supreme Court by way of revoking laws or determining that policy is unlawful constitute only a fraction, albeit a significant one, of the messages that the Supreme Court transmits to other branches. The principal part of the dialogue occurs by way of non-binding messages. The number of judgments in which the Supreme Court determined that national security policy, which the State undertook, is contrary to law is rather low compared to the many advisory messages the Court conveys.

The Supreme Court's approach in the area of national security, both in judgments constituting precedents given throughout the period and in other judgments, are characterized by a reliance on advisory dialogue.

The difficulties inherent in exercising judicial review in its full and ordinary sense in times of emergency led the Supreme Court to develop a wide variety of tactics of alternative judicial review. Even if they lack the effect of binding decisions, these tactics enable the Court to exercise partial judicial review and express its opinion with regard to conducting combat in real time.

Figure 13.2 below schematically presents the principal forms of transmitting messages in interim decisions that were analyzed in the study.

We have seen in previous chapters that almost every judicial decision, including decisions pertaining to the panel of justices or to a question of giving an interim order, can serve—and often does serve—as a platform for transmitting messages to other branches of government. It is not necessary for these decisions to be noted specifically in the bottom line of a decision. The Court can transmit messages to other branches by altering the panel of justices, the language, the customary procedure, and the timing. Players in the field and particularly repeat players recognize the possibility that every decision may serve as a platform for conveying a message and, therefore, are required to develop the ability to study the Supreme Court's messages well.

The legal adversarial procedure as developed by the Israeli Supreme Court affords it the capacity to conduct a dialogue in the course of a hearing at the center of which are initiatives of the parties submitting the petition, making an argument, or lodging an application. The Court perceives the parties' messages and furthers the dialogue by decisions that relate to the messages transmitted to the Court. Conducting a dialogue in so

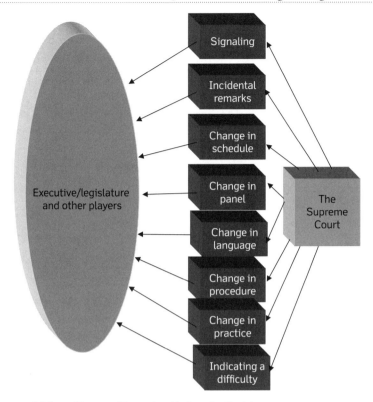

FIGURE 13.2 Advisory Messages Transmitted in Interim Decisions

many different ways and on several levels at the same time requires comprehensive attention. For interpreting, analyzing, or reviewing decisions of the Israeli Supreme Court
we must assume that the Supreme Court conducts dialogue all the time with the other
branches and it does so while using all kinds of platforms available to it. Each message
and each platform has its advantages and disadvantages. A verbal remark that the law
must be changed is different in nature and effect from a similar remark that is included
in a judgment. A message transmitted by signaling differs in nature and intensity from
a message transmitted by indication or recommendation. The Court developed these
features of advisory dialogue to relay complex and sophisticated messages to the players
in the field at the time of hearing a petition and at the time of giving a judgment.

Figure 13.2 above also illustrates the extent to which the Court's methods for transmitting messages are highly varied and sophisticated. Signaling, as may be recalled,
comprises messages that relate in a non-binding manner to the question of constitutionality or legality of a certain issue that is being heard by the Supreme Court or that
has some connection to an issue being heard by the Court. However, as we have seen,
focusing on signaling, as a principal tactic for transmitting advisory messages, misses
the finer means the Supreme Court employs in transmitting messages to other branches
and the impact of these messages. Indeed, it will not always be possible to state definitely

that a certain course of action of the Court was directed toward transmitting an advisory message. Frequently, it will be difficult for the players to evaluate, particularly in the early stages of a petition, whether the Supreme Court intended to transmit a message and what are the message's contents. For this reason, players in other branches are required to make every effort to locate these messages and interpret them, and they are likely inadvertently to conclude that there is a message or to reach conclusions pertaining to the contents of a message even where the Court did not intend this or intended something else entirely.

USE OF A VARIETY OF MEANS FOR TRANSMITTING MESSAGES

The dialogue on the subject of national security does not end with the conclusion of a petition's hearing. The Supreme Court is a master of the art of transmitting sophisticated messages to other branches in its judgments. Figure 13.3 in the next page presents the formats for transmitting the principal messages in Supreme Court judgments.

Figure 13.3 demonstrates the rich and varied tactics employed by the Supreme Court with regard to dialogue. It shows that the Court has developed an exceptionally broad repertoire of methods of transmitting non-binding messages to other branches in its judgments. Indeed, comparative law literature offers many examples of the use of advisory dialogue by different courts in different parts of the world; nonetheless, it is highly doubtful that another instance of such wide, diverse, sophisticated, and intimate use of legal text to promote policy objectives by way of non-binding dialogue exists elsewhere.

CONCLUSION

The Israeli Supreme Court has selected advisory dialogue as its principal tool for applying judicial review to issues of national security, particularly during times of crisis or in cases that require an urgent decision. The Court is available at any time to any person—whether it is a weekend, holiday, day, or night, and it is prepared to decide any issue so that it will be able to have some bearing on the rights of petitioners appearing before the Court in real time. However, 24/7 availability is not enough to guarantee judicial review in real time. In order to meet this challenge, the Court developed a broad repertoire of tools and tactics for transmitting messages. These messages are broadcast continually to the players—from the time the petition is submitted, while it is being heard, and until a judgment is given in the case. At times the messages are conveyed even beyond the decision being taken when the Court keeps a petition pending till all issues relating to its application are resolved.

It is the combination of these tools and tactics that enables the Court to carry out judicial review in real time. Without this arsenal, even if the Court were prepared to

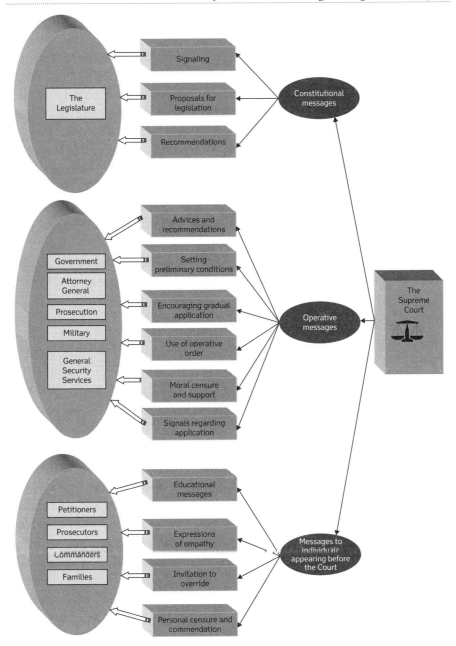

FIGURE 13.3 Non-binding Formal Messages Transmitted in Judgments

apply judicial review in real time, it is doubtful whether the Court would be able to do so in practice.

The Supreme Court's intensive use of advisory dialogue has several significant implications for the legal system and the study of judicial review in the field of national security. Every evaluation or interpretation of the Court's judgments must take into account the dialogue that occurred during the course of the hearing or at the end of it. Relating only to the bottom line of a judgment often misses the mark with regard to a true interpretation or significance of the hearing that was held and its effect on how Israel contends with national security challenges in the realm of law. In many cases, the non-binding messages the Court transmits by way of advisory dialogue during a hearing or in a judgment have a critical effect on the limits of the State's use of violence. This conclusion appears to be correct in relation to any court that takes a discursive approach to judicial review. The binding messages and the non-binding messages are nonseparable. *Together, both express the Supreme Court's normative position on questions of values that the Court has been asked to decide.*

Furthermore, in many cases it is impossible to say that the decision to revoke policy is more significant than the advisory message that was conveyed along with it. In many cases, it will also not be precise to determine that a decision does or does not contribute to human rights solely according to the question whether the Supreme Court determined that a certain policy is lawful or not. In many cases, Supreme Court judgments in the field of national security contribute to furthering human rights even when a petition is rejected, if along with the rejection an advisory message is transmitted that may restrict to a considerable extent the State's ability to apply the offensive policy. At times, it is precisely those judgments in which the Supreme Court intervened in policy that can permit the continued use of a certain policy in a manner that requires doubt to be cast as to whether the state of human rights in the issue indeed improved, at least to some degree, in the manner that the petitioners or the public expected.

The Supreme Court judgment in the *Bargaining Chips* case is a good example of such case. According to the classic distinction, the binding message in this judgment is that the State does not have the authority to hold detainees as bargaining chips. The remaining matters that were discussed in the judgment appear as incidental remarks of ostensibly less significance. However, examination of the judgment in accordance with the principles and tools outlined above leads to the conclusion that the message concealed in the judgment's margins are no less significant to an understanding of the Supreme Court's position on the moral question that was brought before the Court and to an understanding of the long-term effect of the judgment on human rights in Israel.

This conclusion is also true with regard to the Supreme Court judgment *On Torture*. An analysis of the judgment on the use of violence, in view of the dialogue that attended it, leads to a renewed appreciation of the judgment. Is the determination that the State is prohibited from using violence while interrogating suspects of terrorism more important than the determination that the Attorney General may refrain from indicting an investigator who used violence vis-à-vis an interogatee? As indicated above, despite the decision of the Supreme Court, since the judgment was given violence has been used in dozens of cases. According to a report by B'Tselem, to date no investigator has been criminally indicted with regard to using violence in the course of an investigation.[24] Certainly, there is no doubt that the number of cases of the use of violence is dramatically less than the number of cases prior to the judgment. However, the advisory message conveyed to the Attorney General illustrates the significance of the Supreme Court's remarks concerning application for an understanding of advisory dialogue and its effect on human rights. In this case, a brief remark at the end of the decision was interpreted by the Attorney General in a way that altered the significance of the application of the prohibition substantively. It was only 10 years after the application of the Court's decision that the Court signaled that it was unhappy with the way its original judgment had been applied.

Practicable messages given in the margins of judgments are also extremely important in understanding the true effect of the judgment on human rights. For example, in the discussion on the question of passive support of terrorism or in the context of house demolitions, the Court managed to restrict the policy through practicable messages. As Justice Mazza indicated, and as reports of human rights organizations demonstrated, "In practice (in fact, not in theory), the power and authority of military commanders to act...were diminished."[25] As opposed to this, practicable messages can lead to a "broader" application of policy that was rejected by the Supreme Court, as we can see in the hearing of the same question during the al-Aqsa Intifada. Practicable messages have a great effect on human rights and on understanding the Court's normative position concerning national security, even though the Court did not intervene in the law's interpretation in these cases and did not place constitutional limits on application of the policy.

More generally, a court that takes a discursive approach leads to a relative devaluation of the significance of the classic distinction between *ratio* and *obiter*. According to the classic distinction, the *ratio* is the essence of a judgment, whereas the obiter dicta are of secondary importance. This distinction partly expresses, and perhaps misleadingly so, the Court's position on the issue that has been brought before it. In certain cases, it does not really describe how a judgment will affect human rights. When the question is asked which part of a judgment affects the conduct of players in other branches, or which part of a judgment contributes to establishing norms or support for human rights, the significance of the ratio of a judgment is not necessarily greater than the significance of the part comprising the obiter dicta. In the Israeli context, there are judgments in which the Supreme Court determined that the policy of a public body is unlawful. However, these

---

[24] *See* B'Tselem, 1987–1997 A Decade of Human Rights Violations (Jan. 1998). *See on this matter also* The Association for Civil Rights in Israel Human Rights in Israel—Current Situation 95 (1996).

[25] HCJ 6026/94, Nazal v. Commander of IDF Forces in Judea and Samaria, PD 48 (5) 338, 346 (1994).

judgments contributed less to the protection of human rights than dozens of judgments in which the Supreme Court advised the Executive by means of dialogue to respect the rights of persons likely to be harmed by the military's actions. In other words, in a world where law is a conversation and the judicial decision is the platform on which it occurs, advisory messages have a great, and, at times, even a critical, effect on the application of policy and on human rights.

14

Judicial Review "under fire"

THE SUPREME COURT'S intensive use of dialogue in matters related to national security facilitates its ability to exercise judicial review in "real time." This feature is so dominant in exercising judicial review that in certain cases, one can compare the work of the Supreme Court while hearing a petition to a kind of "humanitarian war room."

The reality in Israel is such that when a military campaign commences, petitions are immediately filed all at once with the Supreme Court requesting the Court's opinion, generally while the fighting is ongoing. These petitions change in content and form at the same time as the fighting is being conducted in the field and as circumstances vary. Often there is only a slim connection between a petition's inception and its conclusion. In one of the petitions mentioned above, the Supreme Court called this kind of petition "a rolling petition."[1] The Court summons the attorneys for the State and at times even the military commanders in the field for a hearing while combat continues, obtains information from them on the situation in the battlefield, and responds with messages for the military as to how the military is to act in conducting combat, all the while leaving the petition pending.

In many cases, the essence of a petition is not the bottom line but rather the dialogue that occured during its hearing. The interim decisions form a framework and provide significance, if not the sole significance of the proceedings. The petition's outcome often is known in advance, and the dialogue that occurs between the parties during its course is in fact the principal consequence of the petition. The petition's role in these instances is to open an effective channel of communication between human rights and humanitarian assistance organizations and the military, and the role of the Supreme Court is that of a mediator. The Court acts as a humanitarian war room and as "a loudspeaker" for human

---

[1] HCJ 11745/02, Community Center for the Development of Beit Hanina v. GOC (General Officer Commanding) Central Command, Tak-El 2003(4) 515, a decision from April 14, 2005.

rights organizations. The Court's intervention during times of combat occurs almost solely as advisory dialogue.

In one case the Court made this point explicitly. It was in 2012 that the Court handed down its judgment in a petition submitted by the Association for Civil Liberties in Israel. In the petition, the Court was asked to declare void the government's decision to declare an emergency situation. This governmental decision is as old as the State of Israel itself. The Court in its judgment made the following statement. "By the nature of things, the role of the Court in the matter at hand often is to serve as a kind of 'babysitter' of government authorities, in order to follow up on the fulfillment of the provisions of the law and the exercise of human rights."[2] The Israeli Supreme Court indeed views sometimes its role as a "babysitter" whose job is to follow up on the respect for human rights and humanitarian law by the other branches.

The discursive approach to judicial review highly influences the manner in which the judicial proceeding is conducted. The traditional view of a judicial proceeding sees it as a means to get to the truth. The proceeding is a corridor to the judicial outcome—the judgment. To this end, facts, legal disputes, and the parties' contentions are brought before the Court.

As opposed to the traditional view, Malcolm Feeley[3] contends in his classic study on the criminal justice system that "the process is the punishment"—introducing the accused into a criminal proceeding with all that this implies with regard to his freedom, his welfare, his financial situation, and his good name. The need to hire the services of an attorney, bear expenses, arrive at hearings, and wait in detention until a verdict is reached are often the true penalty that an accused suffers. According to Feeley, with regard to a criminal trial, it is often the proceedings that are the real punishment for the accused.

It is possible to apply Feeley's approach metaphorically to the context of the Israeli Supreme Court judicial review of national security matters. The Supreme Court's use of advisory dialogue often leads to a situation in which the Court's proceeding is the essence—not the proceeding's outcome. In many instances, and certainly with respect to military campaigns, the hearing of a petition and the dialogue that occurs during its course are what matters—and not necessarily the decision that constitutes the bottom line. This is how in the Court's view discipline and deterrence from violations of human rights and international law could be achieved.

The proceeding that was conducted in HCJ *Halutz*, in this respect, is a classic case in point. In fact, it is doubtful whether it is possible to understand the course that the Supreme Court undertook in this case other than as the wish to use the petition to censure Halutz regarding his statements in his well-known interview and to transmit in this manner an instructive message to the military. The reply to the question of what is the real meaning of the judgment in HCJ *Halutz* is not whether the statements made by Halutz in the *Haaretz* interview are sufficiently grave to justify his being disqualified from serving

---

[2] HCJ 3091/99, The Association for Citizens Rights v. the Knesset (unpublished, 5 August 2012, para. xiii.
[3] *See* MALCOLM M. FEELEY, THE PROCESS IS THE PUNISHMENT (1979).

in his position, as the bottom line of the judgment determines. This conclusion was foreseen both by the parties and by the Court, as the Court itself indicated when it noted that it is difficult "to reconcile the relief requested by the petitioners within the confines of this petition and the conclusion they seek to reach from the interview conducted with Maj.-Gen. Halutz."[4] Instead, the proceeding itself and the incidental remarks of the justices made during the hearing and, at the end, in the judgment must be viewed as the principal substance. According to this approach, interpretation of the judgment does not turn on the question of whether the Supreme Court acted in this judgment according to the rulings that directed it with regard to public service appointments. Rather, the significance of the judgment and its interpretation lie in the fact that in order to transmit the message that military commanders should be sensitive to the humanitarian consequences of their actions and should not treat it as "collateral damage," the Court did not strike out the petition *in limine*. Instead, the Court used it as an impetus and means to convey instructive messages, even if non-binding, to the Israel Defense Forces (IDF) and its commanding officers. Thus, in the matter of *Halutz*, too, "the process is the punishment."

The conclusion that often the mere willingness to adjudicate national security matters in real time is no less important than the final outcome can rest as well on an analysis of the same judgments in which the Supreme Court serves as mediator or communicator between the military and human rights organizations, particularly during times of combat. As we saw in the Supreme Court judgments during Operation Defensive Shield, Operation Rainbow, and Operation Cast Lead, the Court intervenes minimally in military decisions pertaining to the manner of conducting combat. Often, the Court's role is exhausted by mediating in dialogue, which occurs between human rights and humanitarian assistance organizations and the military while combat is taking place. However, the Supreme Court views its entry into this field, legalizing it and the non-binding messages that it transmits to the military and the commanding officers, as an objective that creates deterrence and discipline. Therefore, it justifies in and of itself the investment of a tremendous amount of judicial energy.

A discursive approach to judicial review also shapes the power relations between the parties even before the Supreme Court has its say. A remark in one direction can affect the State's decision to concede or not to concede, or its decision whether to continue to maintain a checkpoint, a curfew, or a detention, or to prevent a meeting with an attorney or the use of violence vis-à-vis an interrogatee. As we have seen, oftentimes the principal achievement of a petition is to further the dialogue between the petitioners and military authorities. This was evident in petitions that concerned integrating humanitarian messages among soldiers and their commanding officers.

We clearly saw this approach in the Court judgment pertaining to petitions that were submitted during Operation Cast Lead. The Court rejected the petitioners' legal claims regarding the manner of conducting combat by the military. However, in the same breath, the Court acknowledged the following: "Every now and then, the role of the

---

[4] HCJ Hess v. Halutz, PD 59 (6) 97 (2005), at 831.

Court in such cases is *to encourage* and monitor compliance with the provisions of Israeli and international law, *even where it knows and trusts that the authorities are unreservedly committed to the appropriate legal framework*. It does so, however, from the judicial perspective aimed at capturing the comprehensive picture. There is therefore constant need for judicial review." [emphasis added][5]

With these words, the Court highlights its view that it is justified to adjudicate national security cases even "under fire" so that the military will make certain to comply with the provisions of international law during times of warfare.

As aforesaid, the Supreme Court makes sophisticated use of several mechanisms that enable and encourage the development of dialogue in this manner. The first is its true commitment to 24/7 availability and its willingness to react to petitions within hours, and decide on the merits if need be within days. The second is the legal procedure, which creates a strict and formal structure for dialogue, and any departure from this immediately calls for its interpretation as an advisory message or potential signaling, with no connection to the question whether the Supreme Court intended to convey a message. The third facilitator of this dialogue is the fact that dialogue in the field of national security often takes place under highly compressed conditions—the number of players in it are limited and they repeat with high frequency. This factor allows the Court to converse directly with the relevant players and to enable them to reach conclusions from any departure, even the slightest, from strict procedural structure or practice that is familiar to them. The fact that dialogue is conducted for the most part with repeat players (both on the part of the State and on the part of human rights organizations) increases the participants' capacity to learn the Court's frame of mind. It also augments participants' motivation to avoid risking obtaining a judgment that contradicts policy that they wish to promote. These players make a greater effort to learn the Court's frame of mind. Accordingly, the players find themselves attentive to any message that the Court wishes to convey in its decisions. Their willingness to comply with these messages is high. The Court makes intelligent use of this fact in order to influence their behavior.

THE INFLUENCE OF REAL TIME DIALOGUE ON THE TIMING OF LANDMARK DECISIONS

Notwithstanding all that has been stated above, we would be remiss if we described the judicial review that the Supreme Court implements as being limited to dialogue. The study of Supreme Court rulings demonstrates that although the Supreme Court makes intensive use of dialogue at times of crisis or in emergencies, its messages must be understood as part of a more wide-ranging exercise of judicial review and the Court was never shy of issuing decisions on some of the most complex questions judicial review of national security in the twenty-first century entails.

---

[5] HCJ 201/09 Physicians for Human Rights v. The Prime Minister, Tak-El 2009 (1) 565.

The Court's approach indeed is to use dialogue during times of combat. However, the messages that the Court transmits during periods of combat enable it also to time the exercise of full and comprehensive judicial review with regard to questions of national security at specifically convenient times, when the level of violence has decreased.

We will clarify this matter. The following figure depicts the number of Israelis killed during the years 1993–2012.[6]

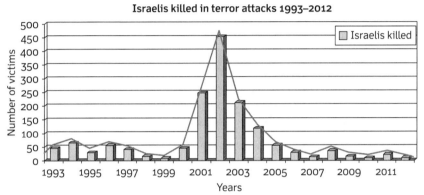

Israelis killed in terror attacks 1993–2012

* In 2010 all killed were during operation Castlead

FIGURE 14.1 Israelis Killed in Terrorist Attacks 1993–2012
Source: Ministry of foreign affairs—Israel.

The next figure shows the number of people killed (both civilian and security services) during the Al-aqsa Intifada month by month.

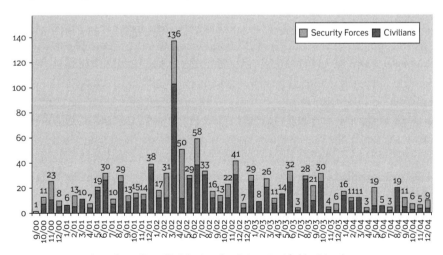

FIGURE 14.2 Number of Israelis Killed during the al-Aqsa Intifad by Month
Source: IDF spokesperson office.

---

[6] In accordance with data from the Foreign Ministry. *See* mfa.gov.il/MFA/MFA Archive/2000_2009/2000/1/ Terrorism+deaths+in+Israel+-+1920-1999.htm.

Figure 14.3 presents the annual data pertaining to the number of persons killed in suicide attacks from the beginning of the al-Aqsa Intifada until the end of 2007:

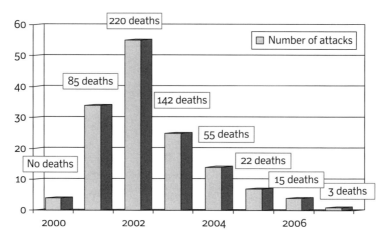

FIGURE 14.3 Annual Data Pertaining to the Number of Persons Killed in Suicide Attacks from the Beginning of the al-Aqsa Intifada until the End of 2007

Source: Shin-Beth.

Roughly speaking, the data show that following the signing of the Oslo Accords there was an increase in terrorist activity. The year 1996 was the relative peak in the number of casualties in terrorist attacks, whereas the following three years indicate a decline to a historic minimum in 1999. It is important to note that in 2000 there were no Israelis killed in terror attacks at all until September 27, 2000, the day that the al-Aqsa Intifada broke out. With the eruption of the al-Aqsa Intifada, the number of suicide attacks and with it the number of casualties in terrorist attacks rose to higher levels, till it reached its highest historical level in March 2002. Thereafter, a decrease occurred in the number of casualties—a decrease of 53 percent between 2002 and 2003, a further decrease of 44 percent between 2003 and 2004, and an additional decrease of 60 percent between 2004 and 2005. The year 2005 marked a "lull" that was announced on January 22, according to which the Palestinian factions agreed to refrain from undertaking terrorist activity against Israel. In the course of this year, 54 Israelis were killed, whereas 2004 saw 118 Israelis killed.[7] Since then, till 2013 the number of terrorism-related casualties remained low with a small increase in 2008.

Further to the data indicated, Appendix B describes the dates of receiving principal rulings that comprise precedents against the State during the most turbulent years, 1996–2005. It analyzes the time of the decision in view of the general tendency of either a relative decrease or the absence of a decrease in the number of Israelis injured in terrorist

---

7 *See* Prime Minister Office, "Five Years of Confrontation Report" (2005)—*see* www.pmo.gov.il/NR/rdon lyres/C7825D77-98A6-4645-992B-437A4F3FACF4/0/shabak2005.doc.

attacks during the same period, considering the time between the date a petition was submitted and the date a decision was given against the State.

The small number of decisions in which the Supreme Court revoked national security policy, based on fundamental rulings on an issue heard before the Court, makes it difficult to reach any unequivocal conclusions from this data. Yet we still are able to draw general conclusions from the data presented in the above-described table.

The first conclusion is that most of the fundamental decisions against the State were given during a period of reduced violence. The second is that during a period of intensive fighting (from February 2002 until the second half of 2003) or during a period of heightened violence, there are almost no fundamental decisions given against the State in national security matters. The single fundamental decision given against the State during a time when the level of violence was relatively high had to do with the matter of screening the film *Jenin, Jenin*. This decision differed from the others in that it did not concern the State's direct national security policy. Rather, it focused on questions pertaining to freedom of speech during a time of hostilities. In this area of case law, the Supreme Court has always been more willing to exercise judicial review during a period of combat, for two reasons. First, freedom of speech is a particularly sensitive issue to the Court, and its protection is understood to be a firm obligation, particularly in times of crisis. Second, arguments that there is a possible causal connection between allowing the screening of the film and harm to national security often appears as not persuasive. In this instance, the hearing was conducted from the perspective of freedom of speech and the film's credibility, and it was difficult—if not impossible—to point to immediate harm to human life due to the decision to permit the film to be publicized. It is further noteworthy that although the judgment was given during a period of violent confrontation and "under fire," immediately after it was given the Court issued a stay of execution order for the judgment following the applicants' Application for a Further Hearing. The Application for a Further Hearing together with the Stay of Execution Order to prevent the screening of the film precluded its screening for an additional six months in practice.[8]

A third conclusion that we may draw from that which has been stated above is that proceedings in which ultimately a fundamental position against the State is accepted are generally spread over a relatively long period of time. The average "lifespan" of a case in a petition to the Israel Supreme Court in 2002 stood at nine months, and in 2003 and 2004 at eight months.[9] Cases in which the Supreme Court took a fundamental stand against the State generally were heard over a period of several years and, on average, two years.

There are several possible reasonable explanations for this disparity. There is the possibility that such cases require longer hearing and longer duration for writing the

---

[8] Further Hearing HCJ 10480/03, Besidan v. Bakhri, PD 59(1) 625 (2004), decision dated Dec. 3, 2003.
[9] SUPREME COURT STATISTICAL REPORTS 2002, 2003, 2004. *See* www.elyon1.court.gov.il/heb/stats/sikum.htm.

judgment. However, the history of the Court shows that the Supreme Court, during the relevant period as well, managed to issue fundamental or lengthy judgments, even in national security matters, in a relatively brief period of time.[10] In any event, it is clear that a hearing of long duration gives the Court a wide berth to time decisions for a date convenient to the Court, if it should opt to do so. A judgment that is recognized as a clear departure from this approach is the *Beit Sourik* one. Here the Court ordered the State to alter parts of the route of the separation barrier due to the harm it caused to residents of the Occupied Territories. An explanation proposed in the literature ties the timing of the decision to the decision given by the International Court of Justice (ICJ) with regard to the separation barrier.[11] It is true that the Supreme Court's giving of the judgment prior to the ICJ's decision served the State well as it reduced the intensity of the conflict between Israel and the international community, and enabled the State to demonstrate that "there are judges in Jerusalem." Giving the judgment within such a brief period, therefore, particularly reinforces the assumption that the Court times decisions against the State in the field of national security so that they will be issued on convenient dates when in the Court's estimation the force of opposition to the decision will be relatively low.

It is very difficult to show in each and every decision whether the Court timed a specific decision or not. Very few judges if any will ever confess to that. However, the more important point for our discussion is that the use of dialogue affords the Court space to maneuver and enables it to time decisions against the State so that they are issued on convenient dates when the level of violence is low. The use of dialogue gives the Court a new tool in its arsenal. It enables the Court, which is asked to decide an issue related to national security, to consider inter alia the question whether the situation is ripe for such a ruling and whether the Court has sufficient information to make a prudent ruling. If the answer to one of these questions is negative, the Court can reject the petition and, at the same time, convey advisory messages concerning the issue. The message conveyed can be that a certain policy is problematic, as the Court often does, or that the Court is likely in the future to re-examine the matter perhaps at a more convenient time. The advisory messages that have been conveyed in decisions given during the times of combat enable the Court to present the decision ultimately to intervene as the continuation of a position it undertook while the fighting was going on.

Several cases that were examined above support the conclusion that the Court indeed takes this approach. To begin with, we saw that the Court immediately rejected the first petition that was submitted on the matter of targeted killings. This decision was given in 2002 when the level of violence was very high. Then the Court began to re-examine its position in a second petition that was submitted and to transmit messages that it is likely

---

[10] *See* HCJ 7015/02, *Ajouri v. Commander of IDF Forces on the West Bank*, PD 56(6) 352 (2002) (the issue of delineating residence).

[11] NAOMI LEVITZKI, THE SUPREMES: WITHIN THE SUPREME COURT 335 (2006).

to reverse its decision. The Court conveyed these massages by ignoring, despite the State's reference, its earlier decision not to intervene, by giving an interim decision that attested to the complexity of the subject, and by appointing a senior panel to hear the case. All these signals clarified for the State that the situation in this case was not straightforward and that the Court was considering intervention. On the eve of the hearing of the petition, the Sharm el-Sheikh Summit of 2005 took place, at which Prime Minister Ariel Sharon announced the cessation of the policy of targeted killings. It must be noted that the announcement was made after months during which there was a steady decrease in terrorist activity against Israel. On learning of the Prime Minister's announcement, the panel of justices hearing the case ordered that the hearing of the petition would not be halted, even though the Court could have ordered the petition to be dismissed and could have noted that the petitioners could bring the issue to court again. The failure to take this step, as indicated above, was a signal that the Court was troubled by the subject and was interested in deciding it. Ultimately, the Court gave its final ruling only after conclusion of the intifada, during a period of relative quiet.

Second, as we have seen, in most of the judgments in which the Court finally intervened in the State's conduct of affairs, the advisory messages that preceded the Court's intervention indicated the Court's tendency and increasing willingness to do so. We saw, for example, how Justice Levy noted in his decision not to revoke the Citizenship Law that the effects of the security situation influenced his choice to solely convey an advisory message of the *Judicial Sunset* kind.

HCJ *Natasha* provides another tangible example of the use of this practice. In this petition, the Supreme Court discussed the matter of the length of periods of detention of security detainees until they were brought before a judge. As may be recalled, together with rejecting the petition, the Court added the following statement: "There is no reason *at this time* for the intervention of this court to curtail the maximum period of detention."[12] [emphasis in original][13] Emphasizing the words *at this time*, which, as noted above, appeared in the original judgment, exposed the Supreme Court's frame of mind with regard to the question at hand. Furthermore, it also disclosed the Court's wish that the petitioners (and the respondents) would perceive the message the Court conveyed that at a later, more suitable time, it might be likely that their petition would be accepted, if the petitioners were to bring the matter again for a hearing before the Court.

It also attested to the fact that the Supreme Court is aware apparently of the question of timing and its effect on Court decisions, at least with respect to adjudication of national security matters. In this case, the Supreme Court "admitted" that the timing

---

[12] HCJ 2307/00, Natasha v. Commander of IDF Forces in the West Bank, Tak-El 2002(1) 979 (2002).

[13] In the legal compendium Takdin, the words *at this time* appear without underlining. However, in the original judgment of the Court, as publicized on the website of the Supreme Court and as distributed to the parties, these words are emphasized by being underlined.

was not right for intervention; however, at a later, more convenient date, the Court was likely to intervene in the matter. As the dialogue with the Court is ongoing and is not cut off when a judgment is given, the Supreme Court can signal the other players that an initial rejection of a petition does not necessarily mean that the matter has indeed been determined, and it is possible that, all in all, this actually concerns waiting until combat has ceased.

A close reading of all the decisions pertaining to Operation Defensive Shield leads to a similar conclusion. Operation Defensive Shield was initiated on March 29, 2002, and concluded on May 10, 2002. As indicated above, during the course of this campaign 29 petitions were submitted to the Supreme Court on the manner in which combat was being conducted by the military or the implications for the local inhabitants. In three cases, the petitions were struck out *in limine*. In one case,[14] in which the Court was asked to order the military to refrain from using airplanes and tanks in the course of fighting in the Jenin refugee camp, the Court accepted the State's position that the petition was not justiciable. In a second instance, the Court accepted the State's contention that the petition submitted pertaining to the prevention of meetings between detainees and their attorneys was too general, and for this reason the Court rejected it.[15] Nonetheless, as aforesaid, at the time that the petition was rejected, the Court signaled the petitioners stating: "*Nonetheless, it is clear that when, within in a reasonable time, conditions will be right that will enable weighing the individual circumstances of each detainee, the respondent will have to consider whether there is reason to give an order prohibiting a meeting with respect to each specific detainee.*"[16] And, indeed, a later petition, which concerned the same question, was discussed substantively and accepted.[17] In addition, in HCJ *La Custodia*, which dealt with the crisis in the Church of the Nativity, the Court accepted the State's position that the matter was not justiciable but it attached advisory messages to this rejection regarding the manner of handling the bodies found within church premises.[18]

The Supreme Court heard and determined all the other petitions substantively. In all of them, except for two,[19] a hearing was held within several days, generally within a day or

---

[14] HCJ 3022/02 Canon v. GOC (General Officer Commanding) Central Command PD 56(3) (2002) 9 [hereinafter HCJ *Canon*].

[15] HCJ 2901/02, *Hamoked: The Center for the Defense of the Individual et al. v. the Commander of IDF Forces in the West Bank*, PD 56(3) 19 (2002).

[16] *Id.* (emphasis added).

[17] HCJ 3239/02 Marab v. Commander of IDF Forces in the West Bank, PD 57 (2) 349 **(2003)** [hereinafter HCJ *Marab*].

[18] HCJ 3436/02, Custodia Internazionale di Terra Santa v. the Government of the State of Israel, PD 56 (3) 22 (2002) [hereinafter HCJ *La Custodia*].

[19] HCJ 3460/02, Dror Halevi—Chairman of the Movement for Separation v. the Prime Minister (unpublished, July 1, 2002) concerned the need to set up a separation barrier in view of the terrorist attacks. Perhaps because the government itself had already discussed the issue, the Court did not find it necessary to determine the matter with any urgency, and even held that the petition was premature. In HCJ 3761/02, Hadir v. Commander of IDF Forces in the Gaza Strip (unpublished, May 28, 2002), the State declared at the same time as the petition was submitted that until a ruling is given on the petition, no actions will be

two, while combat continued. Of the 29 petitions that were lodged, two were accepted.[20] In these two, the judgments were handed down long after the cessation of hostilities. The *Neighbor Procedure* decision that constituted a precedent[21] was given three years after the end of Operation Defensive Shield. The decision with regard to mass arrests that also constituted a precedent[22] was given 10 months after the campaign's conclusion. In a third petition that was partially accepted[23] the judgment was given seven months after the campaign ended. In all these petitions, except for those that were accepted, the hearing was held and the ruling was given within the time period of the military campaign or within several days following its conclusion. Generally, the judgments were read out loud in the courtroom shortly after the hearing on the parties' pleadings. All petitions that were determined during or near the period of combat were rejected. And in all of them, except for the same three stated above, the ruling was given on the substance of the matter.[24]

If we examine the use of advisory messages we see that even where the petition is rejected in substance, in 11 of 27 petitions that were determined during or near the time of hostilities, the Court transmitted advisory messages during the hearings or at the stage of handing down the judgment. For example, in HCJ 2901/02, *The Center for the Defense of the Individual V., The Commander of IDF Forces in the West Bank*,[25] the Court accepted the State's contention that the petition is too general, but at the same time signaled the petitioners that at another time, the Court would be likely to reconsider its position on the subject of mass detentions, as it indeed did later on. In HCJ 2936/02 the Court conveyed to the military that

> This commitment of our forces, based on law and morality—and, according to the State, even on utilitarian considerations—*must again be presented to the fighting forces down to the level of the lone soldier fighting in the field*, while issuing concrete instructions to prevent to the extent possible, even in severe situations, incidents that are inconsistent with the rules of humanitarian assistance. [emphasis added][26]

---

taken to implement the order for seizing land, which the Commander of the IDF Forces issued. It is reasonable to assume that for this reason the Court did not deem it urgent to hear and rule on the petition.

20. HCJ 3799/02 Adallah v. GOC (General Officer Commanding) Central Command PD 60 (3) 67 (2005) [hereinafter HCJ *Neighbor Procedure*], and HCJ *Marab, supra* note 19.

21. HCJ *Neighbor Procedure, supra* note 22.

22. HCJ *Marab, supra* note 19.

23. HCJ 3278/02, Hamoked Lehaganat Haprat v. the IDF Commander, PD 57(1) 385 (2002) [hereinafter *Ofer Detention Facilities*].

24. In practice, with regard to the petitions that were struck out *in limine*, the Court was favorable to the State's position in substance. *See, e.g.,* HCJ *Canon, supra* note 16: "The threshold contention argued by the State is acceptable to us. We also believe that the reliefs cannot be awarded, practically and institutionally, to prevent, or at least to minimize, the injury to civilians."

25. HCJ 2901/02, The Center for the Defense of the Individual et al. v. the Commander of IDF Forces in the West Bank, PD 56(3) 19 (2002).

26. HCJ 2936/02, Physicians for Human Rights v. the Commander of IDF Forces, PD 56(3) 3 (2002).

The Court acted similarly in 2977/02, in which it added at the end of the judgment: "It is presumed that the Respondent—and it has not been contended otherwise before us—has instructed and will instruct the fighting forces to do everything necessary to avoid the possibility of needless injury to the innocent."[27] During the evacuation of bodies in the *Jenin* affair,[28] the Court used advisory messages extensively to bring the parties to agreement on the issue, and advised the Military to have representatives of the Red Crescent and other local entities join in resolving the issue. The Court added similar statements with regard to the claim that a massacre occurred in the refugee camp. Subsequently in HCJ 3116/02, the Court reiterated this recommendation.[29] In the *Ofer Detention Facility* affair, which concerned the detention conditions of detainees arrested during the campaign, the Court intervened primarily through advisory messages in order to bring about some improvement in the conditions, and advised the military commanders to allow the possibility of visits of representatives of human rights organizations.[30] In HCJ *La Custodia*, the Court accepted the State's position that the matter is not justiciable but advised the State to permit the removal of bodies from the church premises.[31] In HCJ *Almedani*, which also concerned a crisis in the Church of the Nativity, the Court advised the State to arrange for food for the priests on the church premises.[32] In HCJ 3900/02, the Court used the judgment to hold a discussion with the petitioners, who protested the government decision to release the terrorists holed up in the church, according to an arrangement that led to concluding the crisis in the church.[33]

In conclusion, the manner in which the Supreme Court exercises judicial review during times of hostilities may be described as follows. In situations in which the level of violence is high or in actual situations of combat that are close to a crisis situation, such as during Operation Defensive Shield or Operation Cast Lead, the Court's use of judicial review is almost completely devoid of judgments that revoke the Executive's policy or declare laws unconstitutional.

Despite this clear trend, almost every time there is a military campaign, petitions are submitted that request the Supreme Court to intervene in events taking place in the field of battle—generally while the fighting is still ongoing. Despite the military situation, the Supreme Court endeavors not to determine that the state of combat is not justiciable. The Court's clear tendency is to monitor the situation in real time using tools it has developed for this purpose, that is, advisory dialogue. The Court also almost completely avoids giving rulings against the State during times of combat. While hostilities are ongoing, advisory dialogue in all its forms is the preferred route for exercising judicial review on the part of the

---

27 HCJ 2977/02, Adalah v. the Commander of IDF Forces in Judea and Samaria, PD 56(3) 6, 7–8 (2002).
28 HCJ 3114/02, Barakeh v. Minister of Defense, PD 56 (3) 11, 15–16 (2002).
29 HCJ 3116/02, Adalah v. the Commander of IDF Forces in the West Bank (unpublished, Apr. 16, 2002).
30 *Ofer Detention Facilities, supra* note 25.
31 HCJ *La Custodia, supra* note 20.
32 HCJ 3451/02, Almedani v. the Minister of Defense, PD 56(3) 30 (2002).
33 HCJ 3900/02, Terror Victims Center v. Ariel Sharon (unpublished, May 8, 2002).

Supreme Court. The less-than-perfect judicial review conducted by the Court during times of hostilities enables it to prepare the ground for deciding more fundamental judgments at a more convenient time. In cases in which the Court would like to review its ruling on an issue at another time, the advisory messages that the Court plants in its rulings prepare the ground for this. Later, at a more convenient time or when the Court has sufficient factual underpinnings for a decision, the Court is likely to complete the job and give a fundamental judgment on the issue, and perhaps even a judgment contrary to the State's position.

The use of advisory messages, the conducting of dialogue with military commanders "under fire", and the providing of directives to the military enables the Court to remain relevant also during times of hostilities and perhaps even to influence to some degree how combat is being conducted in terms of its humanitarian aspects. This of course may be a less-than-perfect model of judicial review. Indeed, as Justice Cheshin wrote on judicial review during times of hostilities, "Also when the trumpets of war sound, the rule of law shall make its voice heard. However, let us admit a truth: in those same places its sound is like that of the piccolo, clear and pure, but drowned out in the tumult."[34]

Nevertheless, the Court believes it is important enough that its voice is heard. The purpose of this enormous judicial effort is to influence the moral and legal manner in which Israel conducts its military actions and national security policies in times of crisis or war without necessarily imposing the Court's decisions on them during the crisis, unless the Court sees a clear violation of international law. The Court indeed sees its role as the State's "babysitter"[35] during a national security crisis. The main tool it uses for this purpose is advisory dialogue.

THE IMPACT OF ADVISORY DIALOGUE

Studies that have been conducted on the judicial impact of a judgment,[36] mainly in the United States, indicate several elements that affect the degree to which these are applied. Although these studies did not examine the effectiveness of advisory messages as such,

---

[34] HCJ 1730/96, Sabih et al. v. the Commander of IDF Forces in Judea and Samaria, PD 50(1) 353, 370–71 (1996).

[35] HCJ 3091/99, The Association for Citizens Rights v. the Knesset (unpublished, 5 August 2012), para. xiii.

[36] Baum demonstrated that there is a relation between the clarity of a Supreme Court decision and the manner of its application by the lower courts. Lawrence Baum, *Judicial Impact as a Form of Policy Implementation, in* PUBLIC LAW AND PUBLIC POLICY (John A. Gardiner ed., 1977). James Spriggs demonstrated in his studies that the United States' administration applies court decisions better when the message that the court transmits in its decision is sharp and clear, and when it anticipates that there will be a price to pay for not applying the decision. James Spriggs, *The Supreme Court and Federal Agencies: A Resource-Based Theory and Analysis of Judicial Impact*, 40 AM. J. POL. SCI. 1122 (1996). *See also* James Spriggs, *Explaining Federal Bureaucratic Compliance with Supreme Court Opinions*, 50 POL. RES. Q. 567 (1997). Spriggs contends "government agencies, as strategic actors, decide whether to comply with court opinions based on their beliefs about the consequences of alternative implementations." *Id.* at 570.

they enable initial conclusions to be drawn pertaining to the potential effectiveness of such messages.

In a study that examined U.S. Supreme Court decisions on the issues of abortion and school desegregation, Gerald N. Rosenberg[37] reached the general conclusion that such decisions have no impact on social processes that would have occurred in the absence of the famous Supreme Court decisions on the subject. Bradeley Canon demonstrated how "cheerleading" by the Court with regard to the abortion question caused opponents of abortion to focus their influence on the political field and caused the Republican government to lead the policy against abortions.[38] Hausegger and Baum[39] found that in cases in which the U.S. Supreme Court invited Congress to overturn a decision of the Court, the chances for the law being amended were twice as high as in cases where the Court did not add an invitation to overturn a decision. However, like Canon, Hausegger and Baum believe that it is impossible to base an empirical conclusion on this fact as it is impossible to know when the process began that led to the amendment of the legislation. (For example, whether the petitioners or their representatives took action behind the scenes at the time that the hearing of the petition was taking place, or whether the legislators were referred at all to this remark, and if they were, whether it was this remark or other considerations that influenced the decision to amend the law.)

Apart from examining the ordinary effectiveness of judicial decisions, examining the impact of advisory messages will require taking into consideration several of these decisions' particular features. First, the impact of advisory messages may be long-term and not necessarily immediate. Second, the impact can be attained indirectly by way of players outside the immediate circle of the participants in litigation, who will be able to make use of such messages to promote issues in the public arena, which only ultimately will be translated into results.[40] Third, an advisory message can be accepted at a time that is convenient for other players so that the timing allows them to rely on the message to justify policy that would have changed in any event, perhaps independent of the advisory message.[41]

Several more conclusions regarding impact may be drawn from the Israeli experience. First, repeat players in other government agencies comprehend advisory messages even if they are not necessarily interested in applying the messages because they are not binding. Second, from the findings it appears that the messages have a certain impact. Several cases mentioned in the study (such as house demolitions, torture, bargaining chips,

---

[37] *See* GERALD N. ROSENBERG, THE HOLLOW HOPE: CAN COURTS BRING ABOUT SOCIAL CHANGE? (1991).

[38] Bradley Canon, *The Supreme Court as a Cheerleader in Politico-Moral Disputes*, 54 J. POLITICS 637 (1992).

[39] *See* Lori Hausegger & Lawrence Baum, *Inviting Congressional Action: A Study of Supreme Court Motivations in Statutory Interpretation*, 43 AM. J. POL. SCI. 162 (1999). *See also* text adjacent to notes 9 and 10 and the relevant references.

[40] *See on this issue* Kevin R. den Dulk & Mitchell Pickerill, *Bridging the Lawmaking Process: Organized Interests, Court-Congress Interaction and Church-State Relations*, 35 POLITY 419 (2003).

[41] As apparently occurred in the case of the house demolitions.

incitement to terror, failure to prevent a crime, and the prosecution's monitoring of the Shin Bet collecting of investigative material) instruct that the other branches are well prepared to study the contents of advisory messages, and these messages have a certain influence on policy formation. Third, it is clear that advisory messages do not have the same effect on other branches as binding judicial decisions. In several instances examined in the study, such as the discussion pertaining to the separation fence, or addressing the detention conditions of detainees, or establishing supervisory procedures of detention conditions, the Israeli Supreme Court's advisory messages did not lead to major policy changes, even though the other branches received these messages, at least for several years. Fourth, some players tend more often to be more receptive to such messages than do other players. These tend to be repeat players, who are also required to report from time to time to the Court and are better prepared to understand its subtle messages. They are also highly motivated to respond to the Court's expectations.[42] This conclusion is further reinforced in view of the intensive use the Court makes of these players, inter alia, through turning to symbolic means (compliments and censure) that are less relevant vis-à-vis the military or the Shin Bet and even of less interest, if any, in the relations of the Court with the Legislature. The case brought in the study with regard to the *Citizenship Law* illustrates that even if the advisory message that was passed in an interim decision was understood by the Minister of Justice and conveyed by him to the Knesset, the Knesset did not deem itself obligated by this message.

Literature on this subject provides a few more insights on elements likely to have an effect on the usefulness of an advisory message. They include the degree of clarity of the message and the degree of decisiveness with which the Court transmits the message. It is reasonable to assume that signaling, which threatens the striking down of a law, will be better respected than a comment, recommendation or intimation. A message that permits a certain policy (Permissive Policy)[43] or allows its extension beyond the constraints that the binding decision creates (such as in the cases on torture, house demolitions without warning, or bargaining chips), will warrant a higher degree of efficacy than a message that asks the Executive not to apply a lawful policy. Studies have also demonstrated that a message that demands a broad amendment of policy will be less effective than a message that requires a change just once or a concrete change in policy.[44]

---

[42] Marc Galanter, *Why the "Haves" Come Out Ahead: Speculations on the Limits of Legal Change*, 9 L. & Soc. Rev. 95 (1974).

[43] Glick defines *permissive policy* as: "Permissive policy refers to Supreme Court decisions that allow governmental institutions very wide latitude in the kind of policies they may adopt." In his study, Glick demonstrates that such policy will be implemented more often on the part of government agencies than policies that are particularly intended to restrict the number of options available to government agencies. Henry R. Glick, *The Impact of Permissive Judicial Policies: The U.S. Supreme Court and the Right to Die*, 47 Pol. Res. Q. 207 (1994).

[44] *See* Baum, *supra* note 3, at n.562.

Based on the foregoing discussion, earlier studies, and the Israeli experience, one could come to the conclusion that the chances that an advisory message will be effective rise, if it is conveyed in a sharp and clear manner; if where a "price-tag" exists for refraining from action in accordance with such message; if the message addresses a player identified with the value system that the Supreme Court represents, the message complies with his interest,[45] and he views himself obligated by Supreme Court decisions, and acts in accordance with considerations of a repeat player.[46]

---

[45] *See* Beth Harris, *Representing Homeless Families: Repeat Player Implementation Strategies*, 33 LAW & SOCIETY REV. 911 (1999).

[46] Galanter, *supra* note 8, ch. 5, n.209.

15

Benefits of the Use of Advisory Dialogue

THE ISRAELI CASE, unique as it may be, provides an excellent case study on the benefits and risks a legal system could gain from intensive review of national security through dialogue. In the next two chapters, I will discuss these benefits and risks. I will do this by presenting them separately. In this chapter, I will illustrate the benefits for the judicial system from such practice. In the next chapter, I will demonstrate what risks the judicial system will face from relying it. In these two chapters, I will refer quite often to the debate in the American literature regarding the use of advisory dialogue by the U.S. Supreme Court. Although the Israeli experience as was shown in previous chapters is unique, many of the rationales provided for or against inter-branch dialogue in the United States are relevant to a broader discussion over the desirability of such practice and go beyond one system or another. Last, in the concluding chapter, I will discuss what lessons we can draw from the Israeli experience and how best advisory dialogue could be utilized in order to promote human rights and the rule of law in national security matters.

Two important benefits, discussed already in length in this book, of advisory dialogue are that it enables meaningful and relevant judicial review of military actions and national security policies and that it allows the Court to provide such review in real time or close to real time. So, for example, when claims that the military was using white phosphorus in the course of military campaigns were brought before the Court, the Court examined the use of white phosphorus in close proximity to the events themselves. It examined whether this use lies contrary to the laws of war (and, in particular, contrary to the principle of distinguishing between civilians and militants), without it, the parties, or the Israeli public seeing any difficulty in this. The Court declared:

> Indeed, the choice of military weapons, which the military employs, is not a matter for this court's examination, as a rule. Nonetheless, it may not be said that each

time issues related to the use of such or other means of warfare arise, the Court will refrain from examining the matter. It is understood that when claims arise for the use of military means in a matter that contradicts the laws of warfare, the Court will be compelled to descend to "the battlefield" and examine the claims raised before the Court. The boundaries for the intervention of this court in these kinds of issues are extremely narrow. Nonetheless, it is reserved and available for unusual and exceptional cases that justify this. When there is concern for harm to established legal norms, this court has intervened more than once in petitions, even if these comprise political or military implications.[1]

It is a huge benefit all who cherish respect for the rule of law that the military understands that the Supreme Court will supervise everything to ensure that combat will be conducted in accordance with the laws of war, and that this supervision will be effected in real time or close to real time. This has a chilling effect on the military and makes it more likely that decisions will be taken and policies will be adopted knowing that they will most likely be subject to judicial review.[2] This would not have been possible if the Court had not used advisory dialogue intensively. In this case, as may be recalled, the Court rejected the petition. However, it did so only after the military assured the Court that new Standard Operating Procedure (SOP) will be issued reassuring that such means would be used only under the most unusual circumstances, and the military would inform the attorney representing the petitioning nongovernmental organization of any amendment to this SOP.

Another important benefit of advisory dialogue, discussed in the previous chapter, is that it allows the Court once intervening to decide on the specific mode of intervention and to time landmark decisions to more convenient times. These however are not the only benefits advisory dialogue offers to the legal system: below I will list several more. In the following chapter I will discuss the drawbacks and risks that await if advisory dialogue is used inappropriately.

ADVISORY DIALOGUE AS A MEANS TO PREVENT CONFLICTS AMONG BRANCHES

A great many studies deal with the conduct of the courts and the manner in which judges' formulate their decisions. Even if we do not decide the question as to which theory of judges' behavior[3] best describes their conduct, the words of James Gibson will still be apt:

Judges' decisions are a function of what they prefer to do, tempered by what they think they ought to do, but constrained by what they perceive is feasible to do.

---

[1] HCJ 4146/11, Hess v. the General Chief of Staff (unpublished, 9 July 2013), para. 5 of the judgment.

[2] *See also* Jack Goldsmith, Power and Constaint 92 (2013).

[3] For a comprehensive review of the theoretical development of research into the behavior of judges, *see* Lee Epstein & Jack Knight, *Toward a Strategic Revolution in Judicial Politics: A Look Back, A Look Forward*, 53 Pol. Res. Q. 625 (2000).

Individuals make decisions, but they do so within the context of group, institutional and environmental constraints.[4]

There is no doubt that one of the most important advantages that advisory dialogue accords a legal system is that the use of advisory messages, to a large extent, reduces the risk of confrontation among branches, particularly during times of emergency, but not only.

Another question is whether preventing conflict in and of itself normatively justifies the use of advisory messages. In the U.S context, Alexander M. Bickel, an advocate of inter-branch dialogue, argued, that in the absence of sword or purse, the US Supreme Court must endeavor to refrain from unnecessary confrontations with other branches that are likely to harm the Court. William N. Eskridge and Philip P. Frickey, too, discussed the significance of the refined dialogue the Court conducts with other branches, in which both endeavor not "to impose" on each other binding decisions (laws on the part of the legislative authority and the invalidation of laws on the part of the Court)— actions that have a destructive effect on dialogue. Eskridge and Frickey believe that in place of "impositions" and confrontations, players in inter-branch dialogue can reach agreements and understandings through advisory dialogue with regard to the limits of power of each of them, and can coordinate their courses of action.[5]

Eskridge and Frickey identify the advantages that the legal system can produce from the use of such messages:

> Compared with formal overrides, signaling is also a less conflictual way for lawmaking institutions to communicate with one another. Without actually striking down federal legislation, the Supreme Court can lay out limitations on congressional authority through dicta in constitutional opinions and narrow constructions of statutes that venture close to constitutional boundaries. The Court rationally sends such signals to avoid unnecessary conflict with an institution that can hurt the Court badly. Congress rationally attends to such signals because the Court in turn can undermine congressional interests by narrowly construing or invalidating statutes.[6]

---

[4] *See* James L. Gibson, *From Simplicity to Complexity: The Development of Theory in the Study of Judicial Behavior*, 5 POL. BEHAV. 7, 32 (1983).

[5] As the authors maintain, "This kind of signaling among lawmaking institutions has the systemic advantage of resolving most institutional disputes without open, mutually destructive conflict. Over a period of time, moreover, signals and actions consistent with those signals can be a way in which interdependent institutions create implicit bargains.... By a series of signals and actions, the coordinate institutions can indicate their priorities and their willingness to reach deals whereby each institution defers to the most important preferences of the others." *See* William N. Eskridge & Philip P. Frickey, *The Supreme Court, 1993 Term Forward: Law as Equilibrium*, 108 HARV. L. REV. 27, 40 (1994).

[6] William N. Eskridge & Philip P. Frickey, *The Supreme Court, 1993 Term Forward: Law as Equilibrium*, 108 HARV. L. REV. 27, 77 (1994).

Eskridge and Frickey maintain that judicious use of incidental statements and constitutional construal allows the US Supreme Court to hold a dialogue with Congress and create implicit bargains with it. In their opinion, these messages have an important practical advantage as the use of such messages, as opposed to invalidating policy or law, allows the Court to clarify its preferences without conflict and at a low level of exposure. Ronald J. Krotoszynski writes the following with regard to this rationale:

> Properly deployed, a constitutional flare facilitates less confrontational judicial interactions with the political branches and reduces the countermajoritarian bite of judicial review. Dialogue between courts and members of the Executive and legislative branch should help to facilitate compliance with constitutional norms, thereby avoiding interbranch strife. This is a prize that makes the game worth playing.[7]

It must be noted that refraining from imposition of views by the Court in the area of national security is a particularly important benefit of advisory dialogue. National security is one specific area where there is not widespread support among the public for judicial intervention, certainly not in times of emergency.[8] By refraining from the invalidation of laws or determining a certain policy as being unconstitutional, and replacing these decisions with advisory messages, a court can diminish, to a large extent, the force of the opposition anticipated with respect to its decision. It also enables the legislature to respond without having to reply to the question that frequently arises in these situations—who is the sovereign authority in the State, the Court, or the legislature?—and, without the force of the decision being a consideration in the response of the legislature.

Neal Katyal and Erik Luna, two more authors among the principal writers on discursivism, proposed that the U.S. Supreme Court make more extensive use of what Katyal describes as judicial "advice-giving." Katyal deemed the use of advice as an ideal provisional solution to the tension between minimalism, as proper practice, and the wish of the Supreme Court to express its position on various issues that are brought before it even when a decision on these matters is not necessary. Eric Luna believed that it is desirable that the Supreme Court explain to the legislative authority, when it invalidates a law, how it should act in order to preclude further constitutional conflicts in the future. Luna called this practice "constitutional road maps."[9]

---

[7] Ronald J. Krotoszynski, *Constitutional Flares: On Judges, Legislatures and Dialogue*, 83 MINN. L. REV. 1, 59 (1998).

[8] GAD BARZILAI, EFRAIM YAAR-YUCHTMAN & ZE'EV SEGEL THE SUPREME COURT IN THE VIEW OF ISRAELI SOCIETY 89–94 (1994).

[9] Eric Luna, *Constitutional Road Maps*, 90 J. CRIM. L. & CRIMINOLOGY 1125 (2000).

Neal Devins,[10] Neal Katyal,[11] Erik Luna,[12] and Ronald Krotoszynski believe that the U.S Supreme Court must be an active partner in the dialogue and initiate the transmission of messages to other branches of Government. However, the Court must do so from a position that recognizes the standing and independence of other branches, including their authority not to act according to the Court's advice.

Employing advisory dialogue in times of emergency, when the courts usually refrain from intervention, affords the Israeli Supreme Court an advantage that purely refraining from intervention or striking out a petition *in limine* is unable to provide. Without the attendant message, there is concern that the other branches will misinterpret the refraining from intervention as granting legitimization. More seriously, it may legitimize violations of the law or actions contrary to international law. Here again literature in the United States could provide us insights as to why nonintervention could be a risky strategy. As Krotozinski writes with regard to the Court's refraining from intervention:

> The passive virtues suffer from a number of shortcomings, most notably a naïve hope that Congress will pay careful attention to acts of judicial abstention.[13]

Accordingly, by using advisory dialogue, the Supreme Court clarifies through advisory dialogue to the other branches what it has decided and what it will refrain from deciding.

ADVISORY DIALOGUE CONTRIBUTES TO THE ADVANCEMENT OF APPROPRIATE LEGISLATION

One other benefit of advisory dialogue in the national security context is that it can assist the legislature in advancing better national security legislation. As we saw with regard to the issue of warning individuals suspected of involvement in terrorist activity, or the question of using violence in Shin Bet interrogations, or of using persons as bargaining chips, the Israeli Supreme Court transmits messages regarding potential legislation. In these messages the Court conveyed signals with regard to the degree of constitutionality of the law to be legislated on the subject, if legislated as a result of its judgment.

In this way, the Court can assist the legislative authority in arriving at more precise formulations of legislation, and a more suitable constitutional balance. Advisory

---

[10] Neal Devins, *The Democracy-Forcing Constitution*, 97 MICH. L. REV. 1971 (1999).
[11] Neal Katyal, *Judges as Advicegivers*, 50 STAN. L. REV. 1709, 1801 (1998).
[12] Luna, *supra* note 9, at 266.
[13] Krotoszynski, *supra* note 7, at 46.

messages can assist the legislators to adopt a law under limitations the Court has already determined. The benefit that the system gains from such use is as follows: If the legislators incorporate the advisory message, this may lead them to avoid legislating unsuitable laws, on the one hand, and to estimate that the chances are good that a law that is legislated in the spirit of the advisory message will be likely to withstand the test of judicial review, on the other. The Court's recommendations are an effective "economic" expression of the dialogue conducted between the Supreme Court and the legislature. In many cases, as the one of "the Bargaining Chips" instructs, many years can go by until the law that the legislature would like to enact will arrive for judicial review in the Court. William Landes and Richard Posner,[14] as well as James Rogers and George Vanberg,[15] view this consideration in the U.S context and concluded that it justifies the use of recommendations for legislation whose purpose is to improve potential legislation. The great advantage of this practice is that it enables the Court to prevent the enactment of injurious laws without having to wait for years until the matter is brought before the Court for decision.

ADVISORY DIALOGUE STRENGTHENS DEMOCRACY, ENCOURAGES THE PERCEPTION OF EQUAL POWERS AMONG BRANCHES, AND PROMOTES PUBLIC DISCOURSE ON FUNDAMENTAL QUESTIONS

In research on linguistics, sociolinguistics,[16] and psychology,[17] many studies have been conducted that discuss the question of why people and bodies with authority tend to refrain from employing formal authority even though they have the ability to do so. The conclusion that arises from these studies is that refraining from the use of sharp unequivocal language that serves to exercise authority enables persons who are in positions of power to raise a certain subject in a non-coercive manner while leaving room for

---

[14] *See* William M. Landes & Richard A. Posner, *The Economics of Anticipatory Adjudication*, 23 J. LEGAL STUD. 683, 686 (1994).

[15] Rogers and Vanberg state, "It might be years after enactment that a law is finally challenged...Such statutes may be in effect for years before they are struck down...Before it is successfully challenged, an unconstitutional statute may discourage legitimate activity; or, conversely, it may encourage reliance which, when the statute is invalidated, will prove to have been ill-founded, thus causing injury to those who have based action upon it." *See* James Rogers & Georg Vanberg, *Judicial Advisory Opinions and Legislative Outcomes in Comparative Perspective: A Game-Theoretic Analysis*, Paper presented at the Midwest Political Science Association Annual Meeting, Chicago, April 19–22, p. 5 (2001).

[16] *See* PENELOPE BROWN & STEPHEN LEVINSON, POLITENESS: SOME UNIVERSALS IN LANGUAGE USAGE (1987).

[17] See Thomas Holtgraves, *Styles of Language Use: Individual and Cultural Variability in Conversational Indirectness*, 73 J. PERSONALITY & SOC. PSYCHOL. 624 (1997); Thomas Holtgraves, *Communication in Context: Effects of Speaker Status on the Comprehension of Indirect Requests*, 20 J. EXPERIMENTAL PSYCHOL. 1205 (1994).

other options.[18] refraining from the employment of formal authority cultivates a sense of cooperation, openness, and equality. Extrapolating this issue to the study of inter branch dialogue can illustrate another advantage of the advisory dialogue. This approach views the use of the advisory dialogue as a means for opening up public discourse while providing other branches and the public with the option of holding such a discussion without the courts having to decide the question in a way that will block the opportunity for this discussion to take place.

A decision to refrain from a direct ruling on an issue and to prefer an advisory message instead does not necessarily ensue from weakness. At times, it ensues from a deeper recognition of the significance of open public social discourse. Neal Katyal,[19] Mark Tushnet,[20] and Jay D. Wexler[21] see this reason for conducting advisory dialogue as an expression of the concept of the division of labor among branches in the absence of the supremacy of judicial review. Refraining from a binding decision, which coerces the Executive or the legislature to accept a certain position, reflects the division of labor among branches of government without the supremacy of one or another. It allows the Supreme Court to demonstrate to the other government branches that indeed the Court supports a certain position, but it prefers not to decide the matter. Rather, the Court would like to persuade the other branches of the correctness and justice of its opinion and to enable them to reach this conclusion of their own accord.

It is appropriate to note in this context that this book focuses on dialogue among branches. However, the Supreme Court's comments also influence the discourse that is being held outside of the Court. When its comments disagree with certain policy related to national security or encourage it, this can allow groups found outside the immediate circle of discussants to rely on it to conduct a public discussion on the question of the desirability of this policy. Greg Myers defines this practice and all its features as "an appropriate attitude for offering a claim to the community."[22] In this case, the advisory message serves as a means for broader public discourse.

This approach ties in with a wider discussion pertaining to the Supreme Court's role in society. For many,[23] the Court is not only a body that resolves disputes between individuals or between an individual and society. This approach views the Court as a social

---

[18] *See* Greg Myers, *The Pragmatics of Politeness in Scientific Articles*, 10 APPLIED LINGUISTICS 1 (1989).

[19] Katyal, *Judges as Advicegivers*, 50 STAN. L. REV. 1709, 1801 (1998).

[20] See Mark Tushnet, *Constitutionalism without Courts? Taking the Constitution Away from the Courts*, 94 Nw. U.L. Rev. 983 (2000).

[21] *See* Jay D. Wexler, *Defending the Middle Way: Intermediate Scrutiny as Judicial Minimalism*, 66 GEO. WASH. L. REV. 298 (1998). According to Wexler, by way of minimalism "the Court can open a dialogue with other governmental actors." *Id.* at 337.

[22] *See* Myers, *supra* note 18, at 13.

[23] Neal Katyal, in his article "Judges as Advicegivers," at 1779, cites Rostow in this context as stating, "Justices are inevitably teachers in a vital national seminar." Eugene V. Rostow, *The Democratic Character of Judicial Review*, 66 HARV. L. REV. 193, 208 (1952).

compass practiced in incorporating a set of social values. Bickel himself indicates "The Court is a leader of opinion, not a mere register of it."[24] Neal Devins, a leading author on discursivism, also views judicial dialogue as a means toward the mutual education of public authorities.[25]

What all this tells us is that a court that engages in dialogue could play an important role in society of being a moral compass.

ADVISORY DIALOGUE ENABLES CHANGE WITHOUT REVOLUTIONS

In the previous chapter, we demonstrated that advisory dialogue apparently has an effect on the timing of Supreme Court decisions and that it is reasonable to assume that the Israeli court tends to time decisions related to national security to coincide with dates of relative calm.

We have also seen that in numerous national security–related cases in which the Supreme Court passed judgment against the State, this was preceded at least by one decision in which the Supreme Court conveyed an advisory message to the parties, preparing the ground and pointing out the direction for change.

Thus, when the Supreme Court would like to initiate social change, which it knows the public is not ready yet to accept, it could use an advisory message to prepare the ground for the change. Such testing will prevent the Court from being harmed (which would occur if the Court was viewed as being unfaithful to its precedents). Presenting change as a development, rather than a transformation, by means of messages embedded in a variety of decisions allows the Court to introduce serious social change without sacrificing the value of stability or its own legitimacy. Advisory messages allow the Court to indicate the direction in which it strives, yet, nonetheless, to choose for itself the suitable pace in which the change in policy will be implemented.

In the national security context, using these measures enables the Supreme Court to refrain from making binding decisions, when, in the Court's estimation, the state of emergency in the country does *not* allow for overturning its previous case law. In these cases, the Court is likely to prefer that change be implemented gradually—as a natural process rather than a radical one. Advisory messages mitigate and blur the change, preparing the ground ahead of additional amendments that will complete the transformation.

This benefit of dialogue was noted by several American scholars. Michael Keene writes, "If advice is dictum, it can provide smooth transitions from the past to the

---

[24] ALEXANDER M. BICKEL, THE LEAST DANGEROUS BRANCH: THE SUPREME COURT AT THE BAR OF POLITICS 236 (1962).

[25] *See* NEAL DEVINS, SHAPING CONSTITUTIONAL VALUES: ELECTED GOVERNMENT, THE SUPREME COURT, AND THE ABORTION DEBATE (1996)] According to Devins, "The Executive, legislative and judicial branches are engaged in an ongoing dialogue, with each branch checking (and perhaps educating) one another." *Id.* at 149.

future."[26] Phillip Kannan denotes: "Often dicta indicate the path that law may take in the future."[27]

The strategic use of such suggestions can serve the Court to prepare the public and other branches of government for a change in policy to be made in another judgment. Delay and deferral at a time of national crisis enables society and social and political systems to process the true implications of the crisis and to adjust to it.

ADVISORY DIALOGUE ALLOWS JUDGES TO COPE BETTER WITH MORAL DILEMMAS

In his book on slavery in the United States,[28] Robert Cover described how justices who opposed slavery coped with cases in which they were compelled to decide matters of slaves who had escaped from their owners. Cover demonstrated how these justices developed legal doctrines and "distorted" existing legal doctrines to preclude punishment of slaves or returning them to their owners.

The fact that judges are often required to give judgments with which they are not in agreement is not a new phenomenon or particular to a certain area of case law. It principally ensues from the tension that exists in every positive legal system between the rules of law and the rules of morality and ethics, and the inevitable clash between a system based on rules and the wish of judges to reach a just outcome in a concrete case.[29]

Such a clash of values occurs as well when judges are required to grant legitimacy to a certain national security policy with which they are not in agreement, even if they are unable to define it as unlawful or unconstitutional. Neal Katyal indicates the following in this context:

> Because courts are generally reluctant to interject their views into military affairs, they are not particularly effective constitutional police for the military. But every time they uphold a military policy with deference-laden review, they legitimize the policy as constitutional.[30]

A court to which a petition is submitted during a time of combat may reach the conclusion that the policy the State has undertaken is not just, but, at the same time, it is not

---

[26] *See* Michael Sean Quinn, *Symposium on Taking Legal Arguments Seriously: Argument and Authority in Common Law Advocacy and Adjudication: An Irreducible Pluralism of Principles*, 74 CHI.-KENT. L. REV. 655, 729 (1999).

[27] *See* Phillip M. Kannan, *Advisory Opinions by Federal Courts*, 32 U. RICH. L. REV. 769, 792 (1998).

[28] *See* ROBERT M. COVER, JUSTICE ACCUSED: ANTISLAVERY AND THE JUDICIAL PROCESS (1975).

[29] *See on this subject* JEAN-FRANCOIS LYOTARD, THE DIFFEREND: PHRASES IN DISPUTE (1988).

[30] *See* Katyal, *supra* note 11, at 1762.

necessarily unlawful or unconstitutional. The court may also decide that this is a question that better falls within the exclusive authority of the Executive or the legislature.

Whatever the non-substantive reasons that lead it to refrain from intervention are, doing so may be interpreted as legitimizing policy that the judge or the Court may believe is harmful. Advisory messages that express the Court's dissatisfaction with the outcome that it has reached enable the Court to refrain from legitimizing this policy, even if the Court does not find such policy to be unlawful or unconstitutional.

The Supreme Court of Israel is very familiar with the risk of nonintervening in controversial national security policies. In most cases, in which the Court determines that a certain policy is lawful, it also justifies the policy morally. As opposed to this, we have seen cases, particularly on the question of house demolitions, in which the Court transmitted messages that consciously refrain from providing moral legitimization for this practice of express dissatisfaction from its use, even though the Court did not feel that the language of the law allowed it to determine the policy to be unlawful.

Few examples could illustrate this benefit of advisory dialogue. As may be recalled, the State presented to the Court in several national security matters the "ticking bomb" dilemma. According to utilitarian principles, the State argued, it is appropriate to use force vis-à-vis an individual in order to save many lives. Nonetheless, it was clear, as extensively explained in previous chapters, that a rule that permits using violence vis-à-vis an individual is contrary to the ontological perception of morality and is likely to be abused by security services. The Court faced a most difficult dilemma.

The statements of Justice Cheshin in his judgment on the *Neighbor Procedure*[31] and the similar statements made by Justice Barak in his judgment in HCJ *On Torture*[32] with regard to the great difficulty the Court experiences illustrate the need that judges have for advisory messages as a means to convey their moral beliefs.

---

[31] "The subject is a difficult one. Most difficult. So difficult is it, that a judge might ask himself why he chose the calling of the judiciary, and not of another profession, to be busy with. It is a no-win situation. [Woe is me, for I answer to my creator; woe is me, with my conflicting inclinations (*see* Babylonian Talmud, Brachot, 61, 1).] No matter which solution I choose, the time will come that I will regret my choice." HCJ 3799/02 Adallah v. GOC (General Officer Commanding) Central Command PD 60 (3) 67 (2005), concurring judgment by Justice Cheshin, para 1.

[32] "Deciding these petitions weighed heavily on this Court. True, from the legal perspective, the road before us is smooth. We are, however, part of Israeli society. Its problems are known to us and we live its history. We are not isolated in an ivory tower. We live the life of this country. We are aware of the harsh reality of terrorism in which we are, at times, immersed. The possibility that this decision will hamper the ability to properly deal with terrorists and terrorism disturbs us. We are, however, judges. We must decide according to the law. This is the standard that we set for ourselves. When we sit to judge, we ourselves are judged. Therefore, in deciding the law, we must act according to our purest conscience and understanding with regard to the law." Justice Barak in HCJ *On Torture*, HCJ 5100/94, The Pubic Committee against Torture in Israel v. the Government of Israel, PD 53 (4) 817, 845 (1999).

In a completely different context, Guido Calabresi cites the *Korematsu* case,[33] which concerned decisions taken in the United States during the Second World War ordering US citizens of Japanese origins into internment camps, as an example of this kind of national security dilemma. Calabresi maintains that the minority opinion of Justice Jackson, who argued that the fact that the US Supreme Court recognized that it is possible to harm the principle of equality in the name of security is worse than other possible solutions that were available to the Court on this matter. According to Calabresi, even if the Court could not intervene in the decision from a political point of view, it should have adopted a solution that prevented legitimizing the outcome that the Court reached. The long-term preservation of the value of equality is more significant to him than the degree to which any judgment is coherent.[34] A more radical example that Calabresi brings us back to the use of violence in interrogations. In this context, he refers to an article written by the jurist Charles Black,[35] which discusses the hypothetical (at the time) question of what a judge would do if he were required to permit the use of violence in an investigation to extract information from a person with knowledge that an atomic bomb was about to be dropped on a city. According to Black, and Calabresi agrees with him, in those situations as well, in which a judge believes that it is ethical to use physical force in an interrogation to prevent an atomic bomb from being dropped on a city, it would be better for the Court to find a way to avoid legitimizing its outcome. Calabresi writes the following on this matter:

> The judge, Black indicates, may waffle, may adjourn court...but the one thing he or she is not apt to do is to enforce the supposed absolute against torture and let the city be destroyed. Are we then correct in characterizing our rule against torture as an absolute one? Yes, Black suggests, because the opposite rule—which would say we balance the need for torture against its harm—would be totally inaccurate. Whom would you trust more to decide both the case of the hydrogen bomb and torture cases generally, as we want them decided? He asked rhetorically, a judge who in hard and easy cases is always declaring that we must balance the costs and benefit of torture, or a judge who announces that our system has an absolute prohibition against torture?[36]

---

[33] Korematsu v. United States, 323 U.S. 214, 245–46 (1944) [hereinafter *Korematsu*].

[34] Dotan compares the ruling in the *Korematsu* case with the judgment of the Court in the deportation of the Hamas members. For the same reasons that Calabresi put forward, Dotan believes that it would have been preferable had the Court refrained from hearing the matter rather than giving a judgment that ratified the government's decision on the deportation matter. *See* Yoav Dotan, *A General Petition and Judicial Politics*, Tel Aviv U. L. Rev. 20 (1997) 149

[35] *See* Charles Black, *Mr. Justice Black, the Supreme Court, and the Bill of Rights*, 63 Harper's Mag. (1961).

[36] Guido Calabresi, A Common Law for the Age of Statutes 173 (1982).

Using the principle espoused by Calabresi and Black for our matter, we are led to the following conclusion. There are situations, certainly in the field of national security, in which judges may find that the language of the law or the principles of the separation of powers limit their ability to express their true moral positions. In such a case of an ostensible clash of values, the judge must choose this or that value and prefer it to any other. However, the use of advisory messages allows the court not to resolve the clash of values and instead to express the tension that exists via an advisory message that serves as a kind of "refuge," "third way," or a means to moderate the intensity of the clash of values.

ADVISORY DIALOGUE ALLOWS THE COURT TO TRANSMIT MESSAGES OF VARYING INTENSITY

One of the features of a judicial decision is that it is binary. The court is compelled to express its opinion on a question whether a certain policy is lawful or unlawful, whether a law is constitutional or not. The court's decision ends the discussion on this question. Integrating advisory messages in judicial decisions enables the courts to cope with the inherent rigidity of a judicial decision. Advisory dialogue permits the court to transmit "softer" messages and to express the court's position on the question in dispute by way of the language it uses, and not necessarily by way of the bottom line.

Here again the U.S experience could offer us some insights on these benefits of advisory dialogue. Lori Hausegger and Lawrence Baum[37] pointed out that "invitations" to overturn a decision or "positive signaling" serve the U.S. Supreme Court in transmitting messages to Congress of variable degrees of intensity. In one case the Court could be satisfied with referring the matter to Congress and, in another, the Court could use sharper language as it advises Congress to amend the law. An analysis of their study indicates that judges use different language according to the intensity with which they wish to convey the signaling to Congress. Michael Quinn writes the following on this matter:

> Obviously, advice can be given in different tones. Sometimes, courts can give advice by saying that they think the legislature really should do such and such, or that some state agency should promulgate some regulations. Sometimes, advising can sound like begging.[38]

---

[37] Lori Hausegger & Lawrence Baum, *Inviting Congressional Action: A Study of Supreme Court Motivations in Statutory Interpretation*, 43 AM. J. POL. SCI. 162 (1999).

[38] *See* Quinn, *supra* note 26, at 729. Eskridge and Frickey too have discussed this quality of advisory messages.

Eskridge and Frikey express similar views. They write as follows:

> Signals express not only an institution's preferences, but also the intensity of these preferences. Strongly directive dicta, committee report language, and presidential signing or veto statements put other institutions on notice that they are in for a fight if they ignore the messages being sent.[39]

This feature of advisory dialogue is of great significance with respect to decisions on national security questions. In this manner, the Court can promote proper policy or law while at the same time expressing the degree of its desire to see change. The use of precise language, which is primary in advisory messages, as opposed to the bottom line of the judgment, which is the essence of the binding part of the decision, enables the Court to transmit messages of varying levels of intensity and to find language—as opposed to a legal conclusion—around which all the justices on the panel can converge.

ADVISORY DIALOGUE ENABLES THE COURT TO OVERCOME DISPARITIES IN APPLICATION OF ITS DECISIONS

The use of advisory dialogue can have several further pragmatic advantages in terms of bridging the gap between a legal rule and the manner of its application in reality. In the *Korematsu* case,[40] Justice Jackson cited the words of Justice Cardozo, who noted the tendency of judicial rules to expand themselves beyond the limits of the logic that produced them.[41] This generally ensues for three possible reasons. First, there is a disparity between the rule produced by the Court and the rule as it is understood and interpreted by the Executive. Second, there is a disparity between the manner in which the Executive interprets a rule and the manner in which it applies it. Third, there is a disparity between the manner in which the rule is applied and the possibility of the Court overseeing this. For the purposes of this discussion, I will refer to these three disparities together as the *application gap*.

In the field of national security, the difficulty of overseeing the application of a legal rule is particularly evident. The Court faces situations in which it cannot ensure that its decision will be applied precisely as it was written—that could be due to the secrecy surrounding many of these policies and the lack in assessing the national security challenges the country is currently facing. In such instances, the Court has two options: to issue a judgment prohibiting the conduct completely or to give a decision that reflects

---

[39] *See id.* at 40.

[40] *Korematsu, supra* note 33.

[41] In the *Korematsu* judgment, Justice Jackson observed "the tendency of a principle to expand itself to the limit of its logic." *See the judgment of Justice Jackson on the matter, id.* at 245–46.

its stand on the issue, while risking that it will not be applied as the Court intended. The use of advisory messages ostensibly offers a third option. The Court determines a delineated and defined legal rule, but tries to regulate the use of policy through its advisory messages.

We saw this practice used in cases in which the Supreme Court believes that certain policy indeed in not unlawful, but has been exposed to harsh reports by human rights organizations pertaining to the manner of its application or its implications. In these cases, the Court encounters a difficult situation: on the one hand, the Court does not feel that it is right to determine that the policy is unlawful, while the security situation that is laid out before the Court appears to justify it. On the other hand, the Court would like to be sure that the military or intelligence services will apply the legal rule as it has been determined. Advisory messages offer a possible solution in such cases, because they are designed to influence those applying the policy to act in a manner that is consistent with the Court's intention and when needed "threaten" these services that the Court or some of its justices are considering declaring the policy unlawful.

ADVISORY DIALOGUE ENABLES THE SUPREME COURT TO OVERCOME THE INHERENT DIFFICULTIES OF ADJUDICATING NATIONAL SECURITY

The area of national security has several unique features that encourage the Court to be more restrained and to prefer advisory dialogue to binding judicial decisions. Many justices believe that they lack the necessary expertise in this field; there is also the power of the argument that pertains to the lives of people justices may also be concerned that in this field it is more likely that a decision may be overturned and harm the status of the Court. These factors cause courts to act cautiously in this field—to attempt to influence but also to acknowledge their limitations. This practical approach is based on the assumption that whether we like it or not, a court's ability to review effectively a variety of issues related to national security is limited. It is based also on the assumption that the public at large understands the term *human rights* during times of war differently than during times of peace.

With regard to many of these questions, the Court is also compelled to give its judicial decisions under the cover of uncertainty with respect to the facts. At times, this ensues from time pressures or the fog of battle that envelops the questions on which the decisions are requested, as we saw in the cases concerning the fighting in Jenin or Rafiah or during Operation Cast Lead. At times, this ensues from a lack of knowledge with regard to the potential implications of a decision that is made under conditions of uncertainty, as occurred in the case of the crisis at the Church of the Nativity and in other combat situations. The uncertainty that envelops judicial decisions about national security also stems from the fact that in order to determine whether policy is lawful or unlawful, the Court must take notice of the policy's actual effectiveness. In considering the degree of harm that will be caused in a specific case by the utilization of certain measures, one must also consider, even if only in utilitarian terms, the harm that these measures may preclude. Accordingly, a shortage of facts, the lack of tools for a true evaluation, or the fog of battle does not allow the Court to decide the question of the measures' effectiveness. In order to decide such difficult questions, the Court must obtain a full set of the facts and of the implications of its decision. As we saw in previous chapters, in many cases this full set of facts is incomplete because fighting is still ongoing at the time that the petition is brought before the Court. At times, the set of facts on the ground is changing all the time. At times, the parties present a set of facts that are conflicting, or the reality of combat does not permit applying the judgment at all. Nonetheless, waiting until the facts can be clarified can make—and in many cases it does make—the petition moot.

For a court that would like to exercise judicial review *in real time*, it is extremely difficult to come to a decision, even if there are no legal or institutional limitations that preclude the court from making a ruling. Given the tremendous difficulty in making a decision under combat conditions, the Israeli Supreme Court uses advisory dialogue as an alternative to decisions, even if at times it is only a provisional alternative.

The Supreme Court, notwithstanding its willingness to intervene in each and every decision, is aware that there are objective restrictions that preclude it from making rational decisions. In several cases, the Court explicitly expressed the effects of these difficulties on its national security decisions. In HCJ 2977/02 *Adalah v. the Commander of IDF Forces in Judea and Samaria*, the Court wrote the following: "The Respondent's position is that at issue are effective combat operations, where occasionally causing damage to homes is unavoidable when these houses are turned into bunkers of sorts, used for shooting at IDF forces. Under these circumstances, the power of the Court to intervene in operational actions through judicial review is limited."[42] Justice Cheshin, also aware of the limitations of the Court, expressed a similar position:

> In war, as in war: Shall the Court tell a military commander what he should do and what he should not do? Indeed, the Court will not tell the commander of a battalion that it would be wise to send a company to the right of the hill rather than to the left. In the same spirit, though to a lesser degree, I would find it difficult to understand how shall the Court order a military commander not to destroy the home of a murdering terrorist—to deter others—solely because the Court perhaps thinks otherwise than the military commander.[43]

---

[42] HCJ 2977/02, Adalah v. the Commander of IDF Forces in the Area of Judea and Samaria, PD 56 (3) 6, 7–8 (2002).

[43] *Id.*, para. 5 of the judgment of Justice Cheshin.

The judgment of Justice Beinisch, too, concerning the fighting in Rafiah illuminates the frame of mind of the Supreme Court in its decisions in this field. Justice Beinisch writes the following: "The circumstances involved in the process of judicial review during a time of actual combat limit the effectiveness of judicial review and make application of the solutions required by the Court difficult."[44] She also provides a certain explanation of the question why the Supreme Court is compelled in these situations to influence decision-making processes in other government agencies through its advisory messages.

> Judicial review, which seeks to examine the need to provide reliefs at a time when combat events are still in progress, requires a judicial procedure of a special kind, and the petition before us is a prime example of this. *The petition was heard while changes and developments in the combat zone were taking place during the actual hearing. The parties that presented their arguments before us based their arguments on continuous reports from the field of combat, and these reports changed the set of circumstances and facts during the course of hearing the petition.* The factual description of ascertaining the particulars of the matter, as aforesaid, finds expression in the President's judgment. *In such circumstances, the judicial review process is limited and suffers from the lack of adequate arrangements with which to ascertain the relevant information in order to examine this in real time, and to grant effective relief with respect thereto.* [emphasis added][45]

The Court discussed these difficulties again in its judgment on the petitions that were submitted during Operation Cast Lead. The Court indicated in its judgment as follows:

> In our case, petitions were submitted at a time when combat activities were still in progress in the field...Our judicial review is being exercised in this case while the hostilities are continuing. *Naturally, this imposes restrictions on the Court's ability to exercise judicial review and to ascertain all of the relevant facts at this stage of the hostilities...Indeed, while hostilities are taking place, it is not always possible to collect all the information that is required for exercising judicial review, in view of the dynamic changes that are continually occurring.* However, the Court endeavors to examine the claims in real time, so that it may grant effective relief or set up an arrangement.[46]

There is no doubt that the difficulty of making a decision that contradicts the policy of fighting under conditions of such high levels of uncertainty is a principal feature of

---

[44] HCJ 4764/04 Physicians for Human Rights v. Commander of IDF Forces in Gaza, Tak-El 2004 (2) 2183, 2186 (2004), para 6 to the concurring judgment of Justice Beinisch.

[45] Id.

[46] HCJ 201/09, Physicians for Human Rights v. the Prime Minister, Tak-El 2009 (1) 565.

decisions related to national security or emergency situations. The fact that the Supreme Court of Israel acquired the authority to exercise such judicial review does not resolve the serious structural problems involved in doing so in the course of combat. A combination of a sense of urgency, an atmosphere of emergency, the uncertainty with regard to the facts, and the fateful nature of the decision are principal features of the dilemmas brought before the Supreme Court, certainly in recent years. The difficulty that is built into case law makes it hard for the Supreme Court to accept decisions against the State. The principal option that the Supreme Court has found is translating the exercise of ordinary judicial review in these situations into the use of intensive advisory dialogue with the Executive. The purpose is, as the Supreme Court indicated in several of its judgments, to make sure that even in times of war the sound of law is heard. It may not be the same practice of judicial review as in calm times but at least the law is not kept silent.

16

The Use of Advisory Dialogue—Disadvantages and Risks

IN THE PREVIOUS chapter, we saw that the use of advisory dialogue offers several important advantages to the Israeli legal system. It indeed allows the Court to provide in "real time" meaningful, even if less than perfect, review of national security policies. Intuitively, it is our sense that this technique is "not harmful" as the messages are formally not binding. Yet if we take this approach, we disregard several significant difficulties inherent in the practice. Before we rush off to propose the use of dialogue to solve the challenge of judicial review of national security, it would be well to consider the significant risks to a legal system from the use, or more accurately the imprudent use, of advisory dialogue.

PROMOTING POLICY BY MEANS OF ADVISORY DIALOGUE COULD HARM THE SEPARATION OF POWERS

As we saw in the Israeli context, messages that the Court transmits via advisory dialogue in several cases depart from questions of law and enter the field of good policy. Here we see that the use of advisory dialogue raises several difficulties pertaining to the proper relations among the branches of government. However, it was to preserve such relations that the need for the separation of powers originally developed. As is most countries, those who sit on the Israeli Supreme Court are not elected public officials and therefore they do not enjoy the degree of legitimacy required to decide questions of government policy. As distinct from a judge, an elected public official interested in promoting a certain policy is required to propose it to the public, to include it in her platform, to explain it to the public, and to enable the public to prefer a different solution or to express an opinion on this choice. The first difficulty presented by the use of advisory messages by the Supreme Court is evidently the blurring of the line between law and policy. Such blurring undermines the principle that elected representatives are those who are required to decide national security questions. Unlike judges, they are exposed to censure of their decisions, and the public can have its say in the event that it does not support this policy.

Christine Bateup adds in this context that judicial advice-giving not only interferes with the domain of the Executive but also harms good relations between the branches of government. Advice-giving blocks the opportunity for open and independent public discourse, and leads to inter-branch distrust. According to Bateup, the use of advisory messages assumes that the legislative authority and other branches of government are unable to apply judicial decisions and to develop constitutional perspectives on their own without the Court's direction. She maintains that this difficulty harms the dialogue among the branches to the point that it denies the possibility of seeing advisory dialogue as part of a constructive constitutional dialogue.[1]

ADVISORY DIALOGUE COULD HARM JUDICIAL PROCEDURE

One of the principles governing a hearing in court is that all parties likely to be harmed directly by the court's decision must be summoned to the hearing of a petition and have their day before the court. This fundamental rule of fair trial is intended to enable the court to decide an issue in dispute with all the relevant aspects of the issue laid out before it. However, this rule applies only with respect to a binding court decision. When the court transmits advisory messages, there is no rule that obligates the court to do so when all parties likely to be affected by the contents of the message are present in the courtroom and have expressed their views on it. Even when all the parties ostensibly likely to be affected by the advisory message are present in court, it is possible that not all the considerations that pertain to the advisory message will be heard at the hearing. First, it is possible that not all the parties are aware of the possibility that the issue may be broadened, as apparently occurred in the *Rafiah* case.[2] Second, it is possible that the players at the hearing are not interested in broadening the issue and wish to discuss the issue with respect to which the Court would like to convey an advisory message. Notwithstanding these difficulties, an advisory message that the Supreme Court transmits can sometimes leave the impression that the Court has discussed the issue to its full

---

[1] "The problems with this account are so great, however, and the description of dialogue provided so theoretically impoverished, that it is questionable whether judicial advice-giving should be described as a theory of constitutional dialogue at all…While the utilization of advice-giving techniques may mean that fewer pieces of legislation are actively struck down by judges, to claim that democratic self-government is enhanced by these techniques is rather disingenuous, as this position does not allow real space for independent political judgment." Christine Bateup, *Expanding the Conversation: American and Canadian Experiences of Constitutional Dialogue in Comparative Perspective*, 21 Temp Int'l & Comp. L.J. 1, 7 (2007).

[2] HCJ 4764/04 Physicians for Human Rights v. Commander of IDF Forces in Gaza, Tak-El 2004 (2) 2183, 2186 (2004).

extent and exhausted it. Krotoszynski, again in the U.S context, discussed the difficulties in advice-giving as follows:

> Practical considerations also counsel in favor of restraint. The absence of a concrete factual dispute—not to mention briefing and oral argument on a particular issue—make it very difficult for federal judges to offer useful advice. Of necessity, advice in the absence of specific facts must be relatively open-ended, perhaps even bordering on vagueness. The utility of such advice is open to question. To the extent that the advice is vague, it is not likely to be particularly helpful to legislators; to the extent that judges attempt to offer highly targeted advice in the absence of a formal record, the advice is likely to be poor.[3]

Although Krotoszynski considered that the constitutional difficulty with respect to the separation of powers does not justify imposing a sweeping prohibition on advice-giving, he believed that in view of this constraint, the use of advice-giving requires a high degree of self-restraint.

Certainly, as he notes, it is possible to alleviate this difficulty to a certain degree. The Court may make certain to clarify that the advice it gives does not exhaust discussion of the issue and does not prevent other parties from bringing the same issue before the Court again. However, it is doubtful whether use of the technique of "reserving rights" will be able to resolve the entire difficulty that transmitting advisory messages raises.

In addition, the use of broad and non-binding language in transmitting advisory messages to avoid a situation in which a message may be interpreted as the expression of an opinion on a matter on which the Court has not exhausted its deliberation is problematic for a different reason. As he notes, insofar as the language the Court uses in an advisory message is broader and less precise, it will be more difficult to make actual use of the message to ascertain the Court's position on the issue at hand. For example, an unclear formulation of signaling can lead to both those in favor of an amendment to a law and those opposed to it viewing the decision of the Supreme Court as supporting their respective positions.

THE DISPUTED QUALITY OF ADVISORY MESSAGES

The above discussion leads us to a more general question. The manner, as well as the speed, in which the Israeli Court transmits messages does not ensure that the quality of these messages will be high and that they are not immune to errors that are likely to lead to incorrect policy. We saw that, at times, the issue on which the Court expresses

---

[3] Ronald J. Krotoszynski, *Constitutional Flares: On Judges, Legislatures and Dialogue*, 83 MINN. L. REV. 1 (1998).

its opinion was not exhausted during the course of the hearing. This is not just a matter of giving the parties their day in court but is likely to have an impact on the message's quality. Particularly for this reason, transmission of an advisory message might lead to less-than-optimal national security policy. The Court's recommendations are not given as part of a structured decision-making process, which takes into account all considerations on the issue. In addition, the Court is not exposed to the positions of others and is not fully familiar with the entire picture of considerations in terms of security, policy, or politics likely to be relevant to the decision.

Here again the debate in the United States could enlighten our discussion regarding the risks of advice. Among those opposed to the use of such advice is Judge Abner Mikva (who incidentally served in a variety of positions in all three branches). In an article written in response to Katyal's piece, Mikva argued that judges have no real advantage as advice-givers over the political echelons.[4] Furthermore, such intervention will lead to a situation in which judges' decisions will be perceived more and more as political.

He further contends that judges lack public legitimacy to make policy decisions. Moreover, they also lack the skills required for this. As he argues, it is not at all clear "that there is something in judges' status or stature that qualifies them to give.... such advice to elected officials."[5] With regard to the Canadian system of law, Janet Hiebert notes that as opposed to judicial decisions, policy decisions must be based on "specialized expertise, relevant information and data, previous trials and failures, comparative experience, and informed best estimates."[6]All these elements, which are an inherent part of Executive decision-making processes, do not and cannot take place in Court.

The issuance of less than optimal advice by the Court can lead to what has been termed by Mark Tushnet as policy distortion.[7] Tushnet writes the following:

> Policy distortion occurs when, due to judicial review, legislators choose policies that are less effective but more easily defensible than other constitutionally acceptable alternatives.

This argument merits further elaboration in the national security context: a military commander or an official who debates different alternatives, ostensibly lawful, to arrange a certain national security policy is likely to prefer the solution that the Supreme Court advised her to take, even if it is not the optimal yet lawful solution, for two reasons. First, as the Court preferred to deliver its recommendation as part of a judicial

---

[4] *See* Abner J. Mikva, *Why Judges Should Not Be Advicegivers: A Response to Professor Neal Katyal*, 50 STAN. L. REV. 1825 (1998).

[5] *Id.* at 1826.

[6] Janet L. Hiebert, *Parliament and Rights, in* PROTECTING HUMAN RIGHTS 231, 240 (Tom Campbell et. al. eds., 2003).

[7] Mark Tushnet, *Policy Distortion and Democratic Debilitation: Comparative Illumination of the Countermajoritarian Difficulty*, 94 MICH. L. REV. 245 (1995).

decision, the military commander or the official is likely to view the recommendation as binding. Even if the legislative authority as a sovereign body can and, at times, does disregard the Supreme Court's signaling and recommendations, other public authorities, particularly law enforcement, the prosecution, and the military, do not view themselves as free to disregard judicial messages. These authorities are then likely to view an advisory message as an alternative to a structured and orderly decision-making process that could have led to the endorsement of an optimal lawful national security policy. Second, the military commander or the official are likely to prefer choosing this recommendation as selecting another option considerably increases the risks to which they are exposed. If a petition against the decision is lodged, adopting the recommendation will limit the chances that the decision will be overturned as the Court has already reviewed this option. Furthermore, choosing the alternative that the Supreme Court tends to prefer enables the officeholder to rely on it when facing the public.

The conduct of military affairs greatly increases this difficulty. When the Supreme Court makes a recommendation, even if non-binding, to a military commander or to the Executive regarding how to conduct a variety of issues related to human life, it places them in a particularly problematic situation. A military commander who believes that the Supreme Court's recommendation is misguided is likely to encounter a difficult situation, as she must persuade her commanders or legal advisers of the justice of her position, the Court's advice notwithstanding. However, if a certain policy is not unlawful and the Court only recommends adopting it, why is a military commander unable to act pursuant to it? Why should she enter into any "legal" dilemma whatsoever and not act in accordance with what she deems proper according to the law?

Examples of risks in problematic messages such as these may be found in many judgments of the Israeli Court. Advisory messages that the Supreme Court transmitted in connection with the fighting in Jenin, the crisis at the Church of the Nativity, and the fighting in Rafiah were given with the factual underpinnings of the cases being highly unstable, and, at times, changing before the ink had a chance to dry on the paper. These judgments pertained to legal issues of considerable weight without enough deliberations of the matter in court. Colonel Daniel Reisner, head of the International Law Division (ILD) in the Judge Advocate General's Office in Israel during Operation Defensive Shield, responded to the hearing and decision of the Court with regard to the crisis in the Church of the Nativity as follows:

> I will present the craziest example that I remember. I was at a terminal about to travel to Europe for work and Menachem Finkelstein [the Judge Advocate General] informs me on my cell phone that a petition has been submitted to the High Court of Justice regarding the siege we imposed on the terrorists, who had barricaded themselves in the Church of the Nativity in Bethlehem. The High Court of Justice instructed the State to reply by the next morning with regard to the question of the legality of the siege. Here I am on my way to a flight and the office is asking me on

the phone if I have any idea where any relevant material is to be found on the question of a siege during fighting, while the soldiers, at the time, are waiting as they hold siege. Thus, that same night from the passengers' terminal, in a cell phone conversation, we invented some theory with regard to the possible analogies, which may be learned from the rules of siege in the classic laws of warfare. Now there is a judgment of the Supreme Court on this method of fighting, of laying siege in the counter terrorism context. This judgment is based on a legal "study" that was improvised in the twinkling of an eye during one night, and I have no idea if this will stand up even to my own criticism, had I had two days to study the matter instead of four hours.[8]

On the same matter, as may be recalled, the Supreme Court, prior to ruling and at the height of the crisis, advised the State that it should definitely consider *finding a suitable solution to the issue of removing the bodies from the Church premises without delay and separate from any other arrangement.*[9] This advice, for which the author does not have the tools to evaluate whether or not it was suitable, had no legal foundation. It was conveyed to the military as a request for a humanitarian gesture, and this is where all the difficulty lies. First, it is highly reasonable to assume that the Supreme Court did not have a sufficient factual basis to determine that this policy is optimal in terms of Israel national security interests. Second, in a time of crisis, why was the military asked to make a humanitarian gesture, if the law does not direct it to do so? Third, how does the Supreme Court know that this humanitarian gesture will help resolve the crisis? It is no less possible that this step was likely to worsen the crisis if the Church invaders interpreted it as a sign of weakness and capitulation or if, for example, the failure to remove the bodies was likely to cause the international community to exert their influence with those barricaded in the Church.

These words of criticism may be balanced by the argument that in many cases the Court's advisory messages seek to promote humanitarian policy or what the Supreme Court has deemed as "common sense." This may be argued, for example, with regard to the Supreme Court's recommendation to include Red Crescent personnel in burying the dead in Jenin, even though the Court determined that the military had fulfilled its duties in this area according to international law. Yet even this example is not so straightforward. The advantages of including the Red Crescent in the work of evacuating the bodies are clear. However, what are the disadvantages or risks inherent in this approach? Can it be said that these have been properly presented to the Court? Moreover, generally speaking, why should the military have to conduct such a process of deliberation

---

[8] *See* THE BATTLE OF THE 21ST CENTURY: DEMOCRACY FIGHTS TERROR (IYUN FORUM—THE ISRAEL DEMOCRACY INSTITUTE) 205 (Haim Pass ed., 2007).

[9] HCJ 3436/02 Custodia Internationale di Terra Santa v. the Government of the State of Israel, PD 56 (3) 22, 24–25 (2002) (emphasis added).

surrounding this issue in consequence of a recommendation that, by definition, did not seek to apply legal norms to the issue?

Therefore, one of the strongest arguments against advice-giving is that a military commander or decision-maker in government echelons who finds herself in the midst of a national security crisis with critical implications for human life and international significance must respect the law, and in particular international humanitarian law, in every decision she makes. And yet it is doubtful whether she must do so in view of a recommendation from the Court, as this recommendation does not ensue from any legal duty that applies to the issue. Responsibility for conducting the fighting is imposed on military commanders and the political echelon. The Supreme Court does not bear public liability for the advisory messages it transmits, even if they are wrong. Military commanders are the ones required to demonstrate courage, daring, and responsibility in making decisions with regard to national security and to bear public liability and, at times, criminal liability, too, if they should fail or if they do not fulfill their duties in accordance with the law. It is difficult to justify why their decisions should be made in view of a recommendation that does not ensue from any duty in law and that limits their freedom of action or impels them to make decisions based on an unstable foundation of facts.

ADVISORY DIALOGUE MAY LEAD TO AMBIGUITY OF NORMS

A great deal has been written on the relation between law and morality. In our case, the fact is that the foundation of our legal system is that the Court must decide legal questions in accordance with *lex lata* (the law, as it exists) and not the ethical or moral position of the Court pertaining to the policy in dispute.

Advisory messages are likely to create a disparity between a decision's legal content and the Court's viewpoint pertaining to the morality of the conduct under discussion. Particularly because of this, the question arises whether it is proper for messages whose entire purpose is to express ethical norms or desired legal approaches to be included in judgments.

In several cases, as we have seen, the Supreme Court of Israel advised the State to implement its judgment in a manner that differs from that implied in the Court's positive legal conclusion. We saw how the Court called on the State Attorney and the Attorney General to act with deliberation, responsibility, moderation, and restraint on various issues or to refrain from applying a certain policy. Introducing these norms into the discretionary power of those applying policy can blur boundaries by decision-makers between that which is lawful and that which is desirable. When the Court determines a norm that is defined in a judgment's binding part but, at the same time, requests or advises the Executive to refrain from applying it or to apply it with caution, restraint, or moderation, the Court's decision might lead to confusion.

The positivist system of law is based on binding judicial decisions that grant public authorities legal certainty in light of which they act. The need for normative certainty is indisputable, certainly with regard to national security. Judgments are intended to clarify the limits of the use of force in the State's struggle to safeguard national security. The use of advisory messages, particularly messages intended to influence policy where there are no clear legal boundaries, makes it more difficult for the Executive to operate with certainty and places the Executive and the public in a state of normative ambiguity with indistinct boundaries. It appears that it is a basic right of a terrorist suspect as well as the public to know via court judgments whether the use of violence vis-à-vis interrogatees suspected of involvement in terrorist activities is permitted or prohibited. A terrorist suspect also has full rights to know whether he is entitled to be warned prior to interrogation by the Shin Bet. Yet, even if this right is of less significance, it is still the right of the Shin Bet investigator to know definitely what value choice society has made when she has to handle a case that in her view belongs to the category of "a ticking bomb," and to know whether she is violating the law and can expect to be charged with an offense. The use of advisory messages, as in the Supreme Court case *On Torture*, does not provide this certainty. The significance of this case and the fact that it dramatically reduced the use of violence by Shin Bet investigators could not be disputed. Nevertheless, by way of the advisory message that was conveyed to the Attorney General, which enabled him to refrain from bringing to trial an investigator who used violence, HCJ *On Torture* left a state of normative ambiguity with regard to what is permitted and prohibited in an investigation of terrorist activity.

ADVISORY DIALOGUE COULD HARM THE POSITION AND CREDIBILITY OF THE SUPREME COURT

We indicated above how advisory messages can influence players in other branches. However, the use of advisory messages can have a negative impact on the Supreme Court's status and credibility as well. It is specifically so in cases where the Court determines that a certain conduct of matters is unlawful but at the same time it does not prohibit its absolute use, and through the use of advisory messages allows some margin. The disparity between the contents of the Supreme Court's fundamental decision and the contents of the advisory message may be construed as "a wink," a lack of sincerity, or an illegitimate subterfuge.[10] The disparity can also be interpreted as a weakness and unwillingness on the Court's part to confront the Executive face to face even though it reached the general conclusion that the policies they undertake are unlawful.

---

[10]   For further discussion of the question of the use of subterfuges in law, *see* GUIDO CALABRESI, A COMMON LAW FOR THE AGE OF STATUTES (1982) *at* n.277; *see also* Daphne Barak-Erez & David Scharia, *Freedom of Speech, Support for Terrorism and the Challenge of Global Constitutional Law*, 2 HARV. NAT'L SEC. J. 1 (2011), at n.289.]

Such situation occurred in the United States following the decision in *Brown v. Board of Education.* The addition of the words *all deliberate speed* in the *Brown* judgment,[11] which ordered the gradual conclusion of interracial segregation in the U.S. education system, in the opinion of many authors undermined the many attempts to terminate segregation. Furthermore, it led to the erosion of efforts by other entities to terminate this regimen.[12] Justice Black also thought that the use of this message was a mistake that enabled the southern states to avoid applying the judgment.[13]

A different risk to the status and credibility of the Supreme Court emerges in cases in which the legislature or the Executive disregard advisory messages that the Court has conveyed. Raviv Drucker and Ofer Shelach maintain in their book *Boomerang* that throughout the course of the al-Aqsa Intifada, there was not one case in which the Judge Advocate General prevented the military echelon from carrying out a targeted killing, even though the Israeli Supreme Court conveyed signals regarding the problematic nature of this policy as early as 2002. The authors argue that the Judge Advocate General ordered his subordinates "to authorize everything that the commanders in the field request."[14]

Indeed, there have been cases clearly indicating that advisory messages, even if not binding, restrain the Executive, as we saw with regard to overseeing the collection of investigative material by the police and the Shin Bet. However, in general, we cannot assume that it is self-evident that the Court's recommendations will be honored and enforced. Advocate Dan Yakir, General Counsel of the Association for Civil Rights in Israel, wrote the following about advisory messages (which he terms "refined messages") that the Supreme Court tends to convey in its judgments:

> *Unfortunately, both the government and the Knesset have not demonstrated to date sensitivity to the refined messages that the Court has sent them. Public authorities only understand an operative order that is clear, definite and decisive.* [emphasis added][15]

This is particularly so when the Knesset or government remains steadfast in adhering to a certain policy. In such cases, it is doubtful whether it is possible to assume that prosecutors and legal counsels would prefer or be able to rely on non-binding advisory messages to prevent use of this policy.

We saw above with regard to house demolitions that the Court's statements influenced a military committee to conclude that Israel must cease this practice. However, four years later, after Justice Barak, who wrote the opinion, and Justice Cheshin, who

---

[11] Brown v. Board of Education, 347 U.S. 483 (1954).
[12] *See* LOREN MILLER, THE PETITIONERS: THE STORY OF THE SUPREME COURT OF THE UNITED STATES AND THE NEGRO 351, 356 (1966).
[13] *See* Charles Black, *The Unfinished Business of the Warren Court*, 46 WASH. L. REV. 3, 22 (1970).
[14] RAVIV DRUCKER & OFER SHELACH, BOOMERANG: FAILURE OF LEADERSHIP IN THE SECOND INTIFADA 162 (2005).
[15] Interview with Dan Yakir, HALISHKA, Issue 61 (June 2006).

wrote a dissenting opinion prohibiting house demolitions, retired, a different panel of Supreme Court justices allowed the State to re-establish this policy. There is no doubt that re-establishment of the house demolitions policy would have been more difficult if not inconceivable had a judgment been given determining that this policy was unlawful.

ADVISORY DIALOGUE AND EXCLUSION

One of the questions that the discussion raises is the effect of advisory dialogue on the Court's relations with human rights organizations. In previous chapters, we saw that the dialogue conducted by the Israeli Supreme Court with these organizations is different in nature and intensity from the Court's dialogue with other branches. As natural as it may be, petitioners as well as human rights organizations in many cases are excluded from the dialogue that the Court conducts with other branches of government, notwithstanding that this dialogue deeply affects their ability to promote human rights compliance.

The Supreme Court ruling to leave the decision on the question of the necessity defense in the hands of the Attorney General regarding the issue of Shin Bet investigators using force is a good example of such difficulties. The decision led to a situation in which human rights organizations were compelled to file a complaint in order to clarify after the fact whether an investigator warranted the benefit of this defense or not. It also makes it more difficult for human rights organizations—notwithstanding their arguments that the policy continues—to attack this policy.

This situation forces human rights organizations to continue collecting information even after the Court has passed judgment, so as to prepare for future confrontations. Insofar as the messages are more veiled and pertain to details of the policy's application, the work is made that much more difficult for human rights organizations.

In addition, intensive dialogue with actors in the other branches damages the sense that the Court maintains the same distance from respondents as it does from petitioners. In this context, it is not superfluous to mention that with regard to national security, petitioners in many cases are members of minority communities, who are likely to feel even prior to the hearing that the legal system does not treat them with equality. Intensive dialogue between the Court and the Executive could strengthen their feeling of exclusion and discrimination.

THE USE OF ADVISORY DIALOGUE DOES NOT NECESSARILY ADVANCE HUMAN RIGHTS

One of the principal arguments in support of using advisory dialogue is that it enables the Court to promote human rights. However, advisory messages can be used in ways that lead to the opposite outcome.

One of the risks in using advisory dialogue as a substitute for binding decisions is that it grants the Court "a third option" apart from rejecting or accepting a petition. So, the Court struggling to decide on a petition may opt to reject the petition and accompany its judgment with an advisory message referring for example to the problematic outcome but refraining from going as far as declaring the policy unlawful or the law unconstitutional. The ostensibly convenient solution of being satisfied with an advisory message that censures a certain policy is likely to encourage justices to choose it even if the picture that emerges requires actual intervention and giving a decisive order.

A third option enables the Supreme Court to bear the banner of human rights by way of advisory messages without a clear, unequivocal, and operative decision attending this action. It may be argued that the Court's support of human rights through statements or advisory messages that may be cited in any local or international forum is often artificial, as, practically speaking, these messages have no weight, as no binding legal validity is associated with them. Messages in which the Court expresses its dissatisfaction with current policy in a manner understood ostensibly as subversive and critical may be interpreted as a conservative subterfuge that allows the Court to serve as a bearer of the banner of human rights, which in fact serves as a mechanism for granting legitimacy to the State.

It may be argued more radically that the Court's use of advisory dialogue must be understood as a subterfuge for reinforcing and fortifying the Court's position without real commitment to judicial review in attendance. The Court obligates the other branches to appear before the Court and accept its institutional superiority, even during times of actual combat. However, in order to preserve and reinforce its position, the Court often does not rule against the principal interests of the Executive. In order not to be viewed by the human rights community as a rubber stamp of the government, the Court promotes a discourse via advisory messages that place the justification, morality, or effectiveness of government policy in doubt—but avoids actually ruling against such policy.[16]

Evidence that the Court understands the benefits to the State apparatus from exercising such judicial review may be found in the statements of Justice Barak, cited in previous chapters. According to Justice Barak, the State of Israel has an interest in being able to cite from a Supreme Court judgment in which the Court relates to the manner in which the military conducted combat. In this lecture, Justice Barak maintained that the State of Israel benefits from being able to rely on a Supreme Court judgment that determines that no massacre occurred in Jenin or that the Supreme Court examined the lawfulness of the siege on the Church of the Nativity.[17] It appears from these statements that the State is likely to obtain legitimacy for its actions "on the legal front," as

---

[16] *See on this subject* Ronen Shamir, *Landmark Cases and the Reproduction of Legitimacy*, 24(3) L. & Soc. Rev. 781 (1990).

[17] Aharon Barak, Concerning National Security and Individual Security, Lecture at a conference of the Israel Bar Association in Eilat (May 6, 2002).

the result of the approval that it receives from the Court. Although it is true that Barak made these statements several years prior to the Goldstone Report, the informational and legal advantage to the State (in case a military commander were to stand trial abroad or at an international tribunal) was already clear to him then, to attorneys representing the State, and to military commanders. This, then, reinforces the conclusion that the advisory messages that the Court conveys at the end of its decisions may serve other purposes apart from the actual proceeding. Advisory messages also point to the common interests of the Court, the prosecution, and the military in conducting such dialogue. The State of Israel, indeed, generally uses Supreme Court texts and decisions at international forums, including in its response to the Goldstone Report. One can, therefore, argue that both the State and the Supreme Court benefit from the use of advisory messages. The State benefits from the nonintervention of the Supreme Court in its policy, whereas the Supreme Court benefits from the option of enjoying the image of a human rights defender, notwithstanding its lack of intervention.

Additional arguments may be made with regard to the harm that the use of advisory messages causes to furthering human rights. As we saw, the Court rules against the State in many cases after advisory messages that were transmitted did not receive proper attention. However, particularly for this reason, the question arises as to why we have to wait several years for a binding ruling. These delays create a lack of uniformity in Supreme Court case law pertaining to human rights and expose the Court to criticism that it approved a certain policy for years that infringes on human rights, though, ultimately, the Court too was persuaded that such policy is illegitimate and immoral.

The way this argument goes is that the use of advisory dialogue, even if it prepares the ground for a revolution, disregards the damage caused to society by an order that grants the military permission to conduct certain activity in dispute. Furthermore, when the Court expresses a significant component in its normative position on a certain issue by way of an advisory message, there is always the risk that the right message will not be understood properly by other branches and may even be misused. And, what will persist in history will be, for example, that the U.S. Supreme Court permitted discrimination against persons of Japanese origin during the Second World War, and that the Israeli Supreme Court allowed for years the use of force against interrogatees, and permitted house demolitions and deportations to be carried out.

17

Conclusion—Judicial Review and National Security

ADVISORY DIALOGUE CAN afford actual advantages to a legal system. It can enable the system to enhance the courts' ability to exercise judicial review on issues related to national security in a way that can minimize infringements of human rights—occasionally in real time and often within days or weeks of the events, rather than years after their occurrence, when the damage to the legal system has already been done and human lives were lost due to wrongful policies.

By exercising judicial review through advisory dialogue courts can overcome several of their institutional disadvantages on questions pertaining to national security. It could mitigate the tension between the wish to promote human rights and the wish to avoid inter-branch conflict in times of emergency. It could help the court overcome the uncertainty of deciding on national security matters without having full access to the facts needed for a binding decision and without knowing the exact national security implications of their decisions. Courts need to act fast if they wish to remain relevant in such times and prevent what may be violations of constitutional law or international law.

Courts also face particularly difficult dilemmas in this area. These dilemmas may not be unique to national security but could present themselves in a rather extreme manner. Tensions between morality and law, between the correctness of a rule and the question of when is the right time to enforce it, are very typical to this field of law. Tensions exist between the wish to create stable rules and the wish to facilitate developments and changes according to varying security related circumstances, and tensions exist between the desire to create appropriate norms with regard to issues of national security and the chances that these will actually be implemented in full. Dialogue with the Executive in such times can assist the courts in contending with these issues, if only as an interim solution until the security situation allows a fundamental decision to be given.

Along with these benefits, the use of advisory dialogue as a technique of judicial review also has its own risks. Advisory dialogue could be seen as an interference in issues most countries leave for the Executive or elected officials to decide. It may lead decision-makers and commanders to prefer the policy that the court promotes, even if it is not optimal. Advisory dialogue may damage the court's credibility, and the experience in Israel demonstrates that advisory dialogue does not always lead to advancing human rights.

The question is whether it is possible to find a way to enable a legal system to utilize the advantages of advisory dialogue while minimizing the risks it faces from using these messages. What lessons could other systems learn from the Israeli experience?

In the discussion that follows, I will propose several rules that ensue from the Israeli experience, without professing to exhaust the discussion. On the contrary: the intention is to advance the legal and public deliberation of the proper use of advisory dialogue between Courts and other branches of government in national security matters.

The first lesson we should always keep in mind is that analyzing the use of advisory dialogue as a principal method of judicial review in one legal system or another must be done while being aware of what distinguishes each system of law. Solutions that seem magical in one system of law can turn into a judicial catastrophe in another. Every legal system willing to examine the use of advisory dialogue must consider whether it is suitable for its own particular features, balances that have developed in it, and constitutional, legal, and political culture within which the courts operate.

In the context of national security, it is particularly noteworthy how a constitution divides powers among the branches. The US Constitution, for example, clearly defines to whom authority is granted to wage war. This division of responsiblity has a major impact on an interpretation of how judicial review has been exercised by the US Supreme Court, both with regard to wars the United States waged in the twentieth century and with regard to its fight against terrorism.

A second lesson we could learn from the Israeli experience is that dialogue is a practice with significant advantages along with considerable risks. There is no way to evaluate its desirability in absolute terms. A more appropriate approach to advisory dialogue is to have rules and "codes of conduct" that will enable a legal system to use the inherent advantages that advisory dialogue affords it to the full extent but restrict to the minimum the risks involved in the imprudent use of this tool.

Focusing on rules and "codes of conduct" for the suitable use of advisory dialogue instead of looking at this issue in absolute terms is supported as well by a practical consideration that should not be discounted. History has shown that even in legal systems where advisory dialogue is not part of the conventional practice of judicial review judges have managed to develop a variety of methods, both formal and informal, for transmitting advisory messages to other branches. Therefore, it is reasonable to assume that in most systems judges will find different methods for conveying advisory messages to other branches. This pragmatic assumption, even if it does not justify the use of the said practice in and of itself, supports the conclusion that it would be well to focus the discussion not on whether this practice is good or bad in absolute terms. Instead, the debate could focus on how a specific judicial system could institutionalize or regulate advisory dialogue so that it strengthens the rule of law, promotes compliance with human rights, and enhances inter-branch dialogue instead of weakening it.

RULES FOR PROPER USE OF ADVISORY DIALOGUE

The discussion of the Israeli case, its successes and failures, leads to several conclusions pertaining to advisory dialogue. I have chosen to formulate these conclusions in the form of rules but they should be more looked at as lessons learned from the Israeli experience.

PREFERRING A BINDING DECISION

The first rule for effective dialogue is that in the absence of a vital interest, the court should determine questions of national security in the traditional manner, that is, by way of binding decisions. The use of dialogue cannot be applied casually. It must be reserved for cases in which there is a significant justification to use an advisory message.

This preference must serve as a guiding principle to the court, particularly when intervention is required to prevent a serious infringement of human rights. When the court recognizes serious infringement of human rights in the State's national security policies, the court must present its conclusion regarding the issue to society in a direct and binding manner. It is doubtful whether intervention by way of an advisory message in these circumstances could be justified.

Use of advisory dialogue could be justified solely in circumstances in which the court has no practical capacity to affect policy or to obtain all the facts necessary to a binding decision on the issue it wishes to address. Where human rights suffer serious infringement and the court does not make a statement in a clear and binding manner, not only are the rights infringed but the court is harmed as well along with the infringement of human rights. No advisory message, as sharp as it may be, can replace a clear and binding decision. For years the Supreme Court of Israel limited its review of torture and house demolitions to advisory dialogue, indirectly lending a hand to maintaining this policy, even if it conveyed very clear messages that it was not satisfied with this policy. The serious infringement of human rights, which the resolute nonintervention of the Court allowed, ultimately harmed the Court as well. Avoidance is ultimately avoidance.

PRUDENT USE OF STANDING, RIPENESS, AND POLITICAL QUESTIONS DOCTRINES BEFORE ACTION

A well-known advantage of the use of advisory messages is in many cases pragmatic. As the courts have real (political and practical) difficulty in influencing policy during times of national crisis, they tend to refrain from intervention by using threshold causes. In the context of Israel, the Court revoked threshold causes of action and decided courageously that situation of a national emergency does not prevent it from looking into the legality of the Executives's response to the crisis. Doing so allowed it to intervene in many issues of national security and to enhance Israel's compliance with international human rights law and humanitarian law.

Each legal system may wish to adopt its own balancing point between avoiding decisions on issues of national security and absolute intervention therein.

However, in legal systems such as Israel's, in which the Israel Supreme Court does not tend to filter petitions brought before the Court, it would make sense to establish an additional preliminary cause for rejecting petitions.[1] There are situations, particularly in times of combat, in which the Court cannot decide an issue specifically, due to "the absence of the ability to obtain a sufficient factual picture for a decision." In such cases, the Court can see in this cause justification for dismissing a petition, to which it can attach in appropriate cases an advisory message, as the Israeli Court has indeed done on occasion, to the effect that at another more appropriate time, the Court will examine the question that the petition raises. Study of Supreme Court case law during the period of

---

[1] *See* HCJ 2901/02, Hamoked: Center for the Defense of the Individual v. Commander of IDF Forces, PD 56(3) 19 (2002); HCJ 3436/02 Custodia Internationale di Terra Santa v. the Government of the State of Israel, PD 56 (3) 22 (2002); HCJ 3022/02 Canon v. GOC (General Officer Commanding) Central Command PD 56(3) (2002) 9.; HCJ 2901/02, Hamoked: Center for the Defense of the Individual v. Commander of IDF Forces, PD 56(3) 19, 21–22 (2002). In HCJ 2977/02 Adalah v. Commander of IDF Forces in Judea and Samaria, PD 56(3) 6, 7–8 (2002), the court writes the following: "The position of the Respondent is that effective combat actions which at times damage residential houses is unavoidable as these houses become a kind of bunker from which shooting occurs at IDF Forces. *In such circumstances, the court's power to intervene in operational actions by way of judicial review is limited*" (emphasis added) In the *Rafiah* case, HCJ 4764/04 Physicians for Human Rights v. Commander of IDF Forces in Gaza, Tak-El 2004 (2) 2183, 2186 (2004), Justice Beinisch wrote the following: "The non-fulfillment of humanitarian duties opens for the injured parties, and generally for practical reasons for the entities representing them, the gates of the court that exercises judicial review during times of combat as during times of peace. *Nonetheless, the circumstances involved in procedures of judicial review during times of actual combat limit the effectiveness of judicial review and make it difficult to apply solutions required by way of the court... The petition was clarified while changes and developments in the field occurred during the course of the hearing. The parties pleading before us based their contentions on ongoing field reports, reports that altered the set of circumstances and facts during the course of hearing the petition. The factual description of clarifying information, as aforesaid, was expressed in the judgment of the president. Under such circumstances, the procedure of judicial review is limited and defective in the absence of sufficient tools to clarify relevant information in order to examine the information in real time and provide effective reliefs in respect thereof*" (emphasis added).

Operation Cast Lead leads to the conclusion that practically speaking, the Israeli Court has already chosen this option.

TRANSPARENCY

In cases where the Court opts to make use of advisory dialogue, the Court must do so with as high a degree of transparency as possible. As we have seen, the Israeli Supreme Court often sends advisory messages during a hearing through oral comments. This practice appears justified when it seeks to promote arriving at a settlement—that is where the proven effectiveness of a verbal remark justifies its being made. However, when the purpose of an advisory message is to express the Court's position on a normative question, there are clear reasons to prefer transmitting the message in a formal judicial decision. This approach will expand the circle of participants in the dialogue and include those who were not present at the hearing, the public, and the media. It will ensure a transparent, candid, clear, and open dialogue with other branches of government on the "public stage."

Making certain that advisory messages that are of significance to other branches of government are conveyed by way of written decisions of the Court and not by way of verbal comments can prevent, or at least restrict, the need to interpret that which occurred at the hearing or to rely on newspaper reports or the attorneys who attended the hearing. A written comment will obligate the players in the other branches to study it and to acknowledge that even if it is not binding, it expresses the Court's position. Written comments, unlike verbal remarks, remain perpetually, and need not rely on "the collective memory" of those who were present in the courtroom or on the reliability of media reports. This also ensures that if history brings again the issue to the Court the advisory message will remain relevant.

MESSAGE CONTENTS

The Israeli experience has much to offer with regard to the proper approach, and this also pertains to the contents of advisory messages and not just the manner in which these are to be used. It could offer us a few more lessons.

ADVISORY MESSAGES ON QUESTIONS OF CONSTITUTIONALITY AND LEGALITY

It is easy to see the advantages of an advisory message that the Court discusses, even if it is non-binding, on questions of legality and constitutionality. We saw earlier that both the Court and other branches can benefit from precluding conflict and encouraging dialogue between them. Advisory messages pertaining to legality or constitutionality can prevent the enactment of unsuitable laws, and assist in promoting laws that are formulated more clearly and precisely, and laws that can realize the objectives of the legislative authority without the Court having to strike them down as unconstitutional. The contention, too, that in conveying advisory messages the Court intervenes in the powers of other branches appears less compelling when this concerns a matter that one way or another is likely one day to arrive for a final decision of the Court. These messages are an example of the proper use of advisory dialogue and of making the most of its advantages.

ADVISORY MESSAGES ON QUESTIONS OF POLICY

Contrary to messages concerning legality or constitutionality, it is more difficult to justify advisory messages that deal with the application of policy. The contents of these messages are likely to depart from the Court's direct authority. The Court has only limited capacity to obtain proper recommendations on these questions, and the potential undesirable effects of such recommendations on decision-makers are likely to lead to "policy distortion."[2] Notwithstanding this general reservation, there are proper types of messages in this area too. As indicated above, there are situations in which the application and interpretation of a law are interdependent. In such cases, an advisory message is likely to serve as a substitute for restrictive interpretation or a more radical ruling that the pertinent policy is unlawful. Due to the potential effect of these messages on questions of legality, the rationales that support allowing the use of messages that deal with legality or constitutionality can also apply to these messages. These rationales apply to a lesser degree when the Court does not see a possibility, at present or in the future, of connecting the manner of applying the law to the manner of interpreting it.

In kind of a departure to this line of thinking Jack Goldsmith argues that in the American context the juridification of national security policymaking has its own merits. According to Goldsmith, "lawyers are trained to think clearly, critically, and analytically, to find weaknesses in evidence or in casual inferences and to consider the broader implications and effects of a decision. They are typically more attuned than most to the context, appearance and political and moral implications of particular actions"[3]

To the extent that this argument is relevant to courts, one could argue that the juridification of national security matters even if does not produce neccessraly legally binding decisions it improves decision-making and provides the Executive with another important perspective that it may not be attuned enough to see under the extreme pressures it is facing in times of national crisis.

---

[2] *See* Mark Tushnet, *Policy Distortion and Democratic Debilitation: Comparative Illumination of the Countermajoritarian Difficulty*, 94 MICH. L. REV. 245 (1995).
[3] JACK GOLDSMITH, POWER AND CONSTRAINT 139 (2013).

ADVISORY MESSAGES WITH CONTENTS THAT RELY ON
NON-LEGAL NORMS

The Israeli Supreme Court also conveys from time to time messages that belong to the ethical world. A good example of such messages are its condemnations of the commander of the air force's statements regarding "collateral damage."

The Court also uses non-legal norms in the guidance it gives to the military or the Attorney General regarding how to implement a specific policy. We saw earlier how the Court advises other public authorities to apply certain lawful policy with "caution," "restraint," "moderation," "deliberation," and "responsibly." The use of such messages places the Executive in a difficult position of normative ambiguity, as it is hard to define what is the appropriate application of a judgment in a "restrained" manner and what is "responsible" policy. Given the inherent ambiguity of such messages, the entities applying a judgment may be left unknowing what is the legal norm that applies to the situation, if the Court's final ruling constitutes the norm, or perhaps if another norm comes into play that calls for the application of the principal norm with deliberation or responsibly.

THE POTENTIAL IMPACT OF ADVISORY MESSAGES

An additional consideration that the Israeli case presents us with is the need to prevent the damage likely to be caused to the Court's position and credibility if government authorities disregard advisory messages. Not all the advisory messages the Court conveyed were respected. Some were blatantly ignored. A preliminary evaluation of the chances that the Executive will respond positively to an advisory message can be useful in these circumstances.

As we discussed earlier some messages are more effective than others. Messages that are conveyed in a sharp and clear manner; carry a "price-tag" for refraining from action in accordance with such message; address a player identified with the value system that the Supreme Court represents and comply with his interests are likely to be more effective.[4] They are likely to become even more effective if the addressee views himself obligated by Supreme Court messages, and acts in accordance with considerations of a repeat player.[5]

These conclusions can assist courts that are considering the use of advisory messages in one context or another. First on how to craft messages. Second, if the message

---

[4] *See* Beth Harris, *Representing Homeless Families: Repeat Player Implementation Strategies*, 33 LAW & SOCIETY REV. 911 (1999).

[5] Marc Galanter, *Why the "Haves" Come Out Ahead: Speculations on the Limits of Legal Change*, 9 L. & SOC. REV. 95 (1974) Galanter, *supra* note 8, ch. 5, n.209.

cannot be crafted in a manner that could allow the Court to assume it will be respected then it would probably be better for the court to refrain from transmitting an advisory message.

CAUTION AGAINST OVERRELIANCE ON GOVERNMENT AUTHORITIES

Another rule of caution that the Israeli case teaches us pertains to the use of players in other government authorities, particularly attorneys, prosecutors, and military commanders, to promote a variety of objectives. Indeed, intensive dialogue with these players enables the Israeli Supreme Court to promote various objectives, including better compliance with human rights. However, such use cannot cover up for other related difficulties. Use of this type of advisory messages reinforces the prevalent view that the Court's distance from the parties is not equal and the Court and the Attorney General's Office are one institutional body. Another difficulty that ensues is making the final outcome of a judicial procedure dependent on the identity, obligations, qualifications, or wishes of a particular party. The fact that the Court relies on this party warrants appreciation but cannot serve as a replacement for a Court ruling.

CONCLUSION

Using advisory messages in reviewing national security matters affords the court and society as a whole highly significant benefits, particularly as often there is no other body that can assure that the State's national security policies, certainly in times of crises, will be implemented while respecting constitutional law and international law. Even those who completely question the use of advisory dialogue must recognize that when other systems are not functioning, the Supreme Court may be the final barrier to protect against a serious infringement of human rights in times of crisis.[6] History instructs that the courts do not tend to intervene through binding decisions in times of crisis. Advisory messages—even if these are "the lesser of two evils"—could save a system from years of infringing on fundamental rights justified by a national crisis.

Furthermore, the mere fact that a court announces its readiness to review the legality of every national security policy even if implemented by the military or by the intelligence service could lead to a chilling effect. It could incentivize the military to refrain from using dubious tools. It could lead to more restrained implementation of controversial yet assumingly legal policies, and it enables human rights organizations to conduct

---

[6] As Sunstein points out, minimalism "is not always the best way to proceed." *See* Cass R. Sunstein, One Case at a Time: Judicial Minimalism on the Supreme Court 46 (1999).

a highly effective dialogue with military authorities and to attain achievements, even if only partial. Knowing that such petitions will be lodged is likely to deter military authorities from choosing certain methods that would not warrant court approval.

These are far too important benefits to be ignored or put aside due to legal traditionalism. Yes, the media, the checks and balances of our democracies, internal controls, and oversight bodies could all do the same. However, history has shown we will be risking our values, and damage our long-term commitment to human rights if we decide to give up the role one important player could play. History has shown that even with the existence of all these checks most democracies violated fundmental rights in times of national crisis, and all these checks including our courts did not prevent unlawful and immoral policies from being implemented, only years later to lead to rethinking and amendments while the damage was already done.

It is a risky policy to accept the argument that in times of crisis other branches of government will consolidate positions on their own that grant human rights an appropriate status in crises. This does not mean that advisory dialogue should be used in all circumstances. Its use must be judicious. Its use should be understood as an outcome of a court's inability in some cases to obtain sufficient facts for a decision during states of emergency. The national security field in times of crisis is characterized by high levels of uncertainty, which makes it almost impossible for courts to exercise judicial review in conventional manners and in real time. Advisory messages, particularly in this area of case law could help courts and society in enhancing the rule of law in times of crisis or high level of uncertainty.

Two additional features of the field of national security call in favor of use of advisory dialogue. First, the threats most countries are dealing with these days have changed dramatically in recent years due to the grave terrorist attacks carried out by al-Qaeda or its inspired individuals or entities and, the involvement of nonstate actors in the conflicts. It led also to the development of novel methods of intelligence gathering, new counterterrorism investigative techniques, criminalization of preventive acts, use of administrative measures, and of course new military and counterinsurgency tools and weapons. The legal field known at times as "law and terrorism" or "national security law" has undergone a process of formation and consolidation unseen since the Second World War. In many respects this formation is still taking place, and countries are still struggling to find the right balance between the tools they possess and the limitations on fundamental rights that they may lead to. Many of these dilemmas have not yet been consolidated finally and fully in internal law or in international law.

Advisory dialogue, as we have seen, from this aspect has the significant capacity to contribute to developing this legal field, to encourage normative discourse among branches and the public at large, and to enable the courts to advance case law in this field step by step.

Another feature that influences the use of advisory dialogue is the fact that the national security reality in many countries is no longer distinguished by times of peace and times of war, but rather by a mixture of the two, which combines periods of calm with periods of emergency or tension. In previous chapters, we saw how the work pattern of the Israeli Supreme Court changes in these different situations. It is fair to assume that the Israeli Court is not the only court that is affected by this new reality. Advisory messages can assist courts in contending better with such tension. Accordingly, courts in suitable cases can use messages whose purpose is to clarify that their decisions do not express the final word and that they are prepared to re-examine the matter under other circumstances.

States of relative quiet enable the courts better to examine the entire set of relevant considerations and to obtain a better picture of the facts of the matter. In these states of relative quiet, the court's ability to make an unpopular decision is greater and, as we saw in the context of Israel and elsewhere, during such times the courts tend to intervene more and reach more balanced solutions. The use of advisory messages until a state of relative calm arrives can allow the court and the public to examine their positions vis-à-vis the relevant question at hand in an organized and rational manner, and then allow the public to accept the court's binding decisions on questions of law and values that new challenges to national security raise. The states of relative quiet afford the court and society an opportunity for true, critical, and extensive analysis, and for binding decisions to be made on the fundamental issue. Under such circumstances, the Supreme Court's true advantage is disclosed as the court is comprised of justices who are not involved in the daily political doings, and, their inherent role is uphold protection of human rights. In states of relative calm, the Supreme Court justices are influenced less by short-term considerations or the pressures to which the legislative authority, the implementers of policy, or the military are exposed during times of crisis or tension with regard to security and combat. Advisory dialogue during times of emergency or periods of tension, along with deferring fundamental decisions to states of relative quiet in cases where it is possible and warranted to do so, can enable the courts to fully realize their utmost duty—that human rights are respected and that the law is not kept silent, in times of peace but no less importantly for our society—in times of war.

Judicial Panels in Judgments Where Fundamental Decisions Constituting Precedents against the State Were Given 1996–2005

Petition	Subject	Decision	Judicial Panel
HCJ *On Torture*	The Shin Bet's authority to use force in "ticking bomb" investigations	The Court determines that the Shin Bet does not have the legal authority to apply force in its investigations	Extended panel of nine justices headed by the President
Further Criminal Hearing Jabrin	Interpretation of the offense of supporting a terrorist organization determined in section 4 (a) of the Prevention of Terrorism Ordinance	The Accused is acquitted by a narrow interpretation of the Prevention of Terrorism Ordinance	Further hearing in the presence of seven justices headed by the President
Further Criminal Hearing Bargaining Chips	The State's authority to hold Lebanese residents as bargaining chips	The Court determines that the State does not have authority to detain the Lebanese residents as bargaining chips	Further hearing before nine justices headed by President Barak
HCJ *Obeid*	Visit by Red Cross representatives with Lebanese detainees who were held as bargaining chips	The Court orders the State to make the arrangements to enable Red Cross representatives to visit the petitioners	Extended panel of five justices headed by President Barak

(*continued*)

Petition	Subject	Decision	Judicial Panel
HCJ *Mahmoud*	A military commander's authority to extend the period of administrative detention of a person after a judge decided, on an appeal of the detention order, to curtail that person's detention	The court determines that as a rule a military commander is not permitted to extend a period of detention after a judge has decided to curtail the period	Ordinary panel—Justice Orr, Justice Zamir and Justice Turkel
HCJ *Marab*	The decision in HCJ "Order 1500"—the order by virtue of which masses of detainees in Operation Defensive Shield were arrested	The Court determines that several central provisions of the order are invalid	Panel comprises President Barak, Justice Dorner, and Justice England
HCJ *Beit Surik*	Route of the separation barrier	HCJ invalidates the route of the separation barrier and determines a framework for exercising discretion in determining the route	Senior Panel— President Barak, Vice-President Mazza, and Justice M. Cheshin
HCJ Neighbor Procedure	Lawfulness of the Neighbor Procedure according to which before IDF forces break into the home of a wanted person, one of the local inhabitants will be requested to enter the house ask the wanted person to step outside or else the military wll storm the house.	The Court determines that the Neighbor Procedure contradicts international law	Senior Panel— President Barak, Justice Cheshin, and Justice Beinisch
HCJ *Sayef v. The Government Press Office*	Decision of the Government Press Office that from the beginning of 2002 and on, it will no longer issue press cards to Palestinian members of the press	The Court revokes the council's decision and orders extension of the validity of the press card of the journalist Sayef and that press cards are to be issued to members of Al Jazeera	Ordinary Panel—Justice Dorner, Justice Rivlin, and Justice Joubran

(continued)

Petition	Subject	Decision	Judicial Panel
HCJ *Jenin Jenin*	The censor's authority to ban screening the film *Jenin Jenin* in public	The Court revokes the council decision and permits the film to be screened	Ordinary Panel—Justice Dorner, Justice Procaccia, and Justice Gronis
Rafiah Case	The decision in HCJ *Fighting in Rafiah*— and deliberation of the question whether the military fulfills various humanitarian duties imposed on it by humanitarian international law during the military actions conducted in Rafiah	The Court determines that military forces are violating many provisions of international law and were not properly prepared for combat ahead of time	Panel consists of President Barak, Justice Turkel, and Justice Beinisch
HCJ *Mar'avah*	The decision pertains to the lawfulness of the separation barrier following the decision of the International Court of Justice at The Hague	The Court invalidates significant sections of the proposed route of the separation barrier	Nine justices headed by the President
HCJ *Bishara*	Do statements of Knesset Member Azmi Bishara, which identify with Hizballah, constitute glorification of terrorism (Apologie du terrorisme) terrorism?	The Court determines that these statements fall within the confines of the essential immunity granted to Knesset members within the framework of fulfilling their duties	Panel of Justices—Justice Barak, Justice Rivlin, and Justice Hayuth

Dates of Principal Rulings Comprising Precedents against the State, in View of the Number of Israelis Injured in Terrorist Attacks 1996–2005

Petition	Subject	Decision	Date petition is lodged	Date decision is given	Duration for which petition is discussed	Was the decision given during a period of decrease in the number of Israelis killed?
HCJ *On Torture*	Authority of the Shin Bet to use violence in the investigation of "a ticking bomb"	The Supreme Court determines that the Shin Bet does not have the authority to use violence in the course of its investigations	Sept. 18, 1994	Sept. 6, 1999	Five years	Yes
Crim. Further Hearing *Jabarin*	Interpreting the offense of supporting a terrorist organization determined in section 4(a) of the Prevention of Terrorism Ordinance	The Supreme Court acquits the accused as it narrowly interprets the Prevention of Terrorism Ordinance	Dec. 2, 1996	Nov. 27, 2009	Four years	Yes, even though the level of violence begins to climb again quite moderately
Crim. Further Hearing *Klafei*	State's authority to hold Lebanese residents as "bargaining chips" and the legal status of "unlawful combatants"	The Supreme Court rules that the State has no authority to hold the Lebanese as "bargaining chips"	Nov. 30, 1997	April 12, 2000	Two years and five months	Yes
HCJ *Obeid*	Visits by Red Cross representatives of Lebanese detainees who were being held as "bargaining chips"	Supreme Court instructs the State to make the arrangements that will allow Red Cross representatives to visit the petitioners	Feb. 8, 1998	Aug. 23, 2001	Three-and-a-half years	No
HCJ *Marav*	Decision on the matter of "Order 1500" —the order by virtue of which detainees of Operation Defensive Shield were held in administrative detention without access to a lawyer and with limited judicial review	Supreme Court determines that several central provisions of the Order are invalid	April 16, 2002	Feb. 5, 2003	Ten months	Yes

Case	Issue	Holding		Date	Duration	
HCJ *Neighbor Procedure*	Lawfulness of "the Neighbor Procedure"	Supreme Court determines that the Neighbor Procedure is contrary to international law and is far too close to the prohibited practice of "human shields"	May 5, 2002	Oct. 6, 2005	Three-and-a-half years	Yes
HCJ *Sayef v. the Government Press Office*	Decision of the Government Press Office that from the beginning of 2002 and on, it will no longer issue press cards to Palestinian press personnel	Supreme Court revokes the decision of the Government Press Office	June 30, 2002	April 25, 2004	One year and ten months	Yes
The *Jenin Jenin* Case	Authority of the censor to ban the screening of the film *Jenin Jenin* in public theaters	Supreme Court revokes the decision of the censor	January 10, 2003	Nov. 11, 2003	11 months	Yes
HCJ *Bishara*	Does the statement made by Knesset Member Azmi Bishara pertaining to Hezbollah constitute glorification of terrorism	Supreme Court determines that this statement falls within the confines of substantive immunity given to any Knesset member	Dec. 24, 2003	Feb. 1, 2006	Two years and two months	Yes
HCJ *Beit Sourik*	Route of the separation barrier	Supreme Court invalidates the route of the separation barrier	Feb. 26, 2004	June 30, 2004	Four months	No

Bibliography

ISRAEL—LEGISLATION

The Citizenship Law and Entry into Israel (Provisional Order) 5763-2003.

Emergency Powers Law (Detentions) 5739-1979.

Evidence Ordinance [New Version]5731-1971—Section 44

The Incarceration of Unlawful Combatants Law 5762-2002.

Knesset Members (Immunity, Rights and Duties) Law (Amendment No. 29) 5762-2002.

Penal Law 5737-1977.- Section 95

Regulation 119(1) of the Defense (Emergency) Regulations 1945.

The Rights of Victims of Crime Law, 5761-2001.

Rules of Criminal Procedure (Enforcement Powers—Arrests), 5756-1996. (Section–35)

Rules of Procedure in the High Court of Justice 5744-1984

ISRAELI CASE LAW

Administrative Detention Appeal 10/94 Anonymous v. the Minister of Defense, PD 53 (1) 97 (1997).

Administrative Detention Appeal 6/96 Anonymous v. the State of Israel, PD 50 (4) 45, (1996).

Administrative Detention Appeal 8788/03 Federman v. the Minister of Security, PD 55(1) 176 (2003).

Civil Appeal 6821/93 United Bank Mizrahi v. Migdal Kfar Shitufi, PD 49(4) 221.

Civil Appeal 6970/99 Abu Samra v. the State of Israel, PD 56(6) 185 (2002).

Crim FH, 7048/97 Anonymous v. Minister of Defense, IsrSC 54(1) 721.

Criminal Appeal 1932/04 Rajabi v. the State of Israel, Tak-El 2005(2) 187 (2005).

Criminal Appeal 2046/04 Fierstetter v. the State of Israel, Tak-El 2005 (1) 3903.

Criminal Appeal 2131/03 Saadi v. the State of Israel (unpublished, Dec. 23, 2003).

Criminal Appeal 307/73 Disoki v. the State of Israel, PD 28 (2) 802 (1974).

Criminal Appeal 3338/99 Pakowitz v. the State of Israel, PD 54 (5) 667 (2000).

Criminal Appeal 3417/99 Har-Shefi v. the State of Israel, PD 55 (2) 735, 813 (2001).

Criminal Appeal 3660/03 Abayed v. the State of Israel (unpublished, Sept. 8, 2005).

Criminal Appeal 4765/98 Abu Saadeh v. the State of Israel, PD 53 (1) 832 (1999).

Criminal Appeal 496/73 Anonymous v. The State of Israel, PD 28 (1) 714, (1974).

Criminal Appeal 5121/98 Issacharov v. the Chief Military Prosecutor, Tak-El 2006 (2) 1093.

Criminal Appeal 5614/92 State of Israel v. Messika, PD 49(2) 669 (1995).

Criminal Appeal 6613/99 Smirk v. State of Israel, PD 56(3) 529 (2002).

Criminal Appeal 6659/06 Anonymous v. the State of Israel, Tak-El 2008(2) 3270.

Criminal Appeal 1226/06 Iyad v. State of Israel (unpublished, Feb. 19, 2006).

Criminal Appeal 9691/03 El Rahman v. the State of Israel (unpublished, Jan. 10, 2005).

Criminal Appeal Alba v. The State of Israel, PD 50(5) 221 (1996).

Criminal File (Haifa) 189/03 State of Israel v. Rajabi, Tak-Machozi 2004(1) 873 (2004).

Criminal File 109/98 (Jerusalem) State of Israel v. Pakowitz, Tak-Mahozi 99 (2) 3415 (1999).

E.A. 1120/02 The Central Elections Committee v. MK Ahmed Tibi, PD 57 (4) 1 (2003).

Further Hearing HCJ 10480/03 Besidan v. Bakhri, PD 59(1) 625 (2004).

HCJ 2461/01 Cna'an v. IDF Military Commander in Judea and Samaria, Pador Elyon 01 (6) 424 (2001).

HCJ 10714/06 Maraba v. the Government of Israel, Tak-El 2007 (3) 3434.

HCJ 1097/03 Alajouri v. IDF Military Commander in the Gaza Strip (unpublished, Jan. 31, 2003).

HCJ 11225/03 Bishara v. the Attorney General, Tak-El 2006 (1) 1398.

HCJ 11745/02 Community Center for the Development of Beit Hanina v. GOC (General Officer Commanding) Central Command, Tak-El 2003(4) 515, a decision from April 14, 2005.

HCJ 124/09 Duwaith v. Minister of Defense, Dinim Elyon 2009 (30) 778.

HCJ 1265/11 The Public Committee Against Torture et al. v. the Attorney General (yet to be published).

HCJ 1321/04 Bari v. Commander of IDF Forces on the West Bank, Tak-El 2004 (1) 2394 (2004).

HCJ 1671/05 Almagor—Terror Victims Association v. the Government of Israel, PD 59 (5) 913, (2005).

HCJ 1715/97 Israel Investments Administrators Office v. the Minister of Finance, PD 51 (4) 367 (1998).

HCJ 1730/96 Sabiah v. IDF Commander in Judea and Samaria District, PD 50(1) 353.

HCJ 1748/06 The Mayor of Dahariya v. the IDF Commander in the West Bank, Tak-El 2007(3) 1109 (2007).

HCJ 2006/97 Abu Fara v. OC Central Command, PD 51(2) 651, 654–55 (1997).

HCJ 201/09 Physicians for Human Rights v. the Prime Minister, Tak-El 2009 (1) 565 [known as HCJ Operation Cast Lead].

HCJ 2056/04 Beit Sourik Village Council v. the Government of Israel, PD 58(5) 807 (2004), a decision dated Mar. 31, 2004

HCJ 2103/96 Al-Din v. the Security Service, Tak-El 96(1) 9 (1996).

HCJ 2150/96 Harizat v. the Attorney General (unpublished, Feb. 21, 2002).

HCJ 2307/00 Natasha v. Commander of IDF Forces in the West Bank, Tak-El 2002(1) 979 (2002).

HCJ 2320/98 Mahmud v. IDF Commander, PD 52(3) 346 (1998).

HCJ 2484/03 Ilariyah v. IDF Commander of the West Bank (unpublished, Mar. 18, 2003).

HCJ 253/88 Sagadiya v. the Minister of Defense, PD 42(3) 801 (1988).

HCJ 2722/92 Elamrin v. Commander of IDF Forces in the Gaza Strip, PD 46(3) 693 (1992).

HCJ 2732/05 Hassin v. the Government of Israel, Tak-El 2006 (2) 3672 (2006).

HCJ 2847/03 Al'ouna v. the Commander of IDF Forces in Judea and Samaria, Tak-El 2003 (2) 3829 (2003).

HCJ 2901/02 HaMoked: The Center for the Defense of the Individual et al. v. the Commander of IDF Forces in the West Bank, PD 56 (3) 19 (2002).

HCJ 292/86 Ha'etzni v. the State of Israel, PD 42(4) 406 (1989).

HCJ 2936/02 Physicians for Human Rights v. Commander of IDF Forces, PD 56 (3) 3, (2002).

HCJ 2967/00 Arad v. the Israel Knesset, PD 54 (2) 188 (2000).

HCJ 2977/02 Adalah v. Commander of IDF Forces in Judea and Samaria, PD 56(3) 6 (2002).

HCJ 3091/99 The Association for Citizens Rights v. the Knesset (unpublished).

HCJ 3109/96 Abu Jabar v. the State of Israel (unpublished, July 7, 2002)

HCJ 3114/02 Barakeh v. Minister of Defense, PD 56 (3) 11, 15–16 (2002).

HCJ 3116/02 Adalah v. the Commander of IDF Forces in the West Bank (unpublished yet, 8 May, 2012).

HCJ 3123/99 Hillman v. the Minister of Internal Security (unpublished, July 7, 1999).

HCJ 316/03 Bakri v. Film Review Council PD 58 (1) 249 (2003) [also known as "the *Jenin, Jenin* case].

HCJ 3195/99 Halef v. Shin Beth (unpublished, May 9, 2000).

HCJ 3239/02 Marab v. Commander of IDF Forces in the West Bank, PD 57 (2) 349 (2003).

HCJ 3417/03 Elan v. the IDF Commander on the West Bank (unpublished, Feb. 24, 2005).

HCJ 3436/02 Custodia Internationale di Terra Santa v. the Government of the State of Israel, PD 56 (3) 22 (2002).

HCJ 3451/02 Almadani v. Minister of Defense, PD 56 (3) 30 (2002).

HCJ 3460/02 Dror Halevi—Chairman of the Movement for Separation v. the Prime Minister (unpublished, July 1, 2002).

HCJ 358/88 The Association for Civil Rights in Israel v. the Central District Commander (Israel), PD 43 (2) 529, 541–42 (1989).

HCJ 3761/02 Hadir v. Commander of IDF Forces in the Gaza Strip (unpublished, May 28, 2002).

HCJ 3799/02 Adallah v. GOC (General Officer Commanding) Central Command PD 60 (3) 67 (2005) [also known as the *Neighbor Procedure* case].

HCJ 3900/02 Israel Trauma Center for Victims of Terror and War v. Ariel Sharon (unpublished, May 8, 2002).

HCJ 3985/03 Bedui v. the Commander of the IDF Forces in Judea and Samaria Tak-El 2003(2) 3649, 3650.

HCJ 4146/11 Hess v. the General Chief of Staff (unpublished yet, 9 July 2013)

HCJ 4211/03 Barkan v. the Minister of Defense, Tak-El 2003 (2) 1485 (2003).

HCJ 4219/02 Gussin v. Commander of IDF Forces, PD 56 (4) 608 (2002).

HCJ 422/03 Abu Dosh v. IDF Commander of Judea and Samaria (unpublished, Jan. 15, 2003).

HCJ 4462/03 Fanon v. Commander of IDF Forces, Tak-El 2003(3) 543 (2003).

HCJ 4573/04 Albasyouni v. the Commander of the IDF Forces, Tak-El 2004 (2) 1288 (2004).

HCJ 4694/04 Abu Attrah v. the Commander of the IDF Forces in the Gaza Strip, Tak-El 2004 (2) 1645 (2004).

HCJ 4764/04 Physicians for Human Rights v. Commander of IDF Forces in Gaza, Tak-El 2004 (2) 2183, 2186 (2004) [also known as the *Rafiah* case].

HCJ 4772/91 Khizran v. IDF Commander of Judea and Samaria District, PD 46(2) 150 (1992).

HCJ 4969/04 Adallah v. GOC (General Officer Commanding) Southern Command in the IDF, Tak-El 2004 (3) 1786 (2004).

HCJ 5100/94 The Pubic Committee against Torture in Israel v. the Government of Israel, PD 53 (4) 817 (1999) [also known as HCJ *On Torture*].

HCJ 5251/02 Arjoub v. IDF Military Commander in Judea and Samaria (unpublished, July 10, 2002).

HCJ 5304/97 Saba v. General Security Service, Tak-El 2000(2) 1869 (2000).

HCJ 5311/02 Abu Hit v. Commander of the Ketziot Detention Facility, PD 02 (2) 385.

HCJ 5422/01 Salah v. The Commander of IDF Forces in Judea and Samaria (unpublished, Aug. 9, 2001).

HCJ 5548/98 Nassar v. the Minister of Defense (unpublished, Oct. 14, 1998).

HCJ 5627/02 Sayef v. the Government Press Office, PD 55(5) 70 (2003).

HCJ 5673/91 Kadr v. Commander of IDF Forces, Tak-El 92(2) 433 (1992).

HCJ 5872/01 Barakeh v. the Prime Minister, PD 56(3) 1 (2002).

HCJ 588/94 Schlanger v. the Attorney General, PD 48(3) 40 (1994).

HCJ 5973/92 The Association for Citizens' Rights v. the Minister of Defense, PD 47(1) 267 (1993).

HCJ 6026/94 Naazal v. IDF Military Commander in the Region of Judea and Samaria, PD 48(5) 338 (1994).

HCJ 6129/02 Vangensu v. the Minister of Defense Tak-El 2002(4) 747 (2002).

HCJ 6296/98 Hasib v. General Security Services, Tak-El 98(3) 1480 (1998).

HCJ 6336/04 Mussa v. the Prime Minister, Tak-El 2004 (4) 2737 (2004).

HCJ 6598/03 Yassin v. the Commander of IDF Forces in Judea and Samaria (unpublished, Apr. 11, 2005).

HCJ 6631/01 Kuzmar v. the Prison Service, Tal-El 2002(1) 480 (2002).

HCJ 6696/02 Amar v. Commander of IDF Forces in the West Bank, PD 56 (6) 110, (2002).

HCJ 677/95 Alzeer v. the Minister of Defense (unpublished, July 10, 1997).

HCJ 6834/02 Abu Hit v. Commander of the Ketziot Detention Facility, PD 02(2) 385.

HCJ 6868/02 Tzalah v. the Commander of IDF Forces, Tak-El 2002 (3), 258 (2002).

HCJ 6972/98 Paritzky v. Minister of the Interior, PD 53(1) 763, 785–86 (1999).

HCJ 7015/02 Ajouri v. Commander of IDF Forces on the West Bank, PD 56(6) 352 (2002).

HCJ 7052/03 Adallah v. the Minister of the Interior, Tak-El 2006(2) 1754 [also known as the *Citizenship Law* matter].

HCJ 7144/01 Gush Shalom v. the Broadcasting Authority, PD 56(2) 887 (2002).

HCJ 7473/02 Bahar v. IDF Commander in the West Bank, PD 56 (8) 488 (2002).

HCJ 7523/11 Almagor Terror Victims Association v. the Prime Minister (unpublished, 17 October 2011).

HCJ 769/02 The Public Committee against Torture in Israel, Tak-El 2006(4) 3958 (2006) [also known as HCJ *Targeted Killings*].

HCJ 7733/04 Nasr v. IDF Commander of the West Bank, Tak-El 2005(2) 3855 (2005).

HCJ 7862/02 Alshaf'i v. IDF Commander of the West Bank, Tak-El 2004(1) 972 (2004).

HCJ 794/98 Obayed v. the Minister of Defense, PD 55 (5) 769 (2001).

HCJ 7957/04 Maraba v. the Prime Minister of Israel, Tak-El 2004 (3) 2982 (2004) [also known as HCJ *Alfei Menashe*].

HCJ 7960/04 Elrazi v. the Commander of IDF Forces—Gaza Strip (unpublished Sept. 29, 2004).

HCJ 8084/02 Abassi v. OC Homefront Command, PD 57(2) 55, 59–60 (2003).

HCJ 9290/99 M.M.T. Center for Victims of Terrorist Attacks v. the State of Israel, PD 54(1) 8, (1999).

HCJ 9353/08 Abu Dahim v. OC Home Front Command (unpublished, 5 January 2009)

HCJ 9682/03 Abu Jahal v. the Minister of Defense (unpublished, Oct. 30, 2003).

HCJ Hess v. Halutz PD 59 (6) 97 (2005).

HJC 610/78 Ayub v. the Minister of Defence PD 33(2) 113 (1978).

Leave for HCJ Appeal1443/04 Bargouti v. the Attorney General (unpublished, Apr. 22, 2004).

Misc. Civil App. 838/84 Livni v. the State of Israel, PD 38 (3) 729 (1984).

Misc. Crim. App. 11493/03 Mahajana v. the State of Israel, PD 59(4) 193 (2004).

Misc. Crim. App. 4857/05 Fahima v. the State of Israel, Tak-El 2005 (3) 479.

US LEGISLATION

Classified Information Procedures Act (CIPA), 18 U.S.C. app. 3 §§ 1–16 (2006).

US CASE LAW

Brown v. Board of Education, 347 U.S. 483 (1954).

Korematsu v. United States, 323 U.S. 214, 245–46 (1944).

Marbury v. Madison. 5 U.S. 137 (1803).

Muskrat v. United States, 219 U.S. 346 (1911).

United States v. Then, 56 F.3d 464 (2d Cir. 1995).

OTHER LEGISLATION

Constitution of India—Section 143

Constitution of Germany—Section 83

Canadian Charter—Sections 1 and 33

UNITED NATIONS DOCUMENTS

A/68/389 Interim report to the General Assembly on the use of remotely piloted aircraft in counter-terrorism operations.

ICJ Legal Consequences of the Construction of a Wall in the Occupied Palestinian Territory, advisory opinion of 9 July 2004

ACADEMIC LITERATURE

Abner J. Mikva, Why Judges Should Not Be Advicegivers: A Response to Professor Neal Katyal, 50 Stan. L. Rev. 1825 (1998).

Aharon Barak, "Between National Security and Individual Liberty." A lecture given at a conference of the Israel Bar Association in Eilat (May 6, 2002).

Aharon Barak, "Concerning National Security and Individual Security." Lecture at a conference of the Israel Bar Association in Eilat (May 6, 2002).

Alexander M. Bickel, The Least Dangerous Branch: The Supreme Court at the Bar of Politics (1962).

Amnon Strashnov, Justice under Fire—the Legal System during the Intifada (1994), B'Tselem Deporting Families in the Territories, Israel's Policy and Application (1993). www.btselem. org/Hebrew/Family_Separation/Implementation.asp

Amos Harel and Avi Issacharoff, The Seventh War—How We Won and Why We Lost the War with the Palestinians (2005).

Barry Friedman, Dialogue and Judicial Review, 91 Mich. L. Rev. 577 (1993).

Beth Harris, Representing Homeless Families: Repeat Player Implementation Strategies, 33 Law & Society Rev. 911 (1999).

Beth Henschen, Statutory Interpretations of the Supreme Court: Congressional Response, 11 American Politics 441 (1983).

Bradley Canon, The Supreme Court as a Cheerleader in Politico-Moral Disputes, 54 Journal of Politics 637 (1992).

Brian J. Daugherity and Charles C. Bolton (eds.), With All Deliberate Speed: Implementing Brown v. Board of Education (2008).

Burt Neuborne, The Myth of Parity, 90 Harv. L. Rev. 1105 (1977).

Cass R. Sunstein, Not Deciding, review of Lisa Klopperberg's Playing It Safe: How the Supreme Court Sidesteps Hard Cases and Stunts the Development of Law, The New Republic, (Oct. 29, 2001).

Cass R. Sunstein, Race-Based Remedies: Reshaping Remedial Measures: The Importance of Political Deliberation and Race-Conscious Redistricting: Public Deliberation, Affirmative Action, and the Supreme Court, 84 Calif. L. Rev. 1179 (1966).

Cass R. Sunstein, The Supreme Court, 1995 Term—Foreword: Leaving Things Undecided, 110 Harv. L. Rev. 4 (1996).

Charles Black, Mr. Justice Black, The Supreme Court, and the Bill of Rights, 63 Harper's Magazine (1961).

Charles Black, The Unfinished Business of the Warren Court, 46 Wash. L. Rev. 3, (1970).

Charles Cameron, Jeffrey Segal, and Donald Songer, Strategic Auditing in a Political Hierarchy, 94 American Political Science Review 101 (2000).

Charles L. Black, The Unfinished Business of the Warren Court, 46 Wash. L. Rev. 3, 22 (1970).

Christine Bateup, Expanding the Conversation: American and Canadian Experiences of Constitutional Dialogue in Comparative Perspective, 21 Temp Int'l & Comp. L.J. 1 (2007).

Christopher J. Peters, Assessing the New Judicial Minimalism, 100 Columbia Law Review 1454 (2000).

Conor A. Gearty, Reconciling Parliamentary Democracy and Human Rights, 118 L.Q. Rev. 248 (2002).

Cynthia R. Farina, Supreme Judicial Court Advisory Opinions: Two Centuries of Interbranch Dialogue, in The History of the Law in Massachusetts: The Supreme Judicial Court 1692–1992, at 353 (Russell K. Osgood ed., 1992).

Dalia Dorner, The Protection of Human Rights in the New Age of Terror, 11 Human Rights Brief (2003). For the full version of the lecture, *see* http://www.wcl.american.edu/hrbrief/11/1dorner.cfm.

Daphne Barak-Erez and David Scharia, Freedom of Speech, Support for Terrorism and the Challenge of Global Constitutional Law, 2 Harv. Nat'l Security J. 1 (2011).

David H. Moore, A Signaling Theory of Human Rights Compliance, 97 N.W. U.L. Rev. 879 (2003).

David Kretzmer, The Law of Belligerent Occupation in the Supreme Court of Israel, 94(885) International Review of the Red Cross (Spring 2012).

David Kretzmer, The Occupation of Justice: The Supreme Court of Israel and the Occupied Territories (2002).

David Scharia, "On Torture Chambers and Acoustic Walls," Politica 10, 61 (2003).

Dorit Beinisch, "The Rule of Law during a Period of Fighting," 17 Mishpat V'Tzava 19 (2004).

Douglas W. Kmiec, The Supreme Court in Times of Hot and Cold War: Learning from the Sounds of Silence for a War on Terrorism, 28 Journal of Supreme Court History 270 (2003).

Edna Arbel, "The Prosecution Copes in a Time of Crisis" 16 Mishpat Vetzava 37, 89 (2002).

Eliezer Witztum and Rut Malkinson "Bereavement and Memorialization: The Dual Face of the National Myth," in Loss and Bereavement in Israeli Society 231 (Eliezer Witztum and Rut Malkinson eds. 1993).

Elyakim Rubinstein, "Security and Law: Trends," 44 Hapraklit 409 (2000).

Eric A. Posner, Law and Social Norms (2000).

Eric Luna, Constitutional Road Maps, 90 J. Crim. L. & Criminology 1125 (2000).

Eugene V. Rostow, The Democratic Character of Judicial Review, 66 Harv. L. Rev. 193, 208 (1952).

Frank Cross, Michael Heise, and Gregory S. Sisk, Exchange: Empirical Research and The Goals of Legal Scholarship: Above the Rules: A Response to Epstein and King, 69 U. Chi. L. Rev. 135 (2002).

Gad Barzilai, Democracy in Wars—Dispute and Consensus in Israel (1991).

Gad Barzilai, Efraim Yaar-Yuchtman, and Zeev Segal, The Supreme Court in the Eye of Israeli Society (1994).

Ruth Gavison, Mordechai Kremnitzer, and Yoav Dotan Judicial Activism (2000).

Gerald N. Rosenberg, The Hollow Hope: Can Courts Bring About Social Change? (1991).

Greg Myers, The Pragmatics of Politeness in Scientific Articles, 10 Applied Linguistics 1 (1989).

Guido Calabresi, A Common Law for the Age of Statutes (1982).

H.W. Perry, Deciding to Decide: Agenda Setting in the United States Supreme Court (1991).

Henry R. Glick, The Impact of Permissive Judicial Policies: The U.S. Supreme Court and the Right to Die, 47 Political Research Quarterly 207 (1994).

Israel Democracy Institute, Is Everything Kosher When Coping with Terrorism: On Israel's Policy of Preventive Killing (Targeted Killing) in Judea and Samaria and in the Gaza Strip 75 (2006).

James B. White, Law as Rhetoric, Rhetoric as Law: Arts of Cultural and Communal Life, 52 U. Chi. L. Review 684 (1985).

James B. White, The Legal Imagination: Studies in the Nature of Legal Thought and Expression (1973).

James Boyd White, Justice as Translation: An Essay in Cultural and Legal Criticism (1990).

James Bradley Thayer, The Origin and Scope of the American Doctrine of Constitutional Law, 7 Harv. L. Review 129 (1893).

James L. Gibson, From Simplicity to Complexity: The Development of Theory in the Study of Judicial Behavior, 5 Political Behavior 7, 32 (1983).

James Rogers and Georg Vanberg, Judicial Advisory Opinions and Legislative Outcomes in Comparative Perspective: A Game-Theoretic Analysis, Paper presented at the Midwest Political Science Association Annual Meeting, Chicago, April 19–22, 2001, at 5.

James Spriggs, Explaining Federal Bureaucratic Compliance with Supreme Court Opinions, 50 Political Research Quarterly 567 (1997).

James Spriggs, The Supreme Court and Federal Agencies: A Resource-Based Theory and Analysis of Judicial Impact, 40 American Journal of Political Science 1122 (1996).

Janet L. Hiebert, Parliament and Rights, in Protecting Human Rights 231, 240 (Tom Campbell et al. eds., 2003).

Jay D. Wexler, Defending the Middle Way: Intermediate Scrutiny as Judicial Minimalism, 66 Geo. Wash. L. Rev. 298 (1998).

Jean-Francois Lyotard, The Differend: Phrases in Dispute (1988).

Jon Gould, The Precedent that Wasn't: Collegiate Hate Speech Codes and the Two Faces of Legal Compliance Theory, 35 Law and Society Review 345 (2001).

Jonathan D. Persky, Ghosts That Slay: A Contemporary Look at State Advisory Opinions, 37 Conn. L. Rev. 1155 (2005).

Joseph Tanenhaus, Marvin Schick, Matthew Muraskin, and Daniel Rosen, The Supreme Court's Certiorari Jurisdiction: Cue Theory, in Judicial Decision Making 111 (Glendon Schubert ed., 1963).

Kent Roach, Constitutional and Common Law Dialogues between the Supreme Court and Canadian Legislatures, 80 Can. Bar Rev. 481 (2001).

Kent Roach, The Supreme Court On Trial (2001).

Kevin R. den Dulk and Mitchell Pickerill, Bridging the Lawmaking Process: Organized Interests, Court-Congress Interaction and Church-State Relations, 35 Polity 419 (2003).

Larry D. Kramer, The Supreme Court, 2000 Term—Foreword: We, the Court, 115 Harv. L. Rev. 4, 13 (2001).

Lawrence Baum, Judges and Their Audiences: A Perspective on Judicial Behavior (2006).

Lawrence Baum, Judicial Impact as a Form of Policy Implementation, in Public Law and Public Policy (John A. Gardiner ed., 1977).

Lee Epstein & Jack Knight, Toward a Strategic Revolution in Judicial Politics: A Look Back, A Look Forward, 53 Political Research Quarterly 625 (2000).

Lee Epstein and Gary King, The Rules of Inference, 69 U. Chi. L. Rev. 1, 106 (2002).

Lee Epstein, Daniel E. Ho, Gary King, and Jeffrey A. Segal, The Supreme Court during Crisis: How War Affects Only Non-war Cases, 80 New York University Law Review 1 (2005).

Loren Miller, The Petitioners: The Story of the Supreme Court of the United States and the Negro 351, 356 (1966).

Lori Hausegger and Lawrence Baum, Inviting Congressional Action: A Study of Supreme Court Motivations in Statutory Interpretation, 43 American Journal of Political Science 162 (1999).

Malcolm M. Feeley, The Process Is the Punishment (1979).

Marc Galanter, Why the "Haves" Come Out Ahead: Speculations on the Limits of Legal Change, 9 Law and Society Review 95 (1974).

Mark Tushnet, Constitutionalism without Courts? Taking the Constitution Away from the Courts, 94 Nw. U.L. Rev. 983 (2000).

Mark Tushnet, Defending Korematsu?: Reflections on Civil Liberties in Wartime, 2003 Wis. L. Rev. 273.

Mark Tushnet, Policy Distortion and Democratic Debilitation: Comparative Illumination of the Countermajoritarian Difficulty, 94 Mich. L. Rev. 245 (1995).

Martin S. Remland, The Importance of Nonverbal Communication in the Courtroom, 2 New Jersey Journal of Communication 124 (1994).

Michael C. Dorf, The Supreme Court, 1997 Term Foreword: The Limits of Socratic Deliberation, 112 Harv. L. Rev. 4 (1998).

Michael H. LeRoy, Institutional Signals and Implicit Bargains in the ULP Strike Doctrine: Empirical Evidence of Law as Equilibrium, 51 Hastings L.J. 171 (1999).

Michael Sean Quinn, Symposium on Taking Legal Arguments Seriously: Argument and Authority in Common Law Advocacy and Adjudication: An Irreducible Pluralism of Principles, 74 Chi.-Kent. L. Rev. 655 (1999).

Naomi Levitzki, The Supremes: Within the Supreme Court (2006).

Neal Devins, Shaping Constitutional Values: Elected Government, the Supreme Court, and the Abortion Debate (1996).

Neal Devins, The Democracy-Forcing Constitution, 97 Mich. L. Rev. 1971 (1999).

Neal Katyal, Changing Laws of War: Do We Need a New Symposium; The Sunsetting Judicial Legal Regime after September 11, 79 Notre Dame L. Rev. 1237 (2004).

Neal Katyal, Judges as Advicegivers, 50 Stan. L. Rev. 1709, 1801 (1998).

Oren Gross, Are Torture Warrants Warranted? Pragmatic Absolutism and Official Disobedience, 88 Minn. L. Rev. 1481 (2004).

Oren Gross, Chaos and Rules: Should Responses to Violent Crises Always Be Constitutional? 112 Yale L.J. 1011(2003).

Owen Fiss, The War against Terrorism and the Rule of Law, 26 Oxford Journal of Legal Studies 235 (2006).

Oz Almog, "Monuments to War Victims in Israel: A Semiological Analysis," Megamot 34 (2) 179 (1992).

Paul H. Grice, Presupposition and Conversational Implicature, in Radical Pragmatics 183 (Peter Cole ed., 1981).

Penelope Brown and Stephen Levinson, Politeness: Some Universals in Language Usage (1987).

Peter W. Hogg and Allison A. Bushell, The Charter Dialogue between Courts and Legislatures, 35 Osgoode Hall L.J. 75 (1997).

Phillip M. Kannan, Advisory Opinions by Federal Courts, 32 U. Rich. L. Rev. 769 (1998).

Raviv Drucker and Ofer Shelach, Boomerang: Failure of Leadership in the Second Intifada 162 (2005).

Richard A. Paschal, The Continuing Colloquy: Congress and the Finality of the Supreme Court, 8 Journal of Law & Politics, 143 (1991).

Richard A. Posner, Judicial Opinion Writing: Judges' Writing Styles and Do They Matter?, 62 University of Chicago Law Review 1421 (1995).

Robert A. Burt, The Constitution in Conflict (1992).

Robert C. Post and Reva B. Siegel, Popular Constitutionalism, Departmentalism and Judicial Supremacy, 92 Calif. L. Rev. 1027, 1041 (2004).

Robert C. Post and Reva B. Siegel, Protecting the Constitution from the People: Juricentric Restrictions on Section Five Power, 78 Ind. L.J. 1 (2003).

Robert C. Post, The Supreme Court 2002 Term, Foreword: Fashioning the Legal Constitution: Culture, Courts and Law, 117 Harv. L. Rev. 4 (2003).

Robert Jervis, The Logic of Images in International Relations (1970).

Robert M. Cover, Justice Accused: Antislavery and the Judicial Process (1975).

Robert Nagel, Indirect Constitutional Discourse: A Comment on Meese, 63 Law and Contemporary Problems 507 (2000).

Robert Nagel, Principle, Prudence and Judicial Power, in Alexander Bickel and Contemporary Constitutional Theory (K. Ward ed., 2006).

Robert Paul Wolff, The Rule of Law (1976).

Ronald J. Krotoszynski, Constitutional Flares: On Judges, Legislatures and Dialogue, 83 Minn. L. Rev. 1 (1998).

Ronen Shamir, Landmark Cases and the Reproduction of Legitimacy, 24(3) Law and Society Review 781 (1990).

Samuel Issacharoff and Richard H. Pildes, Between Civil Libertarianism and Executive Unilateralism: An Institutional Process Approach to Rights during Wartime, 5 Theoretical Inquiries in Law 1 (2004).

Shai Nitzan, "The Fight against Terrorism as Warfare—Legal Aspects," in The Battle of the 21st Century: Democracy Fights Terrorism 130 (The Israel Democracy Institute) (Haim Pass ed., 2007).

Shiri Crabes, National Security, Secret Evidence and Preventive Detentions: The Israeli Supreme Court as a Case Study, in Secrecy, National Security and the Vindication of Constitutional Law (David Cole, Federico Fabbrini, and Arianna Vedaschi, eds., International Association of Constitutional Law 2012).

Stewart McAulay, Lawrence M. Friedman, and Elizabeth Mertz, Law in Action: A Socio-Legal Reader (2007).

Stuart A. Scheingold, The Politics of Street Crime: Criminal Process and Cultural Obsession (1991).

The Battle of the 21st Century: Democracy Fights Terror (Iyun Forum—the Israel Democracy Institute) (Haim Pass ed., 2007).

Thomas Holtgraves, Communication in Context: Effects of Speaker Status on the Comprehension of Indirect Requests, 20 Journal of Experimental Psychology 1205 (1994).

Thomas Holtgraves, Comprehending Indirect Replies: When and How Are Their Conveyed Meanings Activated?, 41 Journal of Memory and Language 519 (1999).

Thomas Holtgraves, Styles of Language Use: Individual and Cultural Variability in Conversational Indirectness, 73 Journal of Personality and Social Psychology 624 (1997).

Tracy E. George and Michael Solimine, Supreme Court Monitoring of Courts of Appeals En Banc, 9 Supreme Court Economic Review 171 (2001).

Tsvi Kahana, Understanding the Notwithstanding Mechanism, 52 Univ. Toronto L.J. 221 (2002).

William M. Landes and Richard A. Posner, The Economics of Anticipatory Adjudication, 23 J. Legal Stud. 683, 686 (1994).

William N. Eskridge and Philip P. Frickey, The Supreme Court, 1993 Term Forward: Law as Equilibrium, 108 Harvard Law Review 27 (1994).

Yaniv Ofek, Deterrence in Attrition: The Support of the Palestinian Public for Terrorism and Violence, a thesis toward a Master's degree, Tel Aviv University (2007).

Yigal Mersel, Judicial Review of Counter-terrorism Measures: The Israeli Model for the Role of the Judiciary during the Terror Era, 38 NYU Journal of International Law and Politics 73 (Nov. 2006).

Yoav Dotan, "Do the Haves Still Come Out Ahead? Resource Inequalities in Ideological Courts: The Case of the Israeli High Court of Justice, 33 Law & Society Review, 1059 (1999).

Yoav Dotan, "Judicial Rhetoric, Government Lawyers and Human Rights: The Case of the Israeli High Court of Justice during the Intifada," 33 Law & Society Review 319 (1999).

REPORTS

B'Tselem 1987–1997 A Decade of Human Rights Violations (Jan. 1998).

B'Tselem Demolition Policy: House Demolitions and Damage to Agricultural Areas in the Gaza Strip—Information Sheet (2002).

B'Tselem Guilty of No Wrongdoing: House Demolitions as Punishment during the Al-Aqsa Intifada 6 (Nov. 2004).

B'Tselem Human Shield—The Use of Palestinian Civilians Contrary to an HCJ Order (Nov. 2002); Human Rights Watch, In a Dark Hour—The Use of Civilians during IDF Arrest Operations (Apr. 2002).

B'Tselem Innocent of Any Crime: Punitive House Demolitions during the Al-Aksa Intifada—Information Sheet (2004).

B'Tselem Legitimizing Torture: HCJ Decision on the Bilbisi, Hamdan and Mubarak Affair; Sources and Comments—Special Report (1997).

B'Tselem Position Paper—Legislation Allowing the Use of Physical Force and Mental Coercion in Interrogations by the General Security Service (Jan. 2000).

B'Tselem Position Paper on the Proposed Law: "Incarceration of Combatants Not Entitled to Prisoners of War Status" (2000).

B'Tselem The Absolute Prohibition of Torture and Abuse of Palestinian Prisoners by the Security Forces of Israel (2007).

B'Tselem Through No Fault of Their Own—Punitive House Demolitions during the al-Aqsa Intifada 39–40 (November 2004).

B'Tselem, Legislation That Permits Physical and Mental Force in GSS Investigations (2000).

Supreme Court Statistical Reports 2002, 2003, 2004. www.elyon1.court.gov.il/heb/stats/sikum.htm

The Association for Civil Rights in Israel Human Rights in Israel—Current Situation 95 (1996).

MEDIA REPORTS

Efrat Weiss and Tal Rosner, "HCJ to Maj.-Gen. Halutz: Present Your Moral Position," Ynet,
    Nov. 18, 2004.

Efrat Weiss, "The Bereaved Families against 'Jenin, Jenin,'" Ynet, Mar. 20, 2003, *available at*
    www.ynet.co.il/1,7340,L-2507177,00.html.

Felix Frisch and Ali Vaked, "Two Bodies Have Been Removed from the Church of the
    Nativity," Ynet, Apr. 25, 2002.

Felix Frisch, "The Statements with regard to the War on Suicide Bombers—Are Banal," Ynet,
    Aug. 14, 2003, http://www.ynet.co.il/articles/0,7430,L-2725796,00.html.

Interview with Dan Yakir, Halishka, Issue 61 (June 2006).

Maj.-Gen. Ben: "Actions against the Families of Suicide Bombers Have Beeen
    Authorized: Deportation and Forfeiture of Property," Haaretz, Aug. 1, 2002.

Moshe Gorali, "Barak: 'I am Conscience-Stricken' with Regard to House Demolitions,"
    Haaretz, June 20, 2003.

Tal Rosner "Barak Fears That the IDF Will Encounter Difficulties in the Use of Civilians,"
    Ynet, Sept. 5, 2004. http://test.ynet.co.il/articles/0,7340,L-2973057,00.html.

Yehonatan Lis and Amos Harel, "Mofaz Seeks to Renew Demolitions of Terrorists' homes,"
    Haaretz, Dec. 5, 2005.

Zeev Segal, "Judicial Restraint Encourages Initiating a Path to Bypass the Law," Haaretz, Aug.
    7, 2002.

Index